A PLAIN ENGLISH REFERENCE TO THE BOOK OF MORMON

TIMOTHY B. WILSON

ISBN 978-1-55517-401-9

Published by Bonneville Books, an imprint of Cedar Fort, Inc.
2373 W. 700 S., Springville, UT, 84663
Distributed by Cedar Fort, Inc., www.cedarfort.com

Printed in the United States of America

10 9 8 7 6 5 4 3 2 1

Printed on acid-free paper

This book, *A Plain English Reference to The Book of Mormon,* reads on a 8th to 9th grade level, making it a useful tool for students of all ages. This book was created to bridge the gap between the text of *The Book of Mormon* and the reading and / or word comprehension and / or signing skills of many people.

Around 570 BC, Nephi wrote:

> *" . . . my soul delighteth in plainness . . . for the Lord giveth light unto the understanding, for he speaketh unto men according to their language, unto their understanding"* — 2 Nephi 31:3

In what ways does the Lord give "light," speaking our language? Through the Spirit, of course, the ultimate teacher, who speaks to the soul, who witnesses of all truth. And through the Spirit, may this reference work help you to better understand the profound testimonies and messages of *The Book of Mormon.*

— Timothy B. Wilson, Author

Feel free to send your questions or comments to the author at timw57@gmail.com.

Mormon was a warrior/prophet who lived in 4th Century Central America. He was told by the Lord to make a history of His people, who were descendants of the house of Israel.

By referring to many records engraved upon thin, rectangular gold or brass plates, Mormon compiled the history of the Lord's dealings with His people in the New World. Before going out to battle for the last time, Mormon gave his book to his son Moroni.

For many years, Moroni wandered alone through central and north America, hiding from his enemies. Before he died, Moroni buried his father's book of gold plates in a hillside in present day Wayne County, New York. There the plates rested for 1,400 years.

To fulfill the covenant that God made with Abraham, Mormon's record was destined to come forth to all of Israel's descendants in the last days. It did come forth to a latter-day prophet—Joseph Smith. As a resurrected being, Moroni gave Joseph charge of the plates in September of 1827. Before returning the plates to Moroni, Joseph was given the power to translate them into English, and *The Book of Mormon* was first published in 1830.

In that book, Jesus states that when Israel's latter-day descendants read *The Book of Mormon*, it will be a sign to them that the Father's work has begun—that He will soon fulfill His covenant to all the house of Israel—to bring them knowledge of their Redeemer and restore them to their lands of inheritance.

Books within The Book of Mormon.:
Who wrote them and what time periods they cover...

The First Book of Nephi — writings of Nephi and selections from the writing of Isaiah (about 600-588 BC)

The Second Book of Nephi — writings of Nephi, and of his brother Jacob, and seletions from the writings of Isaiah (about 587-545 BC)

The Book of Jacob — writings of Jacob and selections from the writings of Zenos (about 544-500 BC)

The Book of Enos — writings of Jacob's son Enos (about 499-421 BC)

The Book of Jarom — writings of Enos' son Jarom (420-361 BC)

The Book of Omni — writings of Jarom's son Omni, of his son Amaron, of his brother Chemish, and of his son Abinadom, and of his son Amaleki (about 360-130 BC)

The Words of Mormon — writings of Mormon (about 385 A.D.)

The Book of Mosiah — writings of Mormon while referring to the record and writings of Zeniff, the records of Benjamin, of his son Mosiah, and of Alma (about 129-93 BC)

The Book of Alma — writings of Mormon while referring to the records of Alma's son Alma (92-74 BC), of his son Helaman (73-57 BC), and of his brother Shiblon (56-52 BC)

The Book of Helaman — writings of Mormon while referring to the records of Helaman's son Helaman (51-24 B.C.), and of his sons, Nephi and Lehi (23-1 BC)

The Third Book of Nephi — writings of Mormon while referring to the record of Nephi's son Nephi (1-35 AD)

The Fourth Book of Nephi — writings of Mormon while referring to the records of Nephi's son Nephi (a disciple of Christ), and of his son Nephi, and of his son Amos, and of his son Amos, and of his brother Ammaron (36-320 AD)

The Book of Mormon — writings of Mormon and of his son Moroni (about 321-400 AD)

The Book of Ether — writings of Moroni while referring to the record of Ether (about 2200-550 BC)

The Book of Moroni — writings of Moroni, including some of Mormon's words (about 401-421 AD)

1 - Nephi writes of his father, Lehi...

I Nephi, was born to good parents who saw that I was educated in the way my father had been. I have experienced many afflictions in my days. But I have always been highly favored by the Lord, and I have received a great knowledge of His goodness and mysteries. Because of these things, I now make this record of my life.

I am writing as my father does—using the Egyptian language (hieroglyphics), but writing according to our Jewish learning. I know this record is true, which I engrave upon metal plates I have made.

Note: Nephi engraved this record on small plates in 570 BC, thirty years after leaving Jerusalem.

My record begins with my father, Lehi, who was born and raised in Jerusalem. He lived there with his own family in the year 600 BC. Not long after our new king, Zedekiah, came to power, many prophets came into our city. They told the people that if they did not repent, they would be destroyed.

When my father heard this he became very concerned for his people. He went out and prayed with all his heart to the Lord, asking what he could do to help save them. While he was praying, a pillar of fire came upon a rock before him. He saw and heard many things that made him shake in astonishment!

After this vision, my father was so overcome by the Spirit that he returned home and collapsed on his bed. As his vision continued he saw the heavens open. He saw what appeared to be God sitting upon His throne, surrounded by countless angels who were singing and praising Him.

My father saw a man come down from heaven whose whole body shone brighter than the sun. He saw twelve others follow, and they shone brighter than the stars.

They came down to the earth, and the first man (who was Jesus) gave my father a book and told him to read from it.

As Lehi read, he was filled with the Spirit of the Lord. He read, "Jerusalem is cursed, for I have seen its wickedness! Unless its people repent, many of them will either be killed by the Babylonians or become their slaves."

My father read about, and saw in vision, many great and marvelous things, after which he exclaimed, "Oh Lord God Almighty! Thy throne is high in the heavens, and Thy power, goodness and mercy are over all the earth. Because of Thy mercy, Thou will spare all who come to Thee!" My father's heart was full of joy because of the Lord's tender mercy in showing him all these things.

I, Nephi, am writing only a small part of my father's visions, dreams and prophecies that he has written in his record and has told to his children. I will make a record of my life, but first I will write part of my father's history on metal plates that I have made.

Note: Nephi's father's history, *The Book of Lehi*, was part of 116 pages of lost manuscripts (see D&C 10,"...the [large] plates of Nephi...", and Words of Mormon 1:3). After arriving in the promised land, Nephi made large plates (1 Nephi 19:1-5). Years later, he made small plates (2 Nephi 5:28-33), which became The First Book of Nephi through The Book of Omni.

My father wrote: "After my vision of the destruction of Jerusalem, I went out and told the people of my city what I had seen and heard. After hearing of my marvelous vision concerning the destruction of Jerusalem, the people made fun of me, for it told them of their wickedness. It also told them of a Messiah who would come down to redeem the world. When they heard all this, they became angry and said they would kill me—just as their fathers had killed the prophets of old."

Now, I, Nephi, will show you that the Lord's tender mercy protects those whom He has chosen (because of their faith)—and whose faith gives them the power to be delivered.

2 - Lehi's family leaves Jerusalem...

The Lord said to my father in a dream, "I bless you because you faithfully told the people the things I commanded you to tell them. However, because of this, they are planning to kill you. To escape them, take your family and go into the wilderness." Lehi obeyed the Lord and left his home, his lands, gold, silver and treasures, and he took only his family, tents and supplies and went into the wilderness.

Note: During the thousand year history of Lehi and his descendants, and in one case around 2,200 BC, *The Book of Mormon* gives seven accounts of a Lehi type exodus. These accounts illustrate how the Lord tells His servants to take their people and "depart into the wilderness." In each exodus account, the righteous people leave their prideful, power-seeking brethren who have sinned against light and knowledge and have brought themselves under condemnation. These examples are a type for a latter-day exodus, as prophesied by Isaiah. (See 2 Nephi 8:10-11, 16:12, 20:20-21, 21:15-16). In addition to Lehi's, six other exodus accounts are found in *The Book of Mormon* (2 Nephi 5:5, Omni 1:13, Mosiah 18:34, Mosiah 22:11, Alma 27:11-4, Ether 1:39-42).

Our family consisted of my father, Lehi, my mother, Sariah, my older brothers, Laman, Lemuel and Sam, and me, Nephi. We traveled south into the wilderness, down the shoreline of the Red Sea. After traveling for three days, we pitched our tents in a valley near a river. Here my father built an altar of stones, made an offering, and gave thanks to the Lord.

The valley where we camped was at the mouth of the river that flowed into the Red Sea. My father named the river after Laman and said to him, "I pray you will be like this river, always flowing into the fountain of all righteousness!" Then my father told Lemuel, "I pray you will be like this valley, firm, steadfast and immovable in keeping the Lord's commandments!"

My father said these things because Laman and Lemuel were both very stubborn. They kept complaining, saying my father was a foolish, visionary man, and that he had taken them away from all their comforts and wealth to die in the wilderness. They complained because they knew nothing about how God deals with His children. Like the Jews, they thought the great city of Jerusalem could not be destroyed. However, Lehi, being filled with the Spirit, spoke to them with the Lord's power. This caused them to fear His judgments—so much that they began to tremble, and for a time they stopped complaining.

Lehi and his family camped in the valley that he had named Lemuel. Although very young, I had great desires to know God's will. So as I prayed with faith, the Lord gave me understanding, and I did not rebel against my father. I told my older brother Sam what the Lord had told me by His Holy Spirit, and Sam believed me. But Laman and Lemuel did not believe me, and in my sorrow over their stubbornness I prayed for them. The Lord answered my prayer, saying, "You are blessed, Nephi, because of your faith and humility before me. I have prepared the best land on earth for you, and if you will obey my commands, I will lead you there. If your older brothers keep rebelling against you, they will be cut off from my presence, and I will not be with them. If you obey my commands, you will become their ruler and teacher. And if Laman and Lemuel rebel against me, I will curse them and their descendants, and they will not have power over yours. But if your descendants also rebel against me, they will not have my protection, and your brothers' descendants will be a trial for yours, reminding them to look to me in righteousness for protection."

3 - Nephi is told to get the brass plates...

After the Lord had told me these things, I returned to my father's tent, wherein he told me, "In a dream, the Lord commanded me to tell you and your brothers to go back to Jerusalem, where Laban, the keeper of the holy records, has the writings of Moses and other prophets, and the genealogy of my forefathers engraved on brass plates. The Lord commanded me to tell you to go to Laban's house where he keeps these brass plates, to ask Laban for them, and to bring them to me in this valley. When I told your brothers to do this they complained, saying what I was asking of them was too hard. I told them it wasn't my commandment, but the Lord's. You must go, Nephi. Lead your brothers, and the Lord will favor you because you have not complained."

I answered my father, "I will go and do as the Lord has commanded, for I know He does not give us commandments without preparing a way for us to obey them." When my father heard this, he was very glad, knowing that I had been blessed by the Lord.

Then my three older brothers and I took our tents and traveled back to Jerusalem. Upon arriving there, we talked about how to get the brass plates from Laban. We cast lots to know who should go into Laban's house and talk with him. The lot fell upon Laman, so he went in and talked with Laban as he sat in his house. Laman asked Laban for the brass plates, which contained my father's genealogy. Laban became angry and threw Laman out of his house, shouting, "You're a robber, and I'll kill you!" But Laman escaped and ran back to tell us what had happened.

We became very discouraged, and my brothers were about to return to my father in the wilderness, but I told them, "As the Lord lives, and as we live, we will not go back to our father until we have accomplished the Lord's command. Let us be faithful like our father, who gave up all his wealth to obey the Lord. Our father knows that this city will be destroyed because the people here are so wicked.

They have rejected the words of the prophets. If our father had also rejected the word of the Lord, which told him to leave, then our entire family would still be here, where we would die. This is why we had to leave.

"And in His wisdom, the Lord told us to come back here for the records so we can preserve the language of our forefathers and the words of the holy prophets, who have spoken by the Spirit and power of God since the world began until now."

By saying these things I persuaded my brothers to be more faithful so we could accomplish our task. Then we went back to our home (in Jerusalem) to gather our gold, silver and treasures to take to Laban's house. This time we all went into Laban's house and told him we would like to buy the brass plates with our gold, silver and treasures. When Laban saw our great wealth, he was determined to have it. Being very cunning and greedy, Laban drove us out of his house and called his servants to kill us. In order to escape the servants, we had to abandon our property, run into the wilderness and hide in a cave.

After resting in the cave, Laman and Lemuel became very angry with me, and also with our father for telling us to get the plates. They started beating Sam and me with a stick.

Then an angel of the Lord came and stood before them and asked, "Why are you beating your younger brother? Don't you know that the Lord has chosen him to be your ruler because of your sins? Now go back to Jerusalem, and the Lord will deliver Laban into your hands." After saying this, the angel left. Just as soon as the angel had left, Laman and Lemuel asked, "How can the Lord deliver Laban into our hands? Laban commands fifty servants, who could kill fifty men, and there are only four of us!"

4 - Nephi is told to kill Laban...

I replied to my brothers, "Let's go back to Jerusalem and be faithful in keeping the Lord's commandments. Since He is mightier than all the earth, surely He is mightier than Laban's fifty, or even his fifty thousand! Let's go and be strong like Moses, for when he spoke the Red Sea parted, and our forefathers walked out of captivity on dry ground. Then Pharaoh's armies followed and were drowned in the Red Sea. You know this is true, and you know an angel has just spoken to you, so how can you doubt? Let's go, for the Lord will deliver us just as He delivered our forefathers. He'll destroy Laban just as He destroyed Pharaoh's armies." After Laman and Lemuel heard this, they were still angry and afraid, but they followed me back to the walls of Jerusalem.

By now it was dark. I told my brothers to wait for me, to hide outside the walls. Then I crept into the city and carefully made my way back to Laban's house. I was being led by the Spirit, not knowing what I was going to do, but I went ahead anyway. As I came near Laban's house, I saw a drunken man stagger and fall down. I crept closer and discovered that it was Laban! I drew his sword from its sheath. The handle was made of pure gold, the workmanship very fine, and the blade was made from the finest steel.

All at once the Spirit told me, "Kill Laban." I replied in my heart, "I have never killed anyone, and I do not want to kill this man." The Spirit replied, "The Lord has delivered him into your hands as He said He would." I knew Laban had not listened to the Lord's commandments. My brothers and I had asked Laban for the records, and he had refused to give them up. Rather than yield to the Lord, Laban had become proud and greedy, and he had taken our wealth after commanding his servants to kill us.

A third time the Spirit spoke, "Kill him, for the Lord has delivered him into your hands. The Lord destroys the wicked to bring about His righteous purposes. It is better for one man to die than for a whole nation to falter and pass away in unbelief."

When I heard this, I remembered the Lord telling me in the wilderness, "If your descendants keep my commandments, they will be protected and allowed to prosper in the choice land I have prepared for them." I knew my descendants could not keep the Lord's commandments found in the law of Moses unless they had a record of the law, which was engraved on the brass plates. And finally, I knew the Lord had delivered Laban into my hands for one reason only—to help me obey His command to obtain the records and bring them to my father in the wilderness. Knowing all these things, I obeyed the Spirit's voice. I took Laban by the hair and swiftly cut off his head with his own sword. Then I put on Laban's clothes and armor, disguising myself as him.

I went to Laban's treasury, where I met his servant who had the treasury keys. Imitating Laban's voice, I told the servant to follow me into the treasury. Because I was wearing Laban's clothes, and because it was dark, the servant thought I was Laban and followed me. The servant asked about the Elders—the Jewish leaders, knowing that Laban had been out meeting with them earlier that evening. I answered him in a way I thought Laban would have. I told the servant I would be taking the brass plates to my elder brethren, who were just outside the city walls, and to follow me there. The servant thought I was talking about the Elder brethren of the church, and he spoke of the Jewish elders many times as he followed me out of the city.

When my brothers saw me coming, they were very frightened and began to run away, thinking I was Laban—that he had killed me and was now coming to kill them. When I called to them in my own voice, they knew it was I and stopped running. Then Laban's servant became afraid and was about to run back to the city. Being large for my age, and with the strength given to me by the Lord, I held onto the servant to keep him from escaping. I said to him, "If you will listen to what the Lord told me, as He lives, you will live." I made an oath with him so that he would not be afraid. The oath was that he would no longer be a servant if he would go with us into the wilderness. I said, "The Lord has commanded us to get the plates, and we should be diligent in keeping His commandments. If you will come with us into the wilderness, you will be an equal among us."

This servant, named Zoram, took courage at my words and made an oath to go and stay with us from that time forward. We wanted him to come with us so the Jews would not find out about us, for they would have come after and killed us. After Zoram had made this oath, we were no longer worried about his loyalty to us. Then we all returned to my father's tent in the wilderness with the brass plates.

5 - Lehi reads the brass plates...

My father, Lehi, was very joyful to see us return. My mother, Sariah, was especially happy, for during our journey she had been mourning. She thought we had died somewhere in the wilderness. She had been complaining against my father, telling him he was a visionary man, saying, "You have led us out of the land of our inheritance. Now my sons are dead, and we will die here in the wilderness." My father had comforted my mother saying, "I know I am a visionary man, for if God had not shown me so many things in a vision, I would not have left Jerusalem, but would have stayed there with my family to die at the hands of the Babylonians. But instead, I have been given a land of promise, over which I rejoice. I know the Lord will protect our sons, and that they will return to us with the plates."

When we finally returned, my father and mother were full of joy, and my mother was comforted. She said, "Now I know without a doubt that the Lord commanded Lehi to go into the wilderness, and that He has protected my sons so they could accomplish their task." My father and mother were so happy upon our return that they offered sacrifice and burnt offerings to the Lord, giving thanks to the God of Israel.

After this, Lehi began to read the brass plates from the beginning. The record contained the five books of Moses, which told about the creation of the world, and also of Adam and Eve, our first parents. The plates also contained a record of the Jews, and of the prophets, from the beginning down to the reign of Zedekiah. They also included many of Jeremiah's prophecies. Lehi found his genealogy written on the plates and discovered that he was a descendant of Jacob's son, Joseph, who was sold into Egypt. Joseph had been preserved by God to save his father, Jacob (Israel), and the rest of his family from starvation. Joseph's descendants were led out of their captivity in Egypt by the same God who had preserved Joseph and his family.

Then Lehi discovered that Laban was also a descendant of Joseph. Laban and his forefathers had been keeping the holy records for many centuries. After reading these things, Lehi was filled with the Spirit and began to prophesy about his descendants: "These brass plates will go forth to all nations and people who are of my descent (of the house of Israel). The brass plates will never be destroyed nor lose their greatness over time." Lehi prophesied many more things about his descendants which are not written here.

Up to this time, my father and I had kept all the Lord's commandments. As we continued to read the plates they became of great value to us, for they enabled us to teach the Lord's commandments to our children. We clearly saw the Lord's wisdom in commanding us to obtain these records and take them with us on our journey to the promised land.

6 - Purpose of making plates explained...

I, Nephi, am not including the genealogy of my forefathers in my record because it's already engraved on the brass plates. It's enough to say that we are descendants of Joseph. I don't have room on these small plates to write everything my father did. I want to save room on them to write the things of God. I want to persuade people to give up their hearts to Christ—the God of Abraham, Isaac and Jacob, and by doing so be saved. What I engrave is not pleasing to worldly people (those whose hearts only want the things of the world), but what I engrave is pleasing to God and to those who are not worldly. I will tell my children, who will continue to engrave this record, only to engrave things of value—things that will persuade their children to come to Christ.

7 - *Laman and Lemuel rebel again...*

After my father finished prophesying about his descendants who would live in the promised land, the Lord said to him, "Your family must not go to the promised land before your sons obtain wives so that they may raise up a righteous people therein."

The Lord commanded my father to tell me and my brothers to go back to Jerusalem again and bring Ishmael and his family back with us to join our journey. So my brothers and I went back to Jerusalem a second time.

Upon arriving, we went to Ishmael's house, and he listened as we told him the words of the Lord. All of Ishmael's family agreed to travel with us to my father's camp in the wilderness. But as we were all traveling to my father's camp, Laman and Lemuel rebelled again. They persuaded two of Ishmael's daughters, and both of his sons, along with their wives and children, to rebel also. They rebelled against me, and against Sam, Ishmael, his wife and their three other daughters. Those who rebelled wanted to go back to Jerusalem.

I asked Laman and Lemuel, "How can you be so hard in your hearts and so blind in your minds? Why must I, your younger brother, always have to speak to you and set an example for you? After all you have seen, how can you rebel against the Lord's word? Have you forgotten that you have seen an angel? Have you forgotten how the Lord delivered us from Laban, and how we obtained the brass plates from his treasury? Can't you see by now that the Lord can do anything for His children who have faith in Him? Now let us be faithful to Him. If we are faithful to Him, we will obtain the land of promise and escape the destruction of Jerusalem, for we know the Lord's word about its destruction will be fulfilled. The Spirit of the Lord will soon completely leave the people of Jerusalem because they have rejected the prophets. They have thrown Jeremiah into prison, and they tried to kill our father, who was compelled to leave the city. The Spirit of the Lord compels me to tell you this: Go back to Jerusalem if you wish, but remember, if you do go back, you will soon die there."

When I finished speaking my brothers were very angry. They grabbed me and tied my hands and feet, intending to leave me bound in the wilderness to be eaten by wild animals. Lying on the ground tied up I prayed, "Oh Lord, according to my faith in Thee, deliver me from the hands of my brothers. Give me the strength to break these ropes."

As I prayed, the ropes loosened and fell off my hands and feet. Then I stood up to speak to my brothers again. They were still angry with me and wanted to seize me again, but one of Ishmael's sons who had rebelled, Ishmael's wife and one of his daughters begged them to stop. As the Spirit touched them, they realized their wrongdoing and stopped.

Clearly seeing their own wickedness because of the Spirit, they were afraid and sorry. Such a change came over them, they bowed before me and begged my forgiveness.

I forgave them completely and told them to pray to the Lord and ask for His forgiveness, which they did. After this incident, we continued traveling toward our father's camp. Upon arriving in the valley of Lemuel, my father and Ishmael gave thanks to the Lord their God and offered burnt sacrifices to Him.

8 - Lehi's dream...

Before our family had left Jerusalem we had gathered seeds so we could raise every type of fruit and grain.

While we camped in the wilderness, my father had a dream—a vision. He told us, "Because of what I have seen, I rejoice in the Lord over Nephi and Sam. I believe that they and many of their descendants will be saved. But I am afraid for Laman and Lemuel, for in my dream, I saw them in a dark, dreary wilderness. In my dream, a man dressed in a white robe came and stood before me. He told me to follow him. I followed him, but I soon found myself in a dark, dreary wasteland. After walking in this darkness for what seemed to be many hours, I began to pray to the Lord to have mercy on me according to His great and tender mercy.

"After praying I came out of the darkness into a large, wide field. In this field, I saw a tree. The Spirit told me the tree bore a fruit that could make one very happy, so I walked to the tree and ate of its fruit. It was sweeter than anything I had ever tasted, and whiter than anything I had ever seen. As I ate, my soul was filled with great joy, and I wanted my family to come and taste it also, for I knew it was the best fruit of all.

"Looking around for my family, I saw a river running near the tree. I looked upstream to see from where it flowed, and I saw that a fountain was its source. Near the fountain were your mother, Sariah, Sam and Nephi, wondering which way to go. I cried out to them, 'Come over here and taste this wonderful fruit,' and they came, ate of the fruit, and were also filled with joy. Again, I looked to the source of the river, hoping to see Laman and Lemuel. I saw them near the fountain and called out, but they would not come to eat of the fruit.

"Then I saw an iron rod running alongside the riverbank, which led to the tree. I also saw a straight, narrow path running alongside the iron rod, which also led to the tree. From the fountain, the straight, narrow path led into a field, which seemed as large and as wide as the whole world.

"In this field, I saw numberless people at different levels coming down into the field. Many of them were moving forward in their efforts to find the path that led to the tree. Many found the path and began coming toward the tree.

"Then a great, dark mist came over the path. Those who had been walking on it could no longer see, and they wandered off the path and became lost.

"Then other people came forward and took hold of the end of the iron rod. They came through the dark mist, holding tightly to the rod until reaching the tree, and they ate of its fruit. After they had eaten, they looked around and were ashamed, for across the river was a large, spacious building standing in the air high above the earth. The building was filled with all types of people—young and old, men and women—all dressed in very fine clothes, laughing and pointing their fingers at those eating of the fruit.

"After tasting the sweet fruit of the tree, many people were ashamed because of those who were making fun of them. So they went away from the tree and became lost on forbidden paths."

My father, Lehi, told us many other details of his dream that I am not including in this record. But to be short in writing, my father saw other multitudes of people take hold of the end of the rod. Holding onto it tightly, they continued until they came to the tree, knelt down in humility, and tasted of its fruit.

He saw other multitudes feeling their way to the large, spacious building. He saw many drowned in the fountain of filthy water, and many lost on strange paths. He saw a great multitude go into the large, spacious building and join in mocking me and those with me eating the fruit, but we ignored them. All those who wanted the approval of the great multitude in the building left the tree and fell away.

Lehi saw that Laman and Lemuel never did come to the tree and taste its fruit. He was afraid they would be cast off from the Lord's presence, and he spoke to them with all the feelings of a tender parent, pleading with them to listen to him and keep the Lord's commandments. He preached to them, hoping that the Lord would be merciful and not cast them off. Then my father prophesied many things to my brothers and again told them to keep the Lord's commandments.

9 - Lehi prophesies of the Messiah...

While living in a tent in the valley of Lemuel, my father saw, heard and spoke all these things, and many more things which cannot be written on these plates. These smaller plates, which the Lord told me to make many years after arriving in the promised land, will not contain our history. The Lord told me to make these plates for the special purpose of making an account of my people's sacred preaching and prophesying. The first plates (larger ones) contain the history of my people—the reign of their kings, their wars and contentions. I don't know why the Lord told me to make another set (small plates), upon which I now write, to contain only the ministry of my people, but I know it's for a wise purpose. The Lord knows all things and has all power to fulfill His words. He prepares a way for all His works to be accomplished among His children.

10 - Lehi prophesies of the Messiah...

Now I will continue this record of my ministry among my people and also finish the record of my father's ministry.

After my father finished telling us all about his dream, and after warning Laman and Lemuel, he spoke about the Jews: "After the great city of Jerusalem is destroyed and many Jews taken as slaves into Babylon, in the Lord's due time they will return again to the land of their inheritance. Six hundred years from the time we left Jerusalem, the Lord God will raise up a prophet among the Jews—a Messiah—even the Savior of the world. All the many prophets have testified of this Messiah, or Redeemer. All people are in a lost, fallen state, and will always be, unless they rely on this Redeemer.

"A prophet will come before the Messiah to prepare the way of the Lord. This prophet will tell the people, 'Prepare the way of the Lord and make His paths straight, for the Lord stands among you, and you do not know Him. He is mightier than I, for I am not even worthy enough to remove His sandals.' This prophet will baptize the Messiah in Bethabara, beyond Jordan. After he baptizes the Messiah he will bear record that he has baptized the Lamb of God, who will take away the sins of the world."

My father prophesied to Laman and Lemuel, "The Messiah will preach His gospel to the Jews, who will not believe Him. Then they will kill the Messiah, but He will rise from the dead. And the Gentiles will come to know Him through the Holy Ghost.

Note: The Gentiles never hear the Lord's voice directly (3 Ne 15:23).

"The house of Israel is like an olive tree, whose branches are broken off and scattered over the earth. Our journey to the promised land is the fulfilling of the Lord's word, spoken by Isaiah, that the house of Israel will be scattered.

Note: Olive Tree. See Jacob chapter 5

"In the last days, after the Gentiles receive the fullness of the Gospel, the house of Israel, or natural branches, will be grafted back into their mother tree. In other words, the house of Israel will come to the knowledge of their true Messiah, their Lord and Redeemer."

This is how my father prophesied to my brothers. I wrote much more of what he said—things important to me, upon my large plates. But I am writing this shorter version on these smaller plates.

All these things were done as my father lived in a tent in the valley of Lemuel.

After my father had told me everything he had seen in visions by the power of the Holy Ghost—given to him because of his faith in the Son of God, I wanted to have the same experience myself. I know that God is the same yesterday, today and forever. The way of salvation has been prepared from the beginning, and it is available to all who repent and come to Christ. All who diligently seek the Lord will find Him, and His mysteries will be unfolded to them by the power of the Holy Ghost. This is how God deals with His children, and His ways never change. Remember this, for you will be judged by all you do. If you are wicked in your mortal life, then you will be found unclean before the judgment-seat of Christ. And since no unclean thing can live with God, you will be cast off forever to a place where God does not live.

11 - Nephi's Vision of the Savior's life...

I cannot deny these things, for the Holy Ghost has told me to write them. Wanting to know what my father had seen, and believing that the Lord could show me, I sat pondering in my heart. Then I was caught away in the Spirit of the Lord to a very high mountain that I had never seen before. There the Spirit asked me, "What do you want?" I answered, "To see what my father has seen." The Spirit asked, "Do you believe your father really saw the tree?" "You know I believe all the words of my father," I replied.

Then the Spirit cried out, "Hosanna to the Lord, the most high God, for He is God over all the earth, even above all. You are blessed, Nephi, because you believe in the Son of the most high God. Because you believe, you will see what you desire to see. First, you will see the tree that bore the fruit your father tasted. Then you will see a Man come down from heaven. By seeing Him you will be able to testify that you have seen the Son of God, that He lives!"

Then the Spirit said, "Look!" I looked and saw the tree. It was more beautiful than anything I had ever seen before, and whiter than the driven snow. I said to the Spirit, "I see the tree, bearing fruit more precious than anything." "What do you desire now?" asked the Spirit. I replied, "To know the meaning of the tree." I talked with the Spirit as I would talk to any man. Although He was in the form of a man, I knew He was the Spirit of the Lord.

The Spirit again said, "Look!" But when I turned to look, He was gone. I looked down from the mountain and saw the great city of Jerusalem and other cities. I saw the city of Nazareth, and in that city I saw a virgin who was very pure and beautiful.

Then I saw the heavens open. An angel came down, stood before me and said, "Nephi, what do you see?" I answered, "A virgin, more beautiful and fair than any other." The angel then asked, "Do you know what the condescension of God means?" I answered, "I know that God loves His children, but not the meaning of His condescension." Then he said, "The virgin you see is the earthly mother of the Son of God." I saw her carried away in the Spirit. After she had been carried away in the Spirit for some time, the angel said to me, "Look!" I looked and saw the virgin holding a child in her arms. Then the angel said, "See the Lamb of God, even the Son of the Eternal Father! Now do you know the meaning of the tree?" "Yes," I answered. "The tree represents God's love which may fill the hearts of all His children, and it is worth more than anything!" "Yes," said the angel, "And God's love is the most joyous thing to the soul."

Then the angel said, "Look!" I looked and saw the Son of God, walking among His people. I saw many fall down at His feet and worship Him. Then I understood the meaning of the iron rod that my father had seen. It represented God's word. The iron rod led to a fountain of living waters and the tree of life. Both the pure fountain and the tree of life represented God's love. Then the angel said, "Look and witness the condescension of God!"

I looked and saw the Redeemer of the world, and the prophet who would prepare the way before Him. The Lamb of God, or Redeemer, was baptized by the prophet. After He was baptized, I saw the heavens open and the Holy Ghost come down upon Him in the form of a dove. Then the Redeemer went among the people, ministering to them in power and great glory. Multitudes gathered to hear Him, but many rejected Him and His words. I saw twelve others follow Him, but after they were carried away in the Spirit, I could no longer see them.

"Look!" said the Angel. I looked, and saw the heavens open once again. Angels came down to the people and spoke to them. I saw the Lamb of God going among them, healing their sick and casting out evil spirits. And then I looked and saw the Lamb of God—the Son of the everlasting God, taken by the people and judged by the world. I saw him lifted upon a cross and slain for the sins of the world.

After He was slain, I saw the multitudes of the earth gather together to fight against the gospel of the twelve apostles of the Lamb. This multitude was gathered in the large, spacious building that my father had seen. The angel said, "Look at the world and its wisdom. Even the house of Israel has gathered together to fight against the gospel of the twelve apostles of the Lamb." And then I understood that the large, spacious building represented the pride of the world. It fell with a great crash, after which the angel said, "This is how all nations, kindreds, tongues and people that fight against the gospel of the twelve apostles of the Lamb of God will be destroyed."

12 - Nephi's vision of his descendants...

Then the angel said, "Look and see your descendants, and also your brothers' descendants." I looked and saw multitudes of people upon the promised land as numerous as the sand upon the seashore. I saw these multitudes gather to battle one another. I saw many wars, and many of my people were killed by the sword. I saw many generations of people come and go, all involved in these wars. I saw so many cities that I could not count them all.

Then I saw a great mist of darkness over the face of the promised land. After awhile, the land became violent with lightning, thunder, earthquakes and all kinds of loud noises. I saw large mountains fall into valleys, and plains were broken up. I saw many cities sink into the ocean. I saw many cities burn, and many collapse from earthquakes.

Then for three days there was complete silence and darkness over the earth. After the darkness left, I saw multitudes of people who had been spared from the Lord's great and terrible judgments. I saw the heavens open. Then I saw the Lamb of God come down from heaven and show Himself to the multitudes. I bear record that the Holy Ghost came upon twelve others, whom the Lamb of God had chosen from among the multitude and had ordained.

Then the angel said, "See the twelve disciples of the Lamb, who are chosen to serve your descendants. Remember the twelve apostles of the Lamb? They will judge the twelve tribes of Israel, and judge these twelve disciples, for they are descendants of the house of Israel.

"By their faith in the Lamb of God, these twelve disciples are purified by His blood. They are righteous forever, and they will judge your descendants."

I looked and saw three generations come and go. They were all purified like the disciples, and their robes were white like the robes of the Lamb of God. I saw many in the fourth generation pass away in righteousness. Then I saw multitudes gathered again to war. The angel then said, "See your descendants and your brothers' descendants," and I saw my descendants gathered to war against my brothers'.

The angel then said, "See the fountain of filthy water and the filthy river that your father saw in his dream? The depths of the fountain represent the depths of hell. The mist of darkness that covers the straight path, and the whole earth, represents the devil's temptations. This mist keeps the people from seeing the true gospel. It also hardens their hearts against the Spirit of the Lord, and many people are lost because of it. The large, spacious building represents the world's pride and vanity. A great and terrible gulf divides it from the tree of life. This gulf represents the justice of God and His Son."

While the angel was saying these things, I watched as my brothers' descendants overpowered mine, for my descendants had been tempted by the devil and had become proud and vain. I saw my descendants completely destroyed, for only my brothers' descendants remained upon the promised land.

Then I saw many generations of my brothers' descendants pass away, fighting battles among themselves. And the angel said, "These remaining people will falter in unbelief." I saw that they had become a dark, loathsome and filthy people, full of idleness and all kinds of sinful traditions.

13 - Nephi's vision of Europeans in America...

Again the angel said, "Look!" I looked and saw many nations and kingdoms. He then asked me, "What do you see?" I told him what I saw, and he told me these were the Gentile nations and kingdoms. Then I saw a great church formed by the Gentile nations. The angel said, "See the most abominable church of all the churches, which captures, tortures and kills God's saints." I saw that the devil was the founder of this great, abominable church. I saw gold, silver, fine silk, fine linen and all types of expensive clothing, and I saw many prostitutes. The angel said, "All these things that you see are what the great, abominable church desires. Its members capture and destroy God's saints for the praise of the world."

Then I saw a great ocean (Atlantic), which divided the Gentiles from my brothers' descendants. The angel said, "You will see that God's anger is upon your brothers' people." I saw a man among the Gentiles (Christopher Columbus). He was separated from my brothers' descendants in the promised land by the great ocean. I saw the Spirit of God come upon him and inspire him to sail across the great ocean. Other Gentiles, who had been in bondage (Puritans, Pilgrims, etc.), also sailed across the ocean to the promised land inhabited by my brothers' people.

Then I saw multitudes of Gentiles upon the promised land. God's anger was upon my brothers' descendants (Native Americans). They were scattered before the Gentiles and many were killed, for the Spirit of the Lord was upon the Gentiles. They prospered and obtained the land for their inheritance. The Gentiles were white, very fair and beautiful, like my people had been before they were all killed.

Now these Gentiles who had gone out of their captivity and had crossed the ocean were humble before the Lord. Because of their humility, the Lord's power was with them.

Then their native (European) kings became angry, and gathered their armies and navies to battle against the Gentiles in the promised land. But God's anger was upon all those who fought against the Gentiles, for I saw the Gentiles delivered out of the hands of all other nations by God's power. And I, Nephi, saw that the freed Gentiles prospered in the land. I also saw a book that they carried among themselves. Then the angel asked, "Do you know the meaning of this book?" "No," I answered. The angel said, "This book, (which will be known as *The Holy Bible*), is a record of the Jews. Because this book will contain the covenants that the Lord made to the house of Israel, it will be of great value to the Gentiles. It will also contain many prophecies of the holy prophets, like those engraved on the brass plates, but not as many. Now when this book first went from the Jews to the Gentiles, it contained the fullness of the gospel, of which the twelve apostles testified in all truth. So according to the truth of the Lamb of God, this book went from the Jews to the Gentiles in purity.

"After this true, pure book went from the twelve apostles, or Jews, to the Gentiles, you saw the formation of that great, abominable church, which is the most abominable of all the churches. This church took out of this book, and out of the gospel, many plain and precious parts. They also took out many parts containing the Lord's covenants with His people. They did this in order to distort the right ways of the Lord, which made it easier for them to blind the people's eyes and harden their hearts against the true, pure gospel of the Lamb."

The angel then said, "Because of that great, abominable church, the Gentiles' Holy Bible will no longer contain many of the plain and precious things that the book of the Lamb of God will have once contained. Their Holy Bible will first go to the nations of the Old World in Europe. Then it will be taken across the ocean to the promised land, to your brothers' descendants, the Lamanites. Now you see that because so many plain and precious things will have been taken out of the gospel of the Lamb, multitudes of people, both Gentile and Lamanite, will stumble in darkness, and Satan will have great power over them.

"The Gentiles, who were brought out of captivity and made powerful by God, will not be allowed to completely destroy your people, who will mix with your brothers' people. This is because the Lord God made a covenant with your father, Lehi, that his descendants would have this choice land for their inheritance forever. Also because of this covenant, the Lord will not allow the Gentiles to remain in their awful state of blindness to the true gospel, which you see they are in because of their incomplete Bible, distorted by that abominable church.

"The Lord will be merciful to the Gentiles by bringing His judgments upon the Lamanites, who will not be mighty before them. The Lamb of God says, 'I will be merciful to the Gentiles by bringing much of my gospel to them, and I will restore many of the plain and precious parts of the gospel to them.'

"The resurrected Christ will appear to your descendants in this promised land. They will write many plain and precious things that He will teach them. At a later time, when your people are destroyed, these writings will be buried. And in the last days, when your brothers' people are faltering in unbelief, these writings will come forth to the Gentiles (Latter-day Saints), through God's gift and power. These ancient writings, which upon being translated will be known as *The Book of Mormon*,' says the Lamb, 'will contain my gospel—my rock and my salvation.' Those who seek to bring forth Zion at that day will be blessed, for they will have the gift and the power of the Holy Ghost. If they continue in righteousness throughout their lives, they will be lifted up at the last day and saved in the everlasting kingdom of the Lamb. And those who publish peace at that day, even tidings of great joy, will be beautiful upon the mountains of Zion."

After the angel said this, I saw the Gentiles take *The Holy Bible* to the Lamanites.

I also saw other books being taken to the Lamanites. These books came forth by the gift and power of the Lamb to the Gentiles—the Latter-day Saints. I saw these books convince other Gentiles, Lamanites, and Jews who were scattered over the earth, that the records of the prophets and twelve apostles were true!

Then the angel said, "These last records you see among the Gentiles will establish the truth of *The Holy Bible*, as written by the twelve apostles to the Jews. It will make the plain and precious things, that were removed from the twelve apostles' writings, known again. It will declare to all the people of the earth that the Lamb of God is the Son of the Eternal Father, the Savior of the world, and that all people must come to Him to be saved.

"For all must come to the Lamb according to His words, which will be found in your descendants' record (*The Book of Mormon*), and in the twelve apostles' record (*The Holy Bible*). These books will be as one, for there is one God and one Shepherd over all the earth.

"The time will come when He will first make Himself known to all nations—to the Jews, and then to the Gentiles. In the last days, He will first make Himself known to the Gentiles, and then to the Jews."

14 - Nephi's vision of the last days...

The angel continued, "And In those last days, if the Gentiles will listen to the Lamb of God when He shows Himself to them in word, power and deed, and not turn their hearts from Him, then He will include them with the house of Israel, and they will be a blessed people upon the promised land forever. Then the Gentiles will no longer be brought down as captives, and the house of Israel will no longer suffer in ignorance.

Note: Gentiles who listen in the last days are mentioned by Moroni (Ether 4:6-8).

"For the Lamb of God said, 'That great pit, dug by the great, abominable church, founded by the devil and his children, and dug with the intent to destroy all people, will be filled by those who dug it as they are completely destroyed in the flesh. Their spirits will not be destroyed, but will be thrown into an endless hell. For the devil's captivity is also God's justice upon all who hear His word, yet choose wickedness.'"

The angel then said, "Nephi, you know about the Lord's covenants that He made with the house of Israel—that those who do not repent will perish, and you realize that if the Gentiles repent, it will be well with them.

"But great judgments will come upon the Gentiles if they reject the gospel and harden their hearts against the Lamb of God, for He says, 'The time will come when I will work a great, marvelous and everlasting work among the children of men—a work that will either convince people to seek for peace and eternal life, or a work that because of people's pride, will allow the devil to justly capture them—to destroy them temporally and spiritually.'"

Then the angel asked me, "Do you remember the covenants that the Lord made with the house of Israel?" "Yes," I replied. "Then look and see the great, abominable church—the mother of wickedness. There are only two churches—the church of the Lamb of God and the church of the devil. Anyone who does not belong to the church of the Lamb of God belongs to the church of the devil—that great church, the mother of all abominations, even the whore of all the earth."

I, Nephi, saw the devil's church. It dominated all the nations, kindreds, tongues and people of the earth. I also saw God's saints, who made up the church of the Lamb of God, spread over all the earth.

Their numbers were few because of the wickedness of the devil's church. Then I saw the devil's church gather multitudes in all the Gentile nations to fight against the Lamb of God. I saw the power of the Lamb come down upon the saints of His church, and also upon the Lord's covenant people (Lamanites, Jews and other tribes) who had been scattered all over the earth, but were now gathering together. They were all armed with righteousness and with God's power in great glory.

Then God's anger was poured out upon that great, abominable church, and there were wars in every nation on earth. When the wars first broke out among the Gentile nations, the angel said, "God's anger is upon the mother of harlots—the great, abominable church—the mother of abominations. In the last days, when this vision comes to pass—when wars begin among all the Gentile nations, then the Father's work will begin, preparing the way to fulfill the covenants He made with the house of Israel."

Then the angel said, "Look!" I looked and saw a man dressed in a white robe. "See John the Revelator, one of the Lamb's twelve apostles," said the angel. "John will see and write the rest of the events of the last days, and also many things which have happened from the beginning of the world. He will also write about the end of the world. What he writes will be just and true. When he gives his writings to the Jews, they will be plain, pure, most precious and easy to understand. John will describe what you have seen, Nephi, and he will also describe what you will yet see. But do not write about what you will yet see, for the Lord God has ordained John to do that.

"There are others who have been ordained by the Lord to see all things concerning the earth, from the beginning to the end. These others will also write their records, which will be sealed up to come forth in purity to the house of Israel in the Lord's due time."

It truly was John the Revelator who wrote about the end of the world. I, Nephi, am forbidden to write what I later saw and heard. What I have written is enough, although it is only a small part of what I saw.

I bear record that the angel showed me everything my father saw. This is a partial record of what I saw and heard while I was carried away in the Spirit to that very high mountain. I give you my witness that everything I have written is true.

15 - Nephi explains Lehi's prophecies...

After returning from being carried away in the Spirit, I went back to my father's tent. There I found my brothers arguing over what my father had told them. My father had said many things to them that could be understood only by asking the Lord for their meaning. But they, being proud, did not ask the Lord. I became very sorry because of their stubbornness, and because of the vision I had just seen, in which I knew that my brothers and their descendants would falter because of their unbelief and wickedness. I was overcome with grief, feeling it was greater than anyone's, for I had seen the destruction of my fair people!

After praying to the Lord I received strength, and I asked my brothers what they were arguing about. They said, "We don't agree on what father meant when he spoke of the natural branches of the olive tree, and of the Gentiles." I asked them, "Have you asked the Lord to tell you their meaning?" "No," they replied. "The Lord doesn't tell us such things."

Then I said, "Why don't you keep the Lord's commandments? Why will you allow yourselves to spiritually die because of the hardness of your hearts? Remember what the Lord said—'If you will humble yourselves before me, and not harden your hearts, but ask of me in faith, believing that you will receive, and diligently keep my commandments, then these things will surely be made known to you.'

"By the same Spirit of the Lord which was in our forefathers, I tell you that the house of Israel was compared to an olive tree. Our family is of the house of Israel, for our father discovered that we are descendants of Joseph. We are like a natural branch, broken off an olive tree, to be planted in the promised land.

"The joining again of the natural branch to the olive tree is compared to our people who will receive the fullness of the gospel in the last days. They will receive it from the Gentiles (Latter-day Saints) many generations after the Messiah will have shown Himself to their forefathers, and many generations after they have faltered in unbelief.

"In the last days, the rest of our descendants will know they are members of the house of Israel—the Lord's covenant people. They will learn of their forefathers, and of their Redeemer's gospel, which He gave to their forefathers. They will also know how to come to their Redeemer and be saved.

"In the last days, they will rejoice and give praise to their everlasting God—their rock and salvation. They will receive strength and nourishment from the natural tree again—the true vine, and come into God's true fold. The Lord will remember them again as members of the house of Israel, and graft them back into their mother tree as natural branches. "Our father means that after the natural branches are scattered by the Gentiles, they will be grafted back in, or in other words, receive the gospel, also by the Gentiles. The Lord will show His power and give His gospel to the Gentiles because the Jews, or the house of Israel, will have rejected the Lord.

"Our father not only spoke of our descendants, but also of the descendants of all the house of Israel, bringing to our attention the covenant that will be fulfilled in the last days, which the Lord made to father Abraham saying, 'Through your descendants, all families throughout the earth will be blessed.'"

I explained many of these things to my brothers—about the Jews being restored to the lands of their inheritance in the last days. Then I repeated the words of Isaiah, who wrote about the restoration of the Jews and of all the house of Israel. I told them that at that time, the house of Israel would no longer be scattered and confused. After I explained these things, my brothers were pacified for awhile and they humbled themselves before the Lord.

A little later they asked me what the tree meant that our father had seen in his dream. I told them it was a representation of the tree of life. Then they asked what the iron rod meant. I said it represented God's word, and that those who held onto it never perished, nor could the devil's temptations overpower and blind them, leading them away from the straight path to the destruction of their souls. I pled with them to listen to this warning from God. I encouraged them with all the energy of my soul, and with all the words of my mind, to obey God's word in all things. Then they asked what the river meant. I explained that it came from a fountain of filthy water, which represents the devil's temptations. The depths of the fountain represent the depths of hell. The river was an awful gulf that separated the wicked from the tree of life, and from God's saints who were eating of its fruit. I told them the gulf represents the awful hell prepared by the devil for the wicked.

I told them our father saw God's justice, which also divided the wicked from the righteous. This justice was as bright as a flaming fire, ascending to God forever. Then they asked me if that fire represented the torment of the body—God's justice in this life, or the final state of the soul after death. I told them the fire represents both temporal and spiritual torment—that the day will come when all will be judged according to the works they did while in their physical bodies—that if they were to die while they were still wicked, they would be cast off from spiritual things—things pertaining to righteousness. I told them that they will stand before God who will judge their works, and if their works in the body were filthy in the days of their probation, then they are still filthy out of the body, and therefore cannot live with God. For if they were to live with Him, they would make His kingdom filthy.

God's kingdom will not be made filthy, and no unclean thing can enter it, so there is another kingdom prepared for those who are filthy. That other kingdom, which is an awful hell, is prepared by the devil. According to the justice of God's word, the final state of all souls is to live with Him or to be cast out of His presence. I told my brothers that this is how the wicked are divided from the righteous, and from the tree of life, the fruit of which is most precious and desirable above all other fruits. This fruit—God's love—is His greatest gift.

16 - Nephi breaks his steel bow...

Then my brothers said, "Nephi, your words are so harsh we cannot bear them." I replied, "I know my words are harsh against the wicked. I have justified the righteous and have testified that they will be lifted up at the last day. Guilty people take the truth to be hard on them, for it cuts them to the very center of their souls. If you were righteous—willing to listen to the truth and to obey God's commandments, then you would not feel that I was speaking harshly to you."

After I had diligently urged my brothers to keep the commandments, they humbled themselves before the Lord, and I was joyful. I had great hope that they would walk the path of righteousness.

All these things were said and done as my father lived in his tent in the valley he had named Lemuel. Of Ishmael's five daughters, I married one, each of my three older brothers married one, and Zoram married the oldest. Up to this time, my father had fulfilled all the commandments the Lord had given him, and I, too had been very blessed by the Lord.

One night the Lord's voice came to my father telling him to continue his journey in the wilderness. The next morning, when my father went to his tent door, to his great astonishment he saw a ball of strange workmanship, made of fine brass, sitting on the ground. Within the ball were two spindles. One pointed the way we should go in the wilderness.

We gathered our provisions that the Lord had given us, and the rest of the things we needed for our journey, including all types of seeds. Then we packed our tents and crossed the river that my father had named Laman. After traveling in a south-southeastern direction for four days, we set up camp in a place we called Shazer.

Then my brothers and I went into the wilderness with our bows and arrows to hunt for food. After finding food, we returned to our families. Then we continued our journey, going south-southeast, staying in the most fertile areas along the borders of the Red Sea.

We traveled for many days, hunting food along the way with our bows and arrows, stones and slings. We followed the direction of the spindle on the brass ball, which led us to the most fertile parts of the wilderness.

After many days, we set up camp again to rest for awhile and to hunt for more food. While hunting, I broke my steel bow, and my brothers became angry with me because I could no longer obtain food. We returned to camp and found our families very tired because of their journeying and suffering from hunger. Soon all the men except myself began to complain greatly against the Lord because of their afflictions in the wilderness. Because of our weakness due to hunger, and because of my broken bow and my brothers' bows which had lost their spring, our situation became desperate. And because my brothers had once again become stubborn, complaining against the Lord, I spoke to them for a long time.

Then I made a bow out of wood, and an arrow out of a straight stick. I took a sling and some stones and went to my father and asked him, "Where should I go to find food?" My father asked the Lord where I should go, for the family had humbled themselves after

I had spoken many things to them in the energy of my soul. The Lord's voice came to my father and chastised him for complaining, and my father became very sorry for having complained against God.

Then the Lord's voice said to him, "Look at the writing on the ball." After my father read the writing on the ball, he started to tremble with fear. When my brothers, Ishmael's sons and our wives read the writing, they also began to tremble. I then realized that the pointers on the ball worked according to our faith in and obedience to the directions they gave us. Also upon the pointers, we discovered some new words that were plainly written, which gave us understanding about the Lord's ways. The writing was changed from time to time according to the faith and diligence we gave to its instructions. From this we learn that by small means the Lord can bring about great things.

I went to the top of a mountain, as instructed by the directions written on the ball. On the mountain, I found wild animals and obtained food for our families. When I returned to camp with food, everyone was overjoyed! They humbled themselves before the Lord and gave thanks to Him.

We regained our strength and continued our journey again in the same direction. After traveling for many days, we set up camp to rest again. And in this place, which we called Nahom, Ishmael died and was buried. His daughters were very sad for having lost their father, and because of their afflictions in the wilderness. They complained against my father, saying, "Lehi brought from our home in Jerusalem to wander in this wilderness. Now our father is dead, and we've suffered from fatigue, hunger and thirst. And after all our suffering we are going to die of starvation in this wilderness!"

They carried on with their complaining against my father, and toward me, asking their husbands to take them back to Jerusalem. Then, to make them angry against me, Laman said to Lemuel and Ishmael's sons, "Let us kill our father, and also Nephi, who thinks he is a ruler and teacher over us, his older brothers. Nephi says the Lord has talked with him, and that angels have ministered to him, but we know he lies. He cunningly says these things to deceive us, to lead us away into some strange wilderness, where he plans to make himself king over us and do with us as he pleases."

But in spite of my brothers, the Lord was with us all. His voice came like thunder and we all heard it. He told my brothers many things and chastised them severely. After this, they repented of their anger and became humble, and the Lord blessed us with food once again.

17 - Nephi is told to build a ship...

Then we took up our travels, heading east. We continued to suffer with affliction in the wilderness as our wives bore children, but the Lord poured great blessings upon us. While eating raw meat (for we were commanded not to make many fires) our wives were healthy and nursed their babies. The women became as strong as the men, and they began to bear the harshness of the journey without complaint.

The miracle of our survival in the harsh wilderness is proof that God's promises will be fulfilled. If His children keep His commandments, He will feed and strengthen them so that they may accomplish His commandments, for the Lord fed us while we traveled in the wilderness.

We camped and traveled in the wilderness for eight years, and finally, we came to a land we called Bountiful because it had so much fruit and wild honey prepared for us by the Lord. Bountiful was by the sea, which we called Irreantum, meaning "many waters." We were very happy to pitch our tents by the seashore and rest, for we had suffered much in the wilderness—so much that I cannot write it all.

After we had been in Bountiful for many days, the Lord's voice came to me, saying, "Go up onto the mountain." I went up and prayed, and the Lord said to me, "Nephi, you will build a ship according to my design that I will show you. You will do this so that I may carry your people to the promised land across this great ocean." I asked the Lord, "Where do I find ore to smelt, to make the tools needed to build this ship?" And the Lord told me where to find the ore.

I, Nephi, made bellows from animal skins to blow a fire. Then I struck two stones together and made a fire. Before this, I had not made many fires because of the Lord's command, for He had said, "I will make your raw meat taste good so that you will not have to cook it. If you keep my commandments, I will be your light in the wilderness and prepare the way before you. I will lead you to the promised land, and you will know that it is I who leads you. After you arrive in the promised land, you will know that I the Lord am God, and that I delivered you from destruction by bringing you out of Jerusalem."

After speaking with the Lord, I did my best to keep His commandments, and I encouraged my brothers to be faithful and diligent as well. Then I made tools from metal ore that I smelted out of the rock. When my brothers realized what I was doing, they said I was a fool to think that I could build a ship good enough to cross the great ocean. They would not help me because they did not believe that I could build a ship or that the Lord had told me to build it.

I became very sorrowful because of their hard hearts and stubbornness. When they saw this, they became glad and said, "We knew that you could not build a ship. We knew you overestimated your abilities. You can't do such a great work. You are just like our father, who is led away by the foolish imaginations of his heart. He has led us to wander for these many years in the wilderness. Our wives have suffered by bearing children in the wilderness. They have suffered everything but death and would have been better off dying in Jerusalem rather than suffering so much out here. For these many years we have suffered in the wilderness when we could have been happily enjoying our possessions in the land of our inheritance. We know the people of Jerusalem are righteous, for they keep all the Lord's statutes, judgments and commandments according to the law of Moses. But our father has judged them and has led us away because he knew we would follow him. And you, Nephi, are just like him!"

I replied, "Do you believe our forefathers would have been led out of the hands of the Egyptians if they had not listened to the words of the Lord? Do you believe they would have been led out of their bondage if the Lord had not commanded Moses to lead them out? You know the children of Israel were in bondage and were given many hard tasks as slaves, and so you know that it was good for them to be led out of bondage. You know that Moses was commanded by the Lord to do this great work, and that by his word the Red Sea divided and the children of Israel walked through on dry ground. You know that the armies who followed them were drowned in the Red Sea. You know that the children of Israel were fed with manna while in the wilderness, and that Moses, by his word according to God's power in him, struck a rock, and water flowed out for the people to drink.

"After being led by the Lord their God, their Redeemer, who went before them by day, who gave them light by night, and who did all things for them that they needed, they still hardened their hearts and rebelled against Moses and against God. And by the Lord's word, He destroyed the children of Israel in their rebellion, or by His word, He led and nourished them in the wilderness. After they crossed the Jordan River, the Lord gave them strength to drive out those who were in the land, to scatter and destroy them. And do you think that the people driven out by our forefathers were a righteous people? No, they were not. And do you think that our forefathers would have been chosen to inherit the land of promise if the people who were already there were righteous? No, they would not have been. The Lord esteems all people equally, yet He favors the righteous. Those who were driven off the land were ripe in wickedness, and the fullness of His anger was upon them. The Lord cursed the land against them to their destruction, and blessed the land for our forefathers so that they could obtain power over it, for the Lord created the earth to be inhabited, and He created His children to possess the earth in righteousness. He raises up a righteous nation and destroys the wicked ones. He leads the righteous into precious lands, and He destroys the wicked, cursing the land for their sakes. He rules high in the heavens, for it is His throne, and the earth His footstool. He loves to bless those who accept Him as their God. He blessed our forefathers, Abraham, Isaac and Jacob, by making covenants with them, and He remembered those covenants by bringing their descendants out of Egypt.

"The Lord purified the children of Jacob (Israel) because they were stubborn and hard in their hearts, as you are. He sent fiery flying snakes among them. After they had been bitten, He prepared a way for them to be healed by simply looking at the brass snake held up by Moses. Because the way to be healed was so simple, many would not look up, and died. They also hardened their hearts from time to time, and reviled against Moses, and also against God. But in spite of all this, you know they were led by His matchless power into the promised land.

"After all this, the children of Israel, now in Jerusalem, have become wicked and are ripening for destruction. I know the day must surely come when they will be destroyed, except for a few who will be taken captive. This is why the Lord commanded my father to depart into the wilderness. The Jews planned to kill him, as you now do, so you are murderers in your hearts like the Jews. You are swift to do iniquity, but slow to remember the Lord your God. You have seen an angel who spoke to you, and you have heard the Lord's voice from time to time. He spoke to you with a soft, gentle voice, but you had become too hardened to feel His words. This is why the Lord has spoken to you with a voice of thunder, causing the earth to quake as if it were about to split open. You know that by the power of His almighty word, He can cause the earth to pass away, the mountains to become valleys, and the valleys to become mountains. Knowing all this, why are you still so hard in your hearts? My soul is full of anguish because of you, and my heart is pained, for I am afraid that you will be cast from God's presence forever. Look at me. I am so full of the Spirit of God that it consumes my strength!"

After I said all this, Laman and Lemuel were angry with me, and seeing my weakness, they were about to take me and throw me into the sea. As they were about to take hold of me I said, "In the name of the Almighty God, do not touch me, for I am filled with the power of God, even unto the consuming of my flesh. Whoever touches me will wither as a dried reed in the sun, and be nothing before God, who will smite him!" Then I told them to stop complaining and plotting against my father and me, and to no longer refuse to help me build the ship. I said, "If God commanded me to do anything, I could do it. If He commanded me to say to this water, 'Be thou earth,' it would be earth! And if the Lord has such great power and has brought about so many miracles among His people, why can't He tell me how to build a ship?" I said many more things to confound Laman and Lemuel. The Spirit of God was so powerful upon them, that they dared not touch me for many days, for they were afraid of withering before me.

After many days, the Lord told me to hold out my arm and touch my brothers, and that He would shock them so they would know it was by His power. I did as the Lord said, and after He shook them they said, "Nephi, we know for sure that the Lord is with you, and that His power has shaken us." Then they fell down before me and were about to worship me, but I told them not to. I said, "I'm your younger brother. Worship the Lord your God, and honor your father and mother so that your days may be long in the land that the Lord your God will give you."

18 - Laman and Lemuel are humbled, yet they rebel again...

My brothers worshiped the Lord and helped me build the ship. We worked the timber in a strange manner, for the Lord showed me from time to time how to fashion the timbers of the ship. It was not made like the ships of man's design, for we built it according to the Lord's design, which He showed me. I often went up to the mountain to pray to the Lord, and He showed me great things.

When we finished the ship, my brothers saw that it was good—the workmanship very fine, and again they humbled themselves before the Lord. Then one night, the Lord's voice came to my father, Lehi, telling him that we should board the ship. In the morning we gathered the large supplies of meat, fruit, honey, seeds and provisions that the Lord told us to gather, and we boarded the ship.

In her old age, my mother had borne two sons in the wilderness. The first was named Jacob, the second, Joseph.

After we boarded the ship, we set out to sea and the wind drove us toward the promised land. After many days of sailing, my brothers and Ishmael's two sons and their wives began to make themselves merry. They danced, sang and spoke very rudely, forgetting that God was carrying them safely across the sea. I was afraid that their rudeness would provoke the Lord to smite us, and that we would be swallowed up in the depths of the seam, so I spoke to them very seriously, but they became angry with me, and said, "We will not tolerate you trying to be a ruler over us."

Then Laman and Lemuel tied me with ropes and treated me harshly. The Lord allowed them to do this in order to show His power and thereby fulfill His words about the wicked.

I could not move being tied, and the pointers on the compass that the Lord had made ceased to move as well. Then a great storm arose. It was such a terrible tempest that my brothers did not know which way to steer the ship, and we were driven back for three days. They became very frightened, thinking they would be drowned in the sea, but they still would not untie me.

On the fourth day, this terrible storm grew stronger still. By the end of that day, our ship was about to be swallowed up in the depths of the raging sea, and my brothers began to realize that God's judgments were upon them—that unless they repented, they would die. So they untied me.

My wrists and ankles had become very sore and swollen, but I did not complain. I looked to God and praised Him all that day. While I had been tied, my father had said many things to my brothers, and to Ishmael's sons, for which they had threatened him. They had also threatened anyone else who had tried to speak on my behalf. My parents had become very sick, being old, and having suffered much grief because of their sons. Their sorrow over the iniquity of my brothers and their years of affliction had brought them near death.

My young brothers, Jacob and Joseph, needed much nourishment, but they suffered because of their mother's afflictions. Even the tears and prayers of my wife and children did not soften my brothers' hearts, that they would untie me. Nothing but God's power, threatening them with destruction, could soften their hearts. Only after they realized they were about to die at sea did they repent and untie me.

Finally freed, I held the compass and it began to work again. And as the storm raged on, I prayed to the Lord, and at last the tempest stopped and the waves became calm. Then I steered the ship as we sailed toward the promised land.

After sailing for many days, we joyfully arrived at the promised land and gave great thanks to God. We went upon the land and pitched our tents. We plowed the land and planted the seeds we had brought from Jerusalem. The seeds grew very well, and we were blessed with abundant crops. As we explored this promised land, we discovered many types of animals in the forests. We found cows, oxen, donkeys, horses, goats and all kinds of wild animals which were useful to us. We also found many types of ore, including gold, silver and copper.

19 - Nephi makes more plates and quotes from the brass ones...

Soon after arriving in the promised land, the Lord commanded me to make large plates. Upon those plates, I transcribed my father's record of our journey in the wilderness, of his prophecies, and many of my prophecies. While making my first set of plates, I didn't know that several years later the Lord would tell me to make this second set (the smaller ones). My first set contains my father's record, his genealogy and a detailed account of our wilderness journey.

On this second set, the Lord told me to write a plain and precious record of the ministry and prophecies to my people. This record was to be for their instruction, and for other wise purposes known to Him. I made a detailed record of my people's warfare on my first set of plates (the larger ones). I have told my people that after I am gone, they should hand down all my plates, from one generation to another, from one prophet to another, until the Lord commands otherwise.

For now, I am writing this sacred history, and at a later time I will tell you how the Lord commanded me to make this second set of plates, upon which I now write this more sacred history. My first set of plates, containing our detailed history, is also sacred. If I make mistakes, like those who have written before me, I forgive myself, not because others have also made mistakes, but because like others, I, too am weak in the flesh.

Some consider what I write to be of great worth, both temporally and spiritually, while others do not value it at all. Some do not even value the very God of Israel and His counsel. But according to what the angel said, the God of Israel will be born 600 years from the time my family left Jerusalem. And because of their iniquity, the worldly will judge Him to be of no value. They will whip and strike Him, and even spit on Him. He will allow this because of His loving kindness and long-suffering toward all people.

The God of Abraham, Isaac and Jacob, who led the children of Israel out of Egypt and preserved them in the wilderness, will yield Himself as a mortal man into the hands of wicked men, to be "lifted up," according to the words of Zenock. To be "crucified," according to the words of Neum, and to be "buried in a sepulcher," according to the words of Zenos, who also spoke of three days of darkness that would be a sign of His death, given to the house of Israel throughout the world.

Zenos the prophet said, "The Lord God will surely visit all the house of Israel at the time of His death and resurrection. He will visit some with His voice because of their righteousness, to their great joy and salvation. And He will visit others with His power—with thunder, lightning, storms, fire, thick darkness, by opening the earth, and by raising mountains. The rocks of the earth will break up, and because of the groaning of the earth, the Spirit of God will come upon many kings on other continents, who will exclaim, 'The God of nature suffers.'

"The people of Jerusalem will be scourged by all nations for crucifying the God of Israel, and for rejecting His signs, wonders, power and glory. They will be defamed and hated among all nations. They will wander and perish for despising the Holy One of Israel and for turning their hearts away from Him." Zenos continues, "However, when the day comes that the Jews no longer turn their hearts away from the Holy One of Israel, He will remember the covenants that He made to their forefathers. He will remember all the people who are of the house of Israel and gather them together from all over the earth. Then all the people of the earth in every nation will see the salvation of the Lord and be blessed."

And I, Nephi, write these things to persuade my people to always remember their Lord and Redeemer. I write these things to all the house of Israel, that my record might come to them as well.

Now I grieve in the spirit, to the point of growing weak, for those who are in Jerusalem. But the Lord has shown mercy on me. He has saved me from perishing in Jerusalem and has shown me its destruction, just as He showed the prophets of old. Surely the Lord showed the prophets of old everything about Jerusalem and about us and our descendants. It is very important for us to have their prophecies that are written on the brass plates. I taught my brothers these things, and I read them many things from the brass plates so they would understand how the Lord has dealt with His people in other lands, and in times past.

I read many things to them written by Moses, and especially by Isaiah, to persuade them to believe in the Lord their Redeemer. I applied all the scriptures to our lives so that we could profit and learn from them.

Before reading some of Isaiah's words I said, "Listen, you who are a branch of the house of Israel, which has been broken off and carried across the sea. Listen to the words of Isaiah, written for all of Israel's descendants. Apply Isaiah's words to your lives so that you may have hope in your Redeemer along with the rest of the house of Israel, for the reason Isaiah wrote was to give us hope!"

20 - Nephi reads Isaiah's words from the brass plates...

The Lord's words, spoken by Isaiah: Listen, oh house of Jacob (Israel), who are baptized, and who make oaths in the name of the Lord and speak of God, yet do it not in truth nor in righteousness. You call yourselves holy, but you do not put the God of Israel first in your lives, whose name is the Lord of Hosts.

From the beginning, I have told you, through prophets, things that have happened. I have spoken and revealed them suddenly. I did this because I knew how obstinate and stubborn you are as a people. I prophesied to you of things that I would do before they happened, fearing that unless I did this, you would say, "Our idols and graven images have caused them to happen."

Having seen and heard their fulfillment, will you now declare them to others? Will you also declare that I have shown you new, previously hidden things? They are things revealed now, but not before. Otherwise, you would say, "We already knew about them (without a prophet)." You did not hear or know of these things before they were revealed to you, for I knew you would be a treacherous people, born into a sinful state.

But in spite of your sinfulness, for my name's sake I will put my anger aside, and for my praise I will not completely destroy you, oh house of Israel, yet I will refine and choose you in the furnace of affliction. I will do this for my own sake, for I will not allow my name to be dishonored nor give my glory to another.

Listen to me, oh house of Jacob, which I have called out of the world, for I am He who was at the first, and who will be at the last. My hand laid the foundation of the earth. My right hand reaches throughout the heavens. I call to them and they obey me at once.

Assemble, all the house of Israel, and listen. Who among you has declared these things to you? It is he, whom I, the Lord, have loved. I will fulfill his prophecies of the house of Israel, and through him bring my justice upon the worldly. I have called and raised him up to prophesy, and he will fulfill his calling well. These are the words of this servant of the Lord:

"Come near me, for I have spoken openly from the beginning—from my first declaration. The Lord God and His Spirit have sent me. The Lord, your Redeemer, the Holy One of Israel, says, 'I, the Lord your God, who teaches you for your profit, and who leads you, have sent you my servant. If only you had obeyed my commandments—then your peace would have distilled upon you as the dews from heaven, and your righteousness would have forever flowed to you as the waves of the sea. Your descendants would have been as many as the sands upon the seashore, and their names would not have been cut off from before me.'

"Now I say, give up your worldliness and flee your conspiring enemies. With a voice of singing, declare to the ends of the earth that the Lord has redeemed all the house of Israel! For the Lord led the children of Israel out of bondage through the desert and caused water to flow out of the rock. Even though the Lord has done all this, and even greater things to save His children, 'There is no peace,' says the Lord, 'for the wicked.'

21 - Nephi continues to read Isaiah's words from the brass plates...

"Listen to me, oh house of Israel, all of you who are broken off and driven out because of my people's wicked pastors. Listen, all of you who are scattered abroad, who are of the house of Israel upon all continents, for the Lord called me before I was born, mentioning my name before my birth. The Lord has made my words strong, but as I was growing up, He refined me in obscurity. He said to me, 'You are my servant of Israel, in whom I will be glorified.' Then I replied, 'But I have worked for nothing, laboring in vain, for only the Lord judges me, and only my God knows my works.' But the Lord, who ordained me before I was born to be His servant to restore Jacob, said that even though Israel is not yet gathered, I will yet be glorious in His eyes, and my God will be my strength.

Note: This is the same servant described in D&C 113:5-6 and 2 Ne 3:24.

"The Lord said to me, 'It is not enough that you will be my servant to raise up the tribes of Israel—Joseph (Ephraim and Manasseh), Judah (the Jews), and the other tribes. You will also be a light to the Gentiles (including LDS Gentiles) and thereby be my salvation to the ends of the earth.'

Note: In many prophecies, LDS are referred to as Gentiles (1 Ne 13:35, 3 Ne 16:6-7, 21:11).

"The Lord, the Redeemer of Israel, said to me, a servant to those in authority, whom men despise and nations abhor, 'Kings will take notice and arise, and princes will also worship me, the Lord, seeing my faithfulness to my people. In my own due time, I will hear the cries of the house of Israel, and through my salvation I will help them. I will preserve them, giving them you, my servant, as their covenant. You will establish the earth and cause them to inherit the desolate places. You, my servant, will say to the prisoners, "You are free," and to those in spiritual darkness, "Come into the light." Then all will be fed as they make their journey, finding rest in all high places. They will not hunger or thirst, nor will the heat or the sun burn them, for He who has mercy on them will lead them to the springs of water. I will make a way to all my nations, raising my highways. Then see, oh house of Israel, all those who come to you from afar—from all over the world.'

"Sing, oh heavens, be joyful, oh earth, for the people of the east will be established. Break forth into singing, oh nations, for you will no longer be broken up, for the Lord will comfort His people and have mercy on His afflicted.

"Those of Zion will say, 'The Lord has forgotten us,' but He will show that He has not. Just as a woman cannot forget her nursing child, neither can the Lord forget the house of Israel—even though they may forget Him. He will say to them, 'Look at these prints upon my hands, continually before me, just as you are. Therefore, I will cause your sons to quickly drive out your destroyers. Look around, oh house of Israel, and see all your tribes gathering around you. And as I, the Lord, live, you will surely be bound together in love. Your gathering tribes will yet make the desolate places too full, even after all your oppressors are removed far away. Then your children, who will be given to compensate for your lost ones, will again say, "This place is too crowded. Give me another place to live." Those of the house of Israel will ask, "Who has given me these children after my first ones were lost—after I was made desolate and moved from place to place? Where have these children been while I was left alone?"

Note: Children in Jeremiah 31:15-17

"The Lord God will reply, 'I raised up my servant to the Gentiles, setting up my standard to the people (including Latter-day Saints).

Note: "Servant" is a metaphor for the words "hand, arm, ensign and rod."
See metaphors for "root of Jesse" in 2 Nephi 21:10-12.

"'They took the gospel to the house of Israel, bringing your sons and daughters to you, supporting them. Many wealthy Gentiles, including kings and queens, will take notice of your plight and greatly humble themselves before you. Then all the house of Israel will know that I am the Lord, for those who wait for me will not be disappointed.'

"Is it likely for those who have been the prey of the mighty warriors—those justly captured—to be delivered? To many it is not, yet the Lord said, 'Even the captives of the terrible and the prey of the mighty warriors will be delivered, for I will contend with him (the Antichrist) that contends with the children of Israel, and I will save them. I will cause those who fight against the house of Israel to fight among themselves, and they will destroy one another. Then all will know that I, the Lord, am their Savior and Redeemer, the Mighty One of Jacob.'"

22 - Nephi explains Isaiah's prophecies...

After I, Nephi, read some of Isaiah's words from the brass plates to my brothers, they asked me, "What does all this mean? Are these things spiritual or temporal?" I replied, "These words were given to Isaiah by the voice of the Spirit, for by the Spirit all things that will happen to God's children are made known to the prophets. These words of Isaiah are both temporal and spiritual, for sooner or later, the house of Israel will be scattered among all nations. Even now there are many tribes not known to the people in Jerusalem, for most of them have been led away. Most of the tribes are scattered over the continents. We do not know where they are, but only that they have been led away. Isaiah prophesied about those who have been led away, and about those who would be scattered and hated among all nations for hardening their hearts against the Holy One of Israel.

"The prophecy of the Lord's hand being lifted up to the Gentiles, and of the Gentiles taking care of the children of those who are scattered, is a temporal prophecy, for the Lord's covenants with our forefathers are temporal. These covenants will insure blessings upon our descendants and upon the descendants of all the tribes of Israel.

"Isaiah's words mean this: After all of the tribes of Israel have been scattered and confounded, the Lord God will raise up a mighty nation upon this land. This mighty nation will scatter our descendants and make them desolate. Then the Lord God will begin to do His marvelous work among the Gentiles—a work that will be of great worth to our descendants. Some of the Gentiles will nourish our descendants, carrying them in their arms and upon their shoulders (bringing them the gospel).

"This marvelous work will also benefit other Gentiles and all of the house of Israel (the Jews and other tribes). Then everyone will know about the covenants that the Father made with Abraham, saying, 'Through your descendants all nations will be blessed.' I want you to know, my brothers, that all the nations of the earth cannot be blessed until the Lord makes His arm bare in the eyes of all nations. This means He will fulfill His covenants with power as He brings His gospel to all the tribes of Israel.

Note: How power is described in D&C 1:14 and 2 Nephi 6:14.

"The Lord will again bring all the tribes of Israel out of captivity and gather them to the their lands of inheritance. They will be brought out of spiritual darkness and come to know that the Lord is their Savior and Redeemer—the Mighty One of Israel.

After the tribes have been gathered, the devil's great, abominable church will war among itself. All nations that war against the house of Israel will war against one another and will fall into the pit they will dig to trap the Lord's people, for all who fight against Zion will be destroyed. That great, abominable church, which will distort the right ways of the Lord, will tumble to the dust with a great fall! For Isaiah said, 'The time comes quickly when Satan will no longer have power over the people's hearts (the millennium), for soon all the proud and the wicked will be burned like a harvested field of wheat. Soon the fullness of God's anger will be poured out upon all people, for the Lord will not allow the wicked to destroy the righteous. The Lord will preserve the righteous by His power, even if He must come in the fullness of His anger to destroy the wicked with fire. This is why the righteous need not fear.'

"I know, my brothers, that these destructions must soon come—even blood, fire and vapor of smoke will come upon those who harden their hearts against the Holy One of Israel. But the righteous will not perish (spiritually or temporally), for the time will come when those who fight against Zion will be destroyed. The Lord will surely prepare a way for His people—fulfilling the words of Moses, who said, 'The Lord your God will raise up a prophet like me, and you must listen to all He says, for those who will not listen to Him will be destroyed.' And I, Nephi, tell you that the prophet Moses spoke of is the Holy One of Israel, even the Messiah, Jesus Christ, and He will judge with righteousness.

"The righteous need not fear, for they will not be confused. But the devil's kingdom built up among the people will have great reason to fear. For according to Isaiah, the time will come in the last days when all churches that belong to the devil's kingdom will fear and tremble as they see their imminent destruction. Those churches created to get gain and power over people, to become popular, seeking physical gratification and material possessions, will be brought down and burned.

"The time soon comes when the righteous must be protected and nourished as helpless calves, and the Holy One of Israel must reign in dominion, might, power and great glory. He will gather His children from all over the earth, numbering each of them, and they will know Him. Then there will be one fold and one Shepherd, and the Lord will feed and protect His children. Because of the righteousness of the Lord's people, Satan will have no power over them. He will not be unloosed for a thousand years, even the millennium, and the Holy One of Israel will reign among His people.

"I know that all these things will happen to people in the flesh, for all nations, tribes and people of all languages will live safely, protected by the Holy One of Israel, if they repent of their wickedness. This is all I will say about Isaiah's words for now. Laman and Lemuel, I hope you will consider that the things written on the brass plates are true—things which testify that we must obey God's commandments. Do not think that our father, Lehi, and I are the only ones who have testified of these things. If you will be obedient to the commandments and remain righteous throughout your lives, then you will be saved on the day of judgment. Amen."

Note: Among the thousands of records available to Mormon, the few that he included in his book contain historical information that strictly follow the pattern set forth by Isaiah's writings. Isaiah's prophecies illustrate the Lord's people who repeat cycles of blessings, apostasy, exile, invasion by their enemies, captivity, and ultimate deliverance through repentance. This is why Isaiah's writings were used and explained by Nephi, Jacob, Abinadi, and even Christ Himself. Isaiah writes about patterns that will repeat themselves in the last days. This is why *The Book of Mormon*, a book written to warn latter-day Israel, is patterned after Isaiah's writings.

1 - Lehi prophesies of the promised land...

After I had taught my brethren, my father, Lehi, spoke many things to them. He reminded them of the many great things the Lord had done for them by bringing them out of Jerusalem, and how merciful God had been to them in sparing their lives upon the ocean during their rebellion. He also pointed out the great blessing of this promised land, which we had obtained, and how merciful the Lord had been in warning us to get out of Jerusalem. He said:

"I have seen a vision, in which I know that Jerusalem has been destroyed. If we had stayed there, we would not have survived. Even though we have been through many afflictions, we have been spared and have obtained this promised land.

The Lord has covenanted with me that He will give this land to me and my descendants forever, and also to those whom He will lead here from other nations. I prophesy, because of the Spirit in me, that no people will come to this land unless the Lord brings them here. For this land is consecrated to those whom the Lord brings to it. If the people upon this land serve the Lord according to the commandments He gives them, they will always be a free people. On the other hand, if they are ever brought into bondage, it will be because they have broken the Lord's commandments. For if the people in this land persist in their sinfulness, the land will be cursed for their sakes, but to the righteous, it will be blessed forever.

"The Lord is wise to keep this land hidden from other nations, for they would overrun it, leaving no place for an inheritance. The Lord made this promise to me: If those whom He brings out of Jerusalem will keep His commandments, they will be the only ones to possess this land. They will prosper, be protected from all other nations and inherit this land forever. But when the time comes that they stop believing and reject the Holy One of Israel, the true Messiah, their Redeemer and their God—after receiving such great blessings, after knowing about the creation of the world and of all people, after having power to do all things by faith, having all the commandments from the beginning, and having been brought by His infinite goodness to this precious land of promise—then His judgments will be upon them!

"Then the Lord will bring people from other nations and give them power to take away their lands, to scatter and kill them. Generation after generation will pass away with bloodshed and destruction among them. I hope that you, my sons, will remember and obey my words, so that these things may not happen. Oh that you would wake up from your deep sleep—the sleep of hell, and shake off the awful chains that bind people and carry them down to the eternal gulf of misery and woe. Awake! Arise and hear the words of a trembling parent, whom you will soon lay down into a cold and silent grave, from where no traveler can return, for soon I will go the way of all the earth.

"But the Lord has redeemed my soul from hell. I have seen His glory, and I am encircled about eternally in the arms of His love. And the desire of my soul has always been that you, my sons, will remember His laws.

"From time to time my heart has been heavy with sorrow because of your pride. I have feared that the anger of the Lord your God will come upon you and cut you off from His presence forever—that a curse will come upon you for many generations—that your descendants will be visited by the sword or famine—that they will be hated by many and be led as captives of the devil. Oh my sons, I hope these things do not come upon you. I hope you and your descendants will always be a choice, favored people of the Lord. But His will be done, for His ways are righteous forever. He has said, 'If you keep my laws, you will prosper in the land. Otherwise, you will be cut off from my presence.'

"My soul longs to have joy in you—to leave this world with gladness because of you. Arise from the dust, my sons. Be men, determined to be of one mind and one heart, united in all things so that you and your descendants will not come down into captivity—that you may not be cursed by a displeased and just God—that your bodies and souls will not be eternally destroyed. Awake, my sons! Put on the armor of righteousness. Shake off those chains which bind you. Learn to know God as you arise and walk uprightly before Him. Stop rebelling against Nephi, for he has seen glorious things and has kept the commandments from the time we left Jerusalem. He has been an instrument in God's hands to lead us to this promised land. If not for him, we would have all died of hunger in the wilderness. Yet you have tried to kill him, and he has suffered great sorrow because of you. I fear for him, that he will suffer again because of you, for you have accused him of seeking power and authority over you. I know he has not done this. He only seeks God's glory and your eternal well-being. You have complained that his words are sharp, and that he has been angry with you, but his sharpness is the power of God's word. What you call anger was the truth that he could not keep from speaking, which boldly told you of your sins. Only God's power within Nephi could compel him to command you. He himself did not command you, the Lord's Spirit did. "Now my sons, Laman, Lemuel and Sam, and also my sons of Ishmael, if you will listen to and obey Nephi, you will not perish, for I will leave you my first blessing. But if you will not do this, I will take my first blessing from you and give it to Nephi.

"And now, Zoram, you were once Laban's servant, but you were brought out of servitude in Jerusalem. I know you are a true friend of Nephi forever. Because you have been faithful, your descendants will be blessed along with Nephi's, that they may live long in prosperity in this land. And nothing but sinfulness among them will disrupt their prosperity in this land forever. If you keep the Lord's commandments, you will be blessed, for He has consecrated this land for the security of your descendants, as well as Nephi's."

2 - Lehi speaks to his youngest sons...

"Now I speak to you, Jacob, my first-born in the wilderness. You have suffered in your childhood because of your brothers' rudeness, yet you know the goodness of God, who will compensate you for your afflictions. Your soul will be blessed, and you will live safely with your brother, Nephi, for your days will be spent in the service of your God. I know you are redeemed because of the righteousness of your Redeemer, for you have seen that in the fullness of time, He will come to offer salvation to all.

"Jacob, you are like the children of a future day, to whom the Lord will appear, for you have seen His glory in your youth. The Spirit is the same yesterday, today and forever, and since the fall of Adam and Eve, the way has been prepared for the free salvation of all their descendants. Men and women have been taught to know good from evil. They are given the law, but it cannot justify them. Breaking the law cuts them off from that which is good in this life and in the afterlife, bringing eternal misery.

"Redemption comes only through the Holy Messiah, for He is full of grace and truth. He will offer Himself as a sacrifice for sin to satisfy the law on behalf of those with a broken heart—those who are truly sorry. This sacrifice answers the demands of the law for them. How important it is to make known to the inhabitants of the earth that they can only live with God through the merits, mercy and grace of the Holy Messiah, who will lay down His life in the flesh and take it up again by the power of the Spirit, bringing to pass the resurrection of the dead, being the first to rise. This makes Him the firstfruits to God the Father. He will stand between us and the Father, and all who believe in Him will be saved. Because He will stand between us and the Father, all will come and stand before Him to be judged according to the truth and holiness in Him. The result of the law that the Holy One has given is for the wicked to receive His punishment, and the result of the atonement that the Holy One will make is for the righteous to receive His happiness.

"Thus, everything has its opposite. If not so, goodness and joy would not be separate from evil and misery. All things would be combined, and there would be no life separate from death, nor mortality separate from immortality. There would be no meaning in such a state, for it would destroy God's wisdom, eternal purposes, power, mercy and justice. For with no law, there is no sin. And with no sin, no righteousness, nor a reward for the righteous or misery for the sinful. And if none of these things exist, then there is no God. And if there is no God, then the earth and everything on it, including us, would not exist, for there would not have been a creation, wherein things act and are acted upon. Instead, there would be nothing.

"My sons, I tell you these things for your profit and learning, for there is a God! He has created all things in heaven and earth...all things that act and are acted upon. To bring about His eternal purposes for men and women, after He created all things, there had to be opposition. This is why the forbidden fruit was created opposite the tree of life—one sweet and the other bitter. By this opposition, God gave Adam and Eve the chance to act for themselves—something they could not do without this choice. And I believe, according to what I have read, that one of God's angels fell from heaven and became a devil, having desired evil before God. After he fell, he wanted everyone to become just as miserable as himself. That old serpent—the devil—the father of lies, told Eve that if she ate of the forbidden fruit she would not die, but would become like God, knowing good and evil.

"After Adam and Eve ate of the forbidden fruit, they were sent out of the Garden of Eden to till the earth and grow food. After leaving the Garden, they had children. Their descendants' lives were lengthened to give them time to repent, and God commanded each generation to repent, showing them how they were lost because of their first parents' transgression.

"If Adam and Eve had not transgressed, they would not have been sent into a fallen world. They would have forever remained in the same condition in which they had been created. They would not have had children, but would have been as children, remaining in a state of innocence (without carnal knowledge or desires), for they could feel no joy or misery without knowledge of good and evil. But all things were done according to God's wisdom. Adam chose to fall from his state of innocence in order to have children, and even in this fallen world, his children are meant to have joy.

"For the Messiah will come in the fullness of time to redeem all of Adam and Eve's children from the fall. Being redeemed from the fall, we are free forever—free to act for ourselves. We will only be acted upon at the great and last day when we will suffer for the sins we did not repent of. In this life we are free to choose captivity and spiritual death according to the power of the devil and join him in his misery, or we may choose freedom and eternal life through Christ, the Great Mediator for all who will repent!

"Now, my sons, I hope you will always look to Christ, obey His great commandments, and be faithful to His words, choosing eternal life, according to the prompting of His Holy Spirit. I hope you will not choose eternal death, according to the evil desires of the flesh, which give the devil's spirit the power to bring you down to his kingdom to reign over you.

"These are my last words to you, my sons. I have chosen the good part according to the words of the prophet (Christ), and my only desire is the everlasting welfare of your souls. Amen."

3 - Lehi speaks to his son Joseph...

"My youngest son, born in the wilderness during our greatest sorrow, may the Lord consecrate this choice land as an inheritance for you, your brothers and your descendants, that it may be for your security forever as you keep the commandments of the Holy One of Israel. The Lord will bless you forever, Joseph, because He will not allow your descendants to be completely destroyed.

"My son, I am a descendant of Joseph of old, who was sold into Egypt, with whom the Lord made great covenants. Joseph of old truly saw our day. The Lord promised him that through his descendants He would raise up a righteous branch of the house of Israel—not the Messiah, but a branch that would be broken off and carried across the ocean. The Lord promised Joseph of old that in the last days, in the spirit of power, the Messiah would be made known to this broken-off branch of Israel, and that this knowledge would bring them out of hidden darkness and captivity, and into the light of freedom!

"The Lord said to Joseph of old, 'I will raise up one of your descendants to be a choice seer.

Note: This "choice seer" was the prophet Joseph Smith, Jr.

"'He will be honored among your descendants. I will command this choice seer to do a great work for his brethren. This work will be of great worth to them, for it will bring them knowledge of the covenants that I made with you and with your fathers. I will make this choice seer great in my eyes because he will obey me in doing only what I command him. He will be great like Moses, whom I said I will raise up to deliver my people—your father's descendants—out of Egypt.

"'And your descendant, this choice seer, will have power to bring my word to your other descendants, convincing them that my words (*The Holy Bible*), which they will already have among them, are true.'

"The Lord continued speaking to Joseph of old: 'Your descendants, and the descendants of your brother, Judah, will write. In the last days, their writings will grow together to confound false doctrines, to end disputes, to establish peace among your descendants, and to bring them knowledge of the covenants that I made with their forefathers. From the choice seer's weakness, I will make him strong in the day when my work begins among all my people. A work that will gather in and restore the house of your father, Israel.'

"Then Joseph of old prophesied, 'The Lord will bless that seer, and anyone who seeks to destroy his work will be frustrated, for I am sure that the Lord's promises about the great things he shall do will all be fulfilled. This seer will bear my name, Joseph. His father will also be named Joseph. This seer will be like me, for the things the Lord will bring through him will bring salvation to my people.

"'I am just as sure that the latter-day Joseph will accomplish his work as I am that Moses will accomplish his, for the Lord promised to preserve my descendants forever.'

"The Lord had told Joseph of old, 'I will raise up Moses, give him power in a staff, and judgment in writing. Moses will not say much, for I will not make him a mighty speaker. But I will write my law with my finger and give it to him. I will also give him a spokesman (Aaron). In the last days, I will raise up your descendant, Joseph the seer, and give him power in translating your descendants' writings. I will also give him a spokesman (Oliver Cowdery), who will write the translation for your latter-day descendants.

"'In my wisdom, the words that the seer will translate will be the words I want your latter-day descendants to have. I know the faith of those who will write to their descendants, whose words will be as if they were warning them from the grave. Even from the dust, they will be crying repentance to their descendants many generations later. The words of their cries will be simple, yet because of their faith, I will make their simple, weak words strong. These words will give their descendants knowledge of the covenants I made to your father Israel, to your grandfather Isaac, and to your great-grandfather, Abraham.'"

After Lehi finished reading what the Lord had said to Joseph of old, he said, "My youngest son, Joseph, this is how Joseph, our forefather of old, prophesied.

"And because of the covenants that the Lord made with him, you are blessed. Your descendants will not be destroyed, for they will read and obey the warnings of their forefathers written in the book (*The Book of Mormon*). And among your descendants, a mighty one will rise up.

Note: A mighty one also mentioned in D&C 113:5-6.

He will say and do much good, and he will be an instrument in God's hands. He will have extremely great faith to work mighty wonders and to do great things in God's sight. He will restore much of the house of Israel—gathering the tribes.

"You are blessed, Joseph, yet you are still very young. Listen to your older brother, Nephi, and all the blessings I have mentioned will come to pass. Remember these words of your dying father. Amen."

4 - Nephi's psalm...

Now I, Nephi, will speak about the prophecies of our forefather, Joseph, who was sold into Egypt. Joseph truly prophesied about all his descendants, and of all prophecies, there are not many greater. His prophecies, written on the brass plates, are about us and our future generations.

After my father finished speaking to his sons about Joseph's prophecies, he called for Laman's children. He told them, "The Lord God said, 'If you keep my commandments, you will prosper in this land. Otherwise, you will not have the presence of my Spirit to be with you. My dear grandsons and granddaughters, I cannot die before leaving my blessing upon you, for I know that if you are taught God's commandments, you will not forget them. If you are cursed, my blessing upon you will insure that the curse will be taken off you and put upon the heads of your parents. It will also insure that the Lord's protection will be upon your descendants forever."

After saying this, Lehi called for Lemuel's children. He left his same blessing upon them and said, "Your descendants will not be completely destroyed, and in the last days they will be blessed."

Then Lehi called for Ishmael's two sons, their wives and children. After he had left a similar blessing upon Ishmael's household, he said to my older brother, Sam, "Like Nephi, you will be blessed all your days. Your descendants will be blessed to inherit this land along with Nephi's, and they will be counted as one."

Soon after Lehi had spoken to his household, according to the feelings of his heart and the Lord's Spirit in him, he died and was buried. Not long afterwards, as I was repeating my father's warnings to Laman, Lemuel and Ishmael's sons, they became angry with me because they did not want to hear any more of the Lord's warnings. But the Lord's Spirit compelled me to speak many things to them, just as it had compelled my father before he died.

Many of our words are written on the larger plates as part of our history. But on these smaller plates, containing a more sacred record, I write the things of my soul, and include many of the scriptures from the brass plates, for my soul delights in the scriptures as I ponder them in my heart. I write them so that my children may learn and profit from them.

My soul delights in the things of the Lord, and my heart continually ponders the many great things I have seen and heard. But even though the Lord has favored me by showing me His great and marvelous works, my heart exclaims: I am a wretched man! Because of the sins of my flesh, my heart sorrows and my soul grieves. I am surrounded by temptations and sins that easily come upon me. When I want to rejoice, my heart groans because of my sins. But I trust God, who supports me. He has led me through my afflictions in the wilderness and preserved me upon the waters of the great ocean. He has filled me with His love—even more love than my natural body could receive. He has confounded my plotting brothers, causing them to quake before me. He has heard my prayers by day, and has given me knowledge through visions by night. By day I have been bold in mighty prayer, sending my voice on high, and angels have come to me. And upon the wings of His Spirit, has my body been carried away to high mountains. I have seen great things—too great to be known out of the Spirit, so I was forbidden to write them.

Having seen so many great things, and knowing that the Lord visits His children in mercy, why should my heart and soul continue in sorrow and the strength of my spirit weaken in despair? Why should I let the devil continue to afflict my soul, to destroy my peace and have a place in my heart? Why am I angry with myself and with the devil because of the weakness of my flesh, which has given in to temptation and sinned? Awake, my soul! Stop sorrowing in sin. Rejoice, oh my heart, and make no room for the devil's despair. Do not be angry again because of my enemies. Be peaceful and strong. Rejoice, oh my heart, and cry, "Oh Lord, I will praise Thee forever. My soul will rejoice in Thee, my God, the rock of my salvation. Oh Lord, redeem my soul. Deliver me out of my enemies' hands. Make me shake even at the appearance of sin! May I no longer be weak to temptations, but be made strong with a broken heart and contrite spirit! Oh Lord, do not shut the gates of Thy righteousness to me, but let me walk humbly before Thee according to Thy strict principles. Oh Lord, encircle me with the robe of Thy righteousness. Help me to escape my enemies. Help me not to stumble, and slow my enemy in his pursuit of my soul. Oh Lord, I have trusted in Thee, and I will trust in Thee forever. I will not put my trust in the ways of man, because those who do this are cursed. I know that God will give liberally to all who ask, as long as they ask for what is right. All my days my voice will go up to Thee, my everlasting God, the rock of my righteousness. Amen."

5 - Nephi's people leave his wicked brethren...

Because my brothers were angry with me, I prayed to the Lord, asking Him to soften their hearts. But their anger continued to grow until they wanted to kill me. They openly said, "Nephi thinks he is our ruler, and we have endured many trials because of him. Let us kill him. Then we will no longer be troubled by his words. We do not have to tolerate him as our ruler. We are the oldest, so we have the right to rule over this people."

I will not write everything my brothers said against me. It is enough to say that they plotted to take my life. The Lord warned me about their plans and told me to leave them—to go into the wilderness along with all who would go with me. So I took my family, Zoram and his family, my older brother Sam and his family, my younger brothers Jacob and Joseph, my sisters, and all else who believed in God's warnings and revelations. We took our tents and whatever we could carry, and we traveled for many days before arriving at our new settlement.

My people decided to name our new home Nephi. They also called themselves the people of Nephi, or Nephites. We kept the Lord's judgments, statutes and commandments according to the law of Moses. The Lord was with us, and we were very prosperous, for we planted seeds and reaped plentiful harvests. We raised flocks and herds of every kind of animal.

I had brought the brass plates and the ball, or compass, made by the Lord. As we prospered, we began to grow in numbers in the promised land. I used Laban's sword as a model to make many swords for protection from the people now called Lamanites, for I knew Laman had taught his followers to hate me, my children and all who called themselves Nephites.

I also taught my people how to construct buildings, and how to work with all types of wood and metals, including iron, copper, brass, steel, gold and silver, all of which we found in great abundance. We built a temple patterned after Solomon's temple. It was very fine, but not built with as many precious materials as Solomon's, for such materials are not found in this land.

I encouraged my people to work hard with their hands and to use their time wisely.

Soon my people wanted me to be their king. I did not want them to have a king, but I did what I could for them as their leader. The Lord's words about my brothers were fulfilled, that I would be their ruler and teacher, for I had been their ruler and teacher before they had planned to kill me. When we left my brothers, the Lord also fulfilled His words to me, which said that if they would not listen to me, they would be cut off from His presence.

The Lord caused a sore curse to come upon Laman and his followers because of their wicked rebellion. Because their hearts had become as hard as flint, He caused their skin to become dark. This helped to keep Laman's people from enticing and mixing with mine, who were white, fair and delightful. The Lord said, "If they do not repent, I will make the Lamanites repulsive to your people. Those who mix with them will bring the same curse upon their children." And this is what happened, just as the Lord said it would.

Also by this curse, the Lamanites became lazy, full of mischief and craftiness, and they hunted dangerous animals in the wilderness. Then the Lord said to me, "The Lamanites will be a trial to your people, reminding them to seek my favor and protection. And if your people do not remember me and keep my commandments, the Lamanites will be allowed to destroy them."

I, Nephi, consecrated Jacob and Joseph to be priests and teachers over my people, and we lived the way of happiness (righteousness). The year was 570 BC, and thirty years had passed since we had left Jerusalem in 600 BC.

Since arriving in the promised land, I had kept a historical record of my people on large plates. Then the Lord said to me, "Make another set of plates for engraving things that are good in my sight—for the profit of your people." Upon this second set—the smaller plates, I have engraved a more sacred record of my people. If my people are pleased with the things of God, they will also be pleased with the engravings on these small plates. If my people want to know more about their history, they can read it from the larger plates, which I keep updated.

And now, ten more years have passed, making it forty years since we left Jerusalem, and already we have had wars with our brethren, the Lamanites.

6 - Jacob relates his and Isaiah's vision...

These are the words that Jacob, Nephi's younger brother, spoke to his people:

My brothers and sisters, I have been called by God and ordained to His holy order. I have been consecrated to serve God by my brother, Nephi, whom you look to as a king or protector, and on whom you depend for your safety. I have often spoken to you, and I will speak to you again because I desire the well-being of your souls. You know I have always been anxious for you to heed the words of my father, Lehi—words that I have diligently taught you. I have also taught you everything that has been written, from the creation of the world until now.

Today I would like to speak about things that concern us now, and that will concern our descendants—things Isaiah wrote for us. These are the things Nephi wanted me to tell you so that you may learn about and glorify God.

Isaiah wrote many things having to do with all of Israel's descendants. And since we are Israel's descendants, Isaiah's words apply to us. I will now read two verses of Isaiah's writings: "The Lord God said to me, 'Watch, for I will raise up my hand to the Gentiles and set my standard before all people. After I do this, the Gentiles will care for your sons and nurture your daughters.

Note: Gentiles who are great will do this (2 Nephi 10:8).

"'You, the oppressed of Israel, will not be disappointed after waiting for me. You will know that I am the Lord when you see Gentile kings and queens humbling themselves before you.'"

Now I, Jacob, will comment on Isaiah's words. First of all, the Lord has shown me in a vision that our people in Jerusalem have been killed and taken captive into Babylon.

Second, the Lord has shown me their return to Jerusalem. Third, He has shown me that the Lord God—the Holy One of Israel—will come and serve His people in the flesh. After this, they will whip and crucify Him.

An angel showed me all these things, and said, "Because the house of Israel, with hard hearts and stiff necks, will do this to the Holy One of Israel, His judgments will come upon them, and many of them will be stricken and afflicted. But because of the prayers of the faithful, the descendants of Israel will not be completely destroyed. They will be hated, afflicted and scattered over the earth, but the Lord will be merciful to them, for when they come to know their Him as their Redeemer, then they will be gathered again to their lands of inheritance."

Jacob continues to relate his vision: If the Gentiles repent, and do not fight against Zion by not joining that great, abominable church, then they, too will be saved.

Note: Moroni describes those latter-day Gentiles who repent in Ether 4:6.

Isaiah wrote these things to give us hope that the Lord will fulfill the covenants He made to His children. But those Gentiles who do not repent, who fight against Zion and the Lord's covenant people, will be humbled before the covenant people, for the Lord's people will not be let down after waiting so long for their Messiah. Isaiah tells us that the Messiah will show His power a second time.

Note: This second show of power is described in D&C 103:15-18.

When the house of Israel believes in Him, He will show His power and great glory by recovering them and destroying their enemies, saving all who believe in Him. Those who will not believe in the Messiah will be destroyed by fire, tempests, earthquakes, wars, plagues and droughts. Then they will know that He is the Lord God, the Holy One of Israel! For can the oppressed be rescued from the tyrants, or can those who have been put in prison by corrupt laws be set free? The Lord tells us, "Yes, even the tyrants' prey and the well guarded prisoners will be delivered. For I, the Mighty God of my covenant people, will deliver them. I will fight those who fight against Israel's descendants. I will cause your oppressors to war among themselves and destroy one another. Then all who remain on earth will know that I, the Lord, am their Savior and Redeemer—the Mighty One of Jacob (Israel).

7 - Jacob reads more of Isaiah's words...

"The Lord will say, 'Have I turned you away or cast you off forever? It was not I who turned away and sold you into bondage, it was you, oh house of Israel, by your sins, who turned from me and sold yourselves into bondage. When I came to deliver you, I was rejected. When I called you to repentance, you would not listen. Do you think that I am not able to redeem you? Simply by my rebuke I dry up the sea and make the rivers a desert. By my power I cause the stars to stop shining as they mourn for Israel.'"

The Lord's servant then prophesies: "The Lord God will give me the gift of speaking, and I will speak wisdom to the house of Israel when they are weary and must have things explained to them day by day. For the Lord will give me wisdom to understand things even as learned people understand. The Lord God teaches me, for I will not be rebellious and turn from Him. I will be taken by those whom I offend and be beaten and spit upon. But the Lord God will help me and give me strength.

Note: The Lord will help His servant—2 Nephi 19:4, 3 Nephi 21:10, Jeremiah 30:8-9

"I will not be confused, and in His strength I will not be ashamed. The Lord will justify my survival. Therefore, I will challenge my adversary and with mighty words smite him. The Lord God will help me destroy all who condemn me, and they will wear out like an old coat eaten by moths. Who among you who fears the Lord and obeys His voice by obeying the voice of His servants is left to walk in darkness? (None of you!) The Lord says to those who walk by the light of their own fires—their mere sparks: 'This is what will come to you from my hand (my servant),—you will lie down in sorrow.'"

8 - Jacob continues to read Isaiah's words...

Through Isaiah the Lord said, "Listen, all who desire righteousness. Remember your fine heritage. Remember Abraham your father, and Sarah your mother. For I, the Lord, called and blessed them. Because of their blessing, I will comfort Zion, and all the deserts will become like the Garden of Eden. And in this paradise, there will be joy, thanksgiving and singing. Listen, my people—my nation. For my law and judgments will be a light for the people. I will be near, my salvation will go forth, and I will judge them.

"The continents will obey me, trusting my power. You will see the heavens, the earth and all its inhabitants pass away. But my salvation will be forever, and my righteousness never-ending.

"Listen to me, you who know righteousness, who have my law written in your hearts. Do not fear what men can do, for they will fade as a cloth eaten by moths. But my righteousness and salvation will endure forever—through all generations of time."

Isaiah continues: "Awake and arise! Clothe yourself with the Lord's power. As the Lord subdued His enemies in ancient times, He will also subdue your enemies! The Lord's power will dry up the sea, making it a highway for His people to escape their enemies. In the last days, this is how the redeemed of the Lord will return.

Note: They will return—2 Nephi 21:15-16, Jeremiah 31:12, D&C 103:15-18

"They, the remnant of Israel, will come, singing to Zion. Everlasting joy, gladness and holiness will be all they know, having forgotten all the sorrow and mourning of the past. For the Lord says, 'I, the Lord, am He who will comfort you, oh house of Israel. Now why should you be afraid of men, who will wither as the summer grass? And how can you forget the Lord, who created you, the heavens and the earth? How can you fear even a furious oppressor, as if he could destroy you? Where is the fury of your oppressor now? Soon those held captive will be set free. They will not die of starvation nor die in prison, for I am the Lord thy God—The Lord of Hosts, who created the roaring waves. I will give you my words and my protection as I make a new heaven and new earth.

Note: A new heaven—Ether 13:3-6

"'I do this for my people—the people of Zion. Awake and arise, oh Jews, who have felt the hand of my wrath. Of all your sons, none can guide or deliver you from this wrath. Only these two sons (desolation and destruction— famine and the sword) will come to you, bringing you sorrow. Then who will I send to comfort you? Your sons have fainted, except these two, which are at the head of all your streets, full of the Lord's rebuke, like a wild bull caught in a net.'"

Isaiah continues: "Now hear what the Lord will do for His afflicted people who have gone astray. After He pleads their cause to the Father and takes away the bitter cup of His fury, the Jews will not drink from it again. The cup will be given to those who have afflicted the Jews—those who have beaten them down and walked over them as if they were dust. Therefore, awake and arise with power, oh Zion! Your city will be holy and beautiful, oh Jerusalem! For soon no one who is unclean will come to you. Your oppression will be over, oh Jerusalem, and you will be free, oh captive daughter of Zion (New Jerusalem)."

9 - Jacob explains resurrection, justice, accountability, then calls his people to repentance...

My brothers and sisters, I, Jacob, have read these things to you from Isaiah so that you will know about the covenants the Lord made with all of Israel's descendants—so you will know that He has spoken to the Jews through His holy prophets since the time of Adam and Eve. The Lord will continue to speak to the Jews until they are restored to the true church and fold of God—until they are gathered home and established in all their lands of promise.

I have read these things so that you will rejoice forever over the blessings the Lord God will bring to your descendants. I know many of you have been searching our scriptures to know of your future. From your searching you have learned that we will all die, but with resurrected bodies we will see God. We know He will be born on earth and will minister to those in Jerusalem. For in His wisdom, the Great Creator will subject Himself to a mortal body and die for all people, that they may become subject to Him.

After Adam and Eve fell, all people were cut off from the Lord's presence. Being cut off, they all became subject to death, which is to leave the mortal body. Because of this death, there must be a resurrection so that the spirit and body will be reunited, able to see God and walk and talk with Him again. This is why the Great Creator's plan included a merciful resurrection.

This resurrection, wherein all are changed to living immortal matter, is only made possible by an infinite atonement—without limits or bounds. Otherwise, the judgment of death would be endless, and all bodies would forever remain as dead mortal matter.

Oh the wisdom of God, His mercy and grace! For if we were to die, never to rise again, then our spirits would become subject to the devil, who fell from the presence of the Eternal God, never to rise again. For without bodies, our spirits would become devils—angels to a devil, shut out from our God's presence, and remain in misery with the father of lies. We would be controlled forever by that being who deceived our first parents, who made himself appear to be an angel of light, and who inspires people to create all types of secret combinations, murder and works of darkness.

Note: "Secret combinations" are groups of people who meet in secret to devise plans that will give them more money, power and glory of the world (3 Nephi 6:27-28, Ether 8:20-25).

Oh how great is the goodness of our God in preparing a way for us to escape the grip of this awful monster—the death and hell of body and spirit. And because the Holy One of Israel has prepared a way for our deliverance, the mortal grave—death—will deliver up all the dead to immortality. And the spiritual grave—hell, will deliver up its captive spirits. Death and hell will be overcome, and the freed spirits will be restored to their immortal bodies by the power of the resurrection of the Holy One of Israel.

Oh how great is our God's plan! For His paradise must deliver the righteous spirits, the devil's hell must deliver the wicked spirits, and the grave must deliver up the bodies of all. The spirit and body will be restored to one another, because everyone, righteous and wicked, must become immortal. We will be living souls, having knowledge as we do now, except our knowledge will be perfect. The wicked will have a perfect knowledge of all their guilt and uncleanness, being exposed before God, and the righteous will have a perfect knowledge of their joy, being clothed in robes of righteousness.

After we have all become immortal souls, we will stand before the judgment-seat of the Holy One of Israel, to be judged according to His holy judgment. Those who were righteous on earth will still be righteous, and those who were filthy on earth will still be filthy—the devil and his angels. They will go away from God with their souls burning within them like flames that ascend forever.

Our God's justice is great because He fulfills all the words and laws He gives us. On the other hand, the righteous saints of the Holy One of Israel—those who have believed in Him and have endured the trials of the world without shame—will inherit God's kingdom, and their joy will be full forever. This kingdom has been prepared for them since before the world was created.

Oh the great mercy of our God, the Holy One of Israel! He will deliver His saints from that awful monster, the devil. He will deliver them from death, hell and that endless anguish which will come to all who separate themselves from Him. Oh how great the holiness of our God, for He knows all things. He will come into the world to save all who will listen to Him. He will suffer the pains of all people—of every man, woman and child descended from Adam and Eve. He will do this so that the resurrection will be brought to everyone, that all may stand before Him at the great judgment day.

He commands all people to repent, to be baptized in His name, and to have perfect faith in Him, the Holy One of Israel, or they cannot be saved in God's kingdom. If they refuse to repent and believe in Him, and are not willing to be baptized in His name, and will not continue in righteousness throughout their lives, then their spiritual progress must end, for the Lord God, the Holy One of Israel, has spoken His law.

Those who have not been given the law—the gospel of repentance—are not condemned. Because of the atonement, the mercy of the Holy One of Israel claims and delivers them.

The atonement satisfies the demands of His justice upon all who have not been taught the law. They are delivered from the devil and restored to the Holy One of Israel, who created them and gave them life. But cursed are those who have been given all of God's commandments, as we have, and who break them, wasting the days of their probation, for their condition is awful!

Note: Being in an "awful state" refers to those given "all" the commandments, or the "fullness" of the gospel, and who then pollute God's "holy church" (3 Nephi 16:10-13, 20:28, Mormon 8:35-38, Ether 8:24).

Oh that cunning plan of the evil one! Oh the vanity, frailty and foolishness of men! When they are educated they think they are wise, and they stop listening to God's counsel. They put it aside, thinking they know better themselves. Their wisdom is foolishness because it doesn't benefit them, and they will die spiritually. But it is good for them to learn many things, as long as they learn how to listen to God's counsel.

The rich, who have many things of the world, are cursed. Because of their worldliness, they despise the poor and criticize the humble, for their hearts are set upon their possessions—their false gods—their riches. They will die spiritually and their possessions will fade away.

Cursed are those who will not listen to or see the truth, for they will die spiritually. Cursed are those who are not pure in heart, who refuse to repent, for a knowledge of their sins will condemn them at the last day. Cursed are those who lie, for they will be sent to hell. Cursed are those who unjustly kill others, for they will die spiritually. Cursed are those who are not sexually pure, for they will be sent to hell. Cursed are those who worship idols, for the devil delights in this. And finally, cursed are those who die in their sins, for they will return to God, still sinful, and see His face.

Remember how awful it is to break the laws of our Holy God and to give in to the devil's enticing. Remember, to be carnally-minded is to die spiritually, but to be spiritually-minded is to live with God forever.

Listen to my words and remember the greatness of the Holy One of Israel. If you say I have spoken hard things against you, then you fight truth, for these are your Creator's words. I know that the words of truth bring fear and anger to those who will not repent. The righteous do not fear the truth, they love it, and are not upset by it.

Oh then, my brothers and sisters, come to the Lord, the Holy One. Remember that His ways are righteous. His path is narrow and it leads straight to Him. At the end of the path there is but one gate. He alone is the keeper of that gate, employing no servant there, for He, the Lord God, will not be deceived. He will open that gate to whomever knocks, but He despises those who are proud of their education and wealth. Unless they give up their pride, seeing themselves as fools before God, and humble themselves before Him, He will not open the gate to them, and the happiness prepared for the saints—those who are truly wise—will be hidden from them.

Oh my brothers and sisters, remember my words. Look as I take off my coat and shake it before you. I pray that God will view this, too. You will know at the last day, when we are all judged by our works, that after I preached the gospel of Christ to you, the God of Israel witnessed that I shook your sins from my soul. Then I will stand before Him, resurrected with brightness, and will not be responsible for your sins.

Turn from your sins. Shake off the chains of the devil, who wishes to bind you down. Come to that God who is the rock of your salvation. Prepare your souls for that glorious day—the day of judgment—when justice will be administered to the righteous. If you are prepared, you will not be afraid, for you will not remember your awful guilt with perfect clarity and have to say, "Holy, holy are Thy judgments, oh Lord God Almighty, for I know my guilt. I transgressed Thy law, and these transgressions are mine. The devil has obtained me, and I have become prey to his awful misery."

My brothers and sisters, it is necessary for me to awaken you to the awful reality of these things. And would I speak so sharply if your minds were pure? Would I need to speak the truth so plainly if you were free from sin? If you were holy, I would speak to you of holiness. But you are not holy, and because you look to me as your teacher, I must teach you the results of sin. My soul hates sin, my heart delights in righteousness, and I will praise the holy name of my God.

Come, everyone who is thirsty. Come to the fountain of salvation, all who have no money. Come, buy and drink wine and milk without money. Do not spend your money on worthless things, working for things that will never satisfy you. Listen closely and remember what I'm telling you. Come to the Holy One of Israel, enjoy His gifts of eternity, and let your soul delight in His abundance. Remember the words of your God. Pray to Him continually by day, and give thanks to Him by night, letting your hearts rejoice. The Lord's covenants are great, and because of them, He will come down to His children with grace and mercy. He has promised us that our descendants will not be completely destroyed because He will preserve them. In future generations, they will become a righteous branch of the house of Israel.

Brothers and sisters, I would like to speak more today, but instead, I will finish speaking tomorrow.

10 - Jacob explains the Lord's covenants...

The next day, Jacob continued speaking: My brothers and sisters, today I will speak to you again about this righteous branch of Israel. The covenants the Lord made to Abraham, Isaac and Jacob are temporal, being fulfilled in the flesh. I have seen a vision wherein I know that many of our offspring will die because of their unbelief. But in His mercy, God will bring His gospel to them again. Our offspring, in the latter days, will again be favored by accepting the gospel, which will give them a true knowledge of their Redeemer.

It is necessary for Christ to come among the Jews—those who are the more wicked part of the world, for no other nation on earth would crucify their God. If mighty miracles were done among other nations, they would repent, knowing that He is their God.

But because of priestcraft and wickedness in Jerusalem, the Jews will turn against Him and crucify Him. For doing this, all types of destruction, famine, disease and bloodshed will come upon the house of Israel, and those who are not destroyed will be scattered among all nations.

The Lord God has said, "After the house of Israel believes in me—that I am Christ, then they will be restored to the lands of their inheritance. This is one of the conditions of the covenant that I made with their ancient forefathers. The house of Israel will be gathered from all over the earth after their long separation, and the Gentile nations will be great in my eyes, for they will help bring the Jews to their lands of their inheritance."

Even Gentile kings and queens will nurture them. Because of this, the Lord's promises to the Gentiles are great! For God has promised, "This land will be for your inheritance, and the Gentiles will also be blessed upon it. This will be a land of liberty to the Gentiles, and they will not have kings to rule over them, for I, the Lord, will protect this land from all other nations, and all who fight against Zion will perish.

"Those who raise up a king against me will perish, because I, the Lord, the king of heaven, will be the Gentiles' king, and a light to them forever, if they hear my words. Because my covenants must be fulfilled—covenants that are fulfilled in the flesh, I must destroy the secret works of darkness, murder and wicked acts. Because I must do this, all who fight against Zion, whether they be Jews or Gentiles, in bondage or free, men or women, will perish. Those who fight Zion are the most corrupt in all the earth, for those who are not with me are against me.

"I will fulfill the promises I made to Israel's descendants while they yet live in the flesh. To fulfill my covenants, I will afflict your descendants (Native Americans) at the hands of the Gentiles. But I will soften the Gentiles' hearts, who will come to love them and be like a father to them. Then the Gentiles will be blessed and become part of the house of Israel. I will consecrate this land as an inheritance to your descendants forever, and also to the righteous Gentiles, who will be counted with them."

God told me, Jacob, that this land is choice above all others, and that He will have all people who live upon this land worship Him. And now, my brothers and sisters, God has been merciful to us by giving us this great knowledge of the future. So let us remember Him and put away our sins. Let us hold up our heads, for we are not too distant from God's love. Our fathers were driven out of Jerusalem, the land of our inheritance, but we have been led to a better land across the sea.

The Lord's promises are great to those who are upon all continents. Since Isaiah speaks of continents (isles), there must be more lands other than this inhabited by our brethren. This is true, because at different times the Lord has led away other tribes of Israel according to His desire. The Lord remembers all whom He has led away, including us. So cheer up your hearts, and remember that you are free to act for yourselves. You may choose the way of everlasting death or the way of eternal life. I advise each of you to give up your heart to God's will, not to the devil's will, nor your own. Remember, after you have given up your heart to God, you must continue in His grace. If you do this until the end of your life, then through His grace you will be saved. May God raise you from death by the power of the resurrection. May He also raise you from spiritual death by the power of the atonement, that you may be received into His eternal kingdom and praise Him through divine grace. Amen.

11 - Nephi writes more of Isaiah's words...

Jacob said many other things to my people, but what I have written is enough. Now I, Nephi, will write more of Isaiah's words, for my soul delights in them. I compare Isaiah's words to the lives of my people, and I teach his words to all my children, for Isaiah truly saw the Redeemer, even as I have.

My brother, Jacob, has also seen Him, so I write Jacob's and Isaiah's words for my children. Their words will prove my words to be true, for God has said that by the words of three He will establish His word. Yet God sends more than three witnesses to prove all His words. My soul delights in proving to my people the truth of the coming of Christ, for every law that God has given since the beginning of the world, including the law of Moses, has been a type, or a representation of Christ.

My soul also delights in the covenants the Lord made with our forefathers. My soul delights in His grace, justice, power and mercy, and in the great, eternal plan that delivers us from an eternal death (spiritual and physical). And most of all, my soul delights in proving to my people that unless Christ comes, we will all perish. If there is no Christ, then there is no God. And if there is no God, then we do not exist, for we could not have been created. But there is a God, and He is Christ, and He will come in the fullness of His own time.

Now I will write some of Isaiah's words so that my people may rejoice for all mankind, for Isaiah wrote to all people.

12 - Nephi writes some of Isaiah's words...

What Isaiah, the son of Amoz, saw concerning Judah and Jerusalem: "In the last days, when the Lord's temple will be established in the chief of the nations (Zion), the righteous throughout all the world will come to it.

Note: The word "mountain" is a metaphor for the word "nation." Two parallel scriptures, 2 Nephi 12:2 and Jeremiah 31:6-7, illustrate this metaphor. Note how "top of the mountains" and "chief of the nations" are used in exactly the same context.

"They will say, 'Let us go to the Lord's nation—to the temple of the God of Jacob. In His temple, the Lord will teach us,' for the Lord's word will come from Jerusalem, and His law from Zion.'

"The Lord and His law will judge all nations and rebuke many. Then they will repent and convert their weapons into farming tools. They will no longer think of war, but of peace. Oh house of Jacob, come back to walk in the Lord's light. You have all gone astray, for each tribe has wicked traditions. The Lord will not protect His people who mix with the unbelieving—those who listen to mystics rather than make covenants with Him.

"The land of the unbelievers is full of silver and gold, and there is no end to their wealth. Their land is filled with transports, and there is no end to their streams of chariots. Their land is also full of man-made idols.

"Because the people are so proud in their sins, refusing to humble themselves before God, He will not forgive them. The wicked will fear the Lord and hide in the rocks, preferring to be buried by mountains rather than face His glory. The proud will be humbled, and the Lord alone will be exalted when He comes, for on that day, which soon comes, all nations that have put themselves above others will be brought down. The day of the Lord will come upon all the finely dressed people who possess so much, and who think they are above others. It will come against all the earth—upon all the proud nations—against every tall tower and fortress—against all the sea vessels that bear fine merchandise. Proud men will bow down, and their pride will be made low, for only the Lord will be exalted in that day, and He will completely destroy their idols.

"Many will go and hide in the cracks of the rocks and in caves because the fear of the Lord will come upon them. The glory of His majesty will smite them when He rises to terribly shake the earth. In that day, a man will throw to the moles and bats the idols of gold and silver that he has made for himself. Again, many will hide in the holes of the rocks and in the tops of the ragged rocks as the fear of the Lord comes upon them. The majesty of His glory will smite them when He comes to terribly shake the earth. Oh descendants of Israel, stop doing things according to the ways of men, who forget that they depend on the Lord for their every breath. For of what worth are the ways of men?

13 - Isaiah's writings on latter-day turmoil and judgments...

"The Lord of Hosts will remove from Jerusalem, and from Judah, their supplies of food and water. The Lord will also remove the mighty man, the man of war, the judge, the prophet, the prudent, and the older leaders. He will remove the captain of fifty, the statesman, the counselor, the cunning craftsman, and the eloquent speaker.

"The Lord of Hosts will make children their princes, for young people will rule over them. People will oppress each other, the young will treat their elders with disrespect, and those without honor will mistreat the virtuous.

"Men will demand that a brother be their ruler, saying, 'You have a robe, be our ruler and do not let this ruin come upon us.' But the brother will respond, 'My house is also barren, and I am not able to heal you, so don't attempt to make me a ruler of the people.'

"Jerusalem and Judah will fall because their words and actions will be against the Lord, provoking Him before His very eyes. The look on their faces will give them away, revealing their sins to be like those of Sodom. Their souls will be cursed, for they will have chosen evil for themselves!

"But tell the righteous that it will be well with them, for they will yet eat the fruit of their labors. The wicked will be cursed and perish, for the reward of their own hands will be upon them!

"The Lord said, 'My people's children oppress them and women rule over them. Oh my people, your leaders cause you to make mistakes and do away with your traditions.'

"The Lord stands to plead before the Father and to judge the people. He will bring the elders and rulers of His people to trial, saying, 'You have taken the goods of my earth all for yourselves, depriving the poor.' The Lord God of Hosts will ask them, 'Why did you do this? Why did you waste their goods and insult their dignity? And because the women of Zion are proud, walking with petite steps, chins in the air, eyes wandering and jewelry tinkling, I will smite them with baldness and expose them unadorned.'

"In the very last days, the Lord will humble those who walk about smartly displaying their fine apparel—chains, bracelets, scarves, bonnets, leg ornaments, headbands, charms, earrings, rings and nose jewels. He will humble those who proudly wear their changeable suits of apparel, shawls, hair ornaments, fine linen, hoods and veils. Then instead of smelling like perfume they will stink—wearing rags instead of fine clothes—being bald instead of having well set hair—being burned instead of being beautiful.

"Your men will fall in battle, and Zion's daughters will mourn, sitting upon the ground, impoverished. Under these circumstances, many women will take hold of one righteous man and say, 'We will support ourselves, just let us be called by your name to take away our shame (to have priesthood protection).'

14 - Isaiah's writings on latter-day judgments and protection...

"During this same time, the Lord's people will be beautiful and glorious, and the fruit of the earth will be delightful to those who have escaped to Zion. After the destruction, those who remain among the living in Zion and in Jerusalem will be called holy. The Lord will wash away the sins of Zion's daughters and cleanse the bloodshed of Jerusalem by the spirit of judgment and burning. Over all of Zion, and over her solemn assemblies, the Lord will form a cloud of smoke by day and a shining fire by night. The glory of Zion will be a refuge and defense for all the righteous. And a tabernacle will shelter them from all the elements.

15 - Isaiah's latter-day description of drought and invasion...

"Then I will sing to my beloved a song about His vineyard:

In a good land, He fenced it, cleared out the stones and planted it with the best vines. He built a watchtower in the middle and put in a winepress. Then He watched for good fruit, but the vineyard only brought forth wild grapes. Now the Lord asks Israel's descendants, 'How well have I taken care of you in all parts of the earth? What more could I have done for you—what have I left undone? When I looked for good fruit, I found only wild grapes. So now I will take away the hedge and let it be eaten up. I will break down the wall and let it be trampled. Your lands will be made desolate from the droughts I will send. I will not care for my vineyard, but allow briars and thorns to grow up all over it.'

"The Lord's vineyard is the house of Israel throughout the earth, and the tribe of Judah is a pleasant plant. But when the Lord looked for fair judgment, He only saw oppressive leaders. When He looked for righteousness, He only saw people crying out for justice. Cursed are those who join house to house until there is no place left, and they are compelled to gather in the center of the land! I know they will be cursed because the Lord of Hosts told me, Isaiah, 'Many great cities will be emptied of their people, and ten acres will produce very little food.'

"Cursed are those who get up in the morning, pursuing strong drink all day and night, who revel in their own music and in their own ways, not caring about the Lord's work nor about how He deals with His people.

Note: "strong drink" is the wine, or ways, of Babylon (2 Ne 27:4, D&C 88:94).

"My people have gone into captivity because they have no knowledge. Their leaders are starved, and they as a people have withered. These multitudes of people will all descend into hell, along with all their glory, pomp and celebrating. For the unjust will be brought down, and those in high positions will be humbled. Only the Lord of Hosts will be exalted, for God will show His holiness by His righteous judgments. After these judgments, His people will be fed in the wasted places of the wicked.

"And cursed are the vain and sinful, who will bring on their own judgments by saying, 'Let the Lord hurry and do His work so we can see it. Let us see the counsel of the Holy One of Israel. Then we will know it is true.' Cursed are those who call evil good and good evil. Cursed are those who consider themselves to be experts and full of knowledge. Cursed are the mighty leaders who drink Babylon's wine (destructive ways), who are bribed by the wicked to take justice away from the righteous.

"Because the Lord's people do these things, despising and throwing away His words and laws, they will be burned like dried weeds as their glory goes up in smoke. For the Lord is angry with His people and will stretch forth His hand against them. Their hills will tremble, and their dead bodies will be torn apart by dogs in their streets. After all this destruction, the Lord's anger will not be turned away, but His judgments will continue. The Lord will lift up an ensign—will hiss unto (call) the enemy—from a far off nation. The enemy will come quickly, without getting tired and without a wrong step. The enemy's army will not stop to sleep nor to set up camps along the way. Their weapons will be ready as they come in swift, loud transports.

Note: Compare this invasion description to 2 Nephi 17:18-20, 18:7, and 23:4-9.

"They will capture those who would not flee to Zion, like a young lion capturing her prey, and no one will be able to free them. These armies will come down against them like the roaring of the sea. Then darkness and sorrow will fill the land, and light from heaven will not be given.

16 - Isaiah's own cleansing and commission...

"In the year that king Uzziah died, I, Isaiah was in the temple. I saw the Lord sitting upon an exalted throne. Angels stood nearby, each with his covering and with power to move about, calling out to each other, 'The Lord of Hosts is most holy, for the whole earth is full of His glory.' As the angels spoke, a door opened and the temple was filled with smoke so that I could no longer see the Lord. Then I realized that I had seen the Lord and exclaimed, 'I am cursed, for I have unclean speech and live among people with unclean speech, yet I have seen the King, the Lord of Hosts!' Then one of the angels came to me, holding a live coal that he had taken from the alter with a pair of tongs. Touching my mouth with it, he said, 'This coal has touched your lips. Your sins are taken away and have been atoned for.'

"Then I heard the Lord's voice ask, 'Whom will I send to these unclean people?' Having been forgiven, I said, 'Here I am, send me!' Then the Lord said to me, 'Go and tell the people that they will continue to hear the Lord's words without understanding them and continue to see His hand in their lives without acknowledging it. Then tell the people what they want to hear, again and again, so that their ears and eyes will grow content and heavy, for they will not hear the fullness of the gospel with their ears, see it with their eyes, and understand it with their hearts. They will not repent, be converted and healed.'

"I asked the Lord, 'How long should I do this?' The Lord answered, 'Until my judgments fall upon them—until their cities are destroyed and emptied.' "But before their cities are destroyed, the Lord will remove His people out from among the wicked. A tenth of the people will return to the cities, only to be consumed, but like the teil and oak tree, their seed, or children, will remain, and will be called holy.

Note: Compare "holy seed" to 2 Nephi 14:3-4.

17 - Isaiah's tells Ahaz not to fear...

"When Ahaz (grandson of Uzziah) was king of Judah, King Rezin of Syria, and Pekah, son of King Remaliah of Israel, both went to war against Jerusalem, but they could not prevail against it. It was known among the house of David (tribe of Judah) that King Rezin had conspired with Pekah (tribe of Ephraim). This is why Ahaz and his people were afraid of being attacked. Then the Lord said to me, Isaiah, 'Take your son, Shearjashub, and go meet Ahaz on the highway at the point where it meets the irrigation canal that comes from the wool cleaners' spring. Tell Ahaz not to fear the fierce anger of Rezin and Pekah. He should not be concerned that Syria (Rezin) and Ephraim (Pekah) have conspired against him by saying, "Let us go up against Judah to conquer it, and to put in Tabeal's son as king," for I, the Lord God, tell you that their plan will not come to pass. Also tell Ahaz that for now, the head of Syria is Damascus and the head of Damascus is Rezin. Samaria is likewise the head of Ephraim, and Remaliah's son, Pekah, is the head of Samaria. But within sixty-five years, Ephraim will not be a united nation. If Ahaz will not believe this prophecy, he will not be established.'

"After giving this message to Ahaz, I, Isaiah, said to him, 'Ask for a sign from the Lord—a sign in the heavens or in the earth.' But Ahaz replied, 'I will not ask for a sign and tempt the Lord.' Then I, Isaiah, said, 'Hear me now, oh house of David. It does not matter if you weary me by not looking forward to the promised signs, but will you also weary my God? The Lord Himself will give you this sign—A virgin will conceive and bear a son, and name Him Immanuel (God with us). By the time He is old enough to eat butter and honey, He will already know how to refuse evil and choose good. But before this, Samaria and Damascus will both have their kings removed. The house of Israel will see days of despair unknown since the time that Ephraim left Judah, for the Lord will bring the king of Assyria upon you, upon your people and your father's house.

"In that day (the last days), the Lord will call in armies from the outer parts of Egypt and Assyria, who will come quickly like flies and bees. They will settle in the desolate valleys and caves near the water holes where thorns and bushes grow. In one day, the Lord will hire the king of Assyria as a razor, who will come from beyond the river to humble the house of Israel.

"After this destruction, the righteous will still be able to feed their animals. In Zion, there will be an abundance of milk, and all who are left in the land will eat butter and honey. In that day, all the places of Babylon that used to flourish with crops and vegetation will be dried up and become a place for briars and thorns. In those places, men will hunt with bows and arrows, searching for food. All the hills that were once plowed and cultivated will not produce food because of the drought. The land will only be good for hungry oxen and cattle to wander over in their search for food.

18 - Isaiah's words about invasion in spite of alliances...

"The Lord said to me, 'Write on a large scroll: Maher-shalal-hash-baz (hurry the plunder, hurry the spoil).' After writing this, I had Uriah the priest and Zechariah witnesses it, that it would be known among the people as a true prophecy. When my wife, the prophetess, bore a son, the Lord told me to name him what was written on the large scroll—Maher-shalal-hash-baz. His name was to be a reminder that before he would learn to say, 'Father' or 'Mother,' the riches of Damascus and the spoil of Samaria would be plundered by the Assyrians.

"The Lord said to me, 'Because these people reject my servants and form alliances with the leaders of other nations, the Lord will bring a large, strong army to overrun their land like a river overflowing its banks. This enemy will overrun Judah even until he gets to the neck (head cities—Old and New Jerusalems), and he will occupy the rest of the land.

"'Because this people associate with their conspiring enemies, listening to the leaders of far off countries, they will be broken into pieces and none will deliver them. If they go to war, they will receive the same fate. Counseling with nations will do them no good. Their resolutions will be ignored, for God will not be with them, but only with the righteous.'

"These strong judgments are what the Lord showed me. He said, 'Do not spend your time identifying and fearing conspiracies as this people do. Do not fear any man.'

I, Isaiah, tell you that you must be sanctified by the Lord of Hosts and fear only Him, for there is only safety in the Lord. But to both houses of Israel—Joseph and Judah—who reject Him, He will be a rock over which to trip, and a curse to those who live in Jerusalem, whose inhabitants will be either killed or captured. I prophesy this because the Lord has told me to write and bind my testimony, and to seal His law for His disciples. After doing this, I will wait for the Lord to come, who for now hides His face from the house of Jacob (Israel).

"My name, Isaiah, means: Jehovah Saves. My sons' names, Shearjashub and Maher-shalal-hash-baz, mean: The Remnant Will Return (to the lands of their inheritance) and Hurry the Plunder, Hurry the Spoil (Assyrian plundering). My children and I are named as the signs and wonders given to Israel from the Lord of Hosts, who will live in the nation of Zion.

"When those in darkness advise you to communicate with your dead, tell them to communicate with the God of the living, and from Him know the desires of their righteous dead. Tell them they should look to the Lord's law, and to the testimony of His servants. If they don't do this, but rather speak according to their own words, they work in darkness. They will be frustrated, angry and hungry, yet they will not humble themselves and repent. They will look up toward heaven, cursing their God and king, and then look down, only to find more trouble, darkness and anguish of spirit. Thus they will be driven into greater darkness on their chosen path.

19 - Isaiah writes about the return of latter-day Israel...

"Nevertheless, this darkness will not be as bad as the darkness the tribes of Zebulon and Naphtali experienced while being afflicted by the Assyrians—nor as bad as the darkness the Lord afflicted upon the route of the Red Sea, beyond Jordan in Galilee of the nations. For the people who live in the land of the shadow of death, walking in darkness, will see a light that will shine upon them! The Lord will multiply the nation of Israel, which will be full of rejoicing! For after Israel's servant suffers at the hand of his oppressor, the Lord will give him power to break his yoke, staff and rod, with which his oppressor will have burdened him.

Note: The Lord will heal His servant (3 Nephi 21:10, Jeremiah 30:8-9).

"Then every battle will be disrupted with the noise of bonfires, wherein bloodstained garments will be burned.

"Because of these things a Child will be born to the house of Israel—a Son will be given, who will govern His people. He will be called The Wonderful Counselor, The Mighty God, The Everlasting Father, The Prince of Peace. He will sit upon David's throne, and by His zeal, He will have no end to His kingdom, government, peace and righteous judgment. The Lord told Jacob (Israel) that all this would come upon his descendants. When all these things happen, all people will know these prophecies, even

Ephraim and Samaria, who speak with pride and arrogance, saying, 'Our system has collapsed, but we will replace it with a new, stronger one. Our leaders have fallen, but we will replace them with new, stronger ones.'

"Because of their pride—refusing to be humbled—the Lord will gather their enemies against them. He will send in their enemies to openly consume Israel. After doing this, the Lord's anger will not be turned away, but will continue, for the people do not turn away from sin nor seek the Lord of Hosts, who smites them. This is why the Lord will humble Israel, cutting off their head and tail, government and commerce in one day. The older, established men are the political head. Those who claim to be prophets, yet who teach false traditions, are the tail, for this people's leaders cause them to err, and those who follow them will be destroyed.

Note: Those who "err" in D&C 33:4 and 2 Nephi 28:14.

"The Lord will have no joy in their young men or mercy on their fatherless and widows, for they are all hypocrites and evildoers, speaking foolishness. After all this, the Lord's anger will not be turned away, but will continue.

Note: The Lord's hand "stretched out still" is the hand of anger against His people, not the hand of mercy (2 Nephi 15:25).

"The wicked will be consumed with evil, which like a fire, will burn within them. Through the Lord of Host's anger, the land will be scorched and the people will be burned by the flashes of heat. Being consumed with evil, the wicked will have no mercy upon one another. They will steal food, but it will not be enough. They will kill for food, but it still will not be enough. And finally, they will eat one another.

"The descendants of Manasseh and Ephraim will fight each other and they will both fight the Jews. After all this, the Lord's anger will still not be turned away, but will continue.

20 - Isaiah writes of latter-day judgments...

"Cursed are those who propose unrighteous laws and then write them into the law books for the people to live by, who do this to lawfully deny justice to the needy, to legally take away the rights of my poor people, to make prey of the widows and to rob the fatherless.

"What will you do when you are visited by desolating armies that will come from afar? What nation will save you then? Where will your wealth be? Without my protection, many will bow down as prisoners and fall among the dead. After all this, the Lord's anger and judgments will continue.

"The Assyrian will act as the rod of the Lord's anger—the staff of His indignation in His hand. The Lord said, 'I will send him against you, a hypocritical nation. I will allow his army to plunder, capture and kill the people, and to tread them down like mud in the streets.' The intent of his heart will not be to be the Lord's instrument, but to destroy and annihilate many nations. He will say, 'Have not all my commanders become kings? Is not Calno (Syria) conquered as Carchemish (Turkey)? Is not Hamath (Lebweh) conquered as Arpad (Tel Erfad)? Is not Samaria conquered as Damascus? I have overcome all these kingdoms, whose graven images were greater than Jerusalem's and Samaria's. And since I have conquered Samaria and her idols, will I not easily conquer Jerusalem and her idols?'

"After the Lord has performed His whole work upon Mount Zion and Jerusalem, He will punish the Assyrian king for his pride and arrogance. For he will also say, "By my strength and wisdom I have done these things. I am a brilliant and valiant commander, who conquered the people and their treasures. I easily conquered the people of all the earth and their riches, like one who gathers eggs without disturbing the chickens."

"But the Lord reasons, 'How can an axe boast that it cuts wood when it has no life—when it was the woodsman's power that cut the wood?' Because the Assyrian king will boast like a lifeless axe, the Lord of Hosts will starve his followers and cause his glory to go up in smoke.

"The light of Israel will call down fire and the Lord will bring down flames. In a single day, the oppressors will be burned like thorn bushes. The fire will consume the Assyrian king and his glory—his armies and the wicked throughout the earth, both body and soul. After this, so few of the oppressors will be left in the earth that a child could count them.

"In these very last days, the remnant of the house of Israel will no longer serve the Assyrian king in oppression. They will serve the Lord, the Holy One of Israel, in truth. These few survivors of Israel, even the remnant, will repent and return to their mighty God.

"At first, only a few will return from the consumed parts of the lands. But at last, these remnants of Israel will become as numerous as the sands of the sea, overflowing the consumed lands. For the Lord God of Hosts will decree that all the wicked in the lands be consumed.

"Because of this, the Lord God of Hosts says, 'Oh my people that live in Zion, do not be afraid of the Assyrian. He may beat you and oppress you for a little while, like Pharaoh once did against the Israelites in Egypt. But soon my anger will destroy him and your oppression will come to an end.'

"For the Lord of Hosts will create a scourge for the Assyrian like the defeat of the Midianites at the rock of Oreb. For just as the Lord miraculously parted the Red Sea, He will raise His rod (His servant) against his oppressor.

Note: This will be a victorious servant in the Lord's hand.
See 2 Nephi 21:1, 10, Jeremiah 30:8-9 and D&C 103:15-16.

For in the very last days, the Assyrian's burdens will be taken off your shoulders and his yoke from off your necks, and this because of the servant's anointing.

"Before that time, the Assyrian will come from the north to Aiath (an old Canaanite settlement). He will travel south, through Migron, stopping at Michmash (west of the Jordan valley). Then he and his armies will march south, through the Michmash Gorge, stopping in Jeba. A few miles to their south, the people in er-Ram, afraid of his power, and those further south in Tell el-Ful, will run in terror. Seeing what is coming, the daughters in Khirbet Kakul will mourn for those living near Jerusalem. They will cry out to their southern neighbors in Khirbet el-'Isawiyeh, 'Oh, poor Anata (near Jerusalem).' As the Assyrian continues south, Shu'fat will be destroyed and the inhabitants just north of Jerusalem will run for their lives. The Assyrian will remain that day on the slopes of Mt. Scopus and will shake his hand against the Mount of Olives.

"Through the Assyrian, the Lord of Hosts will cut off Jerusalem's government leaders with terror. Those in high positions will be cut down and the proud will be humbled. The Lord will use iron to cut down the thickets of the forests—the most corrupt branches, and Lebanon will fall by a mighty one.

21 - Isaiah writes of the Lord's servants (rod and branch)...

"A rod (servant) of the Lord—a descendant of Jesse as well as of Ephraim, will come forth and be given much power. A branch will also grow from this same lineage of Jesse.

Note: The Lord's rod and branch explained in D&C 113:4—6.

"The Lord's Spirit will rest upon this branch—the spirit of wisdom, understanding, counsel, might and knowledge. Because he will fear the Lord, the Lord's Spirit will make him quick to understand truth and he will not judge merely by what he sees or hears. This servant will judge the poor with righteousness. On behalf of the humble, he will judge fairly. He will command the earth, and at his command, the wicked will be destroyed. He will be covered with righteousness and faithfulness to the Lord.

Note: This mighty servant is mentioned in 2 Nephi 3:24 and D&C 103:15-16.

"After the wicked are killed, the world will live in peace. Wolves will live with sheep, wild cats will sleep by calves, and children will play among them. Bear cubs will also sleep next to calves, and lions will eat straw instead of hunting other animals. A baby will play near a snake's nest, and the young child will play near the cockatrice's den. No one will hurt or destroy any living thing throughout all the Lord's holy nation, for as water fills the seas, so shall the knowledge of the Lord fill the earth. In that great millennial day, this branch, descended from Jesse—the root of Jesse—will be a source of truth to the people of the earth. The Gentiles will seek his wisdom, and his rest will be glorious.

"Just before that time, the Lord will set His hand (through His servant) a second time to recover the remnant of His people, whom the king of Assyria will have oppressed—the survivors on all continents. The Lord will establish him as an ensign for all nations to come to. He will assemble the outcasts of Israel and the scattered Jews from all over the earth.

"The descendants of Ephraim will no longer envy Judah (the Jews), whose enemies will be destroyed. In turn, the Jews will no longer despise Ephraim. Together, Judah and Ephraim, supported by their conquered enemies, will subdue the eastern nations.

"The Lord will completely destroy the tongue of the Egyptian sea and the river, dividing them into seven streams, allowing the remnant of Israel to walk across on dry ground. A great highway will be provided for the survivors of Israel to walk upon. Many will come out of Assyria, just as the children of Israel walked out of Egypt.

Note: Isaiah describes a second exodus, just as Joseph did in D&C 103:15-18.

22 - Isaiah describes latter day rejoicing...

"In these very last days, the house of Israel will say, 'Oh Lord, we will praise Thee. Though Thou was angry with us, Thine anger is turned away and Thou has comforted us. Behold, God is our salvation. We will trust in Him and not be afraid, for the Lord JEHOVAH is our strength, our song and salvation. Now with joy we will drink water from the wells of salvation. Praise the Lord, call upon His name, declare His doings among the people, tell that His name is exalted!'

"All will sing to the Lord because everyone on earth will know that the Lord has done wonderful things. So rejoice, all who will live in Zion, for the Holy One of Israel is great, and He will live among you!

Note: The Lord among His people D&C 103:20, 3 Nephi 21:25, Jeremiah 30:22

23 - The Assyrian conquers Babylon...

This is the demise of Babylon that Isaiah, son of Amoz, saw: "To the Assyrian king the Lord says, 'Lift your banner against the great nation. Sound the advance and give the signal to go in to their capital. I, the Lord, have already commanded my sanctified ones to leave. I have called out my mighty ones from among the wicked because my anger is not upon those who rejoice in my highness.'

"Then the Lord of Hosts will stir up many nations to gather in battle, and their noise will be tremendous. They will come from a far country, from beyond the horizon, as the Lord's weapons of His indignation, to destroy the whole land. Cry out, for the day of the Lord is very near, that comes with destruction from the Almighty. Because of this invasion, all will be faint and every man's heart will pound with fear. They will be filled with sorrow, amazed at the scope of the destruction, and their faces will burn from the heat of the blasts.

"Watch for this day of the Lord, which will be cruel, both with wrath and fierce anger, to lay the land desolate, for He will destroy the sinners from the face of it. Because of the darkness over the land, the stars, the moon and even the sun will not be visible.

"The Lord says, 'I will punish the world for its evil and the wicked for their sins, and I will cause the arrogance of the proud to end. So many will be destroyed, that a man will be as scarce as fine gold. In my fierce anger, I, the Lord of Hosts, will shake the heavens, and the earth will be moved out of her orbit. Then, like a hunted deer or wandering lamb, every man will return to his own people, running back to his homeland. All the proud and the wicked will die by the sword. Their children will be dashed to pieces before their eyes. Their houses will be spoiled and their wives ravished.

"'I will stir up their enemies against them, who will not come for riches, but to kill. They will not spare young men, pregnant women, nor children.

"'Then Babylon, the glory of kingdoms, the beauty of the Chaldeans, will be like Sodom and Gomorrah when God overthrew it. It will never be lived in again from generation to generation. Nomads will not camp there nor shepherds herd their flocks there. Only wild beasts of the desert will live there. The houses of Babylon will be full of owls, and idle, demonic creatures. The wild beasts of the islands will howl in their desolate houses and reptiles in their pleasant palaces. This time soon comes, for Babylon's days will not be extended.'

24 - Babylon to be destroyed...

"The Lord will have mercy on Israel, choosing them again and returning them to their own lands. Gentile converts will be adopted into the house of Israel, and they will bring the house of Israel to their place from the far ends of the earth, returning them to their lands of promise. Israel's descendants will then rightfully possess these lands, capturing and ruling over their oppressors, who will become their servants and handmaids.

"In those very last days, when the Lord delivers Israel's descendants from sorrow, fear and hard, forced labor, they will repeat this proverb against the king of Babylon, the Antichrist: 'Who has put an end to the oppressor and the golden city, Babylon? The Lord! He has broken the staff of the wicked and the scepters of the rulers. He who struck the people in wrath continually, who ruled the nations in anger, is now persecuted, and nobody will help him.

"'The whole earth is at rest and is quiet. Those remaining break into singing! The people of Joseph and Judah rejoice over your demise, saying, "Since you have been cut down, no one attacks us." Hell has made special arrangements for you, stirring up the dead—even all the wicked chiefs and kings—to meet you. These men will taunt you, saying, "Have you become weak like us? Your glory is brought down to hell. Your music is no longer heard, and worms cover you."

"'How you have fallen from heaven as Lucifer, the son of the morning! You have been cut down to the ground, you who once weakened the nations! This is your reward, because like Lucifer, you said in your heart, "I will ascend into heaven. I will exalt my throne above the stars of God. I will also sit upon the mount of the congregation, in the heights of the north. I will ascend higher than the clouds, becoming like the Most High."

Yet you, king of Babylon, will be brought down to hell—to the depths of the pit.

"'Those who happen to see you will ask, 'Is this the man that made the earth tremble, who shook kingdoms? Is this the man who turned the world into a wilderness, who destroyed cities and took so many prisoners? All the kings of the nations lie in tombs among their kindred, but you are not given a grave. Your body is like the remains of those killed by the sword, thrown into a gravel pit after being trampled. You will not even be buried with those slaughtered in battle because you have destroyed your land and have killed your people.'

"If his children were to survive, they would also be evil-doers. Therefore, prepare to destroy the children of the king of Babylon because of their father's sinfulness. Do not let them rise up again to possess the land or to fill the world with cities. 'For I will rise up against them,' says the Lord of Hosts, 'cutting off Babylon's name and descendants. I will destroy its people and turn it into a swamp, sweeping it with the broom of destruction.'

"The Lord of Hosts reaffirms, 'Surely as I have foreseen and planned it, so will all this come to pass. I will call the Assyrian king (the Antichrist) into my land, and in my nation tread him under foot. Then his yoke and burden will be taken off my people's shoulders.'

"This is the plan for the whole earth. This is the hand stretched out over all nations. Since the Lord of Hosts has declared this to be, who will dispute? The Lord's hand is stretched out, and who will turn it away?"

In the year that king Ahaz died came this prophecy:

"Do not rejoice in victory just yet, you Philistine descendants (Palestinians), now that King Ahaz, the Jewish leader, is dead. His descendant will be as a fiery flying serpent (as a seraph—a powerful servant of the Lord). "The Lord says, 'I will protect the first-born. Their poor and needy will be fed, resting in safety. But I will kill your people in Palestine with a drought. Then he will kill your survivors.

"'Then moan and cry in your city, you enemies of Judah, you Palestinians, when you are completely dissolved, for a pillar of smoke will come from the north, and none will survive beyond their designated time to die.'

"After this destruction, what will then be the message to the nations? That the Lord has founded Zion, in which the poor of His people will trust."

25 - Nephi explains Isaiah...

Now I, Nephi, will explain some of Isaiah's words. Many of my people do not understand them very well because they do not understand the way that the Jews prophesied. I have not taught my people much about the Jews because the Jews worked in darkness and sin.

I have written some of Isaiah's words on my small plates so that my people in this generation and in generations to come will know that God's judgments will come upon all nations. Because Isaiah's words are not plain, listen my people who are of the house of Israel. Listen to what I have to say about them.

Isaiah's words are plain to those who are filled with the spirit of prophecy. I will give you my plain prophecy, for my soul delights to teach in all plainness. My soul delights in Isaiah's words because like Isaiah, I, too came from Jerusalem. I have seen the Jews' methods of learning, and I know that by their methods they understand the prophets. No other people understand the prophets the way the Jews do, unless they, too, have learned their methods. I have not taught my children these methods, but I have told them about God's judgments, prophesied by Isaiah, that have come upon the Jews.

Now I will write my own prophecy plainly so that all may understand:

When Isaiah's prophecies come to pass, all people will clearly know that his words have been fulfilled. If any of my people feel that Isaiah's words are not great, I direct my prophecy to them. Isaiah's words will be of great worth to those who live in the last days because that is when people will understand them. I include Isaiah's words for the good of those who will live in the last days.

Many generations of Jews have been destroyed at various times, but none were ever destroyed before the Lord's prophets warned them to repent of their wickedness.

Other prophets warned the Jews just after my father left Jerusalem, but they hardened their hearts. I prophesy that the Jews have been destroyed, except for those captured and taken to Babylon. I know these things because of the Spirit that is in me.

Even though the Jews have been captured, they will return again to possess Jerusalem and the lands of their inheritance. But they will continue to have wars until the Only Begotten of the Father of heaven and earth is born and shows Himself to them in the flesh.

Even then, they will reject Him because of their iniquity, hard hearts and stubbornness. They will crucify Him, but after three days, He will rise from the dead, and all who believe in His name will be saved in God's kingdom. My soul delights in prophesying of Him, for I have seen His day. My love for Him causes me to magnify His holy name.

After the Messiah rises from the dead and shows Himself to those who believe in His name, Jerusalem will be destroyed again, for those who fight against God and His church are cursed.

The Jews will be scattered among all nations. The city of Babylon will also be destroyed, so the Jews will be scattered by other nations. The Lord will use these other nations to scatter and persecute the Jews for many generations, until the time comes when the Jews will begin to believe in Christ. And when they begin to believe in Christ, they will believe these prophecies, and the Lord will convert them, setting His hand (servant) a second time to restore His people from their lost and fallen state. To do this, the Lord will begin a marvelous, wonderful work among all people. This marvelous, wonderful work will bring His words to them. These scriptures will judge the house of Israel at the last day because they will come forth to convince them of the true Messiah—that they no longer need to look forward to a Messiah.

If another Messiah should come, he would be a false Messiah, deceiving and flattering the people. But there is only one true Messiah that the prophets spoke of, the one that the Jews will reject when He first comes in the flesh. According to the prophets, the Messiah will come 600 years from the time we left Jerusalem. According to God's angel, His name will be Jesus Christ, the Son of God.

Now, my brothers and sisters, I have spoken plainly so that you cannot misunderstand. As the Lord God lives, and has worked miracles for the children of Israel through His servant, Moses, there is no other name given under heaven except Jesus Christ whereby all can be saved. For this reason, the Lord God promised me that my writings will be preserved and handed down from generation to generation. Through my writings, the promise that He made to Joseph of old—that his descendants will never perish in ignorance of Christ as long as the earth exists—will be fulfilled. This is why my writings will go from generation to generation as long as the earth exists, according to God's will and pleasure. And the nations who will have my words will be judged by them.

We work diligently to engrave on these plates, to persuade our children and our brothers and sisters to believe in Christ, and to be reconciled to God. We also know that by His grace we are saved after doing all we can ourselves.

Even though we believe in Christ, we keep the law of Moses, looking forward to Christ until He fulfills the law. We know Christ will fulfill the law of Moses, so the law has become dead to us. We are made alive in Christ because of our faith in Him, yet we keep the law of Moses because of the commandments.

We talk of Christ, we rejoice in Christ, we preach of Christ, we prophesy of Christ, and we write our prophecies. We do this so our children may know to whom they may look for a remission of their sins. We speak about the law of Moses so that our children may know the deadness of it after it has been fulfilled. This knowledge will help them look forward to Christ's way of life. It will also help them understand why the law of Moses was given, so they will not harden their hearts against Christ as He fulfills the law of Moses. For you, my people, are stubborn. This is why I have spoken so plainly to you—so that you cannot misunderstand. The words I have spoken will stand as a testimony against you because they are enough to teach anyone the right way. The right way is to believe in Christ and not deny Him. By denying Him, you also deny the prophets and the law. Christ is the Holy One of Israel, and you must bow down before Him and worship Him with all your might, mind and strength—with your whole soul. If you do this, then you will not be cast out. But until Christ comes, you must keep God's performances and ordinances until the law of Moses is fulfilled.

26 - Nephi prophesies of 34 to 385 AD...

Nephi speaks to his descendants: After Christ rises from the dead, He will show Himself to you. You must be careful to live by the laws that He will give you. In a vision I have seen that many of your generations will pass away, troubled by great wars.

And when the Messiah comes into the world you will be given the signs of His birth, and also the signs of His death and resurrection—a great and terrible day for the wicked, for that is the day they will perish. This will happen because the cries of the prophets and the saints, whom the wicked will reject and kill, will go up to God from the ground against the wicked.

The Lord of Hosts says, "All the proud who do wickedly will be burned. Those who kill the prophets and saints will be swallowed up by the earth and mountains will cover them. Tornadoes will carry them away, and earthquakes will cause buildings to crush them, grinding them to powder. They will be visited with thunder, lightning, earthquakes and all types of destruction, for the Lord's angry fire will burn them like kindling."

Oh the pain and anguish of my soul for the loss of my people that will perish! For I, Nephi, have seen their destruction, which almost consumes me before the Lord's presence. But I must cry to my God, "Thy ways are just."

However, those of you among my righteous descendants who listen to the prophets and faithfully look forward to Christ and the promised signs, even while being persecuted, will not die. The Son of righteousness will appear to you and heal you. Then you will have His peace for three generations. Many of your fourth generation will also have His peace.

But after this, destruction will come quickly to you, my people. For even though it pained my soul to see it, I have seen your destruction and know that it will come to pass. After four generations, you, my descendants, will sell yourselves for nothing. The reward for your pride and foolishness will be destruction. Because you will give way to the devil and choose his works of darkness rather than light, you must go down to hell. For the Spirit will not always stay with you. When the Spirit leaves you, your destruction will come quickly, and this grieves my soul.

Just as the Jews need to be convinced that Jesus is the very Christ, the Gentiles must also be convinced that He is the Christ, the Eternal God. They must be convinced that He shows Himself to all who believe in Him by the power of the Holy Ghost, even to every nation, working mighty miracles, signs and wonders among them all, according to their faith.

But listen, for now I prophesy to you about the last days—the days when the Lord will bring these words (*The Book of Mormon*) to all people: After my and my brothers' descendants falter in unbelief—after being subdued by the Gentiles—after the Lord will have camped against them, and laid siege against them with horses, and raised forts against them, humbling them to the dust—even after they are considered to be nothing, the words of the righteous will be written, and the prayers of their faithful forefathers will be answered. And the latter-day Lamanites will no longer be forgotten as a people. Their ancestors, who will have been destroyed, will speak to them from out of the ground, from where the book will come. Their voices will be as familiar spirits, for the Lord will give them power to whisper to their descendants (through *The Book of Mormon*). For the Lord God said, "The Nephites will engrave their history on metal plates. When the plates are buried, the unbelieving Lamanites will not have access to them because they would destroy them. Then the Nephites, even their terrible warriors, will be destroyed suddenly.

About 1,100 years later, many of the remaining Lamanites (Native Americans) will be driven and killed by the Gentiles who will come to this land. Then the Gentiles will lift themselves up in the pride of their own eyes, stumbling by building up many churches that deny God's miracles and power. They will preach their own wisdom for profit and worldly approval while taking advantage of the poor. They will build up many churches, which will be the cause of envy, contention and slander.

The Gentiles will also have secret combinations, like the ancients, which come from the devil—the founder of murder and works of darkness. He will lead the Gentiles by the neck with a weak cord until he binds them with his strong cords forever.

Listen my beloved brethren, for the Lord God does not work in darkness. Because of His love, everything He does is for the benefit of the world. He will even lay down His own life to draw all people to Him and to offer His salvation freely to all. Does the Lord say to anyone, "Depart from me?" No. He says, "Come to me, all people of the earth. Buy milk and honey without money and without price." Has He ordered us out of the synagogues and chapels? No. Has He told anyone that they may not partake of His salvation? No. He has given it freely for all and has commanded His people to persuade all others to repent. Has the Lord forbidden anyone to enjoy His goodness? No. All people are equally privileged to partake of it freely.

However, the Lord does forbid priestcraft among us. Priestcraft is setting oneself up as a light to the world, teaching others for gain and fame, claiming to teach truth while ignoring the needs of Zion. The Lord helps to keep us from practicing priestcraft by commanding us to practice charity, which is love. If we do not have charity, then we are nothing. And if the Gentiles have charity, they will not allow the laborer in Zion to perish. True laborers in Zion are those who build up Zion. If they labor with their hearts set upon money, they will perish (physically and spiritually).

The Lord God has also commanded us not to murder, lie, steal, envy or take His name in vain. We should not fight with one another or commit adultery, for whoever does these things will perish. None of these sins come from the Lord, for He only does good among us in all plainness. He invites everyone to come to Him and enjoy His goodness—black, white, rich, poor, male, female, Jew and Gentile. And He remembers those who have not been taught His laws, for all people are equal to Him.

27 - Isaiah's prophecies of last days...

More of Isaiah's words: "In the last days, which are the days of the Gentiles, all the Gentile nations and Jews throughout the world will be drunken with all types of sin. When that day comes, the Lord of Hosts will visit them with thunder, earthquake, great noise, storms and devouring fire. All the multitudes of the nations that fight against Zion and distress her will not be satisfied! All you sinners, stop and wonder, for you will shout in distress and cry. You will be drunk and stagger, not full of alcohol, but full of all types of sin—the wine of Babylon. The Lord will allow the spirit of deep sleep to come upon the wicked, for they will close their eyes to the truth, rejecting the prophets and rulers. And when the people refuse to listen to the prophets, the Lord hides them."

In the last days, the Lord will bring these plates to the Gentiles—words written by those who lived long ago. Part of these plates will be sealed—parts containing a revelation from God, describing everything from the beginning to the end of the world. Because of wickedness, this revelation will remain sealed. However, the unsealed plates (the first part of *The Book of Mormon*), will be given to a man (Joseph Smith) who will deliver its words—the words of those who lived long ago—to another man (Martin Harris).

At first, none of the sealed plates will be translated. They will remain sealed by the power of God until the Lord reveals them. When the sealed plates are translated, they will be read throughout the world by the power of Christ. From this new book (the rest of *The Book of Mormon*), all things will be revealed to the people of the earth—things that have been and will be among them, until the end of the earth.

When the plates are given to Joseph Smith, they will be hidden from the world. Besides Joseph, three other witnesses will see them by God's power. They will testify that the plates exist, and that the translation is true. God will allow others to see the plates, who will also bear testimony of God's word to the world. This translation will fulfill the prophecies that say the faithful forefathers' words will speak as if from the dead.

To fulfill this prophecy, the Lord God will begin to bring the words written on these plates to the world. The Lord will establish His word with as many witnesses as He needs, and cursed are those who reject God's word! For the Lord will say to Joseph Smith, "Give some of the unsealed words to another (Martin Harris), so that he may bring them to an educated man (Professor Charles Anthon) to read." The educated man will say, "Bring me the whole book, so that I may read it." He will say this, wanting money and glory from the world rather than to glorify God. The first man will say, "I cannot bring you the book, for it is sealed." And the educated man will reply, "I cannot read a sealed book."

Note: See Joseph Smith History 1:62-65 (Pearl of Great Price).

After this, the Lord will again give the plates and the power to translate them to Joseph, who will have little confidence, saying, "I am not a scholar." The Lord will answer Joseph, "Scholars will not be allowed to read them, for they have rejected them. I am able to do my own work, so you will read the words that I will give to you. Do not touch the sealed plates, for I will bring them to the world in my own due time. I will show all people that I am able to do my own work. After you have translated the words that I have commanded you, and after you have shown the plates to the witnesses I promised you, hide the plates up to me again so that I may preserve the sealed words that you have not read. For behold, I am a God of miracles. I will show the world that I am the same yesterday, today and forever, and that I work among people according to their faith. This people speak well of me, but they do not know me. Their hearts are far from me, and they fear me according to their own false ideas. Because of this, I will begin to do a marvelous work and a wonder among them. It will cause the wisdom of their wise scholars to vanish and their powers of reasoning to fail them. And cursed are those who work in darkness, trying to hide their ways from me, saying, 'Who sees us and knows what we do? Surely, this new scripture will amount to nothing.'

Note: New scriptures are described in 1 Ne 5:17-19, 14:1, 2 Ne 27:10, 28:27-32, Alma 37:3-4, 3 Ne 23:4, 26:6-10 and Ether 3:28, 4:4-6.

"But I, the Lord of Hosts, will show them that I know all their works. For can they whom the Lord created and established say that He has no understanding? I will show the people of the world that soon Lebanon—the Jewish settlements—will be turned into a fruitful field and esteemed as a forest."

Isaiah's words: "For in the last days, those blinded by living in spiritual darkness—deaf to the voice of the Spirit—will listen to the words written in this book and will see the Lord's light and truth. The humble will be given an increase—their lands of inheritance, and their joy will be in the Lord. The poor will rejoice in the Holy One of Israel, for as surely as the Lord lives, they will see their terrible enemy brought to nothing.

"Also, those who mock others, and who look for a chance to sin, will be cut off from the land. Those who trick people in their words, making them law breakers, entrapping those who stand up for righteousness, who reject justice for money, will be destroyed from the face of the land. Then the Lord who redeemed Abraham will say to Israel's descendants, 'You will no longer be ashamed or afraid.' His children will be with Him, fearing the God of Israel and sanctifying His name—the Holy One of Jacob. Then those who were in spiritual darkness will come into the light, and those who complained ignorantly will learn doctrine."

28 - Nephi prophecies of the last days...

My brothers and sisters, I, Nephi, have spoken to you as the Spirit has prompted me, for I know these prophecies of Isaiah will come to pass. The words of *The Book of Mormon* will be very valuable to all people, especially to our descendants—a branch of Israel's household. In the last days, people who do not know the Lord will create churches and claim they are the Lord's. Their priests will argue with one another, teaching according to their learning, for they will not allow the Holy Ghost to inspire their words. They will deny the power of God—the Holy One of Israel—by saying, "Listen to me because God does not speak today. He has already done His work and has given His power to His children. If others say the Lord does miracles, do not believe them. God does not do miracles today. His work is done."

Many will say, "Eat, drink and be merry, for life is short. Fear God, but not too much because He will justify a little sin. Lie a little. Use the law to take advantage of others. Sue your neighbor. There is nothing wrong with this. If we are guilty, God will scold us for awhile and then save us in His kingdom." Many will teach these false, vain and foolish doctrines. Being proud, they try to hide their works of darkness from the Lord, and the blood of the saints will cry from the ground against these people. Because of their pride, false teachers and doctrine, they will become corrupt.

By spending their money on their fine churches and fine clothing they will rob the poor. Because they will think so well of themselves, in their pride, wickedness and immorality, they will persecute the humble and poor in heart. They will hold their heads up high and all will go astray, except for a few of Christ's humble followers. But even these humble followers will make many mistakes, being taught according to the concepts of men, and not of God. The wise, the well-educated, the rich, and they who are so proud of their accomplishments, who preach false doctrines and are not chaste, who distort the right way of the Lord, will be cursed with a great cursing," says the Lord God Almighty, "for they will be cast down from my presence."

Cursed are those who favor the unjust over the just. Cursed are those who reject goodness, saying it is worthless! For in the last days, the Lord God will speedily visit the people of the earth, and those who are fully ripe in sin will not survive. "But if the people of the earth repent of their wickedness, they will not be destroyed," says the Lord of Hosts. But that great, abominable church, the whore of all the earth, must tumble to the dust with a great fall! The devil's kingdom must be shaken, giving its members good reason to repent. Otherwise, the devil will surely grasp them with his everlasting chains and incite them to anger, and to die in their anger. For in the very last days, the devil will rage in people's hearts, inciting them to become angry with anything that is good.

The devil will pacify others, giving them a false sense of security. Those pacified will say, "All is well here in Zion because we are so prosperous." But in reality, the devil is cheating them—carefully leading them to hell. The devil will tell them what they want to hear. Things like, "There's really no devil or hell." He will whisper these lies into their ears until he grasps them with his awful chains, and at last he will obtain power over them forever.

The devil's captives will be held by his power—death and hell. All who have been seized must stand before God's throne to be judged according to their works. After being judged, they must go into the place prepared for them where their souls will be in endless torment, like a burning lake of sulfur.

Because of this terrible, final judgment, cursed are those who are at ease in Zion! Cursed are those who say, "All is well," and who listen to men's counsel, denying God's power and the gift of the Holy Ghost. Cursed are those who say, "We have already received the gospel. We don't need any more," and with little faith in Christ, tremble with anger as God's truth is preached to them. Those who have faith in Christ gladly receive more truth, and cursed are those who will say, "We have already received the word of God. We have enough and don't need any more."

The Lord God said to me, "I will give only a few precepts at a time. Those who heed what I give them will be blessed with wisdom, and I will give them more. But I will take the gospel out from among those who say, 'We have enough.'

Note: The Lord gives more of His words (3 Nephi 26:8-9, Ether 4:7) or takes them away (3 Nephi 16:10-13, Ether 12:35), depending upon how we heed them.

"Cursed are those who put their trust in man's teachings, unless they are taught by the power of the Holy Ghost. Cursed are the Gentiles, because even though I will continually extend my arm (protective covenants) toward them, they will deny me. But if they will repent and come to me, I will receive them.

29 - The Lord warns the Latter-day Gentiles through Nephi...

"I will begin to do a marvelous work among the Gentiles, remembering the covenants that I made to Israel's descendants, and I will deliver my people a second time.

Note: This marvelous work is yet to come (2 Nephi 27:11, 21-23, Ether 4:15).

"I will remember the promises that I made to you, Nephi, and also to your father, Lehi. My promise was that I would not forget your descendants. I will remember them by bringing them the words of their forefathers (the entire *Book of Mormon*), which will go with power throughout the earth and become a standard to Israel's descendants.

"Because these words will have power, many Gentiles will say, 'We already have a Bible, so there cannot be any more.' Oh fools, who have their Bible from the Jews, my ancient covenant people. Do the Gentiles thank the Jews for the Bible? Do they remember the pain the Jews suffered, and their work and diligence before me in bringing salvation to the Gentiles? No, they do not remember these things, but instead the Gentiles curse the Jews. They hate them and do not make any effort to recover them. But everything the Jews have suffered will be done to the Gentiles, for I, the Lord have not forgotten my people.

"You fools who will say, 'We already have a Bible. We do not need more scripture.' How did you get your Bible except from the Jews? Don't you realize that there is more than one nation, and that I, the Lord your God, created all people and remember them? I rule the heavens and the earth and will bring my word to all nations. Why do you fear to receive more of my word? Don't you know that the testimony of two nations is a greater witness to you that I am God, who remembers one nation like another?

"I speak the same words to one nation that I do to another. When the two nations meet together, their testimonies will also join together. I will do this to prove that I am the same yesterday, today and forever, and that I speak according to my own pleasure. Just because I have chosen one group of people to speak to, do not think that I cannot choose another, for my work is not finished, and it never will be. Do not think you have all my words because you have a Bible, or that I have not caused more to be written. For I command all people everywhere to write the words I speak to them, and I will judge the world according to their works—according to what I have commanded to be written. I will speak to the Jews, to the Nephites, to the ten tribes, and to all nations, and they will all write their own scriptures. In the last days, these groups will exchange and have one another's scriptures—

The Holy Bible, the complete *Book of Mormon*, and other ancient scriptures of those who have been led away. Then my people—members of the house of Israel—will be gathered home to the lands of their possessions. My word will also be gathered into one book. I will show those who fight against my word, and against my people, that I am the same God who covenanted with Abraham that I would remember his descendants forever."

30 - Nephi prophesies of last days...

Now my beloved brothers and sisters, do not think that you are more righteous than the Gentiles, for unless you keep God's commandments, you will all perish as well. What I said earlier does not mean that the Gentiles will be completely destroyed. All the Gentiles who repent are the Lord's covenant people, and all the Jews who do not repent will be cast off. The Lord only makes covenants with those who repent and believe in His Son, the Holy One of Israel.

Now I will prophesy more about the Jews and the Gentiles. After *The Book of Mormon* is published by the Gentiles, and the plates are again hidden, many will believe its words.

The Gentiles who believe that *The Book of Mormon* is true will take its message to the rest of our descendants, the Lamanites, who will then know about us—how we came from Jerusalem, and that they are descendants of the Jews. Like their forefathers, they will come to know the gospel of Jesus Christ. They will rejoice, knowing that God has blessed them. They will come out of their spiritual darkness, and in only a few generations they will become a pure and delightful people.

Then the scattered Jews will begin to gather. Those of them who believe in Christ will also become a delightful people. After this, the Lord God will begin His work among all nations, kindreds, tongues and people to restore Israel's descendants throughout the earth.

And with righteousness the Lord God will judge the poor. With fairness He will chastise those who persecute the meek, and by His servant's command He will cause the wicked to be destroyed.

For the time will soon come when the Lord will cause a great division among the people. He will destroy the wicked and spare His people, even if He must destroy the wicked with fire. He will do this through His righteousness and faithfulness.

After the wicked are destroyed by fire, wolves will live in peace with a lambs. The leopard will lie down next to a young goat, the calf and a young lion, and a little child will lead them all. Cows and bears will feed together, their young ones sleeping nearby. The lion will eat straw like the ox, and a toddler will play near a snake's nest. They will not hurt or kill in all His holy nation because as the waters cover the sea, the earth will be full of the knowledge of the Lord. All people of all nations will have knowledge of all things. All secrets will be revealed, all works of darkness will be shown in the light, and all sealed records will come forth. Everything that was ever revealed to people in the past will be revealed at that day, and Satan will not have power over people's hearts for a thousand years.

31 - Nephi speaks of Christ's baptism...

Note: Nephi's prophecies (2 Nephi 25:7—30:17) were not directed to the people of his day, but to future members of the house of Israel.

Now I, Nephi, end my prophesying to you, my beloved people. I can only write a few of the things that I know will happen, and a few of the words of my brother Jacob.

What I have written so far is enough, except I must speak a few words about the doctrine of Christ. I will speak as plainly as I can, just as I spoke when I prophesied. My soul delights in plainness, for this is how the Lord works among His children. He gives us His light by speaking to us in our own language, according to our own understanding.

Remember the prophet, John the Baptist, whom the Lord showed me, who will baptize the Lamb of God who will take away the sins of the world? Now if the Lamb of God, being holy, needs to be baptized, how much more do we need to be baptized, being unholy?

I ask you, my beloved brethren, how will the Lamb of God fulfill all righteousness by being baptized? Even though He is holy, He will show all people that He will humble Himself before the Father with a mortal body, witnessing to His Father that He will be obedient and keep His commandments. After being baptized with water, the Holy Ghost will come upon Him in the form of a dove. This sets the example to all people, showing them just how straight the path, and how narrow the gate through which they should enter.

For Christ said to all, "Follow me." And how can we follow Jesus unless we keep the Father's commandments? The Father said, "Repent and be baptized in the name of my Beloved Son." And the Son's voice came to me, saying, "The Father will give the Holy Ghost, as He did to me, to all who are baptized in my name. So follow me and do what you have seen me do."

I, Nephi, know that you must sincerely follow the Son, with honest intentions, not trying to deceive others before God as a hypocrite. If you follow the Son, repenting of your sins, witnessing to the Father that you are willing to take the name of Christ upon you, by baptism, by following your Lord and Savior down into the water according to His word, then you will receive the Holy Ghost. Then the baptism of fire and of the Holy Ghost will come and you will be able to speak as the angels, shouting praises to the Holy One of Israel.

The Son's voice also came to me, saying, "If you repent, witnessing to the Father that you are willing to keep my commandments by being baptized, and receive the baptism of fire and of the Holy Ghost, and speak with the tongue of angels, and after all this deny me, then it would have been better for you if you had never known me." I also heard the Father say, "Yes, the words of my Beloved are true and faithful. Those who continue in righteousness throughout their lives will be saved."

Now, my beloved brothers and sisters, because of what I have heard, I know that unless you follow the example of the Son of the living God by continuing in righteousness throughout your lives, you cannot be saved. So do the things that your Lord and Redeemer will do; be baptized as He. His baptism was shown to me so that I could tell you how to repent, be baptized and receive a remission of your sins by fire and by the Holy Ghost.

And then you are on the straight and narrow path; you have entered at the gate. By being baptized, you obey the Father's and the Son's commandments and are promised the gift of the Holy Ghost, who witnesses of the Father and of the Son.

After you have been baptized and have received the Holy Ghost, have you done everything? No, you have not, for you could not have done these things without relying entirely upon Christ—having an unshakable faith in Him, who is mighty to save you.

You must keep your faith in Christ strong, having a perfect brightness of hope, loving God and all mankind. If you keep your faith strong by feasting on Christ's words, and continue in righteousness throughout your life, then the Father will say, "You shall have eternal life." This is the only way and name given under heaven by which God's children can be saved in His kingdom. This is the doctrine of Christ—the only true doctrine of God the Father, of His Son, Jesus Christ and of the Holy Ghost, who are as one God forever. Amen.

32 - After baptism comes the Holy Ghost...

My beloved brethren, why do you wonder about what to do after you are baptized? Do you remember me telling you that after you received the Holy Ghost you could speak with the tongue of angels? Now, how could you do this unless it were by the Holy Ghost?

Angels speak by the power of the Holy Ghost, so they speak Christ's words. This is why I told you to heed Christ's words, which will tell you everything that you should do.

If you cannot understand what I have told you, it is because you do not ask God for the answer. If you do not ask, you will not come into the light, but will die spiritually in the dark. Again I tell you, if you are baptized and receive the Holy Ghost, He will tell you what to do at all times.

This is all I will say about Christ's doctrine for now. More of His doctrine will be given when He comes to teach you Himself; doctrine that you should obey. The Spirit stops me from telling you any more. I can only sorrow because people are so stubborn and refuse to believe. They will not search out knowledge or understand great knowledge when it is given to them in plain words.

Brothers and sisters, I, Nephi, know that you are still wondering what to do. I am sorry to say that if you were listening to the Spirit, you would know that you must pray, for it is the evil spirit who teaches you not to pray. You must always pray, never forgetting to pray to the Father in the name of Christ before doing anything for the Lord. If you do this, He will bless all that you do, so that it will benefit your soul.

33 - Nephi's weak writing to be made strong...

I, Nephi, cannot write everything that my people were taught. I am not a very good writer. I'm a much better speaker than a writer, because when one speaks by the power of the Holy Ghost, that power goes right to the hearts of those who hear.

But many people harden their hearts against the Holy Spirit, giving it no place in them. Because of this, they do not value the written word. I consider what I have written to be of great value, especially to my descendants. Every day I pray, and at night I weep over them because of what they will do. I cry to my God in faith, knowing that He will hear me. I know the Lord will answer my prayers by blessing my people, for even though my writings may be weak, they will be made powerful through the Holy Ghost when they are read by my descendants. They will persuade them to do good and will give them knowledge of their ancestors. My writings will speak of Jesus in order to persuade my descendants always to believe in Him, and thereby gain eternal life.

My words are harsh against sin because they are the simple and plain truth. Only those filled with the devil's spirit will be angry with my writings. I glory in plainness, in truth, and in my Jesus because He has redeemed my soul from hell. I have charity for my people, great faith in Christ, and faith that I will meet many souls, spotless and sanctified, at His judgment-seat. I have charity for the Jews—the people of my heritage. I also have charity for the Gentiles, but no hope for any of them unless they are reconciled to Christ and stay on the straight path that leads to eternal life.

I speak to my descendants, to the Jews, and to all the people of the earth. If you believe my words, then you will believe in Christ, for He has given me the words that I now write to benefit you. These words teach all people in all places to do good. If you think my words are not Christ's words, then judge them for yourselves. But I know, that at the last day Christ will show you with power and great glory that these are His words. Before His bar, we will stand face to face, and then you will know that He commanded me to write these things in spite of my weakness. I pray to the Father, in the name of Christ, that many of us, if not all, will be saved in His kingdom on that great and last day.

To all you descendants of the house of Israel, and to all people throughout the earth, I speak as one calling from the dust. Farewell, until that great day arrives.

And you who will not accept God's goodness, who will not respect the words of the Jews, my words, or the words of the Lamb of God, I bid you an everlasting farewell, for these words will condemn you at the last day. Because the Lord commanded me to write, what I seal on earth will be brought against you at His judgment bar. Amen.

1 - Jacob is trusted with the plates...

In the year 545 BC, fifty-five years after Lehi's group had left Jerusalem, my older brother Nephi gave me, Jacob, a commandment regarding the small plates, upon which these words are engraved. He told me to write only a few things on these small plates—things that I thought were most precious. He told me to include only a little history of his people, the people of Nephi. He said the history of his people should be engraved on his large plates. Nephi told me to preserve all these plates, and to hand them down from generation to generation. He told me to engrave any sacred preaching, great revelations and prophesying, and to engrave as much of this as possible for Christ, and for the sake of our people. Because of our faith in the Lord and great concern for our people, we had been shown what would happen to them. We also had many revelations and the spirit of prophecy, and we knew about Christ and His kingdom that would come.

We worked very hard among our people to persuade them to come to Christ and to enjoy God's goodness, that they might someday enter His rest. Otherwise, God would vow in His anger that they would not enter, just as He did when the children of Israel fell into temptation in the wilderness. We hope that with God's help we might persuade all people not to rebel against Him—not to provoke His anger, but to believe in Christ, who would suffer and die on the cross while bearing the shame of the world. Because of these desires, I, Jacob, take it upon myself to fulfill the instructions from my brother Nephi.

When Nephi was old and realized that he would soon die, he anointed a man to be king and ruler over his people as the people had desired. The people loved Nephi very much, for he had been their great protector, defending them with Laban's sword, and he had worked for their temporal and spiritual welfare all his life. Because they loved him so much, the people wanted to remember his name. So they decided that whoever reigned from then on would be called Nephi—second Nephi, third Nephi, etc., according to the reign of the kings. Those who reigned as king from then on were known as Nephi, and not by their actual names. Then Nephi died.

All those who were not Lamanites were called Nephites, although there were also Jacobites, Josephites, Zoramites, Lamanites, Lemuelites and Ishmaelites.

I, Jacob, will not refer to them by these names, but will refer to those who try to destroy Nephi's people as Lamanites. And I will refer to those who are friendly to Nephi as Nephites.

The Nephites, under the reign of their second king, started the wicked practice of desiring and indulging themselves with many wives and mistresses, like David of old and his son Solomon had done. They also began to dig for great amounts of gold and silver, for they were becoming prideful. So I, Jacob, having been called by God, taught them in the temple.

Nephi had consecrated my brother Joseph and I to be the people's priests and teachers. We increased in our commitment to serve the Lord, feeling responsible for the people's sins if we did not teach them God's word as best we could. We taught them with all our might so we would not have to answer for their sins.

2 - Jacob calls his people to repentance...

After Nephi died, I spoke these words to the Nephites:

"My beloved brothers and sisters, I am responsible to God to fulfill my obligation to serve you, so I will not have to answer for your sins. This is why I have come to give you God's words in the temple today. You know that I have taught you diligently. So far, this has not been a hard task. But today it is hard because I am weighed down more than ever with anxiety over the welfare of your souls. Until now, you have obeyed the Lord's words that I have given you. But listen to me, for by the help of the all-powerful Creator of heaven and earth, I know your thoughts—how you are beginning to work in sin, which is very offensive to God, and to me. It sorrows my soul and causes me to shrink with shame before the presence of my Maker, for I must testify to you about the wickedness of your hearts. I'm also sorry that I must speak so boldly about you in front of your wives and children, for many of their feelings are very tender, chaste and delicate before God, which is pleasing to Him. They have come to hear the pleasing word of God—the word that heals the wounded soul. My soul is burdened because I am compelled by a strict command from God to admonish you for your crimes, and enlarge the wounds of those who are already wounded, instead of consoling and healing them. And those who have not been wounded, instead of feasting upon the pleasing word of God, they will have their souls pierced and delicate minds wounded. But as hard as this, I must obey God's strict command and tell you about your wickedness in the presence of their pure and broken hearts, and do it under the gaze of the Almighty God's piercing eyes.

"I must tell you the truth according to God's plain word. For as I was praying, His word came to me, 'Jacob, go to the temple tomorrow and tell your people the words that I will give you.' Now my brothers and sisters, these are the words:

"Many of you have begun to search for gold, silver and all types of precious ores that are plentiful in this land of promise, given to you and your descendants. God has smiled upon you most pleasingly, and by His providence you have obtained many riches. Because some of you have obtained more than others you have become lifted up in the pride of your hearts. You lift your heads high because of your expensive clothing, and you criticize

others, thinking that you are better than they. Now, do you think God justifies you in doing this? No, He condemns you. And if you continue to do this, His judgments must quickly come upon you. I wish He would show you how He can level you to the dust with just one glance of His eyes! I wish His Spirit would take the desire to sin away from you so you would listen to His commands and not let the pride of your hearts destroy your souls!

"You should know all your brothers and sisters' needs as you do your own and be generous with your things, so generous that you all become equally rich. But before you seek riches, seek God's kingdom. After you have obtained a hope in Christ you will have riches, if you want them to do good—to buy food and clothing for those in need, to liberate those in debt, and to give relief to the sick and afflicted.

"I have spoken to you about pride. And those of you who afflict and despise your neighbors because you are so proud of your possessions—things with which God has blessed you—what do you say for yourselves? Don't you think your pride offends your Creator, to whom everyone is equally precious? For God created us all from the dust, to keep His commandments and thereby glorify Him forever.

"This is all I will say about your pride. If I did not have to speak to you about a more serious sin, my heart would rejoice greatly because of you. But God's word burdens me because of your crimes. The Lord told me, 'This people are becoming sinful. They do not understand the scriptures. They try to excuse their immorality because of what is written about David and his son Solomon, who both had many wives and mistresses—a serious sin before me. I led this people out of Jerusalem by the power of my arm to raise up righteous descendants of Joseph of old. To do this, I, the Lord God, cannot allow this people to do what David and Solomon did.' Now my brethren, hear me and obey the Lord, for every man should have only one wife and no mistresses. For the Lord said: 'I, the Lord God, delight in the chastity of women, and immorality of any kind is a very serious sin before me. My people will keep my commandments or the land will be cursed for their sakes. If I need to raise up many righteous people, I will command accordingly. Otherwise, they must obey this law. I, the Lord, have seen the sorrow and have heard the mourning of my people's daughters in Jerusalem, and in all my people's lands, because of their husbands' wickedness. I will not allow the cries of the fair daughters of this people, whom I have led out of Jerusalem, to come up to me against my people's men. For if they seduce and capture the hearts of my people's daughters because of their tenderness, I will visit them with destruction for committing sexual sins like those of old.'

"My brethren, you know that these commandments were given to our father, Lehi. Now you have come under great condemnation for doing what you know is wrong. Your sins are greater than those of the Lamanites. Because of your bad examples, you have broken your wives' tender hearts and have lost your children's confidence. The sobbing of their hearts goes up to God, and because of God's strict word that has come down against you, many of their hearts have died, pierced with deep wounds.

3 - Jacob speaks out against adultery...

"I, Jacob, now speak to the pure in heart. Look to God with determination, praying to Him with great faith, and He will comfort you in your trials. He will plead your cause and send down justice upon those who try to destroy you. All you who are pure in heart, lift up your heads and receive God's pleasing words. If you are committed to doing right, you will enjoy His love forever. But those of you who are not pure in heart are greatly cursed. Unless you repent, the land is cursed for your sakes. The Lamanites, who are also cursed, but who are not sinful like you, will destroy you. Unless you repent, the Lamanites will soon possess the land of your inheritance and the Lord will lead the righteous out from among you. The Lamanites, your brethren, whom you hate because of their sinfulness and curse of dark skin, are more righteous than you, for they have not forgotten the Lord's commandment to have only one wife and not to commit these types of sins. Because they keep this commandment, the Lord will not destroy them. He will be merciful to them and one day they will become a blessed people. Their husbands love their wives, their wives love their husbands, and they all love their children. They hate you and do not believe in God because of their fathers' false traditions. So how much better are you than they in the sight of your Creator? Oh my brethren, I am afraid that unless you repent, their skin will be lighter than yours when you stand next to them before God's throne.

"I command you, by the word of God, not to hate them because of their dark skin and sinfulness! Remember your own sinfulness, and that their sinfulness came because of their fathers. Remember how you have grieved your children's hearts because of your bad examples. Your sinfulness may bring them to destruction, and if so, their sins will be upon your heads at the last day. Oh my brethren, listen to me. Awaken your souls from the sleep of death. Loosen yourselves from the pains of hell so that you will not become angels to the devil. Do not be thrown into a lake of fire to your second death (dead to righteousness forever)."

I, Jacob, said many other things to Nephi's people, warning them against sexual sins and every kind of sin, telling them the awful consequences of them. But not even one percent of what these people did can be engraved upon these smaller plates. However, many of their proceedings are engraved on the larger plates—their wars, disputes and the reigns of their kings. Some of these smaller plates that I am now engraving upon are called Jacob's Plates, even though my brother Nephi made them.

4 - Jacob values prophecies and records...

I have spoken many times to my people, but I can only write a small part of what I said to them because engraving on plates is so difficult. We do it, knowing that the things we engrave on metal plates will endure. Any other materials we write on (parchment, skin, etc.) will not endure. The little that we do engrave on our plates will give our children, and also our beloved brethren, the Lamanites, a little knowledge of us, their forefathers. We work diligently to engrave these plates, hoping that the Lamanites and their children in the last days will receive them with thankful hearts, and learn with joy, not sorrowing nor resenting Laman and Lemuel, their first parents. We keep our records so that they will know that we knew of Christ, and that we had a hope of His glory hundreds of years before He came, and that holy prophets who lived before us also had a hope of His glory.

Those prophets believed in Christ and worshiped the Father in His name, as we do now. And like them, we keep the law of Moses, which points our souls to Christ. And our sacrifices are considered righteous, as was Abraham's, who offered his son Isaac—a symbol of God's offering of His Only Begotten Son.

We search the prophets' writings and have many revelations in the spirit of prophecy. With all these witnesses, we have hope. Our faith becomes so strong that we can command the trees, the mountains and the ocean in the name of Jesus, and they obey us. But the Lord shows us our weaknesses so that we may know it is by His grace and great kindness to His people that we have this power. The Lord's works are great and marvelous! How deep His mysteries are! It is impossible for people to know all His ways, and no one knows His ways without revelation. This is why you should not despise revelation from God.

By His word, man, woman and the earth were created. So if God created the earth and everything on it by speaking, why can't He command all the elements of the earth as He so desires? Pondering this, do not try to counsel the Lord. Take His counsel, for you know He counsels in wisdom, justice and great mercy over all His works. Be reconciled to Him through the atonement of Christ, His Only Begotten Son. If you do this, then through Christ's power, you may be among the first to be resurrected and presented to God. So have faith in Him, and obtain a hope of glory in Him before He shows Himself in the flesh. Do not wonder that I tell you these things, for why should we not speak of the atonement of Christ, and seek a perfect knowledge of Him, of the resurrection, and of the world to come?

Those who prophesy should be understood by the people, for the Spirit speaks the truth and does not lie. He speaks of things as they really are, and as they really will be, explaining eternal truths to us plainly to save our souls. We are not the only witnesses of these things, for God also told them to the prophets of old. But the Jews were stubborn. They despised plain words and killed the prophets, looking for things that they could not understand. Because of their blindness, which came from looking beyond the mark, God gave them exactly what they wanted. He took away His plain words and gave them many things they could not understand. This is why they stumbled spiritually and fell.

Now I, Jacob, am led by the Spirit to prophesy, for I sense by the workings of the Spirit in me, that because the Jews stumble, they will reject the stone upon which they might have built a safe foundation.

Note: Christ is the cornerstone upon which to build. See Helaman 5:12.

According to the scriptures, this stone will become the great, last and only sure foundation upon which they can build. And how will it be possible for the Jews, after rejecting their sure foundation, to ever build upon it and make it their cornerstone? I will tell you how, as long as I do not get shaken from my determination in the Spirit and stumble because of my anxiety for you. Speaking to all members of the house of Israel, the Lord's prophet, Zenos (who was martyred), told us exactly how the Jews will make Christ their cornerstone after rejecting Him for centuries:

Note: The reference to Zenos being a martyr is found in Helaman 8:19.

5 - Jacob reads Zenos' writings of "the olive tree", a metaphor of the House of Israel...

The Lord said the house of Israel (the Jews, or Judah, the lost tribes, and the tribe of Joseph) is like a tame olive tree, which a man planted in his vineyard and took care of. The tree grew, became old, and started to decay.

Note: Abraham was the beginning of the olive tree, planted in Canaan around 1900 BC. His grandson Israel (Jacob) went with his twelve sons into Egypt. Their descendants were delivered from slavery in Egypt and wandered until Joshua led them back into Canaan around 1350 BC. The house of Israel began to grow in righteousness under King David and Solomon, but by 931 BC, its government had begun to decay spiritually and politically.

Seeing this, the Master of the vineyard said, "I will prune out its wicked leaders, divide it into two kingdoms, and water it by sending many prophets, who will declare righteousness to the people (prophets such as Jehu, Elijah and Isaiah). Then perhaps the house of Israel will repent, sprouting new, righteous young branches, and not die."

So He pruned it, dug around it, and watered it—sending many prophets to both kingdoms

After much time, part of the house of Israel began to grow in truth, but the main branches at the top of the tree (their kings) began to die spiritually (by worshipping idols).

Seeing this, the Master of the vineyard said to His servant, "Losing the entire house of Israel, the whole olive tree, would grieve me. Therefore, bring in the branches from a wild olive tree (the Assyrian and Babylonian kings). We will pluck out and burn the dying main branches (the apostate kings of Israel) and replace them with wild branches."

The Lord of the vineyard said, "I will pluck out the young and tender branches and plant them in other parts of my earth. Then I will not lose the whole house of Israel if the roots die, and I will still preserve the good fruit (those who keep their covenants). Now take the branches of the wild olive tree and graft them into the tame tree."

Note: The northern kingdom of Israel was invaded by the Assyrians in 722 BC.
The southern kingdom of Judah was invaded by the Babylonians in 587 BC.

The servant did as he was told and grafted the wild branches into the olive tree. But in His mercy, the Lord of the vineyard cared for the house of Israel's spiritual roots.

Note: Through Daniel, Esther and Nehemiah, the Lord caused the house of Israel's roots to be nourished.

Then He said, "The tender branches will be preserved for myself, that I may lay up their fruit before the last day, for it would grieve me to lose the house of Israel and its fruit." The Master hid the natural branches that had been plucked out in separate places upon His earth. He planted them here and there according to His will and pleasure.

After many years had passed, the Lord said to His servant, "Come, let us go down to the vineyard." They both went down to labor, and the servant said to his master, "Look at the tame olive tree, the roots of Israel!" The Lord of the vineyard saw the mother tree in which the wild branches had been grafted. The tree had begun to bear much good fruit (keeping the laws and commandments of Moses).

Note: The mother tree was the Babylonian captives of Judah, now returned to Jerusalem. Lehi saw them in vision (1 Ne 10:3).

Even though wild branches had been grafted into the mother tree, it bore good fruit, just as good as the fruit of the natural branches that had been transplanted to other places. The Lord then exclaimed to His servant, "Look, the branches from the wild tree have taken hold, getting strength from the spiritual roots of the house of Israel (the prophets of Judah). The wild branches are now bearing tame fruit! It is good that we brought in the wild branches (many who converted to the Lord) or else the tame roots would have died by now, having no branches to nourish them. Now I will have much fruit (covenant people) before the last day. "Come, let us now go to the other parts of the earth to see if the transplanted natural branches of the house of Israel are also bearing good fruit."

They went to the other parts of the earth, and the Master said to His servant, "Look at these!" The servant saw the first tree (scattered Jews and/or tribes) bearing much good fruit. The Master told the servant to harvest the fruit, for He had nourished that tree for a long time. Then the servant asked his master, "Why did you plant the first branch in the poorest spot in the vineyard?" The Master replied, "Do not counsel me. I knew this was a poor spot, and so I nourished it for a long time. Now you see that it has brought forth much good fruit (many people keeping their covenants).

"Look over there, where I planted another branch (scattered Jews and/or tribes). You know this spot of ground was poorer than the first. But look at them. I have nourished them for a long time and they bring forth much good fruit. Harvest that tree as well."

And the Lord of the vineyard again said to His servant, "Look over here, where I planted and nourished another branch (scattered Jews and/or tribes). It bears much fruit.

"And look over here and see the last branch that I planted (Mulek, Lehi, Ishmael and their families) in a very good part of my earth. I have nourished them for a long time, but now only part of them are righteous, bearing good fruit (the Nephites). The rest of them (the Lamanites) bear wild fruit that is not good. Let the Nephites completely destroy the wild branches (their brethren the Lamanites) who don't bear good fruit." But the servant said, "Let the Nephites preach to the Lamanites a little longer. Maybe the Lamanites will yet bear good fruit for you to keep on the day of judgment." Then the Lord of the vineyard and His servant nourished the entire earth.

A long time passed, and the Lord said to His servant, "Come, let us go down in the earth, for the end is near, and I must have good fruit (celestial souls) for myself before the last day." They went to the tame olive tree again (the mother tree) whose natural branches had been broken off, and whose grafted-in wild branches had born good fruit. Now all types of fruit burdened the tree. The Lord of the vineyard tasted each type of fruit from the mother tree, sorted and counted them, and said, "We have taken care of this tree for a long time. In the past the wild branches were fed by the natural roots and this tree gave me much good fruit. It still bears much fruit, but now it is all bad (general apostasy in Jerusalem). This tree no longer profits me, in spite of all our work, and I will be sad to lose it now. What do we need to do for this tree to help it bear good fruit again?"

The servant answered, "The wild branches that we brought in, which once bore good fruit, are all corrupt again. However, the original roots are still good." The Lord of the vineyard replied, "But even with good roots, this bad fruit is worthless to me. I also know the roots are good. Because of their great strength, they once nourished the wild branches, which for a time bore good fruit. But now look. The corrupt branches (governing powers) have overrun the spiritual roots. This is why their fruit is bad. Because this tree bears so much bad fruit, it will die unless we do something to save it. "Let us go down to the other parts of the earth to see if the other natural branches are also bearing bad fruit." And sure enough, all of the natural branches (scattered Jews and/or tribes, and the descendants of Mulek, Lehi and Ishmael) had also become corrupt. The wild fruit of the last tame tree (the Lamanites) had overcome the part of the tree that had once borne good fruit (the Nephites, who had rebelled against the light and had been swept off the earth). Upon seeing this, the Lord of the vineyard wept while saying to His servant, "What more could I have done for my vineyard? I knew all the fruit had become corrupt, except for these (the Nephites). Now even they who once bore good fruit have become corrupt and are gone! Now all the people of the earth are good for nothing except to be burned. Look at this branch of the last tree (the Nephites) which has withered away. I planted it in the best part of my earth—in the choicest land! You saw me remove what was here before (the Jaredites) so that I could plant this tree (the Nephites) in its place. You saw this tree bear good fruit and wild fruit. Because I did not destroy the wild branches (the Lamanites) long ago, they overcame the good branch. Now in spite of all the care we have given to my earth, all the people in it have become corrupt. I had hoped to save them—to have preserved their souls to myself before the last day. But look at them. They have all become like wild olive trees, good only for burning. Losing all of them grieves me.

"What more could I have done? Have I ever stopped nourishing my vineyard? (Sending prophets, giving scriptures to the people, etc.). It grieves me to cut down all the trees of my vineyard and burn them. Who has corrupted my vineyard?" The servant answered his master, "The proud people (the lofty branches) have overcome their spiritual roots. They have grown too proud and rich to be fed by their spiritual roots. The lofty branches have stolen the strength (governing power) from their spiritual roots, starving and overcoming them. Isn't this why your world has become corrupted?" The Lord of the vineyard replied, "Yes. Now let's cut down the trees and burn them, for I've done everything I can to save them." But the servant said, "Spare them a little longer." The Lord answered, "I will spare them a little longer, for it would be a sad thing to lose all the trees of my vineyard. Let us gather the branches planted in the outer parts of my earth (the Jews, the ten tribes, and the tribe of Joseph) and bring them back to their spiritual roots. Let us pluck out the branches with most bitter fruit (the most wicked), and replace them with the natural branches. I will do this to save their roots for my own purpose. The roots of the house of Israel are yet alive. To preserve these roots, I will graft their original, natural branches back into them, even though the branches have become corrupt. When these corrupt natural branches are strong again, maybe then they will bear good fruit for me, that I may yet have glory in the fruit of my orchard."

Then the Lord and His servant took branches from the mother tree that had become corrupt, and grafted them into the transplanted natural trees, which also had become corrupt.

Note: This transplanting was the Jewish/Lamanite dispersions, caused by the wicked Gentiles.

Then they took the corrupt branches from the transplanted natural trees and grafted them back into their mother tree.

Note: This grafting is the gathering of the Jews, Lamanites, and dispersed tribes of Israel to their lands of inheritance, to be caused by the righteous Gentiles (1 Ne 15:15-18, 3 Ne 21:22-28, and Mormon 5:14-15, 20).

The Lord of the vineyard said to the servant, "As we do this, only remove the most wicked from the corrupt natural trees before doing as I have said. As we do this, we will send prophets to these corrupt natural branches once again. We will destroy only the most wicked (those most ripe). We will do this so that the good, spiritual roots of the house of Israel will again be able to nourish their corrupt natural branches, and help them overcome evil. Because I have saved the natural branches and their roots, perhaps the people of the house of Israel throughout my earth will bear good fruit once again, and I will have joy in them.

"Now go. Give power to other servants, that we may all labor together diligently with our might in the earth, preparing the way, that I may yet have natural, good fruit again (the most precious fruit of all)! Let us labor with our might this last time, for the end is near. This is the last time that I will destroy the wicked of my earth.

"Gather the corrupt natural branches of the house of Israel back to both Jerusalems. But bring the gospel to the Gentiles first (the latter-day restoration). Then gather the scattered Jews last. Gather in Ephraim and Manasseh (Joseph), the ten tribes, and Judah (the Jews), that they may all be taught the gospel one last time. Nourish the house of Israel one last time, for the end will soon come.

"If these last grafts bring forth good fruit, then according to their strength and numbers, clear their way for them to grow even more by destroying the wicked. Do not destroy the wicked all at once, but only as fast as the natural, good fruit can take their place. By doing this, Israel's descendants will rely on me, and I will not lose them. Their roots (spiritual power) and high branches (governing power) will be kept equal in strength until they will again bear enough good fruit to completely overcome the bad. Otherwise, I would lose the good fruit, which would grieve me.

"This is how I will sweep the wicked from my earth. I will bring the corrupt natural branches back to their mother tree (gathering), and I will graft corrupt branches from the mother tree into the transplanted corrupt natural trees (dispersion). After the natural branches have come together (the mingling of latter-day Israel), they will again bear good fruit as one, natural tree, and all the wicked in the world will be removed during this last cleansing."

Then the Lord of the vineyard sent His servant, who gave other servants power to preach and cleanse. These servants were few when compared to the hosts of the wicked. The Lord of the vineyard said to them, "Go and labor in my earth with all your might, mind and strength because this is the last time I will work in my earth, for the end is near. If you labor mightily with me, you will have joy in the fruit that I will preserve to myself against the day of judgment, which soon comes."

Then the servants labored with their might, obeying all the commandments of the Lord of the vineyard, who labored with them. The natural, good fruit grew again in the earth. The servants did as they were commanded, keeping the spiritual roots and the governing tops of the trees in balance.

Note: This balance is between the Lord's word and His law, which will go out from Zion (the old and new Jerusalems (2 Ne 12:3).

They did this by destroying only part of the wicked at a time, allowing the natural branches to grow in their place. The servants labored with all diligence, according to the Lord's commandments, until all the wicked had been swept off the earth and the Lord had preserved to Himself the natural fruit. Now all of Israel's house had become unified in love, as one body, and were all equal. The Lord of the vineyard had preserved to Himself the natural fruit (His righteous children) which had been most precious to Him from the beginning.

When the Lord of the vineyard saw that His fruit was good, and that all the corrupt had been destroyed, He called up all His servants and said to them, "We have nourished my earth for the last time, and you have seen me do my will, preserving the good, natural fruit, like it was in the beginning. You are all blessed for having diligently labored with me in my earth, keeping my commandments, bringing the natural fruit to me again and destroying all the wicked. Because of the good souls of the earth that you have gathered, you will have joy with me in my house. I will preserve these souls to myself for a long time after the last day, which soon comes. I have nourished my people and have destroyed the wicked for the last time. When evil comes upon the earth again, I will gather the good and the bad. I will preserve the good to myself and throw the bad out to their own place. Then the final judgment will come, and I will celestialize my earth with fire."

6 - Jacob explains Zenos' writings...

"Now, my brothers and sisters, I, Jacob, said that I would prophesy to you, and this is my prophecy...what Zenos wrote about Israel's descendants, by comparing them to a tame olive-tree, will surely come to pass!

"When the Lord again sets His hand, sending His powerful servant, like Moses, to deliver His people, it will be the last time that powerful servants will preach and destroy throughout the world.

Note: powerful servants referred to in 2 Ne 6:14-15 and D&C 103:15-18.

"Soon after this, the end will come. How blessed are those who will labor diligently in His earth, and how cursed are those who will be cast out into their own place before the world is celestialized with fire.

Note: D&C 43:23-33.

"How merciful is our God, who will remember Israel's descendants, both their spiritual roots and their governing branches. He extends His arms to them continually, but they are stubborn, contentious and will not come to Him. However, those who do not harden their hearts will be saved in His kingdom.

Because of this, my beloved brothers and sisters, I call upon you to repent and sincerely come to God with all your hearts, holding onto Him as He holds you. While His arms of mercy are extended toward you in the light of the day, do not harden your hearts. If you want to hear His voice today, then do not harden your hearts against Him and die spiritually.

After being nourished by God's good word for so long, will you openly rebel, only to be cut down and thrown into the fire? Will you reject the words of so many prophets who have spoken about Christ? Will you deny His power and the gift of the Holy Ghost? Will you drive off the Holy Spirit, mocking the great plan of redemption that has been laid before you? Don't you know that if you do these things the power of the redemption and the resurrection, which is in Christ, will bring you to stand with shame and awful guilt before God?

Then, according to the power of the justice of God's word, which cannot be denied, you must go away from Him into that fire that separates the wicked from the righteous. Into those flames and smoke that go up forever. Knowing this reality, repent and enter in at the straight gate. Then stay on the narrow path, holding onto God's word until you obtain eternal life. Oh be wise! What more can I say? Farewell, until I meet you again before the pleasing bar of God, which bar strikes the wicked with awful dread and fear. Amen."

7 - *Jacob meets with Sherem...*

After some years had passed, a man named Sherem came among the Nephites. He began to preach that there would be no Christ. He preached many flattering things in order to overthrow Christ's doctrine. He worked hard and led many hearts away. He knew that I, Jacob, had faith in Christ, who would come, so he tried many times to speak to me.

Sherem was a well educated man, and he had a perfect knowledge of the people's language. He was a very flattering and powerful speaker, having power from the devil. He was hoping to shake me from the faith in spite of the many revelations and things that I had seen, for I truly had seen angels who had spoken to me. I had also heard the Lord's voice speak to me from time to time, so I could not be shaken.

When Sherem finally got his chance to speak to me, he said, "Brother Jacob, I have been looking forward to meeting you for some time now, for I have heard, and also know, that you preach what you call 'the gospel' or 'the doctrine of Christ.' You have led many people to change the ways of God and not keep the law of Moses, which is the right way. You are attempting to convert the law of Moses into the worship of a being whom you say will come many hundreds of years from now. I, Sherem, declare to you that this is blasphemy, for no one knows such things—no one can see the future."

Then the Lord God poured His Spirit into my soul, enabling me to confound Sherem in all his words. I said to him, "Do you deny Christ, who will come?" He answered, "If there were a Christ, I would not deny Him, but I know there is not a Christ. There never has been nor will there ever be one." I asked him, "Do you believe the scriptures?" He said, "Yes." I said, "Then you do not understand them, Sherem, because they truly testify of Christ. None of the prophets have written or prophesied without speaking of Christ. I have seen and heard Christ in vision, and by the power of the Holy Ghost, it has been made known to me that if no atonement were made, then everyone would be lost."

Sherem replied, "Show me a sign by the power of this Holy Ghost, whom you know so much about." I answered him, "Who am I to tempt God by asking Him to show you a sign to prove to you what you already know is true? Even if you saw a sign, you would still deny Christ because you are of the devil. It's not up to me, but if God smites you, that's His sign to you that He has power, and that Christ will come. Oh Lord, Thy will be done, not mine."

As I, Jacob, said this, the Lord's power came upon Sherem and he collapsed. He was barely kept alive for many days. Then one day Sherem said, "Gather the people together tomorrow, for I am going to die soon."

The next day a crowd gathered and Sherem spoke plainly to them. He denied the things that he had taught them. He confessed the reality of Christ, of the power of the Holy Ghost, and of the ministering of angels. He said that he had been deceived by the devil's power. He spoke of hell, of eternal punishment and of eternity. He uttered, "I'm afraid because I think I have committed the unpardonable sin, for I have lied to God. I denied the Christ, yet said that I believed the scriptures, which truly testify of Him. Because I have lied to God, I'm afraid for my soul. But I now confess my evil works to God."

Sherem could say no more, and he died. Having seen Sherem confess just before dying, the multitude was greatly astonished. As God's power came upon them and overcame them, they all fell to the earth. This pleased me, Jacob, because I had asked my Father in heaven for such an event. He had heard my cry and had answered my prayer. God's love and peace was restored among the people. They searched the scriptures, and Sherem's lies died with him.

The Nephites had many ideas about how to restore the Lamanites to the knowledge of the truth, but they were all in vain because the Lamanites delighted in war and bloodshed. They had an eternal hatred against us, their brethren, and continually tried to kill us. So we, the people of Nephi, fortified ourselves against them with our weapons and strength, trusting in God, the rock of our salvation. By doing this, we were able to conquer our enemies.

As I, Jacob, now grow old, I finish my record on the small plates that Nephi gave me. The Nephite history is kept on Nephi's larger plates. The best way I can describe our lives is by saying that they passed like a dream. We were a lonesome and solemn people—wandering outcasts from Jerusalem, born in tribulation in the wilderness and hated by our brethren, who caused wars and contentions. And so we mourned out our days.

When I, Jacob, realized I would soon die, I told my son Enos to take charge of all the plates. I repeated the commands of my brother Nephi to Enos, and he promised to obey them. This is the end of what little I have engraved. I hope many of my brethren, the Lamanites, will be among those who read my words. Farewell, and may blessings attend you.

1 - Enos is forgiven and prays for others...

I, Enos, know that my father, Jacob, was a just man. He taught me in his language, and he taught me about the Lord's kindness, and of His warnings. Blessed be the name of my God for giving me such a father!

Now I will tell you about the struggle I had before receiving a remission of my sins. One morning, I went to hunt in the forest. While there, I pondered the words of eternal life and of the joy of the saints that I had often heard my father speak. My soul longed for this joy, so I knelt down before my Maker and cried to Him in mighty prayer, asking Him to bless my soul.

I prayed all day long, and when night came, I still prayed loudly so that my voice would reach the heavens. Then a voice came into my mind, saying, "Enos, your sins are forgiven and you will be blessed." I knew that God could not lie, so my guilt was instantly swept away. I asked the Lord, "How is this done?" In my mind the Lord answered, "This is done because of your faith in Christ, whom you have never seen nor heard before. Many years will pass before He will show Himself in the flesh.

Now, go forth in peace. Because of your faith, your soul has been healed." When I heard this, I became concerned for the welfare of my brethren, the Nephites. So I poured out my whole soul to God for them. While I was struggling in the spirit, the Lord's voice came into my mind again, saying, "I will visit your brethren according to how well they keep my commandments. I have given them this holy land and will only curse it because of iniquity. Therefore, I will visit your brethren as I said I would, but I will bring down their sins upon their own heads, and they will be sorry."

After hearing this, my faith in the Lord became so strong it could not be shaken. I prayed very hard to Him, struggling for my brethren, the Lamanites.

After I had prayed diligently, the Lord said to me, "I will grant your desires because of your faith." And this is what I, Enos, had asked the Lord to do: "If my people, the Nephites, ever fall into sin and are destroyed, and the Lamanites survive, will Thou, oh Lord God, by the power of Thy holy arm, save a record of my people, the Nephites, so that it will come to the Lamanites in some future day—so that they, too will be brought to salvation?" I asked the Lord to do this, knowing that He alone could do it, for our preaching to the Lamanites and attempts to restore them to the true faith had been useless. In their anger, the Lamanites had sworn to destroy us along with our fathers' traditions and records. Knowing that the Lord God could preserve our records, I cried to Him without stopping, for He had said to me, "Whatever you ask, in the name of Christ, believing that you will receive, will be granted."

I had faith and prayed to God to preserve the records, and He covenanted with me that He would bring our records (The complete Book of Mormon) to the Lamanites in His own due time. I knew that it would be done according to the covenant that He had made, so my soul was at peace. The Lord said to me, "Your fathers also required me to save their records and to bring them forth in the future. This will be done for them as well, according to their faith. Their faith was strong like yours, Enos."

After having this experience, I went out and prophesied of the future among the Nephites, testifying of things that I had seen and heard. Upon these plates, I now testify that we, the people of Nephi, tried very hard to restore the Lamanites to the true faith in God, but our labors were in vain. The Lamanites' hatred was fixed, and they were led by their evil nature. They had become a wild, ferocious and bloodthirsty people, full of idolatry and filthiness. They ate beasts of prey, lived in tents, and wandered around the wilderness wearing loincloths. They shaved their heads and became skilled with the bow and arrow, scimitar and axe. Many of them ate only raw meat, and they were always trying to kill us, the Nephites.

We tilled the land and raised all types of grain and fruit. We also raised all types of cattle, goats and horses. There were many prophets among us, but the Nephite people had become too proud to listen to them. Nothing but constant, harsh and plain preaching about war, death, the length of eternity, and the judgments and power of God would keep them from quickly going down to destruction.

I, Enos, have seen many wars between the Nephites and the Lamanites during my lifetime. It is now 421 BC, and I am growing old. It has been 179 years since my grandfather, Lehi, left Jerusalem. All my life, God's power has compelled me to preach and prophesy to this people. I have declared the word according to the truth in Christ, and I have rejoiced in His word more than anything in the world. Now I will soon go to my resting place with my Redeemer. And I will rejoice in the day when my mortal body becomes immortal and stands before Him. Then I will see His face with pleasure, and He will say to me, "Come to me; you are blessed. There is a place prepared for you in my Father's mansions."

Jarom preaches and deals with war...

Now, I, Jarom, will obey my father, Enos, who gave me these plates before he died. I will write a few words so that this record and genealogy, begun by my great-grandfather, Lehi, will continue. There is not much room left to engrave upon these plates, and since they are kept for the spiritual benefit of our brethren, the Lamanites, I will not engrave much, for I do not need to repeat the plan of salvation that my fathers have already revealed in their writings. It is more important for much to be done among the Nephites because they are so hard hearted and blinded with pride. In spite of this, God is very merciful to them and has not yet swept them off the land.

Many Nephites have many revelations, for not all of us resist the Holy Spirit. Those who do not resist have communion with Him according to their faith.

In the year 400 BC, twenty-one years after my father, Enos, gave me these plates, we, the Nephites, had become strong in the land. We were protected because we kept the law of Moses and the Sabbath day holy. We did not profane or blaspheme, and the laws of the land were very strict.

We and the Lamanites have populated much of the land, but the Lamanites are much more populous than we. They are a wild people who love murder, and they drink the blood of animals. They have come to battle against us for years, but our kings and leaders have been mighty men in the faith of the Lord, who have taught the people His ways. This is why we have been able to repel the Lamanites and force them out of our lands. We have also fortified our cities and lands of inheritance against their attacks. We have multiplied greatly and have become rich with great amounts of gold, silver and precious things. We've had many fine craftsmen, who have worked with wood, and who have built fine buildings and machinery. Others are skilled in metalwork, using copper, brass and steel to make all types of farming tools and weapons. Our fine tools and weapons have kept the Lamanites from prevailing against us. The Lord's word has been verified that He spoke to our forefathers: "As you keep my commandments, you will prosper in the land."

Our prophets have threatened the Nephites according to God's word, telling them that if they did not keep the commandments, and fell into transgression, they would be destroyed off the face of the land. Because of this great warning from the Lord, the prophets, priests and teachers work hard, patiently preaching to their people, the Nephites. They teach them the law of Moses, that it was given to persuade us to look forward to the Messiah, and to believe in Him as if He had already come. These righteous men keep us, the Nephites, from being swept off the land of promise by constantly urging us to repent.

By the year 362 BC, for most of the time since Lehi had arrived in the promised land, there has been warfare between the us and the Lamanites. I, Jarom, finish my writing because there is not much room left to engrave on these small plates. Refer to Nephi's larger plates to find a record of our wars, as the Nephite kings have written, or have ordered to be written. I now give these plates to my son Omni, to keep according to my fathers' command.

The plates are passed on...

My father, Jarom, commanded me, Omni, to continue writing our genealogy on these small plates of Nephi. Most of my life has been spent as a warrior, defending my people against the Lamanites. But I myself am a wicked man and have not kept the Lord's statutes and commandments as I should have. By the year 324 BC, we had gone through many periods of war and peace. It is now 318 BC, and I have guarded these plates forty-four years. I now give them to my son Amaron.

Now I, Amaron, write a few things in my father's book. By 280 BC, most of the wicked Nephites had been destroyed by the Lamanites. After saving Lehi's family from their enemies in Jerusalem, the Lord verified His warning to Lehi's posterity: "If you do not keep my commandments, you will not prosper in the land." This is why the Lord has already visited the wicked Nephites with great judgments. But He has spared the righteous from being killed by their enemies. I will now give these plates to my brother Chemish.

Now I, Chemish, write a few things in this same book in which my brother Amaron wrote. I saw him engrave his entry on these plates the same day he gave them to me. Our fathers have been commanded to keep this record in this way. Now I give these plates to my son.

I, Abinadom, am Chemish's son. I have seen many wars between my people, the Nephites, and the Lamanites, in which I have killed many Lamanites with my own sword while defending my brethren. The history of this people is written on the large plates, which the kings keep and hand down from generation to generation. Every revelation and prophecy I know of has been written, so I will not add to this sacred record.

Now I, Amaleki, am Abinadom's son. I will tell you a little about Mosiah, who was made king over the land of Zarahemla. He had been warned by the Lord to get out of the land of Nephi and to go into the wilderness. He was told to take with him all those who would listen to the Lord's voice. Mosiah obeyed the Lord and went into the wilderness with as many as would listen. They were led by much preaching and prophesying and were constantly warned by the word of God. The Lord led them by the power of His arm as they made their exodus through the wilderness and came to this land of Zarahemla. Here they discovered a people, led by a man named Zarahemla. They were very happy when they understood that the Lord had sent Mosiah with the brass plates containing the Jews' records.

Note: In addition to bringing the brass plates out of the land of Nephi, Mosiah and Amaleki's father, Abinadom, brought Nephi's large and small plates, and other sacred things (the Liahona compass, Laban's sword, and the interpreters). These things were passed down until Mormon received them (W of M 1:10, Mosiah 1:15-16, 29:42, Alma 37:14, W of M 1:11).

The people of Zarahemla were happy to have the brass plates from Jerusalem, for their ancestors had also come from Jerusalem when Zedekiah, king of Judah, was carried away captive into Babylon. Like Lehi, their ancestors had been brought by the hand of the Lord across the ocean to the very place where Mosiah discovered them. This place had been settled for 320 years.

Mosiah noted that the people of Zarahemla were very numerous, even though they had been having wars as well. Because they had not brought any records from Jerusalem, their language had become corrupted, and Mosiah could not understand their speech. They had also lost the knowledge of their Creator. And so Mosiah had his language taught to them. After they learned the language, their leader, Zarahemla, recited his genealogy from memory. This genealogy is not written here, but on other plates (not translated). The people of Zarahemla and the people of Mosiah united, and Mosiah was appointed to be their king.

During his reign, a large engraved stone was brought to Mosiah, and he interpreted the engravings by the gift and power of God. The engravings were the history of a man named Coriantumr, and of his people who had all been killed. The first people of Zarahemla had found Coriantumr, who had lived with them for nine lunar months. The engravings on the stone also told of Coriantumr's forefathers—how they had come from the tower of Babel when the Lord confused their language. They told of the Lord's severe yet fair judgments that had come upon Coriantumr's people, and that their bones were scattered on the ground in the northern land.

I, Amaleki, was born in the days of Mosiah. He has since passed away, and now his son Benjamin reigns here in Zarahemla. During King Benjamin's reign, I have seen a serious war and great bloodshed between the Nephites and the Lamanites. But the Nephites under King Benjamin have driven the Lamanites out of the land of Zarahemla.

I am old now and have no children. Since I know King Benjamin is a just man before the Lord, I will soon give him these plates. The messages on these plates invite all people to come to God, the Holy One of Israel, and to believe in prophesying, revelations, and the ministering of angels, to believe in the gift of speaking in tongues, and in the understanding of languages, and in all good things, for good comes from the Lord and evil comes from the devil.

My beloved brothers and sisters, I invite you to come to Christ, the Holy One of Israel, and to partake of His salvation. Allow His power to redeem you. Come to Him and offer your whole soul to Him, continuing to fast, pray, and to stay righteous throughout your lives. If you do this, then as the Lord lives, you will be saved.

Now I will tell you about a large number of Nephites who left Zarahemla and went through the wilderness on a quest to return to the land of Nephi (the place from which our fathers had come with Mosiah). They believed the land of Nephi was rightfully theirs as an inheritance. Their leader was a physically strong man. He was also very stubborn, and this caused fighting to break out among those making the quest. Only fifty of his men survived this fighting in the wilderness, and they returned to the land of Zarahemla. Then these fifty gathered another large group and went into the wilderness again.

I, Amaleki, had a brother who went with them. I have not seen nor heard from him since he and the group left. Now I am old and will soon die. These small plates of Nephi are full, and I have finished my engraving upon them.

The plates are passed on...

THREE HUNDRED EIGHTY-FIVE AD: I, MORMON, am about to give my plates to my son Moroni. I have seen the death of almost all my people, the Nephites. I believe my son will witness their entire destruction. May God spare him long enough to write about my people, and about Christ, so that someday his writings may be of value to my people's descendants among the Lamanites.

After I had engraved the Nephite history down to King Benjamin by referring to Nephi's large plates, I found Nephi's small plates. They contain many of Nephi's words and a brief account of the prophets from Jacob down to King Benjamin. What pleases me most about Nephi's small plates is their account of the prophecies of Christ's coming. My ancestors knew that many of these prophecies had been fulfilled in their day. I know the prophecies of my day have been fulfilled, and that the prophecies not yet fulfilled surely will be. Because these prophecies will be fulfilled, I will pattern the rest of my record after them. I will do this as I continue referring to Nephi's large plates. And I cannot engrave even one percent of the history of my people, the Nephites.

Because these small plates are so choice to me, I am putting them with my plates before continuing my engraving. I know the record of these small plates will also be choice to my brethren, the Lamanites, in the last days. I am putting the small plates with mine because the Lord's Spirit tells me to. I do not know exactly why, for I know not the future, but it must be for a wise purpose known to the Lord, who works His will through me.

My prayer to God is for my brethren, the Lamanites, to once again know God, to know of Christ's redemption, and to again become a delightful people.

Now I, Mormon, continue to engrave my record as I refer to Nephi's large plates. I do this according to the knowledge and understanding God has given me.

When King Benjamin received Nephi's small plates from Amaleki, he put them with Nephi's large plates that had been handed down by the kings from generation to generation. All these plates have been handed down by King Benjamin, from generation to generation, until I, Mormon, have received them. I pray to God that they will always be preserved, and I know they will be, for great things are written on them. On the great and last day, my people, the Nephites, and our brethren, the Lamanites, will be judged by what is engraved upon these plates.

Now back to King Benjamin. His own people, the Nephites, fought a great deal among themselves. Then the Lamanite armies came from the land of Nephi to attack them. King Benjamin gathered armies to defend his people, and he himself used Laban's sword while battling the Lamanites.

Because the Nephites were strengthened by the Lord, they killed several thousand Lamanites and chased the rest of them out of their lands of inheritance. Among the Nephites, there had been false Christs who were silenced and punished according to their crimes. There were also false prophets, preachers and teachers among the Nephites who had caused much of the fighting as well as defecting to the Lamanites, and they were also punished. With the assistance of the holy prophets among his people, King Benjamin had seen to this justice. King Benjamin was a holy man, who reigned in righteousness. There were many other holy men in the land who spoke God's words with power and authority. They spoke sharply because the Nephites were stubborn. With the help of these holy men, and by laboring with all the strength of his body and soul, King Benjamin established peace again in the land.

1 - King Benjamin teaches his sons...

This peace among all the people in the land of Zarahemla lasted for the rest of King Benjamin's days. He had three sons, Mosiah, Helorum and Helaman. He had them taught in the language in which his forefathers wrote—modified Egyptian. He did this so that they would become men of understanding, knowing about the prophecies that the Lord had given to their forefathers (engraved on Nephi's plates). He also taught them about the records engraved on the brass plates, saying, "My sons, I want you to remember that if it were not for these plates which contain these records and commandments, we would now be in ignorance, not knowing the mysteries of God. It would have been impossible for our forefather, Lehi, to have remembered all these things and to have taught them to his children without the help of these plates. Lehi had been taught in the Egyptian language. This is why he could read the brass plates and teach them to his children. They in turn taught their children Egyptian, fulfilling God's commandments, even down to this present time.

"My sons, if it were not for these brass plates that have been preserved by the hand of God, our forefathers would have faltered in unbelief. We would be like the Lamanites, who know nothing about God's commandments and mysteries. They do not believe these things because they are misguided by their forefathers' false traditions. Remember this, for these sayings and records are true. These plates that Nephi made, which contain our forefathers' words from the time they left Jerusalem until now, are also true. Remember to search them diligently so that you may profit from them. I want you to keep God's commandments so that you will prosper in the land according to the promises that He made to our forefathers."

King Benjamin taught many more things to his sons which are not written here. As he grew old, and realized that he would soon die, he felt it was necessary to confer the kingdom upon one of his sons. And so he called for Mosiah, named after his grandfather, and said to him, "My son, I want you to make a proclamation throughout all the land of Zarahemla. Tell the people to assemble tomorrow, when I will proclaim that you are now a king and ruler over this people, whom the Lord our God has given us. Tomorrow I will also give this people a name to distinguish them from all the people that the Lord God has brought out of Jerusalem. I will do this because they have been diligently keeping the Lord's commandments. It will always be their name unless they become sinful. For if this people, who are now highly favored of the Lord, become wicked and adulterous, the Lord will deliver them to the Lamanites by taking away their strength and protection. Then He will no longer save them by His matchless and marvelous power as He saved our forefathers. If the Lord had not extended His arm to save our forefathers, they would have all fallen victim to the Lamanites, who hated them."

After King Benjamin said this to his son, he put him in charge of the kingdom. He also gave Mosiah the brass plates, Nephi's plates, Laban's sword and the Liahona—the ball with spindles, made by the Lord, which had led Lehi and his people through the wilderness when they diligently obeyed the Lord. When anyone in Lehi's group had been unfaithful, the whole group did not progress in their journey. They were driven back and suffered hunger and pain. They felt God's displeasure in order to remind them of their duty to Him.

Mosiah did as he was asked and made a proclamation to all the people in the land of Zarahemla to go up to the temple to hear his father speak.

2 - King Benjamin speaks to his people...

The next day all the people went up to the temple to hear King Benjamin. The Nephites had become very numerous, even too numerous to count. They brought the firstborn of their flocks as sacrifices and burnt offerings according to the law of Moses. They gave thanks to the Lord their God, who had brought their forefathers out of Jerusalem and had delivered them from their enemies. They were also grateful for the just men who had been appointed to be their teachers, and for Benjamin, a just man, who had been appointed as their king. These just men had established peace in the land of Zarahemla and had taught the people to keep God's commandments, that they might rejoice and be filled with love toward God and all mankind.

Each family—a man with his wife, sons, daughters and grandchildren, from the oldest down to the youngest, set up separate tents around the temple. Their tent doors faced the temple so they could stay in their tents and still hear King Benjamin.

The multitude was so large that all the people could not fit inside the walls of the temple. So King Benjamin had a tower made. When he spoke from this tower many more people could hear him. But as he started to speak, not everyone could hear him, so King Benjamin had his words written and sent among those who were too far away to hear. And these are his words:

"My brothers and sisters, I have not commanded you to come here to make light of what I will tell you, but to open you hearts and minds, so that God's mysteries may be unfolded to your view. I have not commanded you to come here to fear me, or to make you think that I am more than a mortal man. Like everyone else, I too, am sometimes weak in body and mind. But I have been chosen by you and consecrated by my father, Mosiah, and I have been allowed to be your ruler and king.

I have been saved by the Lord's matchless power to serve you with all the might, mind and strength that He gives me. I have spent my life in your service, not seeking gold, silver or any kind of riches from you. I have not allowed slavery or confinement in dungeons. I have not allowed murder, plunder, stealing or adultery. I have not condoned any kind of wickedness, but I have taught you to keep all the Lord's commandments. And I have even labored with my own hands to serve you so that you would not be burdened with taxes. You, yourselves, know all these things.

"I do not say these things to boast or to accuse you. I say these things so that you will know that I can answer to God with a clear conscience today.

"Saying that I have spent my days in your service does not mean that I am boasting, for I have only been serving God. You will be wise when you learn that serving your brothers and sisters is serving your God. If I, your king, work with my own hands to serve you, then shouldn't you do the same for one another? And if I, your earthly king (who serves God by serving you), deserve thanks, then how much more should you thank your Heavenly King!

"If you gave God all the thanks and praise that you could, for creating and protecting you, and for giving you reason to rejoice and live in peace, it would not be enough. He lends you breath to live, to move about, to do as you wish, supporting you from moment to moment. If you served Him with all your souls forever, you could never do enough to profit Him. Yet all He requires of you is to keep His commandments. He has promised you that if you keep His commandments, you will prosper in the land. And you see that He has blessed you.

But since He created you, giving you your life, you are still in debt to Him. He does not require payment for your life, but only for you to keep His commandments. When you do this, He immediately pays you with blessings. Since you still owe Him for your life no matter what you do, how can you boast? Can you, yourselves, say that you are great? No, you are no greater than the dust of the earth, for it was the Creator's dust from which you were created. Even I, whom you call your king, am no better than you, for I, too, am made from dust. You see that I am old, and am about to give up this mortal body to its mother earth.

"I have asked you to gather here so that I might be found blameless, so that your blood will not come upon me when I stand before God to be judged for the things I have done for you—things that I have been commanded to do. I do this to rid my robes of your blood before I die—that I might die in peace and my immortal spirit join the choirs above in singing praises to a just God. I also need to tell you that I can no longer be your teacher nor your king. For even now, my whole body shakes while I attempt to speak to you. But the Lord supports me, and He has commanded me to tell you that my son Mosiah is now your king and ruler.

"Now, my brothers and sisters, continue to keep the Lord's commandments that my father, Mosiah, and I have given to you. Because you have been keeping these commandments, you have prospered, and have been protected from your enemies. If you continue to keep God's commandments that will be given to you by my son Mosiah, you will continue to prosper in the land, and your enemies will never have power over you. But beware of contentions among you, oh my people, which arise when you obey the evil spirit. There is a curse pronounced upon those who obey that spirit. If you have a knowledge of God's laws and transgress them, choosing to obey the evil spirit, and then die in your sins, your souls will not progress (will be damned).

"All of you, except your little children, have been taught these things. You know that after you have given your Heavenly Father all the service and substance He requires, you will still owe Him, never being able to fully repay. You have also been taught from the brass plates, which contain the ancient prophecies of the holy prophets down until the time our forefather, Lehi, left Jerusalem. You also know everything that has been spoken by our forefathers, who said what the Lord commanded them to say. This is why their words are just and true. After having been taught all these things and knowing that they are true, if you go against them, you withdraw yourselves from the Lord's Spirit. Then you will no longer have Him as a guide to keep you on the paths of wisdom, which lead you to blessings, prosperity and safety. If you go against what you know is true, then you are in open rebellion against God, obeying the evil spirit. You become an enemy to all righteousness. In this condition, the Lord cannot help you because He cannot send His Holy Spirit to live in unholy temples.

"If you do not repent, but choose to remain an enemy to God until you die, then the demands of divine justice will suddenly awaken your immortal soul to a clear awareness of your own guilt. This will cause you to shrink from the Lord's presence and will fill your heart with guilt, pain and anguish, like an unquenchable fire with flames that go up forever and ever. Mercy has no claim on such a person. His final doom, or judgment, is to endure this never-ending torment.

"I have spoken plainly so that you may all understand, both old and young alike. Wake up and remember the awful situation of those who have fallen into transgression. But more than this, I want you to consider the blessed and happy state of those who keep God's commandments. They are blessed in all things, both temporal and spiritual. If they are faithful to the end of their lives, they will be received into heaven to live with God in a state of never-ending happiness. Oh remember, remember that these things are true because the Lord God has spoken them.

3 - King Benjamin quotes an angel...

"Listen carefully, brothers and sisters, because I have things to tell you about the future. An angel from God told me these things, saying, 'Awake!' I awoke and saw him standing before me. He said, 'Listen, because I have come to give you news of great joy, for the Lord has heard your prayers and has judged you to be righteous. You will rejoice with your people when you give them this news.

In not many years the Lord Omnipotent, who reigns for all eternity, will come down from heaven with power among His people. He will live in a mortal body, performing mighty miracles—healing the sick, raising the dead, causing the lame to walk, the blind to receive their sight, the deaf to hear, and curing all types of diseases. He will cast out the evil spirits that live in people's hearts. He will suffer temptations, pain, hunger, thirst and fatigue that would certainly kill an ordinary man. His suffering and anguish for the sins of His people will be so great that He will sweat blood from all of His pores. He will be called

Jesus Christ—the Son of God—the Father of Heaven and Earth—the Creator of all things from the beginning. His mother will be called Mary. He will come to save His own—those who have faith in Him. But after doing all this for His chosen people, they will treat Him like an ordinary man, and say, "He is possessed by a devil." Then they will whip and crucify Him.

"'After three days, He will rise from the dead and stand to judge the world. He will do all of this to qualify as the one who can make a perfect judgment upon all people. His blood will atone for those who sin in ignorance—those who die not knowing God's will for them.

But there is great cursing upon those who do know God's will and rebel against it, for among such, only those who repent and rely upon the Lord Jesus Christ will be saved. The Lord God has sent His holy prophets to give this news to all the people of the world. Those who believe in Christ and change their ways will be forgiven of their sins and may rejoice as though Christ had already come.

"'Because the Lord's covenant people—the house of Israel—were stubborn, He gave them a lower law—the law of Moses. He showed them many signs, wonders, types and shadows of His coming. Their holy prophets also spoke of His coming. But the children of Israel still hardened their hearts, and they did not understand that the law of Moses was given to prepare them to accept the atoning blood of Jesus Christ. It is impossible for little children to sin. Even if they could sin, the law of Moses could not save them. Because Adam and Eve fell from God's presence, all their children are in an imperfect state. This is why Christ's blood will atone even for their little children.

"'It is important to know that there is no other name or way that can save anyone other than Christ, the Lord Omnipotent, for His judgments are just. Infants who die are saved in His kingdom because they are innocent. But those who know God's laws and refuse to humble themselves as children damn their own souls, for they do not believe that their salvation has always been through the atoning blood of Christ, who is Lord over all things.

"'Because of the fall of Adam and Eve, all of their descendants are born into a fallen, natural state. As mortals, with natural desires to serve themselves, they are enemies to God forever. But if they allow the Holy Spirit to guide them, rejecting their natural desires, then they become saints through the atonement of Christ the Lord. They become as submissive, meek, humble, patient and as full of love as children. They again become willing to learn all the lessons that the Lord sees fit to teach them, as if they were again children.'

"Standing before me, the angel concluded, 'In the last days, all people throughout the world will know of the Savior. When that time comes, only little children, and those who have become like them through repentance and faith in the Lord God Omnipotent, will be found innocent. When you have given your people the knowledge that the Lord your God commanded you to give them, they will only become innocent in His sight if they have repented, with faith in their Savior.'

"I, Benjamin, have said everything that the Lord God commanded me to say. The Lord said that these words will stand as a bright testimony against this people on judgment day, when all will be judged according to the good or evil that they have done. If they have done evil, they will see their own guilt and sins, which will cause them to cower in the Lord's presence. They will be in a state of misery and endless torment from which they cannot return, having already damned their own souls. Mercy will never claim them, for they will receive God's justice as Adam and Eve received it (through the fall) for eating of the forbidden fruit. Their torment will be like a lake of fire and burning sulfur, with unquenchable flames and smoke that will go up forever. This is what the Lord commanded me to say. Amen."

4 - The Spirit fills the people with joy...

After King Benjamin finished quoting the angel, he saw the multitude bowing upon the earth, for the fear of the Lord had come upon them. They had realized that in their carnal state they were lower than the dust of the earth. They all shouted with one voice, "Oh have mercy, and apply the atoning blood of Christ to us, so that our sins may be forgiven—that our hearts may be purified. We believe in Jesus Christ, the Son of God, who created heaven, the earth and all things, and who will come down among His people."

Then the Spirit of the Lord came upon them, and they were filled with joy, having received a remission of their sins and a peace of conscience, because of their great faith in Jesus Christ, of whom King Benjamin had spoken.

Then King Benjamin said to the multitude, "My friends, brothers and sisters, my family and my people. Listen and understand the rest of my words. The knowledge of the goodness of God has made you realize your nothingness in your fallen state. You now know the goodness of God, His matchless power, wisdom, patience and His long-suffering toward all people. You know that the atonement, planned from the beginning of the world, brings salvation to those who trust in the Lord and diligently keep His commandments throughout their lives.

"This salvation is offered to Adam and Eve's descendants until the end of the world. This salvation, and the conditions for it, come only through Christ. Believe in God, and that He created all things in heaven and earth. Believe that He has all wisdom and power. Believe that we cannot comprehend everything that the Lord comprehends. Believe that you must leave your sinful ways and not go back to them. Humble yourselves before God, sincerely asking the Lord to forgive you. And if you believe these things, see that you do them.

"I repeat, now that you know the glory of God, or His goodness, having tasted of His love, having been forgiven, and having received His great joy, I want you to remember the greatness of God, and your own nothingness. Remember His goodness and patience, humbling yourselves as much as you can, praying to the Lord daily with faith in Christ, who will come. If you do this, you will always rejoice and be filled with God's love. You will always retain a remission of your sins. And your knowledge of justice and truth, which are the glory of your Creator, will always grow.

"Because you will lose your desire to hurt anyone, you will live in peace and deal justly with one another. You will not let your children go hungry or go about ill-clothed, and you will teach them to obey God's laws, that they may not serve the devil by fighting and arguing with one another. The devil is the master of sin, an enemy to all righteousness. He is the evil spirit, of whom our forefathers wrote. Teach your children to walk in the ways of truth, to take God seriously, and to love and serve one another.

Help those who need your help, and give your substance to those who need it. Do not turn away those who ask for your help, saying, 'This foolish man has brought on his own misery. I will not relieve his misery by giving him food or money. He deserves to suffer for his own mistakes.' Anyone who does this has great need to repent or he will spiritually perish forever, having no place in God's kingdom. For we are all beggars. We all depend upon the same Being, even God, for everything we have—food, clothing and all our prosperity.

Today you have been calling on His name, begging for a remission of your sins. And have you begged in vain? No, for God has poured out His Spirit upon you, and you could not even speak because your hearts were filled with so much joy. God, the one on whom you depend for your lives, and for everything you have and are, gives you whatever you ask, if you ask in faith for what is right, believing that you will receive it. Then how much more you should give your substance to those who are in need! If you judge and condemn those who ask you for substance just to survive, then you will be condemned for holding it back. For what you think is yours is really God's, including your life. Yet while under this condemnation, do you ask God's forgiveness, or change your ways? Cursed are such people, for their substance will perish with them.

I am speaking to those who are rich in the things of the world. And the poor who turn away the needy should say, 'I cannot help you because I have nothing to give, but if I had something, I would give it to you.' If you who are poor feel this way in your hearts, then you are guiltless. Otherwise, you are condemned for not being willing in your hearts to give up things that you do not even have.

In order to keep a forgiveness of your sins each day, that you may walk guiltless before God, give your substance to the poor. Having more, the rich must give more. Having less, the poor will give less. Yet everyone must feed the hungry, clothe the ill-clothed, and visit and relieve the sick according to their wants, both spiritual and temporal. To obtain eternal life, it is necessary to do these things. But you must do them in wisdom and order, for you are not required to give more than you are able.

"Whoever borrows something from his neighbor and does not return it when he says he will commits sin, and he may also prompt his neighbor to sin by becoming angry with him.

"I cannot tell you all the ways you can sin because there are too many. But this much I can tell you. If you do not watch yourselves—your words, actions, and even your thoughts, and keep God's commandments, having faith in the coming of our Lord until the end of your lives, then you must perish spiritually. So remember these things and do not perish."

5 - From faith to knowledge and covenants...

After saying these things to his people, King Benjamin sent messengers among them to ask if they believed his words. All of the people looked up at King Benjamin and shouted with one voice, "Yes, we believe everything you have told us. We know it is the truth because the Spirit of the Lord Omnipotent has brought about a mighty change in our hearts. We no longer have any desire to do evil, but only to do good continually. We have seen what is coming through the infinite goodness of God and the manifestations of His Spirit. If it were necessary, we could prophesy of all things. Because we first had faith in what you, our king, told us, we are now overjoyed to have a great knowledge of it ourselves! We are willing to make a covenant with our God to do His will, and to be obedient to His commandments in all things for the rest of our lives. We do not want to bring a never ending torment upon ourselves, and experience God's wrath, as the angel described."

King Benjamin responded to the multitude, "This is what I wanted to hear. The covenant you have made is a righteous covenant. Because of the change made in your hearts through faith in His name, and because of the covenant you have made, you will be called the Children of Christ, for today you have been spiritually born of Him, and have become His sons and daughters. Only as Children of Christ can you be made free, for no other name could free you and save your souls from hell. Remember that all who have entered into this covenant with God should be obedient to Him for the rest of their lives. Those who do this will be found at the right hand of God, where Christ is. Those who are righteous will know their name, for they will be called 'The Children of Christ.'

"Those who do not take the name of Christ upon themselves must be called by another name, and will find themselves on the left hand of God. Children of Christ is the name that I said I would give to you—a name that will never be forgotten in your hearts unless you sin. Remember always to keep this name written in your hearts so that you will not be found on the left hand of God, and so that you will recognize His voice and know the name by which He will call you. For how can you know someone that you have not served, who is a stranger to you, far from the thoughts and intentions of your heart? Does a shepherd keep his neighbor's goat? No. He will not even allow it to feed among his sheep. He will drive it out, away from his flock. Your fate will be like the goat's if you do not recognize your Shepherd's voice and are not one of His sheep.

"Be strong and immovable, always doing good works. If you do this, then Christ the Lord God Omnipotent will seal you His. Then you will be brought to heaven—to everlasting salvation and eternal life, through the wisdom, power, justice and mercy of Him who created all things in heaven and earth, who is God above all. Amen."

6 - Mosiah is made king...

After speaking, King Benjamin felt that it was necessary to write down the names of all those who had entered into a covenant with God to keep His commandments. Everyone in the multitude, except their little children, had entered into the covenant and had taken the name of Christ upon themselves. Then King Benjamin consecrated his son Mosiah to be a ruler and king over his people, giving him charge of everything concerning the kingdom. Benjamin appointed priests to teach the commandments of God to the people, and to help them always remember the oath they had made. Then he dismissed the multitude and they all returned to their homes with their families.

In the year 124 BC, at age thirty, Mosiah began to reign in his father's place. About 476 years had passed since Lehi had left Jerusalem. King Benjamin lived three more years and then died in 121 BC.

King Mosiah walked in the ways of the Lord, observing His judgments, statutes and commandments. He told his people to farm the earth. Like his father, he himself farmed so that he would not be a burden to his people.

7 - *Sixteen men search for their brethren...*

After three years of peace, King Mosiah wanted to know about his people who had gone to live in the city of Lehi-Nephi, for none of his people had heard from them since they had left the land of Zarahemla. Mosiah's people constantly bothered him, asking permission to send out a search party. So King Mosiah finally allowed sixteen of their strong men to go up to the land of Lehi-Nephi to find out about their brethren.

The next day the search began. The group was led by Ammon, a strong and mighty man, and a descendant of Zarahemla. He and his men did not know the course they should take to get to the land of Lehi-Nephi, so they wandered for forty days in the wilderness.

Finally they camped on a hill, and to the south they saw the land of Shilom. From their camp, Ammon took three of his brethren, Amaleki, Helem and Hem, and went down into the land of Nephi. Outside the city walls, they approached the king of the people in the land of Nephi and the city of Shilom. The king's guard quickly surrounded and captured them, and they were thrown into prison.

After spending two days in prison, they were brought before the king and untied. They stood before him and were commanded to answer his questions. The king said, "I am Limhi, son of Noah. My grandfather, Zeniff, led people up out of the land of Zarahemla to inherit this land, which was once the land of our forefathers. After arriving here, the people he had led voted him to be their king. Now why were you bold enough to come near the city walls when I was outside the gate with my guards? I could have had my guards kill you, but I wanted to ask why you were so bold. You are permitted to speak."

Ammon bowed himself before the king, and upon rising said, "Oh king, I am very thankful before God that I am yet alive and am permitted to speak. I will speak with boldness, for I'm sure that if you had known me, you would not have had me bound. I am Ammon, a descendant of Zarahemla. I have come from the city of Zarahemla to find out what happened to our brethren, whom your grandfather, Zeniff, brought out of our land."

When Limhi heard this he was very happy and said, "Now I know for sure that my brethren in the land of Zarahemla are yet alive! Now I will rejoice, and tomorrow I will cause my people to also rejoice! For we are in bondage to the Lamanites, paying a high tax which is hard to pay. And now our fellow Nephites will deliver us out of our bondage, out of the hands of the Lamanites, and we will be their slaves if they wish. For it is better to be slaves to Nephites than to pay tribute to the Lamanite king." After saying this,

King Limhi commanded his guards to free Ammon and his brethren and allowed them to go to the hill north of Shilom and bring the rest of their men into the city, to eat, drink and rest from their long, hard journey.

The next day, King Limhi sent a proclamation among all his people to assemble at the temple to hear him speak. After they had gathered, Limhi said to them, "Oh my people, lift up your heads and be comforted, for soon we will no longer be controlled by our enemies, in spite of all our futile resistance. I believe we may yet be effective in our struggle.

So lift up your heads, rejoice, and put your trust in that God who was the God of Abraham, Isaac and Jacob—the same God who brought the children of Israel out of the land of Egypt, to walk through the Red Sea on dry ground—He who fed them with manna in the wilderness, and did many more things for them. Trust that same God who brought our fathers out of Jerusalem, and who has kept and preserved His people even until now. We know it is because of our sinfulness that He has brought us into bondage.

"You are all witnesses today that my grandfather, Zeniff (who was made king over this people), being over-zealous to inherit the land of his forefathers, was deceived by the cunning and craftiness of King Laman. He entered into a treaty with Zeniff, giving him possession of part of the land—the city of Lehi-Nephi, the city of Shilom, and the surrounding area. King Laman did this in order to bring Zeniff and his people into bondage. Even now we must pay a fifty percent annual tribute to King Laman of all our grain, increase of flocks and herds, and of everything we own, or else he will kill us. Isn't this a terrible tax? Isn't our affliction great? What great reason we have to mourn! Yes, we do have great reason to mourn, for many of our brethren have died in vain, all because of sinfulness. For if this people had not been so sinful, the Lord would not have allowed this great evil to come upon them. But they would not listen to Him. Instead, they fought among themselves and killed one another.

"Before that war, they killed Abinadi, a prophet of the Lord. He was a chosen man of God, who told them of their great wickedness. He prophesied of many things, and of the coming of Christ. He told them that Christ was God, the Father of all things, and that He would come down among His people to take upon Himself a body of flesh and blood in the image of man, who was created in God's image. Because Abinadi said these things, they killed him. They also did many other things to bring God's wrath down upon them. This is why we are so sorely afflicted and in bondage. For the Lord has said, 'I will not protect my people when they transgress. I will keep them from prospering, and everything they do will become a stumbling block before them. If my people plant filthiness, then they will harvest its chaff in the whirlwind—the east wind, which will affect them like poison, bringing immediate destruction.' Now this promise of the Lord is fulfilled, and you are stricken and afflicted. But if you will turn to the Lord with full purpose of heart, trusting and serving Him with all diligence of mind, then He will deliver you out of bondage according to His own will and pleasure."

8 - King Limhi presents plates to Ammon...

King Limhi said many other things to his people which are not written in this book, telling them all about their fellow Nephites living in Zarahemla. Then he had Ammon tell them everything that had happened in Zarahemla, from the time that Zeniff had left there until Ammon and his fifteen companions went out to search for them. Ammon also repeated and explained King Benjamin's last speech to King Limhi's people, so that they would know and understand Benjamin's prophecies of Christ. After all this, King Limhi dismissed the multitude and they returned to their homes.

Then Limhi brought a set of plates to Ammon which contained the record of his people from the time his grandfather, Zeniff, left the land of Zarahemla. When Ammon finished reading this record, Limhi asked him if he could interpret languages. Ammon told him that he could not.

Limhi then explained to Ammon, "Being grieved over the afflictions of my people, I sent out forty-three men into the wilderness to find the land of Zarahemla, to ask their fellow Nephites to deliver us out of bondage.

"These men became lost in the wilderness for many days. They never found the land of Zarahemla, and returned home, having traveled through a land of many lakes and rivers. They discovered a land covered with the bones of people and animals, and with the ruins of all types of buildings. The land had once been populated with as many people as the hosts of Israel.

"To prove their findings, my men brought back twenty-four plates of pure gold, filled with engravings. They also brought large breastplates in perfect condition, made of brass and copper, and rusty swords with the handles rusted away.

"No one in this land is able to interpret the language engraved on the plates. This is why I asked if you could translate. If not, perhaps you know someone who can translate. I want these records to be translated into our language, for maybe they will tell us about any of the survivors of those who were destroyed, and where these plates came from. Or maybe the plates will tell us about the very people who were destroyed. I am very curious to know how they were destroyed."

Ammon replied, "I know of a man who can translate ancient records by simply looking at them through what are called interpreters. This is a gift from God. No man can look into them unless he is commanded to, or else he would look for what he should not and perish. Whoever is commanded to look into them is called a seer, or one who sees.

"The man who has this high gift from God is King Mosiah, king of the people of Zarahemla." Limhi said, "A seer must be greater than a prophet!" Ammon explained, "A seer is both a revelator and a prophet. No man can have a greater gift from God unless he possesses God's power, which no man can. But a man can be given great power from God. A seer can know the past and the future. Through a seer, all things are revealed, secret things are shown, and hidden things come to light. God has provided this method for a man, through faith, to work mighty miracles and become a great benefit to his fellow beings."

King Limhi was overjoyed at hearing this news. He thanked God by saying, "No doubt a great mystery is contained within these plates. These interpreters must have been prepared for the purpose of unfolding all such mysteries to all people. Oh how marvelous are the works of the Lord. How long He suffers with His people. How blind and dense people are in their understanding, for they will not seek to be governed by wisdom. They are like a wild flock running from the shepherd, and once scattered, they are chased and eaten by wild animals."

9 - A history of Zeniff's people, engraved by him (chapters 9—11) ...

Now I, Mormon, will transcribe some of Zeniff's own writings:

I, Zeniff, was taught both of the Nephite languages (Hebrew for speaking and reformed Egyptian for engraving). I also knew of our forefather, Nephi, and of the land that he and his people had settled. I was sent out to spy on the Lamanites that had taken over the land of Nephi—to see how our army could destroy them. But when I saw the good things they were doing, I did not want them to die. I returned to our camp, requesting of our leader to make a treaty with the Lamanites. But our leader, a strict and bloodthirsty man, ordered our men to kill me. I was spared because many disagreed with our leader, and a battle broke out between fellow Nephites. Father fought against father and brother against brother. Only fifty of us survived the battle, and we returned to Zarahemla to tell the sad tale to the wives and children of those who had been killed.

And yet I, being over-zealous to inherit the land of our fathers, gathered many who also wanted to regain the land of our forefathers. We started out again on our journey into the wilderness. We suffered with hunger and fatigue because we were slow to remember the Lord our God. After many days of wandering, we camped in the place where our brethren had killed one another, near the land of Nephi. Then I went into the city with four of my men. We went to ask the Lamanite king if I might go in with my people and possess the land in peace.

Laman, the king, covenanted with me that I could possess the land of Lehi-Nephi and the land of Shilom. He even commanded his people to leave the land so that my people could take possession of it. After coming into the land, we began to construct buildings and to repair the city walls of Lehi-Nephi and Shilom. We farmed the land and raised corn, wheat, barley and other crops. We also planted all types of fruit from seeds, and began to multiply and prosper in the land. But from the beginning, King Laman was craftily planning to bring my people into bondage. This is why he gave us the lands so easily.

After we had lived in the land for twelve years, King Laman started getting restless, for he saw that we were growing stronger. He knew that if he did not overpower us soon and bring us into bondage, that it would be too late.

The Lamanites were lazy and idolatrous. They wanted to bring us into bondage to glut themselves with the labors of our hands and to feast upon our flocks. So King Laman began to stir up his people to fight with mine, and we began to have wars in the land.

During the thirteenth year of my reign, in the southern part of Shilom, my people were watering and feeding their flocks and working their lands. Then a very large Lamanite army attacked them and began to kill them in their fields, taking their flocks and corn. My people ran from the army. Those who were not overtaken ran to the city of Nephi and called upon me for protection. I armed them with bows and arrows, swords, scimitars, clubs, slings and with all the weapons we could invent. Then I went with my people to battle against the Lamanites.

Note: a scimitar is a sword with a short, curved one-edged blade.

We went with the strength of the Lord against them, for we all cried mightily to Him to deliver us from our enemies, remembering how our forefathers had been delivered.

God heard our cries and answered our prayers. We went forth in His might against the Lamanites, and in one day and a night we killed 3,043 of them and drove the rest out of our land. I, myself, with my own hands, helped bury them. And to our great sorrow, 279 of our brethren had been killed.

10 - Nephites rely on God for strength...

After this war, we established our kingdom again in peace. I told my people to make every kind of weapon to be used if the Lamanites attacked us again. I set guards around the land to watch for Lamanites and to protect my people and my flocks, and we continued to live in the land of our forefathers for an additional twenty-two years. Our men continued to farm the land, raising all types of grain and fruit, and our women spun all types of cloth and fine linen. We peacefully prospered in the land during those twenty-two years. Then King Laman died, and his son began to reign in his stead. He encouraged his people to rebel against my people and to prepare for war.

I had sent my spies around the land of Shemlon to find out what the Lamanites were doing. My spies saw a very large Lamanite army coming into northern Shilom, armed with bows and arrows, swords, scimitars, stones and slings. They had shaved their heads and wore nothing more than a leather loincloth. Knowing their plans, we hid our women and children in the wilderness.

All of our young and old men who were able-bodied were armed and placed in ranks according to their age. Then we fought the Lamanites. Even I, Zeniff, in my old age fought. We went to battle strengthened by the Lord.

The Lamanites were ignorant of the Lord and of His strength. They depended on their own strength, being strong as to the strength of men, and they were wild, ferocious and blood-thirsty. They believed in the false traditions of their forefathers, Laman and Lemuel, who had taught their children that Lehi's sins had caused him and his family to be thrown out of Jerusalem, that they had been treated badly by Nephi in the wilderness and while crossing the ocean. Laman and Lemuel had also taught their children that they were wronged after arriving in the land of their first inheritance.

The truth was that Nephi was favored by the Lord, who heard and answered his prayers because he had been more faithful in keeping the Lord's commandments. This is also why Nephi had been Laman and Lemuel's leader during their wilderness journey.

Laman and Lemuel had hated Nephi because they had not understood how the Lord deals with His people. They were angry with Nephi because they hardened their hearts against the Lord while crossing the ocean. They still hated Nephi upon arriving in the promised land, saying he had taken the leadership of the people away from them, and they planned to kill him. They hated Nephi because the Lord had told him to take the brass plates and to go into the wilderness. Because he did this, they said Nephi had robbed them.

Laman and Lemuel taught their children this eternal hatred toward Nephi and his followers. They taught their children to murder, rob and plunder the Nephites, and to do everything in their power to destroy them. This is why King Laman deceived me with his cunning, lying craftiness and fair promises. All he wanted was to bring my people into this land so he could destroy them, and we have suffered for many years in this land.

I, Zeniff, told all these things to my people to motivate them to fight with their might while putting their trust in the Lord. Then we fought the Lamanites face to face. We drove them out of our land again, killing too many of them to count. Then we returned to our land, and my people tended their flocks and raised food again. Since I was growing old, I conferred the kingdom upon one of my sons, Noah. This is all that I will engrave. May the Lord bless my people. Amen.

11 - Zeniff's son Noah is corrupt, and Abinadi cries repentance...

Now I, Mormon, will write about Zeniff's people while referring to the records of King Benjamin and his son Mosiah (chapters 11-22).

King Noah did not follow the ways of his father, Zeniff. Rather than keep God's commandments, Noah followed the desires of his own heart. He had many wives and mistresses. He also allowed his people to commit adultery and other sins that were offensive to the Lord. He imposed a twenty percent tax on everything the people owned and acquired. This meant that his people had to give him one fifth of all their gold, silver, copper, brass, iron, cattle, sheep and grain. Noah did this to support himself, his priests, and all their wives and mistresses. He completely changed the way the kingdom was run, replacing all the humble priests his father had consecrated with new, proud ones. Noah and his priests were supported in their laziness, materialism and immorality by Noah's high taxes, which the people worked hard to pay.

Soon the people had also become materialistic, being deceived by the vain and flattering words of their king and his priests. King Noah built many elegant and spacious buildings, finely decorated with wood and precious metals. Noah had a spacious palace built with a throne in the middle of it. This palace was lavishly decorated with precious metals and woodwork.

Noah also hired fine craftsman to decorate the inside of the temple with wood, copper and brass. The seats for the high priests, trimmed with pure gold, were placed above the other seats. A pulpit was built for them to lean on and to rest their arms while they spoke vain and lying words to the people.

King Noah had a very high tower built next to the temple, upon which he could overlook all the surrounding lands, including his land of Shilom and the Lamanite land of Shemlon. With the tax money, Noah ordered many buildings to be built in Shilom and a great tower to be built on a hill north of Shilom. That hill had once been a hiding place for the Nephites' forefathers when when fleeing from their lands.

Note: Read about "fleeing the land of Nephi" in Omni, 1:12-13.

Noah loved his riches, and he spent his time in riotous living with his wives and mistresses. His priests also spent their time with prostitutes. Noah told his people to plant vineyards and to build wine-presses in order to make lots of wine. He and his people soon became drunkards.

Then small groups of Lamanites began to attack his people, killing them in their fields. King Noah responded by posting guards around the land, but he did not post enough guards, so the Lamanites killed them and stole the people's flocks. This is how the Lamanites, in their hatred, began to destroy the Nephites under King Noah's reign. After these attacks, King Noah sent out his armies, who drove the Lamanites back and then returned, boasting of their victory. They were very proud, boasting in their own strength, saying that fifty of them could fight thousands of Lamanites. They delighted in war because of their wicked king and his priests.

Then a man named Abinadi went among the people and began to prophesy, "The Lord has commanded me to tell you that you are cursed, for He has seen your great sins, wickedness and immorality. Unless you repent, He will visit you in His anger. Unless you repent, and turn to the Lord your God, He will deliver you into the hands of your enemies, who will afflict you and bring you into bondage. Then you will know that the Lord is your God, that He demands loyalty, and that He punishes the sins of His people. Unless you repent and turn to the Lord, you will be brought into bondage, and no one but the Lord the Almighty God will be able to deliver you. Then when you cry to the Lord, He will be slow to hear you, and He will allow your enemies to keep afflicting you. And then unless you repent in the depths of humility, crying mightily to the Lord your God, He will not hear your prayers, nor will He deliver you."

After Abinadi said this to the people, they became angry with him and tried to kill him, but the Lord delivered him out of their hands. When King Noah heard what Abinadi had said, he was very angry and said, "Who does Abinadi think he is, judging my people? And who is the Lord, saying that He will afflict my people? Guards, bring Abinadi to me. He is trying to stir up my people to fight among themselves. For doing this, he will die!"

Because the people had been blinded to the truth, they would not listen to Abinadi. They were determined to find him and see that he was killed, but he was nowhere to be found. King Noah also hardened his heart against the Lord's word and did not repent of his evil deeds.

12 - Abinadi's warnings are rejected...

Two years later, Abinadi came among them again, this time in disguise, saying, "The Lord commanded me, 'Abinadi, go and prophesy to my people, for they have hardened their hearts against my words. They have not repented of their evil doings, so I will visit them in my fierce anger.' This generation is cursed, for the Lord said to me, 'Stretch forth your hand and prophesy: Thus saith the Lord, this generation will be brought into bondage because of their sins. They will be slapped in the face, driven by their enemies and killed. Vultures, dogs and wild animals will eat their carcasses. King Noah's life will be as worthless as an old coat that is burned in a furnace. And at that time, he will know that I am the Lord. Then I will afflict my people with drought, famine and pestilence, and they will suffer. I will allow burdens to be placed upon their backs, and they will be driven like dumb mules. I will send hail and the east wind to afflict them. Insects will eat their grain, and I will afflict them with a great pestilence. I will do all this because of their great sinfulness.

"If they do not repent after all this, I will completely destroy them off the face of the earth. But they will leave their record, which I will preserve for future nations that will possess their lands. By reading their record, these future nations will be given a vivid warning not to repeat their sins.'"

This is how Abinadi prophesied against the people, and they became angry with him again. They tied him, carried him to King Noah and said, "This man has prophesied evil about your people, saying, 'God will destroy all of you'. He has prophesied about you, saying, 'King Noah's life will be as worthless as an old coat that is burned.' He said your burned body will be like a dry stalk of corn that is trampled by people and animals—that your ashes will be like ripe thistle blossoms blowing in the wind across the land.

He pretends the Lord has said these things to him, and that all this will come upon you, oh King, unless you repent. And now, oh King, what great evil have you done, and what great sins have your people committed to deserve this man's judgment and God's condemnation? This man has lied about you and has prophesied in vain. We know how strong we are. We will not come into bondage or be captured by our enemies. You have prospered in the land and will continue to prosper. Here is the man. We deliver him to you to do whatever you want with him."

King Noah had Abinadi put into prison. Then he called his priests to counsel with him. The priests told King Noah they wanted to question Abinadi, so the king had him brought before them.

The priests began to question Abinadi, wanting to accuse him of a crime. But to their astonishment, Abinadi answered their questions boldly and confounded them. One priest asked, "What do these written words mean, words taught by our forefathers:

'How beautiful will be the sight of him among the nations—he who will bring good news, announcing peace and salvation, who will say to Zion, "Your God reigns." Your watchmen will sing aloud together, for they will be equal when the Lord establishes Zion. Break forth in joy, singing together, you who are in the war-ravished places of Jerusalem, for the Lord has comforted His people and has redeemed you. He has shown His great power as all the nations watched, and throughout the earth, all will yet see the salvation of our God.'"

Abinadi answered, "How can you call yourselves priests? You pretend to teach this people, and pretend to understand the spirit of prophecy—yet you ask me what that means? If you do understand these things, you certainly do not teach them. Because of this, you have distorted the Lord's ways and are cursed! In your hearts you have not desired understanding. This is why you are not wise. So, what do you teach this people?"

The priests replied, "We teach the law of Moses." Abinadi responded, "If you teach the law of Moses, then why don't you keep it? Why do you set your hearts upon riches? Why do you commit adultery with prostitutes, causing this people to also commit sin? This is why the Lord has sent me to prophesy a great evil against this people. Don't you know that I speak the truth? Yes, you do know, and you should be trembling before God. Soon you will be stricken for your sinfulness, for you have said that you teach the law of Moses, but you know nothing about it. Does salvation come by the law of Moses? What do you say?"

They answered that salvation did come by the law of Moses. Then Abinadi said, "I know you will be saved if you keep the commandments that the Lord gave to Moses on Mt. Sinai, saying, 'I am the Lord thy God who has brought you out of bondage in Egypt. Do not worship any God but me. Do not create images for worship that look like anything in heaven or on earth.'" Abinadi then asked, "Have you obeyed these commandments and taught this people to also obey them? No, you have not."

13 - Abinadi questions the priests...

Upon hearing this, Noah said to his priests, "Why do you keep this crazy man around? Take him away and kill him!" The priests stepped forward to take hold of Abinadi, but he boldly said to them, "Do not touch me! God will strike you if you do, for I have not yet delivered the Lord's message to you nor explained Isaiah's words as you asked me to. Until I do this, God will not allow me to be killed. For I must fulfill the commandments that God has given me. Noah, because I told you the truth, speaking God's words, you are angry with me and say that I am crazy."

Because the Lord's Spirit was upon Abinadi, no one dared touch him. His face shone very brightly, the way Moses' face shone while he spoke with the Lord on Mt. Sinai. With God's power and authority, Abinadi said, "Now that you realize you do not have the power to kill me, I will finish my message.

"I know my words cut you to the center of your hearts, for they testify of your sins. My words fill you with wonder, amazement, and anger! After I deliver my message to you, it will not matter where I go, as long as my soul is saved. But whatever you do with me will be a type and shadow of the future.

"Now I will read the rest of God's commandments. I see that they are not written in your hearts because you have studied and taught sin for most of your lives. The Lord said, 'Do not create images for your worship that look like anything in heaven, on earth, or in the water. Do not worship them, for I the Lord thy God demand loyalty. My judgments will come against those who hate me, even until their third and fourth generations. But I will show mercy to thousands of the descendants of those who love me and keep my commandments.

Do not take the Lord's name in vain, because He will not consider those who do this to be guiltless.

Remember to keep the Sabbath day holy. Do all your work in six days, but on the seventh day, the Sabbath of the Lord thy God, do not do any work—not you, your son, daughter, servants, cattle, nor your guests. The Lord made heaven, earth, the sea and everything in them in six days. Then the Lord blessed the seventh day—the Sabbath, making it a holy day.

Honor your father and mother. If you do this, the Lord your God will give you a long life upon the land of your inheritance.

Do not kill. Do not commit adultery. Do not take what is not yours. Do not lie about your neighbor. Do not covet your neighbor's spouse, nor anything that belongs to your neighbor.'"

After saying this, Abinadi asked Noah's priests, "Have you taught the people to keep these commandments? No, you have not, for if you had, the Lord would not have sent me to prophesy evil about this people. You have said that salvation comes by the law of Moses. I tell you that it is necessary to keep the law of Moses for now, but in the future it will not be.

"Salvation does not come by the law of Moses alone, for if the atonement were not made by God Himself for the sins of His people, they would all die spiritually—even after keeping the law of Moses

"It was necessary for the Lord to give the children of Israel a very strict law because they were stubborn, quick to sin, and slow to remember the Lord their God. If this strict, daily law of performances and ordinances had not been given to them, they would not have remembered God and their duty to Him. All of their performances and ordinances were types of things to come. But did the children of Israel understand the law? No. Most of them did not understand it because of their pride, which kept them from realizing that they could only be saved through God's redemption.

"Moses prophesied to them about the coming of the Messiah, and that God would redeem His people. All of the prophets since the world began have said the same. They have all said that God Himself would come down among His people, take the form of a man, and go forth in mighty power upon the face of the earth, and that He would be oppressed and afflicted, and then bring to pass the resurrection of the dead."

14 - Abinadi quotes Isaiah...

"Even Isaiah said, 'Who has had faith in my revelations, which faith allows the Lord to show His power—to reveal His arm on their behalf? For Jesus Christ will grow up before the Father like a tender plant, like a root coming out from dry ground. He will look like any other man, so the people will not accept Him as their Savior. He will be despised and rejected, and will become a man of sorrow, acquainted with grief. The people will turn away from Him, considering Him to be of little worth.

'Surely He will bear the grief and sorrow for our sins, but the people will think that it is God who is smiting and afflicting Him. He will be wounded for our transgressions, bruised for our sins, chastised for our peace, and whipped that we might be healed.

'All of us are like sheep gone astray. Because we have gone our own way, the Lord will take all our sins upon Himself. Oppressed and afflicted, He will not speak, but will be silent, like a lamb brought to the slaughter. He will not be put into prison, nor will He receive a fair trial.

'And after He is dead, having been killed for my people's sins, who will be called His children? He will be buried among the wicked and the rich, even though He will do no evil nor speak deceitfully to anyone. The Savior will be bruised, and will grieve. The Father will offer His Son, who will live again to see His children. For the Father will witness and be satisfied with the travail of His Son's soul. By His knowledge, the Savior will justify many, for He will bear the sins of His people. Because the Son will pour out His soul and be killed, and will make an intercession for our sins, the Father will give Him an inheritance among the great.

'And in turn, the Son will give an inheritance to His children.'"

Note: Concerning an inheritance, see D&C 84:37-38.

15 - Abinadi explains Isaiah...

"I want you to know that God Himself will come down among His people to redeem them. Because He will have a mortal body, He will be called the Son of God. Because He will do the Father's will in the flesh, He will be called the Father. And again, because He will be conceived by the power of God, He will be called the Father.

"And because He will be partly mortal, He will be called the Son. The Father and His Son are one God, the very Eternal Father of Heaven and Earth. As the Son in the flesh submits to the Holy Spirit, His desires become the desires of the Father, and the Savior will not give in to temptation. He will allow Himself to be mocked, scourged, thrown out, and disowned by His people.

"After suffering all this, and after working many mighty miracles among His people, He will be led, as Isaiah said, 'Like a lamb to the slaughter, to be crucified and slain,' giving up His will to the will of His Father. This is how God will break the bands of death and gain victory over it. He will give the Son the power to intercede on our behalf—to plead our cause through His mercy.

"The Savior will be able to do this because He will take the sins of all people upon Himself, redeeming them and satisfying the demands of justice. He will break the bands of death and go into heaven with mercy and compassion toward all people, standing between them and justice.

"And who will be called His children? After offering His body and spirit for sin, He will see His children, whom He has spiritually borne. And who do you think His children will be?

Note: The Children of Christ. See Mosiah 5:7, 26:18 and 24.

"They will be those who believe the holy prophets, who prophesy that the Lord will come to redeem His people. They will be those who look forward to Him for a remission of their sins, patiently waiting to inherit God's kingdom. For Christ will bear the sins of His people and die for them to redeem them from their transgressions. These people are called 'The Children of Christ.' All the holy prophets who have spoken of Christ since the world began are also His children, for they have published peace, bringing good news of salvation to Zion, saying, 'Your God reigns!' The sight of them will be beautiful among the nations.

"Those who continue to publish peace will also be beautiful to see among the nations! And again, those who publish peace from now until all eternity will be beautiful among the nations! But this is not all. For how beautiful it will be to see the Lord among the nations, who will redeem His people, granting them salvation and bringing good news as the founder of their peace.

"Without the redemption of Christ, which was planned from the beginning of the world, all would die and never rise again. But the bands of death will be broken, and the Son will reign with power over the dead, bringing to pass their resurrection!.

"The first to be resurrected will be the righteous who lived before Christ. The first resurrection will also include the prophets and all who have believed and kept God's commandments. They will be raised to live with their Redeemer and have eternal life through Christ's redemption.

"Those who die in ignorance of Christ, who have not had salvation preached to them, will also be redeemed by the Lord and be a part of the first resurrection—have eternal life. And little children who die also have eternal life.

"But you priests should be trembling before God, for since the world began the Lord has never redeemed those who have willfully rebelled against Him and died in their sins—those who knew His commandments but would not keep them. Such people will have no part in the first resurrection. This is why you should tremble. For salvation cannot come to you in your condition. The Lord cannot deny Himself by redeeming men such as you when justice has its rightful claim.

"In the last days, the Lord's salvation will be declared to every nation, tribe and people, in all languages. The Lord's watchmen—His righteous servants—will sing aloud together, for they will be one when the Lord again brings Zion.

"Then it will be declared, 'You in the war-ravished places of Jerusalem, break forth into joy, singing together, for the Lord has comforted and redeemed you. All have seen the Lord show His great power, and now the people from all parts of the earth will yet see His salvation!'"

16 - Abinadi tells the fate of the wicked...

Then Abinadi stretched out his hand and said, "The time will come when all the people of the earth, in every nation, tribe, and of every language, will witness the Lord's salvation. They will understand the truth together, and confess before God that His judgments are just. After this, the wicked will be cast out to their own place. They will have good reason to moan, cry, wail and clench their teeth, for they will not be redeemed, having ignored the Lord's voice. After they die, the wicked will still be carnal and devilish, and the devil will still have power over them. After the devil tricked Adam and Eve, they fell into this lower world. This is why their descendants are carnal, sensual and devilish when they are without God's Spirit. And in this fallen state, we would all be lost forever if God did not redeem us.

"But all those who choose to remain in their fallen state, to be controlled by their owncarnal nature, going the way of sin and rebellion against God, will remain in the devil's power. For them it will be as if no redemption had ever been made, for like the devil, they will be God's enemies.

"If Christ does not come to earth, there will not be any redemption from sin. If Christ does not rise from the dead, breaking the bands of death and gaining a victory over the grave, there will not be a resurrection. But there will be a redemption and a resurrection! The grave will not have the final victory because Christ will come. He is the light and life of the world, putting an end to darkness and death forever.

"Because of Christ, all mortals will be resurrected and then brought to stand before the bar of God, to be judged by Him according to their good or evil works. If their works were good, they will be resurrected to endless life and happiness. If their works were evil, they will be resurrected to endless damnation, which is to become one of the devil's subjects.

"The damned will have lived on earth according to their own carnal wills and desires—having never prayed to the Lord while His arms of mercy were extended to them—having never repented after being warned of their sins.

"You priests should now tremble and repent of your sins, remembering that you can only be saved in and through Christ. If you teach the law of Moses, then teach that it is a symbol of things to come. Teach that redemption comes through Christ the Lord, who is the very Eternal Father of our salvation. Amen."

17 - Alma defends Abinadi...

When Abinadi had finished speaking, the king commanded the priests to take him away and kill him. But one of Noah's young priests, Alma, a descendant of Nephi, believed Abinadi's testimony of their sinfulness. Alma pled with King Noah not to be angry with Abinadi, but to let him go in peace. This just made Noah more furious. He had Alma thrown out, and sent his servants after him to kill him, but Alma escaped and hid.

During the next several days while in hiding, Alma wrote down everything Abinadi had said. After throwing out Alma, King Noah told his guards to surround

Abinadi, tie him, and throw him into prison.

After three days, and after counseling with his priests, King Noah called for Abinadi and said to him, "We have found you guilty of a crime punishable by death, for you have said that God Himself will come down among the people. If you do not recall all your evil words about me and my people, then you will be put to death!"

Abinadi responded to the king, "I will not recall my words, for they are true. I have allowed you to capture me so that you will know for sure that my words are true. If necessary, I will die, but regardless of what happens to me, my words will stand as a testimony against you. And if you do kill me, you will shed innocent blood, and this will also stand as a testimony against you at the last day."

These words were so powerful to King Noah that he became afraid of God's judgments and was about to let Abinadi go. But the priests objected, accusing Abinadi by exclaiming, "He has reviled the king!" Then Noah became angry again and delivered Abinadi to the priests. The priests took Abinadi, tied him, and burned him with dried wood.

When the flames began to scorch him, Abinadi cried out, "Your children will burn others who believe in the salvation of the Lord their God. And you will be afflicted with all types of diseases because of your sinfulness. You will be killed and scattered like a wild flock driven by wolves. Your children will be hunted and captured by your enemies, and finally suffer, as I do, the pains of death by fire. God will execute vengeance upon those who destroy His people. Oh God, receive my soul."

Note: Abinadi's prophecies of the priests' descendants being hunted and killed by fire was fulfilled (Alma 25:3-8).

After saying this, Abinadi fell, having suffered death by fire. He was murdered because he would not deny God's commandments, and he sealed the truth of his words by his death.

18 - Alma teaches outside the city...

Alma, who had repented of his sins, went secretly among the people, teaching them Abinadi's words. Many believed him as he taught about the resurrection and the redemption that would come through the power, suffering and death of Christ, who would be resurrected, and then go up into heaven. Alma taught in private so that King Noah would not find out about him. The people who believed Alma met in a place called Mormon, named by King Noah. This was a place outside the city where many wild animals came during certain times of the year. In this place, Alma lived near a pure spring. During the day he hid in a small thicket of trees near the spring while the king's men searched for him. The believers came to this place to hear Alma speak. After many days, all the believers, now a large group of people, had come to hear him.

Alma preached repentance, redemption and faith in the Lord. He said, "Here are the waters of Mormon. And here you have come to enter the fold of God. You desire to be called His people, and are willing to bear one another's burdens, making them light. You are willing to mourn with those who mourn, comfort those who need comforting, and stand as witnesses of God at all times, in all things, and in all places for the rest of your lives. You desire this so that you may be redeemed by God and rise in the first resurrection to eternal life. Since this is the desire of your hearts, do you have anything against being baptized in the name of the Lord, as a witness before Him that you have entered a covenant to serve Him and keep His commandments, that He may pour out His Spirit upon you even more?"

When the people heard this, they clapped their hands for joy, exclaiming, "This is the desire of our hearts!"

Then Alma went into the water with Helam, one of the first believers, and cried, "Oh Lord, pour out Thy Spirit upon Thy servant, that he may do this work with holiness of heart."

After saying this, the Lord's Spirit came upon Alma. He said, "Helam, having authority from the Almighty God, I baptize you as a testimony that you have entered a covenant to serve Him for the rest of your life. May the Lord's Spirit be poured out upon you, and may God grant you eternal life through the redemption of Christ, whom He has prepared from the foundation of the world." After saying this, both Alma and Helam went under the water. They arose and came out of the water rejoicing and filled with the Spirit.

Then Alma baptized another man, but this time he did not go under the water himself. In the same way, Alma baptized everyone who had come, about 204 of them, and they were all filled with the grace of God. From then on they were called the church of God, or the church of Christ. All who were baptized by the power and authority of God were added to His church.

Then Alma, having authority from God, ordained one priest for every fifty people in the church, to teach them of God's kingdom. Alma commanded the priests to teach only what he had taught—things that the holy prophets had spoken—repentance and faith in the Lord who would redeem His people. Alma also commanded them not to argue, but to have one faith and one baptism, with their hearts knit together in unity and love for one another.

By preaching this way, Alma's people were taught, and they became the children of God. Alma commanded them to keep the Sabbath day holy and to give thanks to the Lord their God each day. He also commanded the priests to work to support themselves.

One day a week was set apart for the people to gather and worship the Lord their God, and to be taught. They also met at other times during the week whenever possible.

The priests did not depend on the people for their support. As compensation for their service they received God's grace, which made them strong in the Spirit, and which gave them a knowledge of God, enabling them to teach with power and authority from Him.

Alma commanded everyone in the church to give of their substance according to what they had. If some had more, they were to give more, while the poor were to give less, and all were to give to those with nothing. They were taught to give by their own free will and good desires toward God. They gave to the needy priests, who spent much of their time building the church, and also to anyone needing food or clothing. Alma said it was a commandment of God to give to one another, both temporally and spiritually, according to the needs and wants among them.

All this happened in the forest near the waters of Mormon, a beautiful place to those who there found their Redeemer. And how blessed they are, for they will sing His praise forever. These things were done on the borders outside the land so that King Noah would not know about them. But the king had discovered this movement and sent out his servants to spy on the people. On the day that Alma's people were gathered to be taught, they were discovered by the spies.

Upon hearing his servants' report, the king claimed that Alma was stirring up the people to rebel against him, and he sent out his army to destroy them. Alma and the Lord's people (about 450 of them) were informed that the king's army was coming, so they took their tents and families and escaped into the wilderness.

19 - Noah's power collapses...

The king's army returned, having searched for the Lord's people in vain. Noah's army was small, and the rest of his people began to be divided among themselves. The minority were those who threatened the king. Among them was Gideon, a strong man who hated the king. He drew his sword and vowed in his anger that he would kill King Noah.

Gideon fought with Noah, and when Noah realized that he could not beat Gideon, he ran and climbed to the top of his tower near the temple. Gideon chased Noah, and was about to climb the tower to kill him, when from the top of the tower, King Noah looked toward the land of Shemlon and saw a Lamanite army approaching. He cried out in the anguish of his soul, "Gideon, spare me, for the Lamanites are coming to kill my people!" King Noah was more concerned for his own life than for his people, but Gideon spared him anyway.

Noah commanded his people to run from the Lamanites. Then he ran ahead of them into the wilderness. As the Lamanites began to catch up with Noah's people and kill them, Noah commanded the men to leave their families behind and run with him. Many fathers disobeyed the king, preferring to die with their families rather than leave them behind. The rest of the fathers ran with Noah.

Note: A few years later in Zarahemla, the abandoned Nephite children of these fathers who ran with Noah disowned their fathers' names and named themselves "Nephi—the children of Nephi" (Mosiah 25:13).

The fathers who stayed with their wives and children had their fair daughters stand and plead with the Lamanites not to kill them. The Lamanites had compassion on the people, being charmed by their beautiful women. But the Lamanites still captured them and forced them to return to the land of Nephi. They allowed them to keep their lands on two conditions. First, they had to bring King Noah to them. Second, they had to pay an annual fifty percent tribute to the Lamanite king. This meant giving up half of everything they owned, and half of what they would acquire each year.

Among Noah's captured sons was Limhi. He did not want his father to die, but being a just man himself, he knew his father had been sinful. Gideon sent spies into the wilderness to find the king and his followers. They found the men who had run away with the king, but not the king and his priests. The men who had gone with the king had sworn in their hearts that they would return to the land of Nephi, and that if their wives, children, and the men who had stayed behind had been killed, they would seek revenge, even if they had to die in the process. Noah had commanded them not to return, but they had heard enough from the king and put him to death by fire. They would have also killed his priests, but they escaped.

Just as they were about to return to the land of Nephi, they met Gideon's spies, who told them that their wives and children had been spared, and that the Lamanites had let them keep their land if they would pay a fifty percent tribute. The men told Gideon's spies that they had killed the king, and that his priests had escaped into the wilderness.

After a peace ceremony with Gideon's men, they returned to the land of Nephi. They rejoiced because their wives and children had been spared, and they told Gideon they had killed the king. Then the Lamanite king made an oath that his people would not kill them.

Because Limhi was the king's son, the kingdom conferred upon him by the people. He made an oath to the Lamanite king that his people would pay the tribute. Then Limhi began to establish his people's kingdom in peace.

The Lamanite king set guards around their land to keep Limhi's people from escaping into the wilderness. These guards were supported out of the Nephite tribute. King Limhi had peace in his kingdom for two years because the Lamanites were pacified by the tribute and did not hurt them.

20 - Noah's priests create a war...

Now there was a place in Shemlon where the Lamanites' daughters gathered to sing, dance and make themselves merry. One day, a small number of them had gathered to sing and dance. King Noah's priests had been hiding in the wilderness, too ashamed and afraid for their lives to return to their wives and children in the city of Nephi. While wandering in the wilderness, they had discovered the Lamanites' daughters and secretly watched them. When only twenty-four of them had gathered to dance, they came out of their hiding places and carried them off.

When the Lamanites found out their daughters were missing, they were angry with Limhi's people, thinking they had taken them. In his anger, the Lamanite king led his army to the land of Nephi to destroy Limhi's people. From the top of his tower, Limhi saw them coming. He gathered his people, and they hid in the fields and forests, waiting for the Lamanites. When they came near, Limhi's people attacked the Lamanites and began to kill them. The battle became fierce as the Nephites fought like lions for their prey. Though they were outnumbered by more than two to one, Limhi's people drove the Lamanites before them. They fought like dragons for their own lives, and for their wives and children.

After the battle, they found the Lamanite king among the fallen, but he was not dead. His army had run away so fast, they had left him wounded on the ground. Limhi's men bandaged his wounds, brought him before Limhi, and said, "Here is the Lamanite king, wounded and abandoned by his army. Now let us kill him!" Limhi responded, "Do not kill him. Bring him closer, so I may see him." Limhi then asked the Lamanite king, "Why did you come to war against my people? My people have not broken the oath that I made to you, so why have you broken the oath that you made to them?" The king replied, "I broke the oath and came to war against your people because they have carried away my people's daughters." Limhi had heard nothing about this matter, so he said, "I will search among my people, and whoever has done this will die."

When Gideon, now the king's captain, heard this, he said to King Limhi, "Please do not search this people or put the blame on them. Remember your father's priests, whom we searched for to destroy? It must be those priests, still in the wilderness, who have stolen the Lamanites' daughters! Tell this to the Lamanite king so that he will pacify his people toward us, for the Lamanites are now preparing to attack us, and we cannot continue to withstand them with our small numbers. Unless the king pacifies them, their great army will kill us all! The Lord's words, spoken by Abinadi, are beginning to be fulfilled because we did not listen to him and repent. Let us pacify the king and keep our oath with him, for it is better to be in bondage than to die. Let us do this and put a stop to the shedding of so much blood."

Limhi took Gideon's advice and told the king about his father's priests who had run away into the wilderness, and who must have stolen their daughters. The Lamanite king was pacified toward Limhi's people and said, "Let us go out and meet my people unarmed. I swear to you with an oath that my people will not kill your people." Then unarmed, Limhi's people followed the Lamanite king and went out to meet the Lamanites. Upon meeting them, the Lamanite king bowed himself down before them and pled in behalf of Limhi's people. Upon seeing the unarmed Nephites, the Lamanites had compassion on them and were pacified. Then they returned with their king to their own land in peace.

Limhi and his people returned to their city of Nephi and began to live in peace.

21 - The bondage of Limhi's people...

After many days, the Lamanites became angry with the Nephites again and surrounded their borders. The Lamanites did not dare kill the Nephites because of their king's oath to Limhi, but they exercised all the authority they could against them as cruel taskmasters. They slapped their faces, made them do hard labor, and drove them like dumb mules. The Lord allowed this as a fulfillment of His word. The Nephites' suffering became great, and there was no way they could escape, for they were surrounded.

Limhi's people began to complain to him, and they asked to fight the Lamanites. Because Limhi was constantly bothered by their complaining, he allowed them to do as they wished. Then they put on their armor and went out against the Lamanites to drive them out of their land. But the Lamanites beat them, drove them back, and killed many.

After this, there was great mourning and lamentation among Limhi's people. They mourned for their lost husbands, fathers and brothers. There were a great number of widows in the land, who cried mightily every day because of their fear of the Lamanites.

All their crying made the rest of Limhi's men very angry with the Lamanites. So they went out again to battle, but they were again driven back, suffering another great loss. Then the men went out a third time, suffering still more losses.

Those who survived returned to the city of Nephi. Finally, they humbled themselves, even to the dust, and they accepted their yoke of bondage, allowing themselves to be beaten, driven and burdened by their enemies. They humbled themselves to the depths of humility, crying mightily to God all day long to deliver them from their afflictions. And the Lord was slow to hear their cries because of their sins. But He did hear them, and He began to soften the hearts of the Lamanites to make their burdens easier. However, the Lord did not see fit to deliver them from bondage immediately. Little by little, Limhi's people began to prosper in the land by raising more grain, flocks and herds, and they no longer suffered from hunger. Because there were many more women than men, King Limhi commanded the men to give food to the widows and their children to prevent them from starving.

Limhi's people stayed in groups as much as possible in order to protect their grain and flocks. They feared the Lamanites, and King Limhi would not dare go outside the city walls without his guards. He told his people to constantly watch for those priests who were in the wilderness, who had stolen the Lamanites' daughters and had caused the great destruction among his people. Limhi and his people wanted to see those priests punished. Furthermore, those priests had come into the city of Nephi by night and had stolen grain and precious things.

It was after this time, when Limhi's people had quit fighting the Lamanites, that Ammon and his men came into the land. When King Limhi saw them outside the city walls, he thought they were Noah's priests. That's why Ammon and his men were tied and thrown into prison. And if they had been Noah's priests, Limhi would have had them killed. When Limhi learned they were not Noah's priests, but fellow Nephites who had come from Zarahemla, he was very joyful.

Before Ammon's arrival, King Limhi had sent forty-three men to search for the land of Zarahemla, but they could not find it, and they became lost in the wilderness. Limhi's men did find a land that had been very populated, covered with dry bones. They thought they had found Zarahemla and had returned a few days before Ammon's expedition had arrived.

Limhi's men had brought a record, engraved on twenty-four gold plates, that they had found in the land covered with bones. Limhi was filled with joy again when Ammon told him that Mosiah had a gift from God to interpret such engravings. Even though Ammon also rejoiced, he and his brethren were filled with sorrow because so many of their fellow Nephites had been killed. They were sorry to hear that King Noah and his priests had caused the people to commit so many sins against God. They mourned for the death of Abinadi and were sad that Alma and his people, who had formed a church of God, were no longer among them. Ammon and his brethren mourned because they did not know where Alma and his people had gone. They would have gladly joined them, for they had also made a covenant to serve God and keep His commandments.

Since Ammon had arrived, King Limhi and many of his people also made this covenant with God. They wanted to be baptized, but no one in the land had the authority from God to baptize. Ammon did not want to do the baptizing because he considered himself unworthy. So at that time no church was formed, but the people waited upon the Spirit of the Lord. They wanted to become a church, like Alma's people, who had escaped into the wilderness. They wanted to be baptized as a witness and testimony that they were willing to serve God with all their hearts, but they had to wait. An account of their baptism will be given later.

22 - Limhi's people escape to Zarahemla...

Ammon, his fifteen men, and King Limhi and his people devoted all their thoughts and energy toward finding a way to deliver themselves out of bondage. After consulting with the people, Ammon and King Limhi called a meeting with everyone to decide on how to deliver themselves. They concluded that since there were too many Lamanites to fight, the only way to deliver themselves out of bondage would be to take their women, children, flocks, herds and tents, and escape into the wilderness. Gideon said to the king, "Oh king, you have listened to my counsel many times as we have fought the Lamanites. If my advice has been useful to you in the past, listen to me now, and I will be your servant to deliver this people out of bondage."

King Limhi listened as Gideon explained his strategy for escape: "The Lamanites who guard the pass through the back wall of the city are drunk at night. So let us send a proclamation among all this people to drive their flocks and herds through that back pass and into the wilderness during the night. I will go according to your command and pay the last tribute of wine to the Lamanites, and they will all get drunk. Then we will go through the secret pass on the left of their camp while they sleep. By going around the land of Shilom, we will escape into the wilderness with our women, children, flocks and herds."

The king accepted Gideon's plan. He had his people gather their flocks, and then sent the regular tribute of wine to the Lamanites. He also sent more wine as a present to them. Happy to have the extra wine, they drank it freely and all became very drunk.

As the Lamanites fell asleep drunk, King Limhi's people, led by Ammon and his fifteen men, departed that night into the wilderness with their flocks and herds. They went around the land of Shilom into the wilderness, bending their course toward the land of Zarahemla. They took all the gold, silver, precious things and provisions that they could carry.

After traveling many days, they finally arrived in the land of Zarahemla. There they were accepted, and joined Mosiah's people as his subjects. With joy, Mosiah received them and the records that their men had found.

Meanwhile, the Lamanites had awakened to find Limhi and his people gone, and had sent an army into the wilderness to capture them. But after two days, the Lamanites not only lost Limhi's trail, but also became lost themselves in the wilderness.

23 - Alma warns against having a king...

Now, back to Alma. He had left the place called Mormon with his people after being warned by the Lord that Noah's army was coming after them. The Lord gave them the endurance to outmarch King Noah's army, which could not catch them. They continued their exodus for eight days in the wilderness. Then Alma and his people came to a very beautiful and pleasant land, a land of pure water. They settled in this beautiful land, and worked very hard to farm it and construct buildings. The people asked Alma to be their king because they loved him. But Alma said, "It is not necessary for us to have a king, for the Lord has said, 'You will not put one man above another or allow one man to put himself above you.' If it were possible for kings to always be just men, then it would be well for you to have a king. But remember the sinfulness of King Noah and his priests.

"I myself was caught in that snare, doing many things which were abominable in the sight of the Lord, which caused me sore repentance. But after I had experienced great suffering, the Lord heard my cries and answered my prayers. He has made me an instrument in His hands to bring many of you to a knowledge of the truth. But I do not glory in this, for I am not worthy to glory in myself. You were oppressed by King Noah, in bondage to him and his priests. Because of them, you were brought into sin. And now that you have been delivered by God's power out of that condition, I want you to hold onto this liberty and remain free, trusting no man to be your king. Also, trust no one to be your teacher or minister unless he is of God—walking in His ways and keeping His commandments."

Alma taught everyone to love their neighbors as themselves, and never to fight or argue with one another. He was their high priest, being the founder of their church. No one received the authority to preach or teach unless it was given to him from God through Alma, who consecrated all the priests and teachers, and only just men were consecrated. The priests and teachers watched over their people, and nourished them with things having to do with righteousness.

Alma and his people began to prosper greatly in the land, which they called Helam (named after the first man Alma baptized). As they populated and prospered in the land, they built the city of Helam. Still, the Lord saw fit to chastise His people in Helam, and He truly tested their patience and faith. But we will see that all who put their trust in the Lord are supported by Him, for the people of Helam were given trials and blessings by the Lord. I, Mormon, will show you that they were brought into bondage, and no one but the Lord their God, even the God of Abraham, Isaac and Jacob, could deliver them. And He did deliver them, showing His mighty power, after which they rejoiced greatly.

As Alma's people were farming the land of Helam near their city, a Lamanite army came into their borders. Terrified by the army, Alma's people ran from their fields and into the city. Alma told them not to be afraid, but to remember that their God would deliver them.

They calmed down and asked the Lord to soften the hearts of the Lamanites so that they would spare them. And the Lord did soften the hearts of the Lamanites as Alma and his people went out and surrendered to them. Then the Lamanites took possession of the land of Helam.

This Lamanite army, which had followed King Limhi's people, had been lost in the wilderness for many days after losing the trail. But they had found those priests of King Noah in a place they had called Amulon. The priests had settled down with the Lamanite daughters they had stolen, and had begun to raise crops. The leader of the priests was Amulon. He pled with the Lamanites, and also sent out his men's wives, the Lamanites' daughters, to plead with their people not to kill their husbands. Because of their wives, the Lamanites had compassion on Amulon and his men, and did not kill them. Then Amulon and his men joined the Lamanites.

The Lamanites were looking for the way back to the land of Nephi when they found Alma and his people in the land of Helam. Now the Lamanites promised to spare Alma and his people and give them their liberty if they would show them how to get back to the land of Nephi. But after Alma had shown them the way back to Nephi, the Lamanites did not keep their promise. Before returning to the land of Nephi, they set guards around the land of Helam to watch Alma and his people.

The rest of the Lamanite army went back to the land of Nephi. Soon after that, part of the Lamanite army returned to Helam, bringing the guards' wives and children.

24 - Amulon becomes a trial to Alma...

After the Lamanites had taken over all these lands, the Lamanite king appointed kings within them. Amulon gained favor in the eyes of the Lamanite king, who appointed him and his men to be teachers over the Lamanites in the lands of Shemlon, Shilom and Amulon. In addition to being a teacher, Amulon was made king and ruler over Alma's people in Helam. However, Amulon was not allowed do anything against the Lamanite king's will.

The Lamanite king, Laman, was named after his father, and he ruled over many people. Because King Laman had appointed Amulon and his men to be teachers in every Lamanite land, the Nephite language began to be taught among all the Lamanites.

The Lamanites were friendly with each other, but they knew nothing about God. Amulon and his men did not enlighten them by teaching them of the Lord, or about the law of Moses, or Abinadi's words. They only taught them how to keep records and write letters.

With this new skill in communications, the Lamanites started a trading system among their cities. They grew richer and began to be cunning and wise as to the wisdom of the world. They delighted in all types of wickedness and plunder, except among their relatives.

Meanwhile, Amulon began to use authority over Alma and his people in the city of Helam. He persecuted Alma's people and encouraged his children to persecute their children.

Having been one of King Noah's priests, Amulon knew Alma. He remembered that Alma had believed Abinadi and had been thrown out. Amulon was angry with Alma because he was subject to King Laman himself. In his anger, Amulon exercised authority over Alma's people and put taskmasters over them.

Alma's people became so afflicted that they cried mightily to God. Then Amulon ordered them to stop their cries. He put guards over them with orders to kill anyone found calling upon God. So Alma and his people stopped raising their voices to the Lord their God, but they still poured their hearts out to Him, and God knew the thoughts of their hearts.

Then the Lord's voice came to Alma's people in their afflictions, "Lift up your heads and be comforted, for I remember the covenant you made with me. I will covenant with you, my people, and deliver you out of bondage. I will also ease the burdens on your shoulders so you will not feel them in your bondage. I will do this so that you may stand as witnesses for me hereafter, knowing without a doubt that I, the Lord God, visit my people in their trials."

Then the burdens on Alma and his brethren were made light. The Lord strengthened them to bear their burdens easily, and with patience they cheerfully submitted to His will.

Their faith and patience was so great that the Lord's voice came to them again, and said, "Be comforted, for tomorrow I will deliver you out of bondage." And the Lord said to Alma, "You will lead this people, and I will go with you and deliver them out of bondage."

All that night, Alma and his people gathered their flocks and grain. And in the morning the Lord caused a deep sleep to come over the Lamanite taskmasters.

Then Alma and his people departed into the wilderness. After traveling all day, they pitched their tents in a valley. They called it the valley of Alma because he had led them there. In that valley, they poured out their thanks to God for being merciful to them, for easing their burdens, and for delivering them out of bondage. They knew that no one but the Lord their God could have delivered them. And every man, woman and child that could speak lifted up their voice in praises to their God.

Then the Lord said to Alma, "Hurry and get this people out of this land, for the Lamanites have awakened and are pursuing you. I will stop them in this valley." Then Alma and his people left the valley and continued their journey. After twelve days in the wilderness, they arrived in the land of Zarahemla, and King Mosiah received them with joy.

25 - All the Nephites reunite in Zarahemla...

After Alma's people arrived in Zarahemla, King Mosiah called a meeting of all the people, most of which were descendants of Mulek. Although many, the Nephites and the descendants of Mulek combined still were not even half the number of Lamanites.

The Nephites and the descendants of Mulek assembled into two groups to hear the readings from the records that had been kept. Mosiah first had Zeniff's record read (the record kept by Zeniff and his grandson, Limhi). Then Alma's account was read, beginning from his own conversion, and ending when he and his people arrived in Zarahemla.

Mosiah's people who had stayed in Zarahemla were completely amazed after hearing these accounts. They did not know what to think. Seeing those who had been delivered out of bondage filled them with joy, yet thinking about their fellow Nephites who had been killed brought them to tears. But when they realized the immediate goodness of God, and how He delivered Alma and his people out of Lamanite bondage, they raised their voices and gave thanks to Him. And when they thought about their brethren, the Lamanites, and of their sinful and polluted state, they were filled with pain and anguish for the welfare of their souls.

The children of Amulon and those other wicked priests—the children who had been abandoned when their fathers had run away with King Noah, had been so unhappy with the conduct of their fathers that they rejected their fathers' names and called themselves the children of Nephi.

Note: These children should not be mistaken for Amulon and his priests' second set of children, borne by the stolen Lamanite daughters. The second set did not escape to Zarahemla with Alma. They were taught to hate Alma's people and their children. Abinadi prophesied that they would cause others to suffer death by fire and then be scattered, hunted and killed.

Now all the people in Zarahemla, even the descendants of Mulek, were called Nephites, because beginning with Mosiah's grandfather, Mosiah, the kingdom had been conferred only upon a descendant of Nephi. When Mosiah finished speaking, he asked Alma to speak. The people divided into large groups, and Alma spoke to each group, preaching repentance and faith in the Lord. Alma called upon Limhi's people, and upon all who had been delivered out of bondage, to remember that it was the Lord who had delivered them.

After Alma had taught the people many things, Limhi and all his people wanted to be baptized, so Alma went into the water and baptized them by immersion. Those whom he baptized now belonged to the church of God.

Then King Mosiah allowed Alma to establish churches throughout all the land of Zarahemla, giving him permission to ordain priests and teachers over each church. There were too many people to be governed by one teacher, nor could they all hear the word of God in one assembly, so they gathered into different groups called churches. Every church had priests who taught according to Alma's words Even though there were many churches, they were all one church—the church of God, and nothing but repentance and faith in God was preached in all the churches. There were seven church groups in the land of Zarahemla, and all who wanted to take upon themselves the name of Christ, or of God, joined the church of God. They were all called the people of God, and the Lord poured out His Spirit upon them, and they were blessed and prospered in the land.

26 - A new generation of unbelievers...

As time passed, many of the rising generation did not believe their fathers' righteous traditions. At the time that their parents had experienced a mighty change of heart under King Benjamin's reign, they were too young to understand. They did not believe what had been said about the resurrection of the dead or about the coming of Christ. Because of their unbelief, they could not understand God's word and their hearts became hardened. Because of their lack of faith, they refused to be baptized or to join the church. They remained in their carnal, sinful state, for they would not call upon the Lord their God.

During Mosiah's reign, the unbelievers were not half as numerous as God's people, but because of dissension among church members, the unbelievers soon became more numerous. The unbelievers deceived many church members with flattery and caused them to commit many sins. It soon became necessary to correct those people in the church who committed sin, and so they were brought before the priests by the teachers. The priests in turn brought them before Alma, the high priest.

King Mosiah had given Alma authority over the church. Alma did not know of these people's sins, but there were many witnesses against them. This kind of thing had never happened before in the church, and Alma's spirit was troubled. He did not feel comfortable judging the accused, and so he brought them before King Mosiah. Alma then said to the king, "Here are many who have been accused by their brethren, having been caught in various sins. The accused are not sorry, so we brought them here for you to judge." King Mosiah replied, "I will not judge them. I prefer that you judge them, Alma."

Now Alma's spirit was even more troubled. He went and asked the Lord what to do, for he was afraid of doing something wrong in the sight of God. After pouring out his whole soul to God, the Lord's voice said to him, "You are blessed, Alma, and those baptized in the waters of Mormon are also blessed. You are blessed because of your great faith, having heard only the words of my servant Abinadi. And those who were baptized are blessed because of their great faith in your words alone.

"You are also blessed because you have established a church among my people. This people, who are willing to bear my name, are blessed, for in my name they will be called, and they are mine. And because you have asked me about the transgressors, you are blessed. You are my servant, and I covenant with you that you will have eternal life. You will serve me, going forth in my name, gathering my sheep. Those who hear my voice will be my sheep. You will receive them into the church, and I will receive them also. For this is my church, and I will freely forgive those whom you receive—those who will believe in my name and be baptized unto repentance. I take the sins of the world upon myself, having created those who sin. And I will give a place at my right hand to those who believe in me throughout their lives. They are called by my name (Children of Christ). If they know me, at the sound of the first trumpet they will be resurrected and have a place eternally at my right hand.

"When the second trumpet sounds, those who never knew me will be resurrected and stand before me. Then they will know that I am the Lord their God—their Redeemer, and that they did not want to be redeemed. Then I will tell them that I never knew them, and they will go into an everlasting fire, prepared for the devil and his angels. This is why I tell you not to receive those who refuse to hear my voice into my church, for I will not receive them at the last day.

"Now go and judge all who transgress against me, according to the sins they have committed. If they confess their sins before you, and before me, and repent in the sincerity of their hearts, forgive them, and I will also forgive them. And as often as my people repent I will forgive their trespasses against me. You will also forgive one another, because anyone who does not forgive his neighbor when his neighbor says that he has repented brings himself under condemnation. Now go, and those who refuse to repent of their sins will not be numbered among my people. Observe this law from this time forward."

Upon hearing these words, Alma wrote them down so that he could judge the people of the church according to God's commandments. Then he judged those who had been found committing sin according to the word of the Lord. Those who repented of their sins and confessed them were numbered among the people of the church. Those who would not confess and repent of their sins were not numbered among the people of the church—they were excommunicated.

Alma regulated all the affairs of the church, and the Nephites began to have peace again. The church prospered as the people walked in obedience before God, and they received and baptized many. Alma and the other priests and teachers were diligent in teaching God's word to the people of the church. They suffered all types of afflictions at the hands of all who did not belong to God's church. Those who committed sins were counseled with God's word, and they were all commanded by God to always pray and give thanks to Him in all things.

27 - Unbelievers persecute the believers...

But the persecution of the people of the church by the unbelievers became so great that the church members began to lose faith and began to complain to their leaders. Their leaders complained to Alma, who laid the case before King Mosiah. After Mosiah consulted with his priests, he sent a proclamation throughout the land, stating that unbelievers could not persecute those who belonged to God's church. There was also a strict command throughout all the churches that there would be no persecutions among them. They were told to treat all people equally. No pride or haughtiness was to disturb their peace, and everyone was to love his neighbor as himself, working with his own hands for his support.

The priests and teachers were also commanded to work with their own hands for their own support, unless they were sick or in great need. By doing this, the Nephites enjoyed God's grace. Peace was restored, and the people became very numerous, spreading out over the land in all directions, building large cities and villages.

As the Lord visited and prospered them, they became a numerous and wealthy people. However, King Mosiah's own sons were among the unbelievers. One of Alma's sons, Alma, was also an unbeliever. He became a very wicked and idolatrous man. He was a man of many words and used much flattery to lead many people after his sinful ways. Alma's son became a great obstacle to the growth of God's church, for he led away people's hearts and caused many to leave the church, giving God's enemy a chance to exercise power over them.

One day, Alma's son Alma and Mosiah's sons were secretly going about to destroy God's church—to lead the Lord's people astray, contrary to the commandments of God and of the king. As they were going about, an angel of the Lord appeared to them. The angel came down as if in a cloud, and he spoke with a voice of thunder, causing the earth to shake beneath them. Alma and Mosiah's sons were so astonished that they fell down and did not hear what the angel was saying. But the angel cried out again, "Alma, arise and face me! Why do you persecute God's church? The Lord has said, 'This is my church, and I will establish it. Nothing will overthrow it except the transgression of my people.' The Lord has heard the prayers of His people, including His servant, Alma, your father, who has prayed with great faith that you would come to know the truth. I have come to convince you of God's power and authority so that the prayers of His servants will be answered according to their faith. And now, can you deny God's power? For does not my voice shake the earth? Can you not see me before you? And I am sent from God! Now I say to you, remember the captivity of your fathers in the land of Helam, and in the land of Nephi. Remember the great things God did for them, for they were in bondage, and He delivered them. Now go your way, Alma, and stop trying to destroy the church, that the prayers for the salvation of your soul may be answered in spite of your rebellion."

After saying this to Alma, the angel left. Alma and Mosiah's sons were so astonished that they fell down again. They had seen an angel of the Lord with their own eyes! His voice had been like thunder, shaking the earth! They knew that nothing but God's power could cause the earth to tremble as if it were about to split open. And Alma was too astonished to speak. He became so weak that he could not speak or even move his hands. He was so helpless that Mosiah's sons carried him to his father, Alma, and told him everything that had happened.

Upon hearing this, Alma's father rejoiced, knowing that it had been done by God's power. He had a large crowd come to see what the Lord had done for his son, and also for Mosiah's sons. Alma's father then called priests together to fast and to pray to the Lord, asking Him to restore Alma's speech and strength—that the eyes of the people would be opened to see and know of God's goodness and glory.

After the priests had fasted and prayed for two days and nights, Alma stood up and began to speak, telling them to be comforted. He said, "I have repented of my sins, and I have been redeemed by the Lord. I have been born of His Spirit! The Lord said to me, 'Do not wonder that all people in all nations must be born of God again. They must be changed from their carnal and fallen state to a state of righteousness—being redeemed by God—becoming His sons and daughters. All must become new creatures, and unless they do this, they cannot inherit God's kingdom.' Unless we change, we must be cast off from God's presence. I know this because I was about to be cast off. But after suffering greatly while unconscious, repenting while close to death, the Lord in His mercy has seen fit to snatch me out of an everlasting burning, and I am now born of God! My soul has been redeemed from bitter pain and compulsive sin. I was in the darkest pit, but now I behold God's marvelous light. While my soul was being racked with eternal torment, I was snatched away and my soul is now free from pain! I had rejected my Redeemer, denying our forefathers' words, but now I know that our Redeemer will show Himself to all, so that all may look forward to His coming. I know that He remembers each person He has created, for at the last day, every person will be resurrected, and then stand before Him to be judged. We will all kneel and confess that He is God. Those who rejected God in the world will confess that their judgment of an everlasting punishment is just. They will quake, tremble and cower when He looks at them and sees them in all their wickedness."

From that day forward, Alma and Mosiah's sons began to teach the people as they traveled throughout the land, telling of what they had seen and heard. They preached God's word in much tribulation, for they were greatly persecuted and even beaten by the unbelievers. But in spite of their suffering, they patiently consoled the church, confirming their faith and encouraging them with great patience to keep God's commandments.

Mosiah's four sons, who taught with Alma, were Ammon, Aaron, Omner and Himni.

They traveled throughout the land of Zarahemla among all the people of King Mosiah. They zealously did everything they could to repair the damage they had done to the church. They constantly confessed their sins and declared everything they had seen. They explained the prophecies and the scriptures to all who wanted to hear. By doing these things, they were instruments in God's hands, bringing many to know of their Redeemer. And how blessed they are for publishing peace and good news, and for declaring to the people that the Lord reigns.

28 - Alma and Mosiah's sons preach...

After King Mosiah's four sons had preached in the land of Zarahemla, they returned to their father. After selecting some men, they asked their father if they and those whom they had selected could go to the land of Nephi to preach God's word to the Lamanites.

They were hoping to bring the knowledge of the Lord to the Lamanites—to convince them of their false traditions and end their hatred towards the Nephites. Mosiah's sons explained to their father, "If the Lamanites knew the truth, they would rejoice in the Lord their God. They would become friendly with the Nephites, and there would be no more fighting in all the land that the Lord has given us."

Mosiah's sons wanted salvation to be declared to everyone, for even the thought of any soul enduring endless torment made them tremble. This is how the Spirit of the Lord worked in them, for they had been the worst sinners of all. The Lord had spared them because of His infinite mercy. But they still suffered great anguish of soul because of their sins, fearing they would be cast off forever. They begged their father over a period of many days for permission to go to the land of Nephi. King Mosiah finally asked the Lord if he should let his sons go among the Lamanites to preach the word.

The Lord said to Mosiah, "Give them permission to go and preach, for many will believe them and gain eternal life. I will deliver your sons out of the hands of the Lamanites."

Then Mosiah granted his sons permission to go and preach to the Lamanites, and so they did. I, Mormon, will give an account of Mosiah's sons later.

After his sons had departed, King Mosiah had no one to confer the kingdom upon, for none of his sons would accept it. So he gathered the brass plates, Nephi's large and small plates, the sacred things to be preserved according to God's commandments (Liahona, Laban's sword, and the interpreters), and his translation from the twenty-four pure gold plates that Limhi had brought to him. Mosiah had translated the plates because his people were very anxious to know about those people whose bones were scattered over the land. Mosiah translated the twenty-four plates using two stones fastened to two rims of a bow. These interpreters were prepared from the beginning of the world, and had been handed down from generation to generation for the purpose of interpreting languages. They had been preserved by the Lord so that He could reveal the sins of His people to all those who would possess this land. And whoever has these interpreters is called a seer (one who sees), like those of ancient times.

Mosiah's translation of the twenty-four plates gave an account that began from the creation of Adam and Eve. It continued through the time when the people at Babel built a great tower—when the Lord confused their language and scattered them over all the earth. The account continued up until the time when the people who had migrated to this continent from Babel had completely annihilated one another.

The record of this great destruction filled Mosiah's people with sorrow, but it also gave them much knowledge, for which they were thankful. The record of these people will be written later.

Note: This record is found in Ether 13:20 through 15:22.

It is very important for all people to know the details of this destruction.

After King Mosiah translated the twenty-four plates, he took the brass plates, all the records and sacred things, and conferred them upon Alma's son, Alma. Then Mosiah commanded Alma to preserve everything, and also to keep his own record of the people, handing everything down from one generation to another, just as they had been handed down from the time Lehi had left Jerusalem.

29 - Alma is given charge of the plates...

After doing this, Mosiah sent messengers among all his people to ask who they wanted to be their next king. The people wanted Mosiah's son, Aaron, to be their king and ruler.

Since Aaron had gone to the land of Nephi, the kingdom could not be conferred upon him. Besides, he and his brothers had already refused the kingdom.

So King Mosiah sent a written message to his people which said, "My brethren (for I think of you as brethren), I call upon you to consider something other than having a king. Aaron, to whom the kingdom rightly belongs, has declined to take it upon himself.

"Now if someone else is appointed in his stead, I am afraid that some of you would argue about it. And who knows whether or not my son, to whom the kingdom rightly belongs, would angrily return to split this people—some for him, and others against him. This would cause great bloodshed among you, for it would be against the ways of the Lord, and many souls would be lost.

"So let us be wise and consider something else, for we have no right to destroy my son or anyone else who may be appointed in his place. If my son turned back to his pride and vanity, recalling what he had said, and claimed his right to the kingdom, then he and all this people would commit many sins. Let us look ahead and do what will keep the peace of this people.

"I will be your king the rest of my life, but let us now appoint judges to take my place when I die, to judge this people according to our law. Together we will create a new way to govern, appointing wise men to judge this people according to God's commandments. Isn't it better to allow God, rather than men, to rule over and judge us? For God's judgments are always just, but man's are not. Now, if it were possible for you to always have just men to be your kings—men who would establish God's laws and judge this people according to His commandments, like my father, King Benjamin, then it would be good to always have kings to rule over you.

"I have taught God's commandments to you as well as I possibly could in order to establish peace throughout the land, and to put an end to wars, stealing, plunder, murder and all types of sins. I have punished those who have sinned according to the law given to us by our forefathers. Because not all leaders are just, it is not necessary for you to have a king, for one wicked king can be the cause of great sinfulness and destruction.

"Always remember King Noah and his wicked people, and the great destruction and bondage that resulted from their sinfulness. If their all-wise Creator had not intervened after they had sincerely repented, they would still be in bondage today! He delivered them because they humbled themselves before Him. Because they cried mightily to Him, He delivered them out of bondage. In all cases, this is how the Lord works with His power among His children. He always extends His arm of mercy to those who put their trust in Him.

"You cannot dethrone an evil king without much bloodshed, for evil kings put their sinful friends in power and surround themselves with guards. They tear up the righteous laws of those who have reigned before them and trample God's commandments. Evil kings invent their own corrupt laws and then kill those who disobey them by sending armies to put down rebellions. Unrighteous kings corrupt the righteous principles of governing.

"It is not good for such sinfulness to come upon you. So choose judges by your vote, that you may be judged according to the correct laws the Lord gave our forefathers.

"It is more common for the minority, not the majority, to want what is wrong. So make it your law to always do your business by majority vote. If the time comes when the majority of the people choose sinfulness, that is when God's judgments will come upon them. That is when He will visit them with great destruction, as He has done before in this land. If one of your judges does not judge you according to the law, then have him brought to a higher judge. If your higher judge does not judge righteously, then have a small number of your lower judges meet together and judge the higher judge, according to the voice of the people.

"I command you to do these things in the fear of the Lord. I command you to have no king, for from now on, you will have to answer to judges for your own sins. Until now, the sins of many people have been caused by the wickedness of their kings, who have had to answer for the sins of their people. This inequality should end in this land, especially among you, my people. This land should be a land of liberty, where all people enjoy their rights and privileges equally, as long as the Lord sees fit for our descendants to remain upon it."

King Mosiah wrote many other things to his people, explaining the burden upon the soul of a righteous king on behalf of his people—of having to bear their lack of faith, their complaints and their sins. Mosiah told them it should not have to be this way, but that the burden should be upon each individual. Mosiah explained all the disadvantages of laboring under an unrighteous king. He told his people that sins under an unrighteous king, such as wars, stealing, plunder, sexual immorality, and too many others to mention, are expressly repugnant to God's commandments.

After King Mosiah sent his written word to the people, they were all convinced that what he had written was true. They gave up their desire to have a king and became very eager to have equality throughout the land. Mosiah's people also expressed a willingness to answer for their own sins. They gathered into groups throughout the land to vote for their judges, according to the law that had been given, and they rejoiced in their God given liberty.

They loved Mosiah very much, and they esteemed him more than any other man. They did not see him as a corrupt, greedy tyrant, for he had not taxed them, nor had he delighted in war. He had established peace in the land, granting liberty to all. The people appointed judges, according to the law, throughout all the land. Alma's son, Alma, was appointed as the first chief judge. He was also the high priest, for his father had conferred that office upon him, giving him charge of all church affairs. Like his father, Alma walked in the ways of the Lord, keeping His commandments. He judged righteously during a period of continual peace throughout the land.

This was the beginning of the reign of the judges among the Nephites throughout the land of Zarahemla At the age of 82, Alma's father, Alma, the founder of their church, died, having lived to fulfill God's commandments. In 91 BC, at age 63, Mosiah died, having reigned for thirty-three years. He was the last of the Nephite kings, who had reigned for more than 450 years.

1 - Alma is the first judge...

In 91 BC, when King Mosiah died, there was no king left to rule over the Nephites. Mosiah, who had been righteous before God, had established laws that the people had accepted and were bound to live by. So the people were ruled by judges rather than by a king.

Alma was the first judge. During his first year as judge, a man named Nehor was brought before him. Nehor was a large, strong man. He had been preaching what he said was the word of God, yet he spoke against the church. He told the people that every priest and teacher should become popular and be supported by the people, and should not have to work with his own hands. He had also testified to the people that everyone would be saved at the last day, so they did not need to fear God's judgment. He told them to lift up their heads and rejoice, for the Lord had created and redeemed everyone, and that in the end, everyone would have eternal life.

Many people believed what Nehor taught, and they began to support him by giving him money. He began to be lifted up in the pride of his heart, wearing very expensive clothes. He even started his own church according to his own preaching.

Before Nehor had been brought to Alma for judgment, he had been on his way to preach to his believers. He had met Gideon, one of the teachers who belonged to the church of God—the same man who many years earlier had been an instrument in God's hands in delivering Limhi's people out of bondage.

Nehor began to criticize Gideon in order to lead more people of the church away. Gideon responded to Nehor boldly, defending the church with the true word of God. Now Gideon was strong in the word of God. Because Gideon had exposed Nehor's lies with the true word of God, Nehor became very angry. He drew his sword and killed Gideon, who was too old to defend himself. Because of this, the people of the church had brought Nehor before Alma to be judged for the crime he had committed.

Nehor stood before Alma and boldly pled for himself. But Alma said to Nehor, "This is the first time that priestcraft has been practiced among this people. You are not only guilty of priestcraft, but guilty of enforcing it with the sword. If priestcraft were allowed to be enforced among this people, it would bring about their entire destruction. You have killed a righteous man! He was a man who has done much good among this people. If we spared you, his blood would come upon us for vengeance. Therefore you are condemned to die according to the laws that have been given to us by Mosiah, our last king, for our people have agreed to live by these laws."

And so, Nehor was taken to the top of Manti Hill. There he confessed before heaven and earth that what he had taught was contrary to the word of God. Then he suffered a disgraceful death. But this event did not put an end to the spreading of priestcraft throughout the land. Many people loved the vain things of the world. They went around preaching false doctrines for money and fame. They pretended to believe what they preached to cover their lies, for liars were punished. By doing this, the law had no power over them. The people dared not steal or murder for fear of the law, for whoever murdered was punished by death.

As time passed, those who did not belong to the church of God began to persecute those who had taken the name of Christ upon themselves. They persecuted and criticized the Christians for humbly preaching God's word without payment. A strict law prevented church members from persecuting non-members and members alike. But in spite of this strict law, many church members began to be proud, arguing with those who persecuted them, even to the point of having fist fights with them. In 90 BC, this pride and contention caused many afflictions and trials to come upon the church. Many proud church members were excommunicated, and many others decided to leave the church on their own.

All this was very hard on the faithful, but they stayed firm in keeping God's commandments, patiently bearing the heavy persecution. When the righteous priests left their work to preach, the people left their work to hear God's word. Then they would all return to their work, for the priests did not feel that they were above working. They were all equal, and every man worked according to his own strength. The righteous saints gave to the poor, the needy, and the sick and afflicted. If a man had more, he gave more, for they all gave according to what they had. None of them wore expensive clothing, but their clothes were neat and attractive. This is how the church worked. It was a system that brought continual peace to its members in spite of all the persecution.

Because of the righteousness of the church, its members all became very rich. They had an abundance of everything they needed—flocks, herds, grain, gold, silver, silk, fine linen and precious things. Yet even with all their riches, they did not turn away anyone who was hungry or who needed clothing, for their hearts were not set upon their riches. They were generous to all people. The righteous gave to the elderly as well as to the young. They gave to those who were in debt as well as to those who were free. They gave to members and non-members alike. The righteous gave to anyone in need, and this is how they all prospered together.

The righteous saints became much more wealthy than those who did not belong to their church, or than those who did not practice charity.

Those who did not take the name of Christ upon themselves indulged in sorcery, idolatry, spiritualism, envying and arguing. They wore expensive clothing and were vain and proud. They participated in persecuting, lying, robbing, committing sexual sins and murder. For doing all this, they were brought to justice as much as possible according to the laws established by Mosiah.

Because the righteous brought sinners to the law to be judged and punished according to their crimes, the wicked became more secretive and did not dare sin openly. So there was still peace among the Nephites until the year 87 BC.

2 - Amlici rebels, fights Nephites...

In this same year, a very cunning man named Amlici began to cause contention. He acted according to Nehor's order (doctrine), and he was wise as to the wisdom of the world. He gained many followers, so many that they became very powerful and wanted

Amlici to become the king over all the people. This was alarming to the people of the church, and to all who had not been persuaded by Amlici, for they knew that according to their law, a man could only become king if the majority of the people voted for him. They knew that if Amlici were elected king, he would take away their right to worship God, for Amlici was a wicked man and wanted to destroy the church of God.

The people came from all parts of the land and assembled into separate groups. Some were for Amlici and some were against him. They argued and disputed with each other as they assembled to vote. The results of their voting were brought to their judges, and the majority of the people had voted against Amlici becoming king.

When the results of the election were announced, those who were against Amlici celebrated, but those who were for Amlici were incited by him to become very angry. They gathered together and consecrated Amlici to be their king.

As soon as these rebellious people had made Amlici their king, he commanded them to take up arms against their brethren, for he wanted power over all the people. The people who followed Amlici were called Amlicites, and the rest were called Nephites, or the people of God. Aware of the Amlicites' intentions, the Nephites prepared to fight them. They armed themselves with swords, scimitars, bows, arrows, stones, slings and with every other kind of weapon. They were organized, and appointed captains, higher captains and chief captains, according to their numbers.

Amlici also armed his men with all types of weapons, and he also appointed rulers and leaders over his people to lead them to war against their brethren.

The Amlicites came upon Amnihu Hill, east of the Sidon River, which ran along the land of Zarahemla. On the hill, the Amlicites began to fight the Nephites. As chief judge and governor of the people of Nephi, Alma went up on the hill with his captains and chief captains, leading his armies to battle against the Amlicites. They began to kill the Amlicites upon the hill, but the Amlicites fought the Nephites with great strength killing many of them. The Lord strengthened the Nephites so that they became mighty in battle. They killed so many Amlicites so quickly that they began to run away. The Nephites went after the Amlicites all that day and killed 12,532 of them. That day 6,562 Nephites were also killed.

When night came, Alma stopped his chase. He and his army camped in the valley of Gideon (named after Gideon who had been killed by Nehor).

Alma sent spies to follow the surviving Amlicites, to learn of their plans and plots, so that he might guard himself against them and keep his people from being destroyed. Alma sent out Zeram, Amnor, Manti and Limher with their men to spy on the Amlicite camp.

The next morning these men came running back to the Nephite camp, very surprised and fearful, and reported, "We followed the Amlicites outside of Zarahemla, to the land of Minon. We discovered that they have joined a very large Lamanite army. Our brethren in Minon are running from them with their flocks, wives and children toward our city! Unless we hurry back to our city, our enemies will obtain it, and our families will be killed!"

Alma quickly led the Nephite army back to their own city, Zarahemla. As they were crossing the Sidon River, the Lamanites and the Amlicites, who seemed to be as numerous as the sands of the sea, came upon them. But the Nephites were again made strong by the hand of the Lord, having prayed mightily to Him that He would deliver them out of the hands of their enemies. The Lord heard their cries, for the Lamanites and Amlicites fell before them in battle.

Then Alma fought Amlici face to face. They fought mightily with their swords. Alma, being a man of God, and having practiced great faith, cried out, "Oh Lord, have mercy and spare my life, that I may be an instrument in Thy hands to save and preserve this people." Then Alma continued the fight with Amlici. He was strengthened and killed Amlici with his sword.

Then the Lamanite king fought with Alma, but the king soon ran from him and sent his guards to fight instead. Alma and his guards killed and drove back the Lamanite king's guards. Alma and his men cleared the west bank of the Sidon River by throwing the dead Lamanites into the river so that the rest of the Nephite army could cross. When they had all crossed the river, the Lamanites and Amlicites ran with terror from Alma, even though they were so numerous they could not be counted. They ran from the Nephites toward the wilderness in the west and the north. The Nephites chased them with their might, killing many. The Lamanites and Amlicites were surrounded and killed, or chased into the wilderness called Hermounts, which was inhabited by wild animals.

3 - *The mark of dark skin explained...*

Many died of their wounds in this wilderness and were eaten by wild animals and vultures. Later their bones were found and piled in heaps.

After this war, the surviving Nephites buried their dead, which were too numerous to be counted. Then they all returned to their lands and houses, and to their wives and children. Many women and children had been killed, many flocks and herds had been destroyed, and many grain fields had been trampled by the great armies. Many bones of the Lamanites and Amlicites who had been thrown into the Sidon River came to rest in the depths of the sea.

Like the Lamanites, the Amlicites identified themselves with red paint upon their foreheads, but unlike the Lamanites, they did not shave their heads. The Lamanites shaved their heads and wore armor and small skins for loincloths. They carried bows, arrows, stones and slings.

The Lamanites had dark skin, which was God's mark upon them—a curse first given to their forefathers, Laman and Lemuel, because of their transgression and rebellion against their brothers, Nephi, Jacob, Joseph and Sam, who were just and holy men.

Because Laman and Lemuel wanted to kill their brothers, they were cursed with this mark of dark skin, and Ishmael's wicked children were also cursed. This was done to identify their offspring. By doing this, the Lord could preserve His people, for the mark was intended to keep the Nephites from being enticed by the Lamanites, from marrying them, and from believing in their false traditions which would prove their destruction.

Also, the Nephites who married Lamanites brought the same curse of dark skin upon their children. And every Nephite who joined the Lamanites had a mark placed on him, and was then called a Lamanite.

Those who did not believe the Lamanites' false traditions were called Nephites. They believed what was written in the records that were brought out of Jerusalem—the correct traditions of their forefathers, and they kept God's commandments. And they have kept these true records of their people, and also of the Lamanites.

The light-skinned Amlicites had put red paint on their foreheads. By marking themselves, God's word to Nephi was fulfilled, saying, "I have cursed the Lamanites and will put a mark upon them. By this mark, their offspring may be separated from yours forever, unless the Lamanites repent of their wickedness and turn to me so that I may have mercy on them. "I will put a mark upon those who mix with your brothers' children and they will also be cursed. I will also put a mark upon those who fight you and your children, and those who leave you will no longer be called Nephites. But I will bless you and anyone who calls himself your offspring."

Now the Amlicites did not know they were fulfilling God's words by painting a red mark on their foreheads. But they had come out in open rebellion against Him, so this curse and condemnation came upon them. Like all who are cursed, they had brought it upon themselves.

Not many days after this battle, another Lamanite army attacked the Nephites at Amnihu Hill. A Nephite army was sent from Zarahemla to drive them out of the land. Alma had been wounded and did not go to battle this time against the Lamanites.

Alma sent a numerous army against the Lamanites. They killed many of them and drove the rest out of the land. Then they returned again and began to establish peace in the land, and for awhile they had no more trouble with their enemies.

All this fighting began and ended in 87 BC, the fifth year of the judges' reign. During this year, tens of thousands of souls were sent to the eternal world to reap their rewards according to their works, whether they were good or evil, to reap eternal happiness or eternal misery according to the spirit that they had chosen to obey, either a good spirit or a bad one. For everyone will receive the reward of whom he chooses to obey. This is the truth according to the spirit of prophecy.

4 - Church is taken seriously because of war...

In 86 BC, there was no fighting in the land of Zarahemla. But the people suffered because they had lost so many men, animals and crops. So great was their suffering that everyone had reason to mourn. They knew they had received God's judgments because of their great sinfulness, and they had now awakened to remember their duty toward Him. They began to establish the church more fully. Many were baptized in the waters of Sidon and joined the church of God. They were baptized by Alma, who had been consecrated to be the high priest over the people of the church by his father Alma.

Eighty-five BC was a year of peace, during which 3,500 souls were baptized into the church of God. But again in 84 BC, the people of the church began to be proud of the wealth they had acquired. Because of their fine silks and linen, their flocks and herds, their gold and silver, and all their valuables, their pride began to show and they started wearing very expensive clothing. Alma and the teachers, priests and elders whom he had consecrated to teach the church were all very sorrowful because of this wickedness that had begun among the people of the church. It sorrowed them to see the people boasting of their accomplishments, and setting their hearts upon their money and the vain things of the world. The people began to despise one another, and to oppress the humble people of the church who did not believe as they did.

After enjoying only one year of peace, there was much fighting among the people of the church. They were envious of one another and had great contentions among themselves, and many church members became even more proud than those who did not belong to God's church. By the end of 84 BC, the progress of the church began to fail, for the non-members saw all the pride and contention of the church members and had no desire to join their church. By 83 BC, Alma saw that the wicked example of the church was leading astray those who had not joined it—a wickedness that was the beginning of the people's destruction. Alma saw great inequality among the people. Many thought they were better than others, and turned their backs on the people who needed food, drink, clothing and physical care.

This inequality caused great sadness among the people. Yet some humbled themselves and gave what they had to the poor and needy. They suffered all types of afflictions because they believed in Jesus Christ who would soon come, as declared to them by the spirit of prophecy. They looked forward to Christ's coming. By giving to the poor, they retained a remission of their sins. They were filled with great joy, for they believed that the will and power of Jesus Christ would deliver them from a permanent death.

Even though Alma was very sorry to see this inequality in the church—so many church members afflicting God's humble followers, the Spirit of the Lord did not fail him.

Following the Spirit, Alma selected Nephihah, a wise elder of the church, and gave him power, by the voice of the people, to make and enforce new laws according to the laws that had already been given. Nephihah was appointed as chief judge and governor of the people, but Alma remained as high priest over the church.

Alma gave up his judgment-seat so that he would have the time to go among his fellow Nephites and preach God's word to them—to help them remember their duty to each other and to bring down all the pride and contention among them. He saw no other way to bring them back to God except by bearing down in pure testimony of Christ against them.

By the beginning of 83 BC, Alma had given up his temporal work as chief judge and did nothing but spiritual work according to the high priesthood of the holy order of God. His work was to testify of God's word, according to the spirit of revelation and prophecy.

5 - Alma calls the people to repentance...

Alma began to testify in Zarahemla and throughout all the land. These are his words, from his own record, to the people in the church at Zarahemla:

"I, Alma, have been consecrated by my father, Alma, to be a high priest over God's church. My father was given power and authority from God to baptize his brothers and sisters and establish a church in the land of Mormon. My father and his people were delivered out of the hands of King Noah's people by God's mercy and power. After being delivered, they were brought into bondage again by the Lamanites. But by the power of His word, the Lord delivered them a second time. He brought them into this land, where His church has been established.

"Now I ask you, the members of this church, have you completely forgotten your fathers' captivity? Have you completely forgotten the Lord's mercy and long-suffering toward them? Most of all, have you completely forgotten that He delivered their souls from hell?

"You see, He changed their hearts. He woke them from a deep sleep, and they awoke to Him. They were surrounded by darkness and the chains of hell, and an everlasting destruction awaited their souls. Then the Lord lit up their souls by the light of His everlasting word. I ask you, my brothers and sisters, were they destroyed? No, they were spared! Were they freed from bondage, and were their souls saved? Yes, for when they were freed their souls grew, and they sang redeeming love, and I tell you that they have been saved! And how were they saved—loosened from the bands of death and the chains of hell? It all happened because my father believed Abinadi, a holy prophet, who spoke the words of God. And because of my father's faith, there was a mighty change made in his heart. Then my father preached God's word to your fathers, and such a mighty change was made in their hearts, that they humbled themselves and put their trust in the true, living God. And because they were faithful to the end, they were saved.

"Now I ask you, have you been spiritually born of God? Have you received His image in your countenances? Have you experienced this mighty change in your hearts? Do you exercise faith in the redemption of your Creator? Do you look forward with faith, seeing your mortal body raised to immortality, to stand before God to be judged according to the deeds done in the body? Will you hear the Lord say to you, 'Come to me, you that are blessed, for your works were righteous on earth.' Or would you think to lie to the Lord, saying, 'Lord, my works have been righteous on earth'—and imagine that He would believe you? Or will your soul be filled with guilt and remorse for your wickedness as you perfectly remember defying God's commandments? Now which do you think will be your case when you are brought before the judgment of God? Will you be able to look up to God that day with a pure heart and clean hands, having His image engraved in your soul? Can you think of being saved when you have given yourself up to become a slave to the devil? On that day you will know that you cannot be saved, for no one can be saved unless his robes have been washed white, purified and cleansed from all stain through the blood of Him whom our fathers spoke of, who will come to redeem His people from their sins.

"How will any of you feel, standing before the bar of God, with your robes stained with blood and all types of filthiness? And what will these stains testify against you? That you are murderers and are guilty of all types of wickedness!

"Brothers and sisters, do you think that anyone like this will have a place to sit down in God's kingdom with Abraham, Isaac, Jacob, and all the holy prophets whose robes are clean, spotless, pure and white? No! Unless you think our Creator is a liar from the beginning, you cannot think this, for those with stained robes will be sent out, for they are the children of the devil's kingdom. In the past, if you have ever experienced a change of heart and have wanted to sing the song of redeeming love, how do you feel now? Have you kept yourselves blameless before God? Could you say to yourselves, if you were to die right now, that you have been humble enough, and that your robes have been cleansed and made white through the blood of Christ, who will come to redeem His people from their sins? Are you stripped of pride? If not, you are not prepared to meet God. You must prepare quickly, for the kingdom of heaven is soon at hand, and those who are proud will not have eternal life. Are any of you envious? Such a person is not prepared, for he will not be found guiltless. I warn you to prepare quickly, for the Lord will soon come, though we do not know exactly when. Do any of you make fun of your brother, speak ill of him, or treat him badly? Cursed are such, for they are not prepared, and the time is near when they must repent or they will not be saved! Yes, cursed are all you workers of sin. Repent, for the Lord God has spoken it! He sends an invitation to all people. His arms of mercy are extended toward them, and He says, 'Repent and I will receive you.' He says, 'Come to me and you will taste the fruit of the tree of life. You will eat and drink freely of the bread and water of life. Come to me with your righteous works and you will not be cut down and thrown into the fire.'

"The time is close when those who bring forth bad fruit will have reason to wail and mourn. Oh you workers of iniquity, puffed up by your pride in the vain things of the world. You, who have professed to have known the ways of righteousness, but have gone astray like sheep without a shepherd, even though the shepherd has called after you. He is still calling after you, but you will not listen to His voice! The Good Shepherd is calling you in His own name, which is Christ. If you will not listen and respond to the name, 'Children of Christ,' then you are not His sheep. And if you are not His sheep, then whose are you? Who can deny that you are the devil's? Whoever does deny this is a liar—a child of the devil.

"For good comes from God and evil comes from the devil. If a man does good works, then he listens to the Good Shepherd's voice and follows Him. But whoever does evil works becomes the devil's child by listening to his voice and following him. All who do this must receive the devil's wages—spiritual death—a death to the things of righteousness, for they are dead to all good works.

"My brothers and sisters, I want you to understand me, for I speak with all the energy of my soul. God has commanded me to speak to you plainly so that you cannot misunderstand. I am called to speak in this way according to the holy order of God, which is in Jesus Christ. I am commanded to stand and testify to you about the things our forefathers said would happen. Do you think that I do not have my own testimony of these things? I testify that I know what I have said is true! And why do you think I am so sure of my knowledge? It is because I have fasted and prayed many days to know these things for myself. I know that they are true, for the Lord God has shown them to me by His Holy Spirit, and this is the spirit of revelation in me.

"Furthermore, it has been revealed to me, according to the spirit of prophecy in me, that the words of our forefathers are true. The spirit of prophecy is also a manifestation of the Spirit of God. I know for myself that what I say to you about the future is true. I know that Jesus Christ will come. He is the Son, the Only Begotten of the Father, who is full of grace, mercy and truth. He will come to take away the sins of everyone who firmly believes in Him. This is the order after which I am called—to preach to you and to everyone in the land—to the old, young, bond and free, crying to them that they must repent and be born again.

"The Spirit says, 'Repent, everyone from the ends of the earth, for the kingdom of heaven is coming soon. The Son of God will come in His glory, might, majesty, power and dominion. The glory of the King of heaven and earth will very soon shine among all people.' The Spirit also speaks to me with a mighty voice, saying, 'Go forth and say to this people: Repent, for unless you repent, you cannot inherit the kingdom of heaven. The axe is laid at the foot of the tree, and every tree that does not bear good fruit will be cut down and thrown into the fire—a fire that cannot be put out. Remember, the Holy One has spoken this.'

"Brothers and sisters, can you ignore these things and trample the Holy One under your feet? Can you build yourselves up in the pride of your hearts? Will you continue to wear expensive clothing and set your hearts upon your riches—the vain things of the world?

"Will you continue to think that you are better than others? Will you continue to criticize your brothers and sisters who humble themselves and walk after the holy order of God? By this holy order they have been brought into this church and have been sanctified by the Holy Spirit, and their works prove their repentance. Will you continue to turn your backs on the poor and the needy and not share your blessings with them?

"And finally, I say to those of you who will continue in your wickedness, you will be cut down and thrown into the fire unless you quickly repent. To those who want to follow the Good Shepherd's voice, I say, come out from among the wicked. Separate yourselves from them and do not touch their uncleanness, for their names will be blotted out and will not be found among the names of the righteous. Then God's word will be fulfilled, which says, 'The names of the wicked will not be mingled with the names of my people, which will be written in the book of life. And I will give my people an inheritance at my right hand.'

"And now, my brothers and sisters, what can you say against this? If you do speak against this, it does not matter, for God's word will be fulfilled. Is there a shepherd who does not watch over his sheep in order to keep wolves from eating his flock? If a wolf comes into his flock, does he drive it out? Yes, and if possible, he will kill it. Now the Good Shepherd calls you, and if you will listen to His voice, He will bring you into His fold, and you will be one of His sheep. He commands you not to let a hungry wolf come in and destroy you.

"Now I, Alma, command you, as God has commanded me, to do good works according to what I have said. I command you who belong to the church. And to those who do not, I invite you to come and be baptized unto repentance, that you may also taste the fruit of the tree of life."

6 - *Alma sets the church in order...*

After Alma finished speaking to the people of the church, which was established in the city of Zarahemla, he ordained priests and elders to preside and watch over the church. He did this ordination by the laying on of his hands, according to the order of God.

Those who had not belonged to the church, but who repented of their sins were baptized unto repentance and received into the church. Those who belonged to the church, yet refused to repent and humble themselves—who were lifted up in the pride of their hearts—were excommunicated and not numbered with the righteous. This is how the priests and elders began to establish the order of the church in the city of Zarahemla.

I, Mormon, want you to understand that God's word was liberal to all, for no one was deprived of his right to assemble and hear the word of God. The children of God were commanded to gather together often, and to join in fasting and mighty prayer on behalf of the welfare of the souls who did not know God. After making these regulations, Alma left the city of Zarahemla and went to the valley of Gideon, east of the Sidon River. In that valley was the city of Gideon, named after the man who was killed by Nehor.

Alma declared God's word to the church established in Gideon. He spoke by revelation, confirming the truth of his forefathers' words. He also spoke by the spirit of prophecy because of his testimony of Jesus Christ, the Son of God, who would come to redeem His people from their sins. Alma did all things according to the holy order of God to which he had been called.

7 - *Alma testifies of Christ...*

In Gideon, Alma preached, "My beloved brothers and sisters, this is the first time I have been able to speak to you, for I have been very busy as chief judge, but now I have given the judgment-seat to Nephihah. The Lord has shown great mercy in allowing me to come to you. I have come, hoping to find you humbling yourselves before God, asking for His grace, so that you would be blameless before Him. I have come hoping that you were not in the same awful dilemma as our brethren in Zarahemla. But God has given me great joy in knowing that the people of Zarahemla are righteous again.

"I trust, according to God's Spirit in me, that I will also have joy over you, for I would rather not experience again the type of sorrow I had over the people of Zarahemla.

"I trust that you are more believing than your brethren—that you are not as proud as they were. I trust that you have not set your hearts upon riches and the vain things of the world, and that you do not worship idols. I trust that you worship the true, living God, looking forward to a remission of your sins with an everlasting faith. For there are many events to come. The most important event is that the Redeemer will come and live among His people. The Spirit told me that He will not come to us while He lives on earth as a man. I do not know when or how the Lord God will come to us, but only that He has the power to do everything that He said He would do.

"The Spirit told me, 'Cry out to this people: Repent, prepare the way of the Lord, and walk in His straight paths, for the kingdom of heaven is near, and the Son of God will come upon the face of the earth.' He will be born of Mary in Jerusalem, the land of our forefathers. Mary will be a virgin—a precious and chosen vessel, who will be overshadowed and conceive by the power of the Holy Ghost, and bring forth a son—the Son of God. He will suffer all types of pain, affliction and temptations to fulfill the words, 'He will take the pains and sickness of His people upon Himself.'

"He will die in order to loosen the bands of death that bind His people. He will be merciful and powerful in the flesh. And He will know by His mortal experiences how to overcome His people's ills (temporal and spiritual).

"The Spirit already knows how this is done, but the Son of God will suffer in mortality, that He may erase the sins of His people, which they commit in mortality. This is my testimony.

"Now, you must repent and be born again, for the Spirit says if you are not born again, you cannot inherit the kingdom of heaven. So come and be baptized unto repentance. Be washed from your sins, showing your faith in the Lamb of God who will take away the sins of the world. He will be mighty to save us and cleanse us from all unrighteousness.

"Do not be afraid to come, and put aside every sin that so easily tempts you and binds you down to destruction. Come and show your God that you are willing to repent of your sins. Make a covenant with Him to keep His commandments, and witness this to Him today by going into the waters of baptism. Those who do this, and who keep God's commandments throughout their lives, will remember that I have told them according to the testimony of the Holy Spirit: 'You will have eternal life.'

"Do you believe these things? Through the Spirit, I know you do, and because your faith in Christ is strong, my joy is great. I am glad that you are not having the same problems your brothers and sisters were having in Zarahemla. I can see that you are on the path of righteousness that leads to God's kingdom, and that you are making His paths straight.

"Through the testimony of His word, you know that the Lord cannot walk on crooked paths. He will do as He said and never turn from what is right. This is why His course is one eternal round—a continuing cycle. He does not live in unholy temples, and filthy things cannot come into His kingdom. At the last day, those who are filthy will remain filthy. I have said these things to awaken you to a sense of your duty to God, to motivate you to walk blameless before Him after the holy order of God, the order by which you have been received into the church.

"Be humble, submissive, gentle and teachable. Be full of patience, long-suffering and temperate in all things. Be diligent in keeping God's commandments at all times, asking for whatever you need both spiritually and temporally. And always return thanks to God for what you receive. Be sure to have faith, hope and charity, and then you will always do many good things. May the Lord bless you and keep your robes spotless, that you may at last be brought in to sit down in the kingdom of heaven with Abraham, Isaac, Jacob and all the holy prophets, never to leave again.

"I have spoken these words according to the Spirit, which testifies within me. My soul rejoices because you have responded so well to my words. Now may God's peace be with you and your families. May it bless your homes, lands, flocks and all that you possess, according to your faith and good works, now and forever. Amen."

8 - Alma is rejected in Ammonihah...

After Alma had taught the people of Gideon many things, too many to be written, and had established the order of the church as he had in the land of Zarahemla, he returned to his home in Zarahemla to rest from his labors. This is how 83 BC ended—the ninth year of the judges' reign over the Nephites.

In 82 BC, Alma went to the land of Melek, west of the Sidon River, near the wilderness. He taught the people in the land of Melek according to the holy order of God—the order by which he had been called to teach. From all over the land that bordered the wilderness, people came to him to be baptized. After Alma finished his work in Melek, he traveled north for three days. He arrived at a city called Ammonihah. (It was a Nephite custom to name the lands, cities and even small villages after the name of the leader who first lived there. This city had been named after Ammonihah.) Alma began to preach God's word to the people in Ammonihah, but Satan had taken great hold upon their hearts, and they would not listen to him. Alma labored in the spirit, asking God in mighty prayer to pour out His Spirit upon the people, that he might baptize them and make their repentance complete. But the people hardened their hearts and said, "We know who you are. You are Alma, the high priest over the church that you have established in many parts of the land according to your tradition. We do not belong to your church or believe in your foolish traditions. Since we are not members of your church, we know you do not have power over us. And since you have given the judgment-seat to Nephihah, you are not even chief judge over us."

After the people reviled and rejected him, and even spit on him, they threw him out of their city. Alma left and traveled toward the city of Aaron. As he went, he sorrowed over the people's wickedness in Ammonihah. His soul was weighed down with great tribulation and anguish. Then one of the Lord's angels appeared to him, and said:

"You are blessed Alma, so lift up your head and rejoice, for you have great cause to rejoice. You have been faithful in keeping God's commandments from the time that I came to give you His first message. I have been sent to you again to command you to return to Ammonihah and preach to the people there. Tell them that unless they repent, the Lord God will destroy them. The people of Ammonihah are planning to destroy the liberty of your people, which is against the statutes, judgments and commandments that the Lord has given them."

After receiving this message, Alma quickly returned to Ammonihah, entering the city from the south side. Alma had been fasting for many days, so he asked a man, "Will you give a humble servant of God something to eat?" The man replied, "I am a Nephite, and I know you are a holy prophet of God, for you are the man that an angel showed me in a vision and told me to receive. Come with me to my house and I will give you something to eat, for I know you will be a blessing to me and my family."

The man who fed Alma with bread and meat was Amulek. After eating his fill, Alma blessed Amulek and his family and gave thanks to God. Then he said, "I am Alma, the high priest over the church of God throughout the land. I have been called to preach God's word among all this people, according to the spirit of revelation and prophecy.

"When I was here before, the people rejected me, and I planned never to come back again. But I was commanded to come back and prophesy to this people again—to testify against their sinfulness. Amulek, because you took me in and fed me, you are blessed. For I was very hungry, having fasted for many days."

Alma stayed with Amulek and taught him for many days before preaching to the people again. By this time, the people were even more sinful than before. Then the Lord's word came to Alma, "Go with Amulek and prophesy to this people, saying: Repent, for the Lord has said that unless you repent, He will visit you in His fierce anger, and not turn it away!"

Alma and Amulek went to declare the word of God, and they were filled with the Holy Ghost. They had been given power, so they could not be kept in dungeons or be killed. But they never showed their power until they had been tied up and thrown into prison. This is how the Lord showed His power to the people of Ammonihah.

Alma and Amulek went about preaching to the people, according to the spirit and the power that the Lord had given them.

9 - Alma and Amulek go and preach...

I, Alma, write that God commanded me to take Amulek with me and preach to the people of Ammonihah. As I began to preach to them, they resisted, saying, "Who are you? Do you really think we would believe the testimony of just one man, even if you told us that the whole earth would pass away?" Now these people did not know what they were saying, for in fact the whole earth will pass away. They also said, "We would not believe you even if you told us that this great city would be destroyed in one day." These people did not know that God could destroy their city in one day, for they were hard in their hearts and stubborn. They said, "Who is God, who sends us the authority of only one man to tell us such great and marvelous things?"

They were about to take hold of me, but something stopped them. Then I stood boldly and testified to them. I said, "You wicked, perverse generation. How could have you forgotten God's commandments and your forefathers' traditions so quickly? Don't you remember that our forefather, Lehi, was brought out of Jerusalem by the hand of God? Don't you remember that he and those with him were all led by God through the wilderness?

"Have you forgotten so soon just how many times God delivered our forefathers out of the hands of their enemies, preserving them from being destroyed by their own brothers? If it had not been for His matchless power, mercy and long-suffering toward us, we would have all been cut off from the face of the earth long ago, and perhaps even now we would be in a state of endless misery and woe. Now He commands you to repent, and unless you do, you will never inherit His kingdom. This is not all. He has commanded you to repent, or He will completely destroy you off the face of the earth, visiting you in His fierce anger, not turning it away. Don't you remember these words He spoke to Lehi, 'If you keep my commandments, you will prosper in the land. Otherwise, you will be cut off from my presence.' I hope you remember that the Lamanites who have not kept God's commandments have been cut off from His presence. But it will be better for them in the day of judgment than for you if you remain in your sins. It will even be better for them in this life than for you, unless you repent. For the Lamanites have been given many promises. They are ignorant because of their forefathers' false traditions, so the Lord will be merciful to them and save their lives. Someday they will be brought to believe His word, and they will come to know that their forefathers' traditions are false. Many of them will be saved, for the Lord will be merciful to all who call on His name. But if you persist in your wickedness, your lives will not be long, for the Lamanites will be sent upon you. They will come when you least expect them, and you will be completely destroyed by the Lord's fierce anger. The Lord will not allow you to live in such sinfulness and destroy His people, the Nephites. He would rather allow the Lamanites to destroy all the Nephites, if they were to fall into sin after being so blessed. The Nephites have been highly favored by the Lord, above every nation, tribe, tongue and people. They have had all things revealed to them according to their desires, faith and prayers—things of the past, present and future. They have been visited by God's Spirit, talking with angels and hearing the Lord's voice. They have been given the spirit of prophecy, revelation, the gift of tongues, preaching, the gift of translation, and the Holy Ghost. They have been delivered by God out of the land of Jerusalem and saved from famine, sickness and disease. They have been made strong in battle, that they might not be destroyed. They have been brought out of bondage again and again. And they have been prospered and made rich.

"Now, if this people, who have received so many blessings from the hand of the Lord, sin against the light and knowledge they have been given, then it will be far better for the Lamanites than for them. For the Lord's promises are made to the Lamanites, but not to you if you sin. The Lord has clearly promised and firmly stated that if you rebel against Him, you will be destroyed off the face of the earth. To save His people from this destruction, the Lord has sent His angels to visit many of His people. They cry mightily, 'Repent, for the kingdom of heaven is near. Soon the Son of God will come in His glory. His glory will be the glory of the Only Begotten of the Father, who is full of grace, equity, patience, mercy and long-suffering. He is quick to hear the cries of His people and answer their prayers. He will come to redeem those who will be baptized unto repentance through faith in His name. So prepare the way of the Lord, for the time is near when all people will receive a reward according to their works. If they have done righteous works, they will receive the salvation of their souls according to the power and deliverance of Jesus Christ. If they have done evil works, they will receive the damnation of their souls according to the power and captivity of the devil.'

"My beloved brethren (for you are my brethren, and you should be beloved), you need to repent. You must realize that your hearts have become very hardened against God's word, and that you have become a lost and fallen people."

I, Alma, could not finish speaking, for the people were angry with me because I had told them they were hard-hearted and stubborn, a lost and fallen people. They tried to take me and throw me into prison, but the Lord did not allow them to take me at that time. Then Amulek began to preach to them, but only part of his words are written in this book.

10 - Amulek testifies on behalf of Alma...

"I am Amulek, the son of Giddonah, who was the son of Ishmael, a descendant of Aminadi, who interpreted the writing upon the wall of the temple, written by the finger of God. Aminadi was a descendant of Nephi, the son of Lehi, who came out of the land of Jerusalem. Lehi was a descendant of Manasseh, the son of Joseph, who was sold into Egypt by his brothers. I have a great reputation among those who know me, having many friends and relatives. I have also worked hard to become wealthy. I had seen the Lord's mysteries and marvelous power that has preserved the lives of this people, but I hardened my heart. I was called many times, but I would not listen. I knew about these things but refused to understand them. Instead, I went on rebelling against God in the wickedness of my heart, even until the fourth day of the seventh month of this year, 82 BC. At that time, I was going to see a close relative when an angel of the Lord appeared to me and said, 'Amulek, go back home, for you will feed a prophet of the Lord—a holy man, chosen by God. He has fasted for many days because of the sins of this people. Take him to your home and feed him, and he will bless you. And the blessing of the Lord will rest upon you and your family.' I obeyed the angel and started for home. On my way, I met the man that the angel had shown me—this same man who has been speaking to you about the things of God today. I know he is a holy man, for an angel told me so. I know the things he has testified of are true, for as the Lord lives, He sent His angel to teach me these things while Alma was staying in my home. And this is because Alma blessed me and my family. He blessed my women and children, my father and all my relatives. And the Lord's blessings have rested upon us according to his words."

When Amulek had finished speaking, many people were astonished, realizing that there was more than one witness who testified in the spirit of prophecy against them, and of the things which were to come. But some men questioned Alma and Amulek, thinking that by their cunning they would catch them in their words, and deliver them to be judged according to the law—to be killed or thrown in prison, according to the crimes they thought they could accuse them of. The men who tried to destroy Alma and Amulek with their words were lawyers. They were hired or appointed by the people to administer the law when their criminal trials came to court before the judges. These lawyers were educated in all the skills and cunning of their people so they would be successful in their profession.

They questioned Amulek, trying to make him contradict himself. They did not think that Amulek could know their plan. As they began to question him, he knew their thoughts and said, "You wicked, perverse generation! You lawyers are hypocrites because you are doing the devil's work—laying traps and snares to catch God's holy ones. You are making plans to distort the ways of the righteous, which will bring down God's anger upon your own heads and totally destroy this people. Mosiah, our last king, spoke well when he said, 'If the time comes when the majority of this people choose wickedness, then they are ripe for destruction.' The Lord has judged you well in your sinfulness. He warns this people by the voice of His angels, who say, 'Repent, for the kingdom of heaven is near. Soon the Lord will come down among His people with equity and justice.' If it were not for the prayers of the righteous, who live in the land, you would have already been destroyed by drought, sickness and war. But because of the prayers of the righteous, you are spared. Now if you drive the righteous out from among you, then the Lord will not hold back. In His fierce anger He will come out against you, and you will soon be destroyed by drought, sickness and war, unless you repent now."

After Amulek said these things, the people were even more angry with him. They shouted, "This man speaks out against our laws which are fair. He also speaks out against our wise lawyers whom we have hired." Then Amulek stretched out his hand and shouted even louder, "Oh you wicked, perverse generation! Why has Satan got such a great hold upon your hearts? Why do you surrender to him and give him power over you? Satan has blinded your understanding of the truth I am telling you. Have I really testified against your law? No, I have spoken in favor of your law—to your condemnation! The foundation of the destruction of this people is being laid by your lawyers and judges!"

After Amulek said this, the people shouted against him, "Now we know this man is a child of the devil, for he has lied to us. He has spoken out against our law, yet says he has not! He also spoke against our lawyers and judges!"

Now, the lawyers made sure that the people remembered their accusations against Amulek. One lawyer in particular, Zeezrom, was Amulek and Alma's greatest accuser. Because he was one of the lawyers with the most expertise, he had a lot of business among the people. Like the other lawyers, all Zeezrom wanted was to get money from the people as he practiced law.

11 - The Nephite units of money...

According to the law written by King Mosiah, every man appointed to be a judge was paid for the time he spent judging. If a man owed another and refused to pay his debt, he was brought before the judge. After the evidence was given, the man was compelled to pay his debt. If he still refused to pay, his property was taken and he was thrown out of the city as a thief and a robber. The judge was paid a senine of gold for a day of judging, or he was paid a senum of silver, which is equal to a senine of gold.

Various measurements of gold and silver were made by the Nephites. They did not measure their gold and silver like the Jews in Jerusalem. They created their own ways of measuring things according to their needs and circumstances. They continued to do this in every generation until the judges' reign, when King Mosiah first established the standard measures.

Gold was measured in units called senines, seons, shums and limnahs. Silver was measured in senums, amnors, ezroms and ontis. A senum of silver was equal to a senine of gold. Either of these were equal to a measure of barley, or any kind of grain.

These were the standard measurements for gold: 1 seon = 2 senines. 1 shum = 2 seons (4 senines). 1 limnah = 1 shum+1 seon+1 senine (7 senines).

These were the standard measurements for silver: 1 amnor = 2 senums. 1 czrom = 4 senums (2 amnors). 1 onti = 1 ezrom+1 amnor+1 senum (7 senums).

This is how they measured smaller amounts: A shiblon = 1/2 senum. They traded a shiblon for half a measure of barley. A shiblum = 1/2 shiblon. A leah = 1/2 shiblum. And 1 antion of gold = 3 shiblons (1.5 senums).

Now, these lawyers had accused Alma and Amulek in order to get gold and silver, for they were paid according to how much time they spent dealing with the law. This is why they stirred up the people to riot and to create all types of disturbances and wickedness. By doing this, they were hired and paid more often for the many law suits that were brought to them. Zeezrom, an expert in the ways of the devil to destroy what was good, asked Amulek, "Will you answer a few of my questions?" Amulek answered, "Yes, if it is according to the Spirit of the Lord, which is in me, for I will not say anything contrary to the Spirit of the Lord." Then Zeezrom said, "Here are six onties of silver (worth 42 senines, or 42 days pay for a judge). I will give them to you if you deny the existence of a Supreme Being."

Amulek replied, "Oh you child of hell, why do you tempt me? Don't you know that the righteous yield to no such temptations? Do you believe there is a God, Zeezrom? Yes, you know there is, but you love money more than Him. You have lied to me before God, never intending to give me your silver. You only wanted me to deny the true and living God in order to obtain a legal way of destroying me. Because you have done this great evil, you will have your reward."

Then Zeezrom asked Amulek the following questions, which Amulek answered accordingly: "You say there is a true and living God?" "Yes, there is." "Is there more than one God?" "No." "How do you know these things?" "An angel made them known to me." "Who will come? The Son of God?" "Yes." "Will He save His people in their sins?" "No, He will not save His people in their sins, for it is impossible for Him to deny His word."

Then Zeezrom said to the people, "Be sure to remember that Amulek said there is but one God, yet he also said the Son of God will come, but He will not save His people. Amulek speaks as if he had the authority to command God!"

Then Amulek said, "You have lied again by saying I spoke as if I had the authority to command God. I said that He will not save His people in their sins. This is true because God cannot deny His word and save His people in their sins. And I cannot deny His word, which is, 'No unclean thing can inherit the kingdom of heaven.' Now how can you be saved without inheriting the kingdom of heaven? And how can you inherit the kingdom of heaven if you are unclean, remaining in your sins?" Zeezrom then asked, "Is the Son of God the very Eternal Father?" "Yes," answered Amulek. "He is the very Eternal Father of heaven and earth, and He created all the things in them. He was at the beginning and He will be at the end, being the first and the last. He will come into the world to redeem His people and to take upon Himself their transgressions. And He will only grant salvation and eternal life to those who believe in Him. The wicked will remain as if no redemption were made, but they will still be resurrected to an immortal body. For the day will come when all will rise from the dead to stand before God and be judged according to their works. The death of Christ will free everyone from the death of their bodies. The spirit and the body will be reunited again in its perfect form. Every limb and joint will be perfectly restored. We will be brought to stand before God, having awareness as we do now. And when we stand before God we will completely remember all our guilt. This restoration will come to all—to the old and the young—to those in bondage and those who are free—to the wicked and to the righteous. Not even a hair of our heads will be lost. Every part of the body will be restored perfectly, and everyone will be brought before Christ the Son, God the Father, and the Holy Spirit, who are one Eternal God. Then each person will be judged according to their good or evil works. I have just told you about the death and resurrection of the mortal body—that our spirits will unite with our immortal bodies, never to be divided."

After Amulek said this, the people were astonished, and Zeezrom began to tremble. Amulek said more things that I, Mormon, have not written.

12 - Alma exposes Zeezrom's lies...

Amulek's words had silenced Zeezrom, catching him in his attempt to destroy Amulek by lying and deceiving. He was now shaking under a consciousness of his guilt. Seeing this, Alma spoke to Zeezrom, explaining the scriptures beyond what Amulek had done.

By now a great crowd had gathered. They heard Alma say to Zeezrom, "You know that your lying and craftiness have been exposed. You have lied to men and to God, who knows all your thoughts. You also know that your thoughts are made known to us by His Spirit. And you know that we know of your very subtle plan, as subtle as the devil's, to lie and thereby deceive this people, that you might turn them against us, to hate us and throw us out. This was the plan of your adversary, who has exercised his power in you. Now remember that what I say to you, I say to all. This was the devil's trap, which he has laid to catch this people—to bring you under his power, and surround you with his chains—to chain you down to everlasting destruction, according to the power of his captivity."

As Alma said this, Zeezrom trembled even more, for he was convinced more and more of God's power. He was also convinced that Alma and Amulek knew the thoughts and intentions of his heart, for they were given the power to know these things by the spirit of prophecy.

Now Zeezrom began to ask sincerely to know more about God's kingdom. He asked Alma, "What does Amulek mean when he speaks about the resurrection of the dead—that all will rise from the dead, both the just and the unjust, and stand before God to be judged according to their works?" Alma answered Zeezrom, explaining, "God gives many people a knowledge of His mysteries. God also gives them a strict command not to say more than

He wants them to say. God gives more of His words to those who diligently obey what He has already given them. Those who do not harden their hearts receive more of His words until they know all of His mysteries. Those who harden their hearts are given less and less, until they know nothing about God's mysteries. Then they are taken captive by the devil and are led by his will down to destruction. This is what is meant by the chains of hell. Amulek has spoken plainly about death, about being raised from mortality to a state of immortality, and about being brought before God to be judged according to our works. On that day of judgment, if we have hardened our hearts against God's words, so that we do not know them, then we will be in an awful state of condemnation. If we have hardened our hearts against God's words, then our words, actions, and even our thoughts will condemn us, and we will not be found spotless before Him. And in this awful state, we would not dare look up at our God. We would be more happy if we could command rocks and mountains to fall on us and hide us from His presence. But this cannot be. We must stand before Him in His glory, power, might, majesty and dominion, and acknowledge to our everlasting shame that all His judgments are just—that He is just in all His works, that He is merciful to all His children, and that He has all power to save those who believe in Him and show by their actions that they have repented. Then a second death comes to those who die in their sins—a spiritual death, for they will become dead to righteousness. At that time, their torment will be like a lake of burning sulfur with flames that go up forever. They will be chained down to an everlasting destruction according to Satan's power of captivity. They will be as if no redemption had ever been made, for they will not be worthy to be redeemed according to God's justice. And in this awful state, they cannot die, for everyone will be resurrected and live forever."

When Alma finished speaking, the people were even more astonished. But there was one among them named Antionah, a chief ruler. He said, "What is this you have said—that we will rise from the dead and become immortal, with a soul that can never die? What about the scripture that says, 'God placed an angel with a flaming sword near the Garden of Eden to keep Adam and Eve from eating fruit of the tree of life and living forever?' If God kept our first parents from becoming immortal, how can we, their offspring, possibly live forever?"

Alma answered, "We believe that Adam and Eve fell by eating of the forbidden fruit. Because of their fall, all their descendants became lost and fallen from God's presence. At that time, if Adam and Eve had eaten of the fruit of the tree of life, they would have lived forever, and God would have been a liar, for He had told them, 'If you eat of the fruit of the tree of knowledge of good and evil, you will surely die.' Now we are a fallen people, and we will all die. But we have been given time to repent. This life became a time of probation, during which we prepare to meet God. It is a time to prepare for that endless state after our resurrection from death. If no plan of redemption had ever been made, which was planned before the world was created, then there could be no resurrection. But a plan was made and it will bring about the resurrection. If Adam and Eve had eaten of the fruit of the tree of life, they would have been miserable forever, having had no time to repent before becoming immortal. The plan of redemption would have had no place, and God's word would have not been valid. But God's word is valid.

This is why all people are born as mortals and then die. After death—the end of their probation, they must come to God's judgment, which is final.

"After God had appointed these things to be, He knew that Adam, Eve and their children had to be given light and knowledge. So He sent angels who spoke with them and allowed them to see His glory. From then on, Adam's descendants called upon God, and He talked to them and taught them the plan of redemption. He did this according to their faith, repentance and holy works. God gave more commandments to His children after they were able to choose between good and evil—after Adam and Eve broke the first commandments in the garden. Their descendants inherited the ability to become like God—to know good from evil—able to choose for themselves, to do good or evil. After making the plan of redemption known to them, God commanded them not to do evil. If they did evil, the penalty was a second death—an everlasting death—an eternal separation from righteousness. According to God's supreme goodness, the plan of redemption cannot redeem those who choose evil because His justice cannot be destroyed. God taught His children the plan of redemption, saying, 'If you repent and do not harden your hearts, then I will have mercy on you through my Only Begotten Son. Therefore, all who repent and do not harden their hearts will be claimed by mercy through my Only Begotten Son. They will receive a remission of their sins and will enter into my rest. But as for all who harden their hearts and become sinful, I swear in my anger that they will not enter into my rest.'

"Adam and Eve broke God's first commandments by eating of the forbidden fruit. This provoked His anger, causing our first death (of the body). And now, if you harden your hearts, your sinfulness will provoke God, who will send down His anger upon you. This second provocation (the first being made by Adam and Eve, which we inherited) will result in the eternal destruction of your souls (being cut off from God). As we realize that these things are true, let us repent and not harden our hearts, nor provoke the Lord our God to bring His anger upon us. Let us not break His second commandments—faith, repentance and holy works.

Then we will enter into His rest which has been prepared according to His word.

13 - The valiant are given the priesthood...

"Now, my brothers and sisters, let us go forward to the time when the Lord God gave these commandments to His children. The Lord ordained priests, after His holy order, to teach these things to the people. Those priests were ordained after the order of His Son so that the people would know that they should look forward to His Son for redemption.

"This is how they were ordained: First, because of their great faith and good works, they were called and prepared from the beginning of the world according to God's foreknowledge. Next, they were placed on earth, being left on their own to choose good or evil. After showing great faith by choosing good, they were called with a holy calling according to the Savior's redemption which was prepared for them. They were called to this holy calling because of their faith, while others rejected the Spirit of God because of the hardness of their hearts and blindness of their minds. If these others had not rejected God's Spirit, then they too might have been called. In other words, in the beginning they were all equally faithful with their brethren. But this holy calling was prepared only for those who would be cleansed on earth, in and through the atonement of thc Only Begotten Son, who had prepared Himself to redeem all people. The reason for being called by this holy calling—for being ordained to the high priesthood of the holy order of God, was to teach His commandments to all people so that they also might enter into His rest. This high priesthood is an order that has always existed. It is without beginning of days or end of years—being prepared from eternity to all eternity according to God's foreknowledge of all things.

"After high priests were ordained with a holy ordinance, they took the responsibility of the high priesthood of the holy order upon themselves. They became high priests forever, after the order of the Son—the Only Begotten of the Father, who is without beginning of days or end of years, who is full of grace, equity and truth. Many were ordained and became God's high priests because of their great faith, repentance and righteousness before Him. They chose to repent and work righteousness rather than to spiritually perish. Because of their correct choices, they were called after this holy order. They were sanctified, and their robes were washed white through the blood of the Lamb. After they were sanctified by the Holy Ghost—having had their robes made white—having been made pure and spotless before God, these high priests found sin to be repulsive. And a great number of them entered into the rest of the Lord their God.

"And now, my brethren, I hope that you will humble yourselves before God, and bring forth works of repentance, that you may also enter into that rest. Humble yourselves even as the people who lived in the days of Melchizedek. He was also a high priest after this same order, who took upon himself the high priesthood forever. It was this same Melchizedek to whom Abraham paid tithes, even ten percent of all he possessed. Now these ordinances were given so that the people might look forward to the Son of God, it being His order. After receiving these ordinances, they looked forward to Him for a remission of their sins, and also to the time when they would enter into His rest. When Melchizedek was King of Salem, his people had become very wicked. By using his mighty faith (having been ordained to this high priesthood according to the holy order of God) he preached repentance to his people, and they repented. He established peace in the land during his lifetime and was called the Prince of Peace, for he was King of Salem, reigning under his father. There were many before Melchizedek, and many after, but none were greater. This is why the prophets make special mention of him in their writings. Now I have said enough and do not need to repeat myself. The scriptures are before you. If you resist their messages it will be to your own destruction."

After saying this, Alma stretched out his arm and cried with a mighty voice, "Now is the time to repent, for the day of salvation is near! Yes, the Lord speaks through

His angels, telling all people in all nations to receive the joyful news. This is why angels have come to us. Because we of the house of Israel are wanderers in a strange land, these things are declared to us in all parts of the earth, and in plain terms so that we may understand. Because of this we are highly favored by the Lord. Even now, angels are declaring this to many people in our land. They do this to prepare the hearts of the people to receive His word when He comes in His glory. We wait for angels to tell us the joyful news of His coming, which will be soon. I do not know how soon, but I hope that it is during my lifetime. Whether His coming is sooner or later, I will rejoice in it. When He comes, angels will make it known to just and holy men. This will fulfill the words of our forefathers, who have spoken of Him according to the spirit of prophecy in them.

"And now, my brothers and sisters, I desire from the center of my heart with great anxiety, and even pain, that you would listen to my words. Throw off your sins and do not put off the day of your repentance. Humble yourselves before the Lord, calling upon His holy name. Watch and pray continually so that you may not be tempted beyond what you can bear. By doing this, you will be led by the Holy Spirit, and you will become humble, meek, submissive, patient and full of love. You will have faith in the Lord, and you will have the hope of receiving eternal life. You will always have God's love in your heart and will be lifted up at the last day to enter into His rest. May the Lord give you repentance so that you will not bring down His anger upon you, nor be tied down by the chains of hell and suffer the second death."

14 - The innocent are burned...

Alma said many other things to the people which are not written in this book. Many people believed him and began to repent and search the scriptures. But most of the people wanted to destroy Alma and Amulek. They were angry with Alma because he spoke so plainly to Zeezrom. They said Amulek had lied to them, and had reviled against their law, their lawyers and judges. They were angry, for Alma and Amulek had testified plainly against their wickedness. They wanted to take the law into their own hands and kill them privately, but instead they tied Alma and Amulek with strong ropes and took them to the chief judge.

These wicked men witnessed against them, testifying that Alma and Amulek had reviled against their law, their lawyers, judges and all the people in the land. Among many other things, they testified that Alma and Amulek said there was only one God, who would send His Son among the people, not to save them, but to throw them into a lake of fire and brimstone.

Zeezrom was astonished when he heard his words being repeated in the men's testimonies. He knew he had caused the blindness of their minds by his lying. His soul began to be tormented as he realized his own guilt, and he began to be surrounded by the pains of hell. He cried out, "I am guilty, and these men are spotless before God!" But the men reviled Zeezrom, saying, "Are you also possessed with the devil?" They spit on him and threw him out. They also threw out the men who believed Alma and Amulek and sent men to throw rocks at them and chase them out of the city.

Then they brought the believers' wives and children to a fire pit, and all who believed or had been taught to believe in God's word were thrown into the fire. Then they brought their records—the holy scriptures—and threw them into the fire. They took Alma and Amulek to the place of martyrdom to see the women and children burning. When Amulek saw the pains of the women and children burning in the fire, he was pained, and said to Alma, "How can we witness this awful scene? Let us hold out our hands and exercise God's power in us to save them." Alma replied, "The Spirit stops me from holding out my hand. For the Lord receives them up unto Himself in glory. He allows the wicked to murder according to the hardness of their hearts so that His judgments and anger upon them will be just. For the blood of the innocent will stand as a witness, and cry mightily against them at the last day." Then Amulek said to Alma, "Perhaps they will burn us, too." Alma responded, "If it is the Lord's will, but our work is not finished yet, so they will not burn us."

After the innocent were burned along with their scriptures, the chief judge of the land came and stood before Alma and Amulek who were bound. He slapped their faces and said, "After what you have seen, will you preach to us again that we will be thrown into a lake of fire and brimstone? You did not have the power to save those in the fire, nor did God save them because they believed in your religion." The judge slapped them again and asked, "What do you have to say for yourselves?" This judge was after the order and faith of Nehor, who killed Gideon. Alma and Amulek did not answer the judge, and he slapped them again and then turned them over to the officers to be thrown into prison.

They all left, but came again the next day. The judge slapped their faces, and so did many others, while saying, "Will you stand again and judge this people and condemn our law? If you have such great power, then why don't you free yourselves?" Then with clenched teeth, they spit on them and said, "How will we look when we are damned?" They said all kinds of things like this to them, mocking and abusing them for many days. They took away their clothes and gave them no food or water. Alma and Amulek suffered this way, tied up in prison.

By the twelfth day of the tenth month in 82 BC, they had suffered for many days in prison. On this day, the chief judge over the land of Ammonihah went into the prison along with many teachers and lawyers. The chief judge slapped them and said, "If you have power from God, then free yourselves from your ropes. Then we will believe that the Lord will destroy this people as you said." One by one, all the teachers and lawyers slapped Alma and Amulek, repeating what the chief judge had said. At last, when they had all finished, God's power came upon Alma and Amulek, and they stood up. Alma cried out, "How long will we suffer these great afflictions, oh Lord? Oh Lord, give us strength to be freed according to our faith in Christ!" Then Alma and Amulek broke the ropes.

When the people saw this, they tried to run, for they were afraid they would be destroyed. They were so afraid, they fell down and could not get out of the prison. Then the earth shook mightily, and the prison walls broke in half and fell to the earth. The chief judge and all the lawyers, priests and teachers who had abused Alma and Amulek were crushed to death by the falling walls.

The Lord had given Alma and Amulek power according to their faith in Christ and they walked out of the prison unharmed. Then they walked into the city of Ammonihah. Multitudes of people who had heard the great noise had run over to the prison to see what had happened. When they saw Alma and Amulek coming out of the collapsed prison, they were very afraid, and ran from them like a goat with her young running from two lions.

15 - Zeezrom is healed...

The Lord commanded Alma and Amulek to leave the city, so they went to the land of Sidom. There they found all the people who had been driven out of Ammonihah for believing Alma's testimony. With great sorrow, Alma told them what had happened to their wives and children. He also told them of his and Amulek's captivity, and of their powerful deliverance.

At that time, Zeezrom lay sick in Sidom with a burning fever, caused by the great tribulations of his mind because of his wickedness. He thought Alma and Amulek had been killed because of his sins. This great sin and many others tortured his mind until it had become very sore, burning without relief. When Zeezrom heard that Alma and Amulek were in Sidom, his heart began to take courage. He immediately sent a message to them, asking them to come. Alma and Amulek quickly went to his house, and to his bedside. When Zeezrom saw them, he held out his hand and begged for them to heal him.

Alma took his hand and said, "Do you believe in the power of Christ to save?"

"Yes, I believe all the words that you have taught," answered Zeezrom. Alma said, "If you believe in the redemption of Christ, then you can be healed." "Yes, I believe according to your words," replied Zeezrom. Then Alma cried to the Lord, "Oh Lord our God, have mercy on this man and heal him according to his faith in Christ."

Then to the great astonishment of all the people, Zeezrom leaped to his feet and began to walk. The news of this miraculous healing spread throughout the land of Sidom.

Then Alma baptized Zeezrom unto the Lord, and from then on Zeezrom preached to the people. Alma established a church in the land of Sidom and consecrated priests and teachers to baptize unto the Lord anyone who desired baptism. ,Many people came from all around the region of Sidom to be baptized. But the people of Ammonihah remained very stubborn. They did not repent of their sins, and they credited all the power of Alma and Amulek to the power of the devil (for they were of the profession of Nehor, and did not believe in repentance).

Amulek had given up all his gold, silver and precious things in Ammonihah for the word of God. He had been rejected by those who were once his friends, and by his father and relatives. Alma established the church in Sidom, and the people began to humble themselves before God, assembling to worship Him before the altar. They watched and prayed continually to be delivered from Satan, death and destruction. After doing and seeing all these things, Alma took Amulek to his home in Zarahemla, took care of him during his tribulations, and strengthened him in the Lord. This is how the year 82 BC ended.

16 - All die in Ammonihah...

There had been peace in Zarahemla for several years, but in 81 BC, on the fifth day of the second month, a cry of war was heard throughout the land. The Lamanite armies had come through the wilderness, into the city of Ammonihah, and had begun to kill the people and destroy the city. Before the Nephites could raise a sufficient army to drive them out of the land, the Lamanites had killed all the people in the city of Ammonihah. They had also killed some Nephites near the city of Noah, and had taken others captive into the wilderness.

The Nephites wanted to free their people who had been taken into the wilderness. Zoram, the appointed chief captain over the Nephite armies, and his two sons, Lehi and Aha, knew that Alma was the high priest over the church. They had heard that he had the spirit of prophecy, so they went to him and asked him where the Lord wanted them to go in the wilderness to search for their brethren. Alma asked the Lord, and after receiving an answer, he told Zoram and his sons, "The Lamanites will cross the Sidon River in the south wilderness, up beyond Manti. Meet them on the east side of the river, where the Lord will deliver your brethren who have been taken captive."

Upon hearing this, Zoram and his two sons led their armies as Alma had instructed. They attacked the Lamanite armies on the east side of the Sidon River and scattered them into the wilderness. By doing this they reclaimed their brethren, and not one of them was lost.

This is how 81 BC ended. The Lamanites had been driven out of the land, and the people of Ammonihah had all been destroyed, along with their great city, which they said God could not destroy because of its greatness. But in a single day it was left desolate, and their bodies were mangled by dogs and wild animals from the wilderness. After many days, their bodies were piled up and covered with dirt. The smell of the dead bodies was so bad that nobody went to Ammonihah for many years. It was called Desolation of Nehors, for they were of the profession of Nehor, and their lands remained desolate.

The Lamanites did not come again to war against the Nephites until 78 BC. Meanwhile, the Nephites enjoyed three years of peace throughout the land. During these three years, Alma and Amulek preached repentance to the people in their temples, sanctuaries and synagogues, which were built like the Jewish synagogues in Jerusalem. Alma and Amulek continually preached the word of God to all who would listen. They did not favor any person above another. Many others were also chosen to preach the word throughout the land.

Soon the establishment of the church became common throughout all the surrounding regions, among all the Nephites. There was no inequality among them, for the Lord poured out His Spirit upon all the people in the land to prepare their hearts to receive the words that He Himself would soon teach them. This was done so that they would not reject the word and go on to destruction, but receive it with joy, as a branch being grafted into the true vine, that they might enter into the rest of the Lord their God. The priests who taught the people preached against lying, deceiving, envying, fighting, stealing, murdering, committing adultery and against every type of evil. They did this hoping to rid the people of these things completely. They also taught the people about the coming of the Son of God, about His suffering and death, and about the resurrection of the dead.

Many people wanted to know where the Son of God would come. To their great joy, they were told that He would come and appear to them after His resurrection. When 78 BC ended, the church was established throughout all the land, having won the victory over the devil. The word of God had been preached in its purity, and the Lord had poured out His blessings upon the people.

17 - Mosiah's sons return after 14 years...

While Alma was traveling south from the land of Gideon to the land of Manti, to his surprise, he met Mosiah's sons, who were on their way to Zarahemla. These were the same who were with Alma when the angel first appeared to him. Alma was very happy to see his brethren and even happier to see that they were still his brethren in the Lord. They had become strong in the truth, for they were men of sound understanding and had searched the scriptures diligently to know the word of God.

But this is not all. They had prayed and fasted often. Because of this, they had the spirit of prophecy and revelation and were able to teach with power and authority from God.

They had been teaching God's word for fourteen years among the Lamanites and had been successful in bringing many of them to the knowledge of the truth. By the power of their words, many souls had been brought before the altar of God to call upon His name and confess their sins before Him. Like Alma, Mosiah's sons had suffered many afflictions such as hunger, thirst and fatigue. They had also labored greatly in the spirit.

Fourteen years earlier, in 92 BC, they had refused the kingdom that their father, Mosiah, and the people had wanted to confer upon them. They had left Zarahemla, taking their swords, spears, bows, arrows and slings in order to hunt for food while in the wilderness.

They had gone into the wilderness with others whom they had chosen, on their way to the land of Nephi, to preach God's word to the Lamanites. They had traveled for many days in the wilderness, fasting and praying for the Lord to give them a portion of His Spirit to stay with them. They wanted to be instruments in God's hands to bring, if possible, their brethren, the Lamanites, to the knowledge of the truth—to the knowledge of the baseness of their forefathers' incorrect traditions.

And they had been comforted, for the Lord had visited them with His Spirit and had said to them, "Be comforted. Go among your brethren, the Lamanites, and establish my word. Be patient in your afflictions, showing a good example to them in me, and I will make you instruments in my hands to save many souls." These words gave Mosiah's sons and their companions courage to go to the Lamanites and declare God's word to them. After arriving in the borders of the Lamanite land, they had separated, trusting in the Lord that they would meet again at the close of their harvest, for they believed that the work they had started was a great one. And it was great, for they had chosen to preach God's word to a wild, hardened and ferocious people—a people who loved to rob and kill the Nephites, whose hearts were set upon gold, silver and precious things. The Lamanites robbed and killed to get these things rather than work for them with their own hands, for they were a very lazy people. Many of them worshiped idols, and the curse of God had fallen upon them because of the false traditions of their forefathers. But the promises of the Lord were still extended to them if they repented. This is why Mosiah's sons had started the work, to perhaps bring them to repentance and to know the plan of redemption. In order to teach more of the Lamanites, they had separated and gone among them, every man alone, according to the word and power of God given to him.

Ammon had been their chief (one who administers), and had administered to each of them, blessing them according to their callings and needs. Then he left and they took their separate journeys throughout the land. Ammon went to the land of Ishmael, the land named after the sons of Ishmael, who had become Lamanites. As Ammon entered the land of Ishmael, the Lamanites captured and bound him. It was their custom to bind all Nephites who fell into their hands and take them before the king, who would then decide whether to have the Nephite killed, made to be a slave, thrown into prison, or thrown out of the land. So Ammon was brought before the king. The king's name was Lamoni. He was a descendant of Ishmael and he ruled over the land of Ishmael. The king asked Ammon if he wanted to live in the land among the Lamanites, or return to his own people.

Ammon said that he wanted to live among the Lamanites for a time, and perhaps until the day he died. King Lamoni was very pleased with Ammon and had him untied. Then he offered Ammon one of his daughters to marry. Ammon responded, "No, but I will be your servant." So Ammon became King Lamoni's servant and worked among his other servants, watching his flocks.

After serving the king for three days, he and the Lamanite servants were driving their flocks to the waters of Sebus where all the Lamanites drove their flocks for watering.

Along the way, a certain number of Lamanites, who had already watered their flocks, began to scatter the king's flocks.

Then the king's servants became frightened, saying, "Now the king will kill us, just as he killed others whose flocks were scattered by these wicked men." They began to cry fearfully while saying, "Look, our flocks are already scattered!" They wept because they did not want to be put to death.

When Ammon saw this, he was filled with joy, thinking to himself, "Now I will show the power of God in me to my fellow-servants by restoring these flocks to the king. Then I will win the hearts of my fellow-servants and lead them to believe in my words." Ammon encouraged the servants by saying, "My brethren, cheer up. Let us go find the flocks and bring them back here for watering. We will save the flocks and the king will not kill us!"

The servants followed Ammon, running quickly to head off the king's flocks and bring them back to the watering place. Then their enemies came to scatter their flocks again, but Ammon said to his brethren, "Surround the flocks so they do not get away again, and I will go and contend with these men."

The servants did as they were told, and Ammon went to contend with the many men who stood by the waters of Sebus. The men were not afraid of Ammon, thinking that one of them could easily kill him. They did not know the Lord had promised Mosiah that He would deliver his sons out of the Lamanites' hands. They did not know anything about the Lord, and they delighted in seeing their brethren die. This is why they had scattered the king's flocks.

Then Ammon began to hurl stones at them with his sling, and with mighty power, he killed six of them. They were astonished at his strength, but they were angry because he had killed some of their men. They were determined to kill Ammon, so after failing to hit him with their stones, they rushed at him with clubs to kill him. But as each man raised his club, Ammon cut off his arm with his sword. The men were astonished and they all ran from Ammon. Ammon had killed six with his sling, and had killed their leader with his sword. He had also cut off every arm that had been lifted against him, and there were many.

After driving his enemies far away, he returned to the king's servants and told them to water the flocks. Then they returned the flocks to the king's pasture. The servants went to the king, carrying the arms which had been cut off by Ammon as a testimony of the things he had done.

18 - Lamoni and his servants marvel...

King Lamoni told his servants to tell him everything they had seen Ammon do. After the king learned how faithful Ammon had been in saving his flocks, and how great his power was in fighting, he was amazed. He said, "Surely this is more than a man. This must be the Great Spirit, sending His great punishments upon this people because of their murders!"

The servants answered, "We do not know if he is a man or the Great Spirit. But we do know that he cannot be killed by your enemies, nor can they scatter your flocks when he is with us because of his skill and great strength. Because of this, we know he is your friend. He has more power than any man, for he cannot be killed."

Upon hearing this, the king said, "Now I know this is the Great Spirit. He came here to save your lives, so that I would not kill you, as I did your brethren. This must be the Great Spirit, of whom our forefathers have spoken."

Lamoni's tradition, which he had received from his father, was to believe in a Great Spirit. Even though he and his people believed in a Great Spirit, they thought that whatever they did was right. Even so, Lamoni still began to be afraid, fearing that he had done wrong by killing his servants. Before this time, Lamoni had killed many of his servants for allowing other Lamanites to scatter his flocks at the watering place. These Lamanites often came to the waters of Sebus to scatter the people's flocks so they could steal their sheep.

Now Lamoni asked his servants, "Where is this man who has such great power?" The servants replied, "He is feeding your horses." Now before the servants had gone to water the sheep, the king had commanded them to prepare his horses and chariots to travel to the land of Nephi. Lamoni's father, the king over all the land, was going to hold a great feast in the land of Nephi.

When King Lamoni heard that Ammon was preparing his horses and chariots, he was even more astonished by Ammon's faithfulness, and said, "I have never had a servant as faithful as this man, for he remembers to carry out all my commands. Now I know for sure that this is the Great Spirit. I want him to come to me, but I dare not ask him."

When Ammon was finished with the horses and chariots, he went to the king. Ammon noticed that the king looked different. He was no longer bold, but in deep thought. Seeing this, Ammon thought he should leave the king alone, and he turned to walk away. But one of the king's servants said to him, "Rabbonah (powerful king), the king wants you to stay." Ammon turned back to the king, and said, "What would you have me do for you, oh king?" The king did not answer, but sat silent for an hour, not knowing what to say to Ammon.

After this time, Ammon asked him again, "What would you have me to do?" And the king still did not answer. Ammon, being filled with the Spirit of God, knew Lamoni's thoughts, and asked him, "Do you wonder because you have heard about what I have done? Why do you wonder so much? I am only a man, and am your servant. I will do whatever you want, if it is right." The king still marveled because Ammon knew his thoughts, but managed to finally ask, "Who are you? Are you the Great Spirit, who knows all things?" Ammon answered, "No." The king asked, "How do you know my thoughts? You may tell me boldly. Also tell me by what power you killed and cut off the arms of those who scattered my flocks. If you will tell me, I will give you anything you want. I would guard you with my armies if you needed them, but I know you are more powerful than all of them."

Now Ammon was wise (cunning—with guile), yet harmless. So he said to Lamoni, "I will tell you by what power I did these things if you will believe all my words." And the king answered, "I will believe all your words." Then Ammon boldly asked the king, "Do you believe in God?" The king answered, "I do not know what you mean." Ammon asked, "Do you believe in the Great Spirit?" "Yes," answered the king. Ammon said, "The Great Spirit is God. Do you believe that God created the earth and the heavens?" "Yes, I believe that He created the earth, and all things in it, but I do not know about the heavens," replied Lamoni. Ammon said, "The heavens is a place where God lives with all His holy angels."

King Lamoni asked, "Is it above the earth?" "Yes," replied Ammon. "He looks down upon all His children, and He knows all the thoughts and intentions of their hearts, for by His hand they were all created from the beginning."

Then King Lamoni said, "I believe everything you have told me. Did God send you?" Ammon explained, "I am a man. In the beginning, man was created in the image of God. I was called by His Holy Spirit to teach these things to this people, that they may learn all that is just and true. A part of God's Holy Spirit is in me, which gives me knowledge and power. This is done according to my faith in God and my desire to serve Him."

Then Ammon began to teach Lamoni, starting from the creation of the world and of Adam. He taught about the fall of man, and about all the records and holy scriptures of the people which had been spoken by the prophets even down to the time that their forefather, Lehi, left Jerusalem. Ammon also told the king and his servants about the journeying of their forefathers in the wilderness—how they suffered with hunger and thirst. He told them about the rebellion of Laman, Lemuel and Ishmael's sons. He explained all the records and scriptures, from the time Lehi had left Jerusalem down to their present time.

This is not all. Ammon explained the plan of redemption, which was prepared from the foundation of the world. He also told them of the coming of Christ, and of all the works of the Lord. King Lamoni truly believed everything Ammon had said. And he cried out, "Oh Lord, have mercy on me and my people, according to Thy abundant mercy which Thou has had upon the Nephites."

After saying this, he fell down as if he were dead. Then the king's servants carried him to his wife and laid him on a bed. He lay as if he were dead for two days and nights. And his wife, sons and daughters mourned over him in the customary way, greatly lamenting his loss.

19 - The Queen believes Ammon...

After two days and nights, the king's servants were about to put him into a tomb. The queen had heard of Ammon's fame, so she sent for him. Ammon went to the queen and asked her what she wanted him to do. She said, "My husband's servants told me that you are a prophet of a holy God, and that you have power to do many mighty works in His name. If this is true, I want you to go to my husband, for he has been on his bed for two days and nights. Some say he is not dead, but others say he is, and they want to take him away. As for me, I do not think he is dead."

This is what Ammon wanted to hear, for he knew king Lamoni was under the power of God. He knew the marvelous light of God's glory, the light of everlasting life, had brought Lamoni such joy that it had overcome his natural body. The cloud of darkness had left Lamoni and he had been carried away in God.

So Ammon went with the queen to see the king. He told the queen, "He is not dead, but he sleeps in God. Tomorrow he will rise, so do not bury him. Do you believe me?" The queen answered, "I have only your word and the word of our servants, but I do believe my husband will rise as you said." Ammon replied, "You are blessed because of your great faith; a faith never known among all the Nephites." The queen sat by her husband all night. In the morning the king awoke, and holding out his hand to the queen he said, "Blessed is the name of God, and you are blessed too, for as surely as you live, I have seen my Redeemer. He will be born of a mortal woman and will redeem all who will believe in Him." Lamoni's heart was so full of joy that he was overcome again. The queen was also overpowered by the Spirit, and she, too collapsed.

Seeing the Lord's Spirit being poured out according to his prayers, Ammon fell upon his knees and began to pour out his soul in thanksgiving to God for what He had done for his brethren. Ammon was also overpowered with joy, and he collapsed near the king and queen. When the servants who had witnessed Ammon's great power saw him on the ground, they began to pray to God, fearing His power. As each servant prayed to God with his might, he fell unconscious.

Soon they had all fallen, except one woman named Abish. She had been converted to the Lord many years earlier because of a remarkable vision her father had received. Abish had never told anyone about her conversion to the Lord. When she saw all the servants, the queen, the king and Ammon fallen, she knew it was by God's power. Abish felt this was her opportunity to help many souls believe in God's power, so she ran from house to house, telling the people to come and see what the Lord's power had done.

A crowd came to the king's house, and to their astonishment, they saw the king, the queen, and their servants lying on the ground as if they were dead. They also saw Ammon, a Nephite. Some said a great evil had come upon the king and his house for letting a Nephite stay in the land. Others argued, "The king has brought this evil upon his own house by having his servants killed, whose flocks were scattered at the waters of Sebus."

The men who had scattered the flocks had also gathered with the crowd. They argued with those who said evil had come upon the king for killing his servants. They were angry with Ammon because he had killed seven of their brethren. The brother of their leader, whom Ammon had killed with his sword, was very angry with Ammon. He drew his sword and rushed to where Ammon lay, and as he lifted his sword to kill him, he fell dead.

Ammon could not be killed, for the Lord had said to Mosiah, his father, "I will spare him according to your faith." Because of this, Mosiah trusted his son's safety to the Lord.

After the crowd saw the man fall dead while trying to kill Ammon, they became afraid. They dared not touch Ammon or anyone else who had fallen. They again wondered what could be the cause of this great power and what these things meant. Many of them said Ammon was the Great Spirit, while others said he was sent by the Great Spirit. Others argued he was a monster who had been sent from the Nephites to torment them. Still others said Ammon was sent by the Great Spirit to afflict them because of their sins, that it was the Great Spirit who had always protected the Nephites by destroying many of their Lamanite brethren.

As the people argued sharply with one another, Abish became sad and began to cry. She then took the queen by the hand with the hope of raising her from the ground. As soon as Abish touched her hand, the queen sat up, stood on her feet and cried out, "Oh blessed Jesus, who has saved me from an awful hell! Oh blessed God, have mercy on this people!" Filled with joy, the queen clasped her hands and said many things to the crowd that they did not understand. Then she took Lamoni's hand, and he sat up and stood on his feet. Seeing his people arguing, Lamoni quickly went among them to rebuke and teach them Ammon's words. Those who listened to the king believed him and were converted to the Lord, but many would not listen and went away.

Then Ammon and Lamoni's servants stood and spoke to the people. They all declared the same thing; that their hearts had been changed, that they had no more desire to do evil. Many of the servants told the people that they had spoken with angels, who had told them of God and His righteousness. Many people believed the servants and were baptized. They became a righteous people and established a church among themselves.

This is how the Lord's work began among the Lamanites, and how He began to pour out His Spirit upon them. From this we learn that the Lord will extend His arm to all who will repent and believe in Him.

20 - Lamoni and Ammon's confrontation...

After the Lamanites had established a church, King Lamoni asked Ammon to go with him to the land of Nephi to meet his father. But the Lord's voice told Ammon, "Do not go to the land of Nephi, for Lamoni's father will try to kill you. Instead, go to the land of Middoni, where your brother Aaron, and also Muloki and Ammah are in prison."

Upon hearing this, Ammon said to Lamoni, "My brother and his friends are in prison in Middoni. I must go there to free them." Lamoni replied, "I know that in the strength of the Lord you can do anything. But I will go with you, for the king there, Antiomno, is a friend of mine. I will flatter him and he will let your brethren out of prison. And who told you that your brethren were in prison?" Ammon answered, "No one but God, who said to me, 'Go and free your brethren who are in prison at Middoni.'" Lamoni told his servants to get his horses and chariots ready to go, and then said to Ammon, "I will go with you to Middoni, and I will plead with the king to let your brethren out of prison."

As Ammon and Lamoni went on their way to Middoni, they met Lamoni's father, the king over all the land. He was sharp with Lamoni, and asked him, "Why didn't you come on the day I held a great feast for my sons and my people? And where are you going with this Nephite, a child of a liar?" Afraid of offending his father, Lamoni answered that he was going to Middoni. He told his father all that had happened in his kingdom—that these things had kept him from coming to the feast. Lamoni expected his father to be happy with this good news, but to his surprise, his father was angry with him, and said, "Lamoni, why would you want to free these Nephites, the sons of a liar? Nephi robbed our forefathers, and now his children have come among us to trick and rob us!"

Then Lamoni's father commanded him not to go to Middoni to free the Nephites, but to go with him back to the land of Ishmael. He also commanded Lamoni to kill Ammon with his sword. Lamoni refused, saying, "I will not kill Ammon, and I will go to Middoni to free Ammon's brethren, for I know they are just men and holy prophets of the true God!"

Upon hearing this, Lamoni's father became very angry and drew his sword to kill him. But Ammon stepped between Lamoni and his father, and said, "You will not kill your son, but if he did die, it would be better for him than you, for he has repented of his sins. If you were to die now in your anger, your soul could not be saved. For your own sake, do not kill your son, for he is innocent, and his blood would cry up from the ground to the Lord his God for vengeance upon you, and perhaps you would lose your soul."

Lamoni's father answered, "Yes, you are right. If I killed my son, I would shed innocent blood. You're the one who has tried to destroy him!" He raised his sword against Ammon who defended the blows. Then Ammon wounded the king's arm so he could not use it. Helpless, Lamoni's father begged Ammon to spare his life. But Ammon raised his sword above him, saying, "I will kill you unless you give me authority to let my brethren out of prison!" Afraid for his life, the king said, "You can have whatever you want, even half of my kingdom!" Ammon saw that he had power over the king, and said, "In addition to letting my brethren out of prison, I want you to let Lamoni keep his kingdom. You must not be displeased with him, but instead let him do as he desires. Unless you promise this, I will kill you!" When Ammon said this, the king was happy, for his life had been spared. He realized that Ammon did not want to kill him, and he was very surprised at Ammon's great love for his son. He said, "Because all you want is to free your brethren from prison and see Lamoni keep his kingdom, I will grant this, and I will not govern Lamoni again. Come to my kingdom when your brethren are out of prison, and bring them with you. I want to see you again and learn more about what you and Lamoni have told me today."

Then Ammon and Lamoni continued their journey to Middoni. Lamoni was favored by Antiomno, the king of the land, who released Ammon's brethren from prison.

When Ammon saw his brethren, he was very sorrowful, for they were naked and had many sores from being tied up. They had suffered from hunger, thirst and all types of afflictions, but they had been patient through it all. It had been their misfortune to be among a more stubborn people who had refused to listen to them. The people had driven them from house to house, and from place to place. The people had beaten them, and had driven them away, until at last they had gone to Middoni, the worst place of all. For in Middoni, they had been thrown into prison, tied with strong ropes, and kept there for many days before finally being released by Lamoni and Ammon.

21 - A report from Aaron...

When Ammon and his brethren first separated near the Lamanite border, Aaron went toward Jerusalem, named after the old Jerusalem across the ocean. The Lamanites, Amalekites and the people of Amulon had built this great city, Jerusalem. The Lamanites were stubborn, but the Amalekites and Amulonites were even more so. They had influenced the Lamanites to become very wicked.

When Aaron came into Jerusalem, he started to preach to the Amalekites in their great church buildings called synagogues. These synagogues were built according to the order of the Nehors, for many of the Amalekites and Amulonites belonged to that order.

As Aaron was preaching, an Amalekite man stood up and argued with him, "What do you mean, you have seen an angel? Why don't angels appear to us? Are your people better than we? You said if we do not repent, we will die. How do you know if we need to repent? How do you know if we are righteous or not? Look around. We have built sacred buildings and have come here to worship God, who we believe will save all men."

Aaron responded to the man by asking him, "Do you believe that the Son of God will come to redeem mankind from their sins?" The man answered, "We do not believe in these foolish traditions. We do not believe that you know the future any more than we believe our forefathers knew the future."

Then Aaron read the scriptures to them about the coming of Christ and the resurrection of the dead—that no redemption could be made for anyone unless it were through the death and suffering of Christ and the atonement of His blood. The people did not want to hear the truth. They wanted to believe they would all be saved no matter what they did. So as Aaron explained the scriptures to them they became angry and interrupted him with their mocking. Aaron left their synagogue and went to a village called Ani-Anti. There he found Muloki, Ammah and his brethren preaching to the people, who also refused to listen to the truth. So they all left and went to Middoni. There they preached the word to many, but few believed them. Aaron and some of his brethren were thrown into prison. The others ran out of the city to other places. In prison, Aaron and his brethren suffered many things until they were freed by Lamoni and Ammon, who fed and clothed them.

After recovering, Aaron and his brethren went out to preach again, going wherever the Lord's Spirit told them to. They preached God's word in every Amalekite synagogue and Lamanite assembly that allowed them. The Lord began to bless them, for they brought many to the knowledge of the truth. They convinced many people that their lives were sinful, and that their forefathers' traditions were false.

Ammon and Lamoni went to Ishmael, Lamoni's land, and Lamoni no longer allowed Ammon to be his servant. He had his people build synagogues wherein they could meet together. He rejoiced over them and taught them many things. He told them they were a free people under him, that they would no longer be oppressed by his father, the king, who had given him reign over Ishmael, and over all the surrounding land. Lamoni told everyone under his reign that they were free to worship the Lord their God the way they desired. Ammon preached about righteousness to Lamoni's people. He taught them diligently each day, and they listened, for they were eager to keep God's commandments.

22 - Aaron teaches Lamoni's father...

While Ammon was teaching in Ishmael, Aaron and his brethren were led by the Spirit to Lamoni's father in the land of Nephi. They went into the king's palace and bowed before him. Then Aaron said, "Oh King, we are Ammon's brethren, whom you have let out of prison. Oh King, if you will spare our lives, we will be your servants." The king answered, "Arise, I do not want to kill you, nor do I want you to be my servants. I insist that you teach me, for my mind is troubled and confused. Ammon's words to me were very great and generous. Tell me, why didn't he come with you as I asked him?"

Aaron replied, "The Spirit of the Lord called him to Ishmael to teach Lamoni's people." The king asked, "What do you mean, the Spirit of the Lord? This is what troubles me. And what did Ammon mean when he said, 'If you repent, you will be saved, and if you do not repent, you will be cast off at the last day?'" Aaron answered, "Do you believe in God?" The king responded, "I know the Amalekites say there is a God, and I have allowed them to build churches wherein they worship Him. And if you say there is a God, I will believe you." When Aaron heard this, his heart rejoiced, and he said, "As sure as you live, oh King, there is a God." The king asked, "Is God that Great Spirit who brought our forefathers out of the land of Jerusalem?" "Yes," answered Aaron. "He is that Great Spirit, and He created all things in heaven and earth. Do you believe this?" "Yes, I believe the Great Spirit created all things," replied the king. "Tell me about these things, and I will believe you."

When Aaron saw that the king would believe him, he began to read aloud from the scriptures. He read about the creation of Adam—how God created man in His own image and gave him commandments, and that because of transgression came the fall.

Then Aaron explained the scriptures he had read. He explained the fall of mankind, his carnal state, and the plan of redemption, prepared from the beginning of the world through Christ, for all who would believe in Him. Aaron said that since mankind had fallen, that we could not earn anything for ourselves, and that only the suffering and death of Christ could atone for our sins, through faith and repentance. Aaron taught that Christ would break the bands of death, that the grave would have no victory, that the sting of death would be consumed by the hope of glory!

After Aaron taught and explained this, the king asked, "What must I do to have this eternal life? What must I do to be born of God—to have this wicked spirit taken from me and receive His Spirit, that I may be filled with joy and not be cast off at the last day? I will give up all I have, even my entire kingdom, to receive this great joy." Aaron replied, "You will have what you hope for, oh King, if you will bow down before God and repent of all your sins—if you will call upon His name in faith, believing that you will receive."

The king immediately bowed down before the Lord upon his knees, and even laid himself down on the ground. He cried out loudly, "Oh God, Aaron has told me that there is a God. If there is a God, and if you are God, then will you make yourself known to me? I will give away all my sins to know Thee, to be raised from the dead and be saved at the last day." And when the king said this, he was struck as if he were dead.

The king's servants ran and told the queen what had happened. She came running and saw him lying as if he were dead. She also saw Aaron and his brethren standing nearby. She was angry with them and commanded the king's servants to kill them. The servants had seen how the king had fallen and they were afraid to lay their hands on Aaron and his brethren. They pled with the queen, "Why do you command us to kill these men when one of them is mightier than us all and will kill us?" When the queen saw the servants' great fear, she became very afraid, too. Then she commanded her servants to call the people to come and kill Aaron and his brethren.

Aaron saw that the queen was determined to have him killed. Knowing the unbelief and stubbornness of the people, and fearing there would be a great disturbance among them, he took the king's hand and said, "Stand." The king received his strength and stood on his feet. When the queen and the servants saw this they became fearful, wondering how it was done. But the king spoke to his household until they were all converted to the Lord.

Meanwhile, a large crowd had gathered because of the queen's orders, and had begun to conspire against Aaron and his brethren. But the king spoke to the crowd, and they were pacified. The king also told Aaron and his brethren to stand before the people and preach the word to them. Then the king sent a proclamation to all his people throughout his land and all the surrounding areas.

The Lamanites' land, which had a sea on the east and the west, was divided from the Nephites' by a narrow strip of wilderness. This narrow strip of land, which ran from the east sea to the west sea, was located south of the land of Zarahemla. It went through the borders of Manti, near the head of the Sidon River. The more idle Lamanites lived in tents near the western seashore, west of the land of Zarahemla, and west of the land of Nephi, in the wilderness—in the place of their forefathers' first inheritance.

Many Lamanites also lived on the eastern shore, where the Nephites had driven them. Being nearly surrounded by Lamanites, the Nephites had taken possession of all the northern lands, starting from the wilderness at the head of the Sidon River, from the east sea to the west sea. The Nephites' land continued north to the land they called Bountiful.

On the north of Bountiful was Desolation, a land once populated and then destroyed. Upon landing there in their ships, the people of Zarahemla (the Mulekites) were the first to discover the bones of this lost civilization (the Jaredites). Then the people of Zarahemla had gone into the southern wilderness. They called the southern land Bountiful because it was filled with all types of wild animals. It took a day and a half for a Nephite to travel in an east or west direction across the neck of land that divided Bountiful from Desolation. And to the south, the lands of Nephi and Zarahemla were nearly surrounded by seas.

The Nephites also lived in the land of Bountiful, from the eastern to the western shores. They were wise to guard the narrow neck with their armies, which kept the Lamanites from overrunning the northern land. The Lamanites could only possess the land of Nephi and its surrounding wilderness area. They could not surround the Nephites, and the Nephites also had the northern country to retreat into, if they so desired.

Now I, Mormon, will continue my account of Ammon, Aaron, Omner Himni and their brethren.

23 - The king opens the way for preaching...

The proclamation that the Lamanite king had sent among all his people told them not to harm Ammon, Aaron, Omner, Himni or any of their brethren who preached the word of God. It was forbidden for anyone to bind them, imprison them, or hurt them in any way. They were to have free access to their houses, temples and sanctuaries so that God's word could be preached throughout all the land.

Lamoni's father, the Lamanite king, desired that all his people to be convinced of their forefathers' wicked traditions. He wanted them to realize that they were all brethren, and that they should not murder, steal, commit adultery, or do any kind of wickedness. The king made this proclamation because he and his household had been converted to the Lord.

After this, Aaron and his brethren went from city to city, from one house of worship to another. Thy established churches and consecrated priests and teachers throughout the land among the Lamanites. They preached and taught God's word with great success. Thousands were brought to the knowledge of the Lord and to believe in the Nephites' traditions. They were taught about the records and prophecies that had been handed down, even to their present time.

Ammon and his brethren preached according to the spirit of revelation and prophecy, and by the power of God, which worked miracles among the Lamanites. And as sure as the Lord lives, all the Lamanites who were converted to the Lord never fell away. They became a righteous people. They laid down their weapons and did not fight against their brethren the Nephites, nor against God, anymore.

Now these are they who were converted to the Lord: The Lamanites in the land of Ishmael, Middoni, Shimlon and Shemlon, and the Lamanites in the cities of Nephi, Lemuel and Shimnilom. All these Lamanites who were converted laid down all their weapons of war. Only one Amalekite was converted and no Amulonites were ever converted. They hardened their hearts, and also the hearts of the Lamanites who lived in their villages and cities.

The king and those who were converted wanted a name to distinguish themselves from those who did not believe. The king consulted with Aaron and many of their priests about the name they would take upon themselves. They decided no longer to call themselves Lamanites, but Anti-Nephi-Lehies. They began to be a very industrious people. They were friendly with the Nephites and openly communicated with them, and God's curse no longer followed them.

Note: This new name that the King, Aaron and the priests came up with , Anti-Nephi-Lehies, expressed the converted Lamanites' new desire—to *emulate* their righteousness forefathers, Nephi and Lehi.

One definition of the word "anti" is "emulator".

After taking up this new name, the converted Lamanites received new lands of inheritance along with complete physical protection (see Alma 27:21-23). The record of this Lamanite awakening is a type for the last days. Knowing this, Mormon and Moroni's final words were directed to the latter-day Lamanites—words which beckon them to use their faith and thereby gain a knowledge of their covenant status (see Mormon 7:1-4,10, Moroni 10:1,33).

24 - Former Nephites stir up the Lamanites...

Then the unconverted Amalekites, Amulonites and Lamanites in the surrounding lands were stirred up by the wicked Amalekites and Amulonites to be angry with their brethren. Their hatred grew, and they began to rebel against their king (Lamoni's father), and they did not want him to be their king any longer. Then they took up arms against the Anti-Nephi-Lehies. During this time, the king conferred the kingdom upon his son (Lamoni's brother) and gave him a new name—Anti-Nephi-Lehi. Then the king died in the same year the Lamanites were preparing for war against God's people.

When Ammon, his brothers, and those who had come up with him realized that the unconverted Lamanites were preparing for war, they all met at Midian. From there they went to Ishmael to hold a council with Lamoni and his brother, Anti-Nephi-Lehi, to discuss what they should do to defend themselves against the Lamanites. None of the Lamanites who had been converted to the Lord would take up arms against their brethren. They would not even make any preparations for war. Their king, Anti-Nephi-Lehi, also commanded them not to take up arms. He said to his people, "I thank my God, my beloved people, that our great God has in His goodness sent our brethren, the Nephites, to preach to us—to convince us of the wickedness of our forefathers' traditions. I thank my great God that He has given us a portion of His Spirit to soften our hearts, and that we have opened a correspondence with these brethren, the Nephites. And by this correspondence, we have been convinced of our sins and of the many murders we have committed. I also thank my God, my great God, for giving us the chance to repent of these things, for He has forgiven us of our many sins and murders that we have committed, and He has taken away the guilt from our hearts through the merits of His Son. And in our lost condition, it was all we could do to repent of our sins and murders that we had committed so that God would take the guilt away from our hearts, and also take away our stains. My best beloved brethren, since God has taken away our stains, and our swords have become bright, let us not stain them again with the blood of our brethren. For perhaps if we stained our swords again, they could not be washed bright through the blood of the Son of our great God, which will be shed to atone for our sins.

"The great God has had mercy on us, and has made these things known to us so that we would not perish. He has given us a knowledge of His Son before He comes, for He loves our souls as well as the souls of our future children. This is why, in His mercy, He visits us by His angels, who teach us the plan of salvation, which is to be known by us as well as by our future generations. Oh, how merciful is our God! Since we have done all we can do to have our stains removed, and our swords have been made bright, let us hide them away, that they may be kept bright. Then on the last day, when we are brought before God to be judged, our bright swords will be a testimony that we did not stain them with the blood of our brethren after He gave us His word, which word enabled us to repent. And now, even if our brethren seek to kill us, we will now bury our swords deep in the earth, that they may be kept bright as a testimony at the last day that we never used them. And if our brethren do kill us, we will go to our God and be saved."

After the king said this, the people buried all their swords and weapons deep in the earth. This was their testimony to God, and also to men, that they would never use their weapons again. They covenanted with God that rather than kill their brethren they would give up their own lives—that rather than take from a brother they would give to him—that rather than waste their time in idleness they would work productively with their own hands.

From this we see that when these Lamanites were brought to believe and know the truth, they were firm, and would rather die than commit sin, for they buried their weapons of war to have peace.

Then the wicked Lamanites came to the land of Nephi to kill the king and replace him with another, and to kill the people of Anti-Nephi-Lehi. When the converted Lamanites saw them coming, they went out to meet them, bowed to the earth before them, and called on the name of the Lord. They continued to do this as the Lamanites began to fall upon them and kill them with their swords. Without meeting any resistance, the Lamanites killed 1,005 of them, and we know they have gone to live with their God and are blessed.

Soon the Lamanites realized that their brethren would not run from the sword, nor resist, but would rather lie down and die, praising God while being killed. Many stopped their killing and repented of what they had done, for their hearts had swollen for those who had fallen. Many Lamanites threw down their weapons and would not take them up again. They became like their brethren, relying upon the mercies of those who then raised their arms to kill them.

More Lamanites joined the people of God that day than the number of those who were killed. Not one of the 1,005 who were killed was a wicked man, and more than that were brought to the knowledge of the truth. From this we learn that the Lord works in many ways to save the souls of His people. Most of the Lamanites who killed their brethren were Amalekites and Amulonites, after the order of Nehor. And not one Amalekite or Amulonite joined the people of God. Only those who were descendants of Laman and Lemuel joined. From this we can plainly discern that when people fall away into sin after having been enlightened by the Spirit of God, they become more hardened, and their spiritual condition becomes worse than if they had never been enlightened.

25 - Abinadi's prophecy is fulfilled...

Because they had killed so many of their own men, the Amalekites and Amulonites became even more angry. They swore vengeance upon the Nephites and stopped killing the Anti-Nephi-Lehies. Because they had sworn this vengeance, they took their armies into Ammonihah and killed everyone in that city. And after this, they lost many battles with the Nephites. Almost all of Amulon's descendants, and the descendants of Noah's other priests, were killed by the Nephite army. Those who were not killed ran into the eastern wilderness and usurped power and authority over the Lamanites, killing many of them by fire because of their belief in the Lord.

After so much suffering and loss, many Lamanites remembered the preaching of Aaron and his brethren in their land. They began to disbelieve the traditions of their forefathers and to believe in the Lord—that He gave great power to the Nephites. By their faith, many Lamanites were converted to the Lord in the wilderness.

Now it was Amulon's descendants who were killing the converted Lamanites by fire. This martyrdom made many Lamanites so angry that they hunted and killed Amulon's descendants, who ran into the east wilderness. Even to this day, those Amulonites are still hunted by the Lamanites. This is how Abinadi's words were fulfilled, for he said the descendants of the priests who were about to kill him would be hunted and killed. Abinadi said, "Your children will be hunted, captured, and suffer death by fire." Abinadi was the first to die by fire because of his belief in God. He had told Noah's priests that their descendants would burn many people after him, and that they would be scattered and killed across the land.

When the Lamanites realized they could not overpower the Nephites, they returned to their own land. Many went to live in the land of Ishmael and the land of Nephi and joined the people of God—the Anti-Nephi-Lehies. They, too buried their weapons as their brethren had done and began to be a righteous people. They walked in the ways of the Lord, keeping His statutes and commandments. They kept the law of Moses, which was necessary, for it was not yet fulfilled. Even though they kept the law of Moses, they looked forward to the coming of Christ, understanding that the law of Moses was a type of His coming. They believed they had to keep those outward performances until Christ revealed Himself to them. They knew that salvation did not come by the law of Moses, but that the law of Moses served to strengthen their faith in Christ. This is how they kept their hope—through their faith in an eternal salvation, relying on the spirit of prophecy, which spoke of things to come.

Now Ammon, Aaron, Omner, Himni and their brethren rejoiced greatly over their success among the Lamanites, seeing that the Lord had answered their prayers and had also verified His word to them in every detail.

26 - The missionaries rejoice...

Ammon said to his brethren, "We have great reason to rejoice. For how could we have known when we left Zarahemla that God would have given us such great blessings? And what are these great blessings? Our brethren, the Lamanites, were in the most terrible darkness, but now many of them have been brought to see the marvelous light of God! This is the great blessing given to us, that we have been instruments in God's hands to do His great work. Thousands of Lamanites now rejoice, having come into the fold of God. The field was ripe, and now you are blessed, for you reaped with your might, working all day long. Now look at your harvest, which will not be lost! They will not be lost at the last day, when the storm and whirlwind come, but they will be gathered together where the storm cannot harm them, and the enemy will have no power over them. They are in the hands of the Lord of the harvest. They are His, and He will raise them up at the last day. Blessed be the name of our God! Let us sing His praise! Let us give thanks to His holy name, for His works are righteous forever! If we had not come from Zarahemla, these Lamanites, our dearly beloved brethren, who have so dearly loved us, would still hate us, and would be strangers to God."

After Ammon said this, his brother, Aaron, rebuked him, saying, "Ammon, I am afraid you are so carried away with joy that you are boasting." Ammon replied, "I do not boast in my own strength or wisdom, but my heart is filled with joy, and I rejoice in my God! I know that I am nothing. I am weak, and I do not boast of myself, but of God, for in His strength I can do all things. We have performed many mighty miracles in this land for which we will praise His name forever. See how many thousands of our brothers has God freed from the pains of hell? They have been brought to sing redeeming love because of the power of His word, which is in us. Isn't this a great reason to rejoice? Yes, we have great reason to praise Him forever, for He is the Most High God and has freed our brethren from the chains of hell.

"Not long ago they were surrounded by eternal darkness and destruction. But God has brought them into His everlasting light and salvation! Now they are surrounded by the matchless bounty of His love, and we have been instruments in His hands by doing this great and marvelous work! So let us glory and rejoice in the Lord, for our joy is full. We will praise our God forever, for who can glory too much in the Lord? Who can say too much about His great power, mercy and long-suffering toward His children? I cannot express the smallest part of what I feel!

"Who could have thought that our God would be so merciful as to snatch us from our awful, sinful and polluted state? We were angrily going about threatening to destroy His church. So why didn't God just consign us to an awful destruction—letting the sword of His justice fall upon us and doom us to eternal despair? My soul cowers at the thought. God did not exercise His justice upon us, but in His great mercy, He carried us over that everlasting gulf of death and misery, and saved our souls. And what natural man or woman can know these things? None, unless they repent. Those who repent and exercise faith, who do good works and always pray, are given the knowledge of God's mysteries. They will be given the power to reveal that which has never been revealed before. They will be given the power, even as we have been given, to bring thousands of souls to repentance.

"Remember how our brothers in the church at Zarahemla laughed when we told them we wanted to preach to the Lamanites in the land of Nephi? Remember how they scorned us, saying, 'Do you really think you can convert the Lamanites to the truth and convince them that their forefathers' traditions are wrong? The Lamanites are stubborn. They delight in bloodshed and spend their time doing the most wicked things. Let us go to war and destroy them and their iniquity before they overrun and destroy us.'

"But we ignored our brethren in Zarahemla and went into the wilderness, hoping to perhaps save a few souls. When we were depressed and about to turn back, the Lord comforted us and said, 'Go among your brethren the Lamanites. Bear your afflictions patiently and I will give you success.'

"And now we have returned after having been among them. We patiently suffered every deprivation. We went from house to house, relying on God's mercy. We taught them in their homes, on their streets and hills, and in their temples and synagogues. We were thrown out, mocked, spit on, and slapped on the face. We had rocks thrown at us and were tied with strong ropes and thrown into prison. And by God's power and wisdom we have once again been delivered. We suffered all this to perhaps be the means of saving some soul. We thought our joy would be full with even a few converts. But are the fruits of our labors few? No, they are many. And we know they are sincere, seeing their love for each other and for us. They would rather sacrifice their own lives than take the life of an enemy. They have buried their weapons deep in the earth because they love their brethren. Has there ever been such great love in all the land? No, not even among the Nephites, for they would take up arms against their brethren and not allow themselves to be killed. But over 1,000 Lamanites have laid down their lives. And we know they have gone to their God because of their love for their brothers and their hatred of sin.

"Do we have great reason to rejoice? Yes, since the world began, no men have ever had greater reason to rejoice than we! My joy is carried away, even to boasting in my God. For He has all power, wisdom and understanding. He comprehends all things, and He is a merciful Being who saves those who will repent and believe in Him. Now if this is boasting, then I will boast, for God is the source of my life and light, my joy and salvation, and my redemption from an everlasting curse. He has been mindful of this people—a branch of the tree of Israel, who are lost from their roots and wander in a strange land. My brethren, we see that God is mindful of every people regardless of where they live. He numbers all His people and shows His mercy over all the earth. This is the reason for my joy and great thanksgiving, and I will give thanks to my God forever. Amen."

27 - The time just before the reunion of the missionaries...

Now as I, Mormon, said before, when the Lamanites who had gone to war against the Nephites realized that they could not destroy them, they returned to the land of Nephi.

The Amalekites were very angry for having lost so many of their people, and when they could not take revenge on the Nephites, they stirred up the wicked Lamanites to be angry enough to begin killing their brethren, the Anti-Nephi-Lehies, once again. And having made a covenant with the Lord not to fight, many of the Anti-Nephi-Lehies were killed by their enemies. They treated Ammon and his brethren like angels sent from God to save them from everlasting destruction. So when Ammon and his brethren saw them being killed, they were moved with compassion and said to their king, "Let us gather this people of the Lord and take them to our brethren, the Nephites, in the land of Zarahemla. Let us escape from our enemies and not be killed." The king replied, "The Nephites will kill us because of the many murders and sins we have committed against them." Then Ammon said, "I will go and ask the Lord, and if He tells us to leave, will you leave?" The king answered, "Yes, if the Lord tells us to leave, then we will go to our brethren and be their slaves until we have made restitution for the many murders and sins we have committed against them." Ammon replied, "Slavery is against our law established by my father, Mosiah. So let us go and rely on their mercy."

The king said, "Ask the Lord, and if He tells us to go, we will. Otherwise, we will die in this land." Ammon went and asked the Lord, who said to him, "Get this people out of this land so they will not be killed, for Satan has a great hold upon the hearts of the Amalekites. They have stirred up the Lamanites to be angry enough to kill their brethren, so take them out of this land. This generation of people are blessed, for I will preserve them."

Ammon told King Anti-Nephi-Lehi everything the Lord had told him. Then they gathered all the people of the Lord with their flocks and herds and left the land. They made their exodus into the wilderness that divided the land of Nephi from the land of Zarahemla, and they came near Zarahemla's border. Then Ammon said to King Anti-Nephi-Lehi, "My brethren and I will go into Zarahemla to see if our brethren there will allow you and your people to come into their land. You wait here with your people until we return."

It was when Ammon was going toward Zarahemla with his brethren that he and his brethren met Alma. Ammon's joy was so full that he was consumed by the joy of his God, and he lost his strength and fainted. Now wasn't this great joy? This is the joy that only the truly repentant and humble seekers of happiness receive. Alma, Aaron, Omner and Himni also had great joy, but not so much that they lost their strength like Ammon. Ammon was revived, and Alma led him and his brethren back to his own house in Zarahemla. They went to tell the chief judge everything that had happened to them in the land of Nephi among the Lamanites.

Then the chief judge sent a proclamation throughout all the land, asking the people how they felt about allowing their brethren, the Anti-Nephi-Lehies, to come into their land. The answer came, "We will give them the land of Jershon as an inheritance (the land near the east shore, adjacent to the southern border of Bountiful). We will protect them with our armies because they have refused to fight, fearing to commit sin again.

"We will post our armies between the land of Jershon and the land of Nephi to guard them from their enemies. We will do this for our brethren on condition that they give us some of their supplies to help maintain our armies."

When Ammon heard this, he and Alma went to the Anti-Nephi-Lehies, who were camping in the wilderness, and told them the good news. (Alma also told them how he had been converted with Ammon and his brothers.) This caused great joy among them, and they went and took possession of the land of Jershon. From then on, the Nephites called those converted Lamanites "Ammon's people."

They were numbered among the Nephites and the church of God. They were known for their zeal toward God and men, for they were perfectly honest and upright in all things. They were firm in the faith of Christ throughout their lives. They looked upon shedding the blood of their brethren with the greatest abhorrence. They never did fight their brethren, nor did they fear death because of their hope in Christ and His resurrection, for they knew that Christ would have victory over death. Rather than take up the sword, many of them died in the most aggravating and distressing manner that could be inflicted by their brethren, the Lamanites. Ammon's people were zealous, beloved, and highly favored by the Lord.

28 - Mormon recounts 92 to 77 BC...

A church was established among them and a Nephite army guarded their land of Jershon.

The army was guarding the Zarahemla border when a Lamanite army came into the land. They had followed the converted Lamanites into the wilderness. The Nephite army fought them in a tremendous battle, like no other battle fought before in the promised land, and tens of thousands of Lamanites were killed and scattered throughout the land. The Nephites also suffered tremendous losses, but the Lamanites were driven away and scattered, after which the Nephites went back to their lands.

This was a time of great mourning and lamentation throughout the land. Widows mourned for their husbands, fathers for their sons, daughters for their brothers, and brothers for their fathers. Surely this was a sorrowful day—a time of soberness, of much fasting and prayer. This is how 77 BC ended—the fifteenth year of the Nephite judges' reign. This is the account of Ammon and his brethren, and their travels in Nephi, of their suffering, and of their incomprehensible joy. It is an account of the reception and safety of the Lamanites who inherited Jershon. And may the Lord, the Redeemer of all mankind, bless their souls forever. This is also the account of the wars that the Nephites fought among themselves, and also with the Lamanites through the year 77 BC. Over this fifteen year period, from 92 BC to 77 BC, many thousands of lives were lost in awful scenes of bloodshed. Many thousands were buried, and many thousands were not buried, but piled up in heaps on the ground. Many thousands mourned the loss of their relatives, having reason to fear they had been cursed forever according to the Lord's promises.

Many other thousands also mourned the loss of their loved ones, yet they rejoiced in their knowledge, according to the promises of the Lord, that their loved ones would be raised to live at the right hand of God in a state of never-ending happiness. From all this we realize how great the inequality of people is because of their sins. We also see the devil's great power, which he gains through his cunning plans to capture people's hearts. We see that the Lord calls His servants to labor diligently in His vineyard. And we see great reason for sorrow and rejoicing—sorrow over mortal death and separation, and joy for those who live in Christ's light.

29 - Alma wishes he were an angel...

Because of all these things, Alma exclaimed, "If only I were an angel. If only I could have the wish of my heart, to shake the earth with my voice, crying repentance to all people! I would declare repentance and the plan of redemption to every soul with the voice of thunder, so that they would repent and come to our God. Then there would be no more sorrow throughout the entire world!

"But I am a man, and I sin in my wish, for I should be content with what the Lord has given me. I should not want anything but the firm judgments of a just God, for I know He rewards men and women according to their desires. I also know that His judgments, which cannot be changed, result in spiritual and temporal salvation or death. I know that good and evil come to all, and that those who do not know right from wrong are innocent. But those who know good from evil are given what they choose—good or evil, life or death, joy or remorse of conscience. Since I know this, why should I want to do more than what I have been called to do? Why should I want to be an angel, speaking to all the ends of the earth? For in His wisdom, justice and truth, the Lord gives portions of His words to people in all nations, in their own language.

"I glory in knowing what the Lord has commanded me to do, for perhaps I may be an instrument in His hands to bring some soul to repentance, and this is my joy. When I see so many of my brethren truly repenting and coming to the Lord their God, my soul is filled with joy. Then I remember how the Lord heard my cry and extended His merciful arms toward me. I also remember the captivity of my father, Alma, and of his people. I know that the God of Abraham, Isaac and Jacob delivered them out of bondage and established His church among them.

"I have always remembered that the same God who delivered my father also delivered my ancient forefathers out of the Egyptians' hands. That same God established His church among my people and gave me a holy calling to preach the word to them. And He gave me great success, in which my joy is full! I do not rejoice in my own success alone. My joy is greater because of my brethren's success in the land of Nephi. They worked very hard, harvesting much fruit, and their reward will be great! When I think of their success, my joy is so great that my soul is carried away as if separated from my body!

May God reward my brethren to sit down in His kingdom with all those who are the fruit of their labors, never to leave again, but to praise Him forever. May God grant this according to my words. Amen."

30 - Korihor begins to preach...

After Ammon's people were established in Jershon, and the Lamanites were driven out, the Nephites buried the dead. The year was 76 BC. So many Lamanites and Nephites had died that they were not counted. And after they were buried, and after the days of fasting, mourning and prayer, there was continual peace throughout all the land. The people kept the Lord's commandments, strictly observing God's ordinances according to the law of Moses, for they were taught to keep it until it was fulfilled. There were no disturbances during all of 76 BC. During most of 75 BC, the seventeenth year of the judges' reign, there was peace also. But toward the end of that year, a man came into the land of Zarahemla, who was Anti-Christ, for he preached against the prophecies of the coming of Christ.

There was no law against one's beliefs, for passing a law that regulated one's beliefs was strictly forbidden by God's commands. For the scriptures say, "Choose for yourself whom you will serve." If a man wanted to serve God, it was his privilege to serve Him. But if he did not believe in Him, there was no law to punish him for not believing.

Murder was punishable by death. And those who committed robbery and adultery were also punished for their wickedness, for the law judged and punished only according to the crimes committed. But there was no law against a person's beliefs, for the equality of the people's right to believe was to be upheld. This Anti-Christ, named Korihor, who could not be restricted by the law, began to preach that there would be no Christ. He said, "Oh you who are bound down under a foolish, vain hope. Why do you burden yourselves with such foolish things? Why do you look forward to a Christ when no one knows the future? What you call prophecies—things that you say have been handed down by holy prophets—are simply your forefathers' foolish traditions. How do you know they are really true? You cannot know about things you do not see, so you cannot know there will be a Christ.

"You look ahead, saying that you see a remission of your sins. But this is the effect of a frenzied mind. Your derangement comes from your forefathers' traditions, which lead you away to believe in things that are not true."

Korihor said many other things, telling the people that an atonement could not be made for the sins of men because every man prospered according to his own genius, conquering according to his strength, and that whatever he did was no crime. This is how he preached and led many hearts away, and inspired them to be proud in their wickedness. Korihor led away many women and men to commit sexual sins—telling them that it did not matter because death was the end of life.

He went over to Jershon to preach to Ammon's people—the converted Lamanites—but they were more wise than many of the Nephites. They tied him and took him before Ammon, their high priest. Ammon had Korihor taken out of Jershon. Then Korihor preached in Gideon with no success, for he was bound again and taken before both the high priest and the chief judge over the land. The high priest, Giddonah, asked Korihor, "Why do you distort the Lord's ways? Why do you interrupt this people's rejoicing by teaching them that there will be no Christ? Why do you speak against all the prophecies of the holy prophets?"

Korihor replied, "I do this because I do not teach your forefathers' foolish traditions. I do not teach this people to bind themselves down under foolish ordinances and performances given by ancient priests to get power and authority over the people, and to keep them in submission and ignorance. You say these people are free, but I say they are in bondage. You say those ancient prophecies are true, but I say you do not know they are true. You say these people are guilty, a fallen people, because of some long ago transgression of a parent. But I say that a child is not guilty of anything his parents do. You also say that Christ will come and be killed for the sins of the world, but I say you do not know this. This is how you lead these people away with your forefathers' foolish traditions, according to your own desires. You keep them down like slaves, to glut yourselves on their labors, so that they do not dare boldly claim and enjoy their rights and privileges. They do not dare use what is theirs for fear of offending their priests, who burden them as they desire. Their priests bring them into submission by convincing them to believe in their own traditions, dreams, whims, visions and made-up mysteries. The priests tell the people that if they do not obey them, that they will offend some unknown being, whom they say is God—a being who never has been seen or known, who never was nor ever will be."

When Giddonah and the chief judge realized how hard Korihor's heart was—that he would revile even against God—they made no reply. They had him bound and delivered to the officers, who took him to Zarahemla to be brought before Alma and the chief judge, the governor over all the land.

Standing before Alma and the chief judge, Korihor blasphemed as he had in Gideon. Korihor reviled against the priests and teachers, accusing them of leading the people away after their forefathers' silly traditions in order to glut themselves on the labors of the people. When Korihor was finished, Alma said to him, "You know we do not glut ourselves on the labors of this people. I myself work with my own hands for my support, and have worked even from the beginning of the reign of the judges until now. I work even though I travel around the land to declare God's word to my people. In spite of the many labors I have performed in the church, I have never received so much as a senine, nor have any of my brethren, except those in the judgment-seat. And even then, we have only been paid for our time, according to the law. Now, if we do not receive anything for our labor in the church, how do we profit other than by rejoicing with our brethren? So why do you say that we preach to get gain, knowing that we receive no pay? Do you really believe that these people have such joy in their hearts because we have deceived them?" "Yes," answered Korihor. Alma then asked, "Do you believe there is a God?" Korihor answered, "No." Alma asked him, "Will you deny again that there is a God, and also deny the Christ? For I know there is a God, and I know that Christ will come. What evidence do you have that there is no God, or that Christ will not come? You only have your word, but I have all things as a testimony that these things are true, and so do you. Will you still deny them? Do you believe that what I say is true? I know you do, but you are possessed with a lying spirit, for you have put off the Spirit of God so that He has no place in you. The devil has power over you, and he carries you about, working his devices to destroy God's children."

Korihor replied to Alma, "If you will show me a sign to convince me that there is a God, and that He has power, then I will believe." Alma responded, "You have had enough signs. Will you tempt your God when you have the testimony of all your brethren, and of all the holy prophets? The scriptures are laid before you, and all things witness that there is a God. Even the earth and all things upon it, its motion, and all the planets that move in their regulated times, all witnesses together that there is a Supreme Creator. With all these witnesses, will you deny them and continue to go about leading people away, testifying that there is no God?" Korihor answered, "Yes, I will deny these things, unless you show me a sign."

Then Alma said, "I am sorry your heart is so hard. You will resist the spirit of the truth until your soul is destroyed. But it is better for your soul to be lost than for you to bring many souls down to destruction by your lying and flattering words. So if you deny God again, He will strike you so that you will not be able to speak again to deceive this people."

Korihor then said, "I do not deny that a God may exist. I simply do not believe in Him. I also say that you do not know there is a God. And unless you show me a sign, I will not believe." Alma said, "I will give this sign to you according to my words. In the name of God, you will never speak again." After Alma said this, Korihor could not speak.

When the chief judge saw this, he wrote to Korihor, "Are you now convinced of God's power? To whom did you expect Alma to show his sign? Did you want Alma to afflict others with a sign? Now that he has shown you a sign, will you continue to dispute?"

Korihor then wrote, "I know I cannot speak, and that nothing but God's power could have brought this upon me. I always knew there was a God, but the devil deceived me. He appeared to me in the form of an angel, saying, 'Go and reclaim this people, for they have all gone astray after an unknown God, for there is no God.' The devil taught me what to say. I taught his words because they were pleasing to my carnal mind. I taught them until I had great success, believing myself that they were true.

This is why I withstood the truth, even until I have brought this great curse upon myself." Then Korihor begged Alma to ask God to take away his curse. But Alma replied, "If this curse were taken away, you would lead the hearts of this people away again. So it will remain upon you as the Lord wills it." The curse was not taken off of Korihor, and he was sent out to wander from house to house, begging for food.

What happened to Korihor was immediately published throughout the land. A proclamation was sent forth by the chief judge to all the people in the land, declaring to those who had believed Korihor that they must speedily repent, or the same judgment would come upon them. The people were convinced of Korihor's wickedness and were reconverted to the Lord, and the sins that Korihor had taught the people to commit came to an end.

As Korihor went begging among the Zoramites (people who had separated themselves from the Nephites), he was run over and trampled to death. From this we see the reward for those who distort the Lord's ways. We learn that the devil will not support his children in the end, but he quickly drags them down to hell.

31 - The word more powerful than the sword...

Not long after the days of Korihor, Alma's heart grew sick again, for he heard that the Zoramites were distorting the Lord's ways, and that their leader, Zoram, was leading his people to bow down to dumb idols. Alma's heart was very sorrowful because of the separation of the Zoramites from the Nephites. The Zoramites had gathered in a land they called Antionum. It was east of Zarahemla, close to the east sea, and south of Jershon. Their land bordered the southern wilderness, which was full of Lamanites. The Nephites were afraid that the Zoramites would form an alliance with the Lamanites and cause a great loss among them. And since preaching had a more powerful effect on the minds of the people than the sword, Alma felt that he and his brethren should use the virtue of God's word in behalf of the Zoramites. So he took Ammon, Aaron and Omner, leaving Himni in charge of the affairs of the church in Zarahemla. From the land of Melek, Alma also took Amulek and Zeezrom. Alma left his oldest son, Helaman, but took his two younger sons, Shiblon and Corianton.

Now the Zoramites were dissenters from the Nephites, for at one time they had been taught God's true words. They had fallen into great error, for they would not keep God's commandments and statutes, according to the law of Moses. Nor would they observe the performances of the church—to always ask God each day to protect them from the devil's temptations. They had distorted the Lord's ways. This is why Alma and his brethren went to Zoram to preach the word to them.

One day a week, which they called the Lord's day, the Zoramites met in their synagogues. To their astonishment, Alma and his brethren saw the Zoramites worshipping in a way they had never seen before. The Zoramites had built a high platform in the center of their synagogue. At the top of this platform there was only room for one person to stand. Anyone who wanted to worship had to stand on top of the platform, hold up his arms toward heaven, and cry with a loud voice: "Holy, holy God, we believe that thou are God, and we believe that thou are holy, and that thou was a spirit, and that thou are a spirit, and that thou will be a spirit forever.

"Holy God, we believe that thou has separated us from our brethren. We do not believe in the traditions of our brethren, which were handed down to them by the childishness of their forefathers. We believe that thou has elected us to be thy holy children, and has made it known to us that there will be no Christ. But thou are the same yesterday, today and forever. And thou has elected us to be saved, while all those around us have been elected to be thrown by thy anger down to hell. For this holiness, oh God, we thank thee. We also thank thee for saving us from the foolish traditions of our brethren, which bind them down to a belief of Christ, leading their hearts to wander far from thee, our God. And again we thank thee, oh God, that we are a chosen and holy people. Amen."

After hearing this prayer, Alma, his brethren and his sons were astonished beyond measure, for every man went and offered up this same exact prayer. They called this high stand Rameumptom, which means, "holy stand." From the top of the stand, they offered this same prayer, thanking their God that they were chosen by Him, for not leading them away after their brethren's traditions, and that their hearts were not stolen away to believe in things to come, which no one knew of anyway. After all the people had offered up thanks in this way, they returned to their homes, never speaking of their God again until they gathered to the holy stand the next week to offer up this same prayer.

When Alma saw this, his heart was grieved, knowing they had become a wicked, perverse people. He realized that their hearts were set upon gold, silver and all types of fine things. He saw their great pride as they lifted up their hearts to boast. And Alma lifted up his voice to heaven, crying, "Oh Lord, how long will Thou let Thy servants live here below in the flesh, to see such great wickedness among the people?

"Oh God, they cry to Thee, and yet their hearts are consumed with pride. Oh God, they cry to Thee with their mouths, while lifting themselves up in great pride because of their love of the vain things of the world. Oh my God, their hearts are set on their fine clothing, jewelry and ornaments made of gold and precious things, with which they adorn themselves. Yet they cry to Thee, 'We thank Thee, oh God, for we are a chosen people unto Thee, while others will perish.' They say that Thou has made it known to them that there will be no Christ. Oh Lord God, how long will Thou suffer such wickedness and unfaithfulness to be among this people? Oh Lord, give me strength to bear my pain, for seeing such wickedness among this people pains my soul.

"Oh Lord, my heart is very sorrowful. Will Thou comfort my soul in Christ? Oh Lord, will Thou give me strength to patiently suffer the afflictions that will come upon me, because of the iniquity of this people? Oh Lord, will Thou comfort my soul and give me success, and also my fellow laborers who are with me, Ammon, Aaron, and Omner, Amulek, Zeezrom and my two sons? Oh Lord, comfort their souls in Christ. Will Thou also give them the strength to bear the afflictions that will come upon them because of the iniquity of this people? Oh Lord, will Thou give us success in bringing them back to Thee in Christ? Their souls are precious, and many of them are our brethren. So give us, oh Lord, power and wisdom to bring our brethren to Thee again."

After Alma said this, he laid his hands upon all those who were with him, and they were filled with the Holy Spirit. Then they separated, and were not concerned about what they would eat, drink or wear. The Lord provided their food and drink. He also gave them strength, so that any of their physical afflictions would be consumed in the joy of Christ. This was done according to Alma's prayer because he prayed in faith.

32 - Alma compares truth (the word of God) to a seed...

Then Alma and his brethren began to preach God's word to the people in their synagogues, houses and streets. After expending great effort, they began to have success among the poor class of people, who had not been allowed to go into their synagogues because they could not afford fine clothing. Because their fellow Nephites had not allowed them to worship God in their synagogues, considering them to be worthless and unworthy, the poor had become poor in heart and were humble and teachable.

As Alma was teaching some of the Zoramite people on Onidah Hill, a large crowd of these poor people came near. Their leader said, "We are despised, especially by our priests, because we are so poor. Our priests have banned us from our synagogues, even though we built them with our own hands. Now we have no place to worship our God. What should we do?" When Alma heard this, he turned around to face the man. With great joy, Alma realized their afflictions had truly humbled them—that they were now prepared to hear the word. Alma stopped speaking to the other group and stretched out his hand to the humble, crying out, "I see that you are lowly in heart, and if so, you are blessed. Your brother asked me what you should do, now that you cannot go into your synagogues to worship. Do you think that you cannot worship God unless you are in a synagogue? And do you think you should only worship God once a week? It is good that you have been cast out from your synagogues because of your poverty, for now you are humble enough to learn wisdom. Because you have been compelled to be humble, you are blessed, for sometimes the humble will seek repentance. And surely, whoever repents will find mercy. And whoever finds mercy and continues in righteousness throughout his life will be saved.

"You are blessed because you are compelled to be humble. But can you see that those who truly humble themselves because of the word are blessed even more? Yes, those who truly humble themselves, who repent of their sins and continue in righteousness throughout their lives will be blessed much more than those who are compelled by their poverty to be humble.

"Blessed are those who humble themselves without being compelled, who believe in the word of God and are baptized without stubbornness of heart. Many say, 'If you will show us a sign from heaven, then we will know for sure and we will believe.' But is this faith? No, for if you know something, you have no need of faith. Those who know God's will and do not do it are cursed much more than those who only believe God's word and then fall into transgression. Judge for yourselves, for there is a reward for those who know, and a reward for those who only believe, and everyone will be judged and rewarded according to what they did with their knowledge, or with their faith.

"Faith is not perfect knowledge. If you have faith, you hope for something which is true, but which you cannot see. Remember, God is merciful to all who believe in His name. First of all, He wants you to believe His word that He gives through angels to men and women. And many times little children have words given to them that confound the wise and the well-educated.

"My beloved brothers and sisters, just because you have asked me what to do in your poverty and affliction, do not think that I judge that all of you have been compelled to be humble, for I believe that some of you would have humbled yourselves regardless of your circumstances.

"Now, as I was saying about faith, it is not a perfect knowledge. You cannot know perfectly that what I am saying is true, for faith is not having a perfect knowledge of things. But if you will listen and try an experiment with my words, using just a little faith (even if you have only the desire to believe), then let your desire work within you until you can make a small place for my words in your heart.

"Let us compare the word to a seed. If you make a place to plant a seed in your heart, and if the seed is good, or true, and if you do not discard it by your unbelief, or by resisting the Lord's Spirit, then it will begin to grow. And when you feel it growing in your heart, you say to yourself, 'The seed (word) must be good, because it is starting to enlarge my soul. It is beginning to enlighten my understanding and satisfy my soul.'

"Now does this experience increase your faith? Yes. But the seed has not grown into a perfect knowledge just yet. As the seed continues to grow and sprout, bringing joy to your heart, you feel that it is good, and that feeling strengthens your faith even more. After having these feelings, are you sure that the seed is good? Yes, you are, for only a good seed would grow. If a seed does not grow, it is not good, and you throw it out. Because you have tried this experiment—planting the seed—you felt it grow and sprout. And now you know it is a good seed.

"Is your knowledge perfect now? Yes, your knowledge in that particular thing is perfect. You do not use faith anymore because you know the seed (word) has enlarged your soul, sprouting up and enlightening your understanding—expanding your mind. Then is this real? Yes, because it is light, which is real and good because it is discernible. Therefore you must know that it is good.

"Now after you have felt this light, do you have a perfect knowledge of the word? No, you only know that the word is good, so do not lay aside your faith. As the seed becomes a tree—as your knowledge increases—continue to use your faith by nourishing the tree with great care. Allow it to establish roots, to grow to maturity, and to bear fruit. If you neglect the tree by forgetting to water it, the tree will not take root. When trials and temptations come, you will fall if you do not have strong roots. And when the Lord of the harvest comes to His vineyard, you will be a barren tree, worthy only to be pulled out and burned. If this is the case, you will not be pulled out because your seed was not good, or because you did not want to be harvested. You will be pulled out because you did not nourish the tree. You will not have borne the fruit that you could have tasted (enjoying God's love).

"Remember, if you do not nourish the word by your faith, looking forward to the fruit, then you will never taste the fruit of the tree. But if you prove to be diligent by using the little faith that you have, and patiently heed His words each day, looking forward to living with your Heavenly Father again, then your faith will become stronger and stronger, until at last you are reunited with Him. If you use diligence, faith and patience in nourishing the seed (word), allowing it to take root in you, eventually you will taste the fruit, which fruit is most precious, sweet and pure. You will feast upon this fruit until you are filled, and you will never hunger or thirst again. Then, my brothers and sisters, you will receive the great, eternal reward for using your faith, diligence and patience with God's word."

33 - How to use faith and how to worship...

When Alma had finished speaking about faith, the people asked him how they should believe in God, how they should plant the seed in their hearts, and how they should begin to exercise their faith. Alma answered, "You said you could not worship God because you have been banned from your synagogues. If you think you cannot worship God without a synagogue, you are greatly mistaken and need to read the scriptures. And if you think the scriptures have taught you this, you do not understand them. Do you remember reading what Zenos, the prophet of old, said about prayer or worship? He said, 'Thou are merciful, oh God, for Thou has heard my prayer, even when I was in the wilderness. Thou was merciful when I prayed for my enemies, and Thou did soften them toward me. Oh God, Thou was merciful to me and heard me when I prayed to Thee in my field. And again, oh God, when I went into my house and private room, Thou heard my prayer. Thou are merciful to Thy children when they cry to Thee, to be heard by Thee and not by men, and Thou will hear them.

"'Oh God, Thou has been merciful to me, and has heard my cries in the middle of Thy congregations. Thou has also heard me when I was cast out and despised by my enemies. Thou did hear my cries and was angry with my enemies, and visited them in Thine anger with speedy destruction. And Thou did hear me because of my afflictions and my sincerity. Because of Thy Son, Thou has been merciful to me. Therefore, I will cry to Thee during all my afflictions, for in Thee is my joy. For Thou has turned Thy judgments away from me because of Thy Son.'"

After reading this, Alma said to the poor people, "Do you believe these scriptures, written by the prophets of old? If you do, then you also believe that Zenos said, 'Thou has turned away Thy judgments because of Thy Son.' Now my brothers and sisters, have you read the scriptures? If you have, how can you not believe in the Son of God? For Zenos was not the only prophet who spoke of the Son of God. Zenock also spoke of Him. Zenock said, 'Thou are angry, oh Lord, with this people, because they will not understand Thy mercies which Thou has bestowed upon them because of Thy Son.' Now my brothers and sisters, a second prophet of old testified of the Son of God. And because the people refused to understand his words, they stoned him to death. This is not all, for these two prophets were not the only ones who spoke of the Son of God. Moses also spoke of Him. A symbol of the Son of God, a brass snake, was held up by Moses in the wilderness, so that whoever would look upon it would live. And many of those who had been bitten by poison snakes looked and were healed. But many of them did not understand the meaning of the brass snake because they were stubborn. They did not believe they would be healed by simply looking up at the brass snake, and they died.

"Oh my brothers and sisters, if you could be healed by simply looking up, would you not look up quickly? Or would you rather harden your hearts in unbelief, being slothful and refusing to look up, and perish? If you do not look up, curses will come upon you. If you do look up, then believe that you will see the Son of God coming to redeem His people—that He will suffer and die to atone for your sins. Believe that He will rise again from the dead and bring to pass the resurrection, so that all people will stand before Him to be judged at the last day according to their works. "I want you to plant this word in your hearts. As it begins to grow, nourish it with your faith and it will become a tree, springing up in you unto everlasting life. Then may God make your burdens light through the joy of His Son. Amen."

34 - Alma and Amulek preach of Christ...

When Alma finished his speaking, he sat down on the ground. Then Amulek stood up and began to teach. He said, "My brothers and sisters, I think it is impossible for you to be ignorant of the coming of Christ, who we have been taught is the Son of God. For I know that you were taught a great deal about Him before you broke away from us in Zarahemla.

"Because your afflictions have now made you humble, you have asked my beloved brother what you should do. To prepare your minds, he has called on you to have faith and patience, even if you only have enough faith to plant the word in your hearts to see if the word, or seed, is good. We know your great question, 'Will the word testify of the Son of God, and that Christ will come?' In many ways my brother has proven to you that the word does testify of Christ's salvation. He has quoted the words of Zenos and Zenock, that redemption comes through the Son of God. He also reminded you of what Moses did, to prove that these things are true.

"Now I, Amulek, will testify to you that these things are true. I know that Christ will come among the children of men to take the transgressions of His people upon Himself. He will atone for the sins of the world, for the Lord God has spoken it. It is essential that an atonement is made, for according to the great plan of the Eternal God, there must be an atonement, or else all mankind must unavoidably perish. For all are hardened, fallen and lost, and must perish unless an atonement is made. It is necessary for a great, last sacrifice to be made, not of man, beast or fowl, but an infinite and eternal sacrifice. No man's blood can atone for the sins of his brother, for if a man commits murder, will our just law take his brother's life? No, the law requires the life of the murderer. Therefore, only an infinite atonement is sufficient to atone for all the sins of the world. An infinite atonement is the one great, last sacrifice. After it is made, there will be no more blood sacrifices. Then the law of Moses will be fulfilled. This atonement is the whole meaning of the law, for every aspect of it points to that great, last sacrifice—the Son of God, who is infinite and eternal.

"This is how He will bring salvation to all who believe in His name. The purpose of this last sacrifice is to bring about mercy, which overpowers justice, and introduces a way for people to have faith, repent, and be forgiven. This is how mercy can rescue us from the demands of justice, and encircle us in the arms of safety. But those who do not use faith and repentance are exposed to the whole law—to all the demands of justice. Only those who have faith and repent are redeemed by this great, eternal plan.

"May God grant you mercy, my brothers and sisters, as you use your faith to repent and call upon His holy name. Cry to Him for mercy, for He is mighty to save. Humble yourselves, and continue to pray to Him. Cry to Him to bless all your flocks when you are in your fields. Cry to Him in your homes, to bless all your household, morning, mid-day and evening. Cry to Him to protect you against the power of your enemies, and against the devil, who is an enemy to all righteousness. Cry to Him to bless your crops and your flocks, that you may prosper in them. But this is not all. Pour out your souls in your closets and secret places, and in your wilderness. And when you do not cry to the Lord, let your hearts be full—drawn out in prayer to Him continually for your welfare, and also for the welfare of those around you.

"But after you do this, if you turn away the needy and the ill-clothed, if you do not visit the sick and afflicted, and if you do not give your substance to those who need it, then your prayers are vain and will not profit you, for you will be hypocrites who deny the faith. If you do not remember to be charitable, you are of no value to God's kingdom.

Note: Benjamin and Moroni spoke of charity. See Mosiah 4:17-18 and Moroni 7:44.

"Now that you have been given so many witnesses, and know that the holy scriptures testify of these things, you must show your repentance. Do not be stubborn, for the time of your salvation is now. If you repent, the great plan of redemption will be brought upon you immediately. For in this life we prepare to meet God by doing His work. Now that you have had so many witnesses, do not delay your repentance. For after this day of life (which is given to us to prepare for eternity), if we have not improved ourselves, then night comes, when no work can be done. When you are brought to that awful crisis, you cannot say that you will repent and return to God, for the spirit which possesses your body when you die will have power to possess your body in the eternal world. If you put off the day of your repentance all of your life, then when you die, you will become subjected to the devil's spirit, who will seal you his. The Lord's Spirit will have left you, and the devil will have full power over you. This is the final state of the wicked. I know this because the Lord said He will not live in unholy temples, but only in the hearts of the righteous. They will sit down in His kingdom, never to leave again, and their robes will be made white through the blood of the Lamb.

"My brothers and sisters, I want you to remember these things and to work out your salvation with fear before God, no longer denying the coming of Christ. Do not resist the Holy Ghost, but receive Him, and take the name of Christ upon yourselves. Humble yourselves, even to the dust. Worship God wherever you are, in spirit and in truth. Live in thanksgiving daily for the many mercies and blessings He gives you. I urge you to pray continually so that you will not be led away by the devil's temptations—that he may not overpower you and that you may not become his subjects at the last day. For he will never reward you with anything good. I also call upon you to have patience while bearing all types of affliction. Do not argue with those who cast you out because of your extreme poverty, or you might become sinners like them. Have patience, and bear your afflictions with a firm hope that you will one day rest from all of them."

35 - Zoramites become angry with believers...

When Amulek was through speaking, he and Alma left the crowd and went over to the land of Jershon. After the rest of his brethren had preached the word to the Zoramites, they joined Amulek and Alma in Jershon. Then the more popular Zoramites consulted with one another about what had been preached, and they became angry, for it destroyed their priestcraft. This is why they had not listened to the words. Then they assembled all the people in the land, and asked them what they thought about the preaching. The rulers, priests and teachers did not let the people know their plans, so the people expressed their opinions. By this deception, the rulers, priests and teachers identified those who were in favor of the preaching, and then exiled them from the land. The many people who were exiled came over to the land of Jershon. In Jershon, Alma and his brethren ministered to them.

The Zoramites remaining in Zoram were angry with Ammon's people for taking in their outcasts. Their wicked chief ruler sent an order to Ammon's people, telling them to send away the Zoramites who had come into their land. He threatened Ammon's people, but they were not afraid of his words. They received all the poor Zoramites that came over to them. They fed and clothed them, gave them lands for their inheritance, and administered to them according to their wants. This made the Zoramites very angry with Ammon's people, and they stirred up the Lamanites to also become angry. By the end of 75 BC, the Zoramites and Lamanites began to prepare for war against Ammon's people and the Nephites.

Ammon's people left the land of Jershon and came over to the land of Melek, and allowed the Nephite army to occupy the land of Jershon. Then a war between the Lamanites and Nephites began in 74 BC.

Note: The account of this war continues at Chapter 43.

Alma and his two sons (Shiblon and Corianton), Ammon, and their brethren returned to the land of Zarahemla, having been instruments in God's hands to bring many

Zoramites to repentance. And those who had been exiled were given lands in Jershon. There they took up arms to defend themselves, their wives, children and lands. Alma was very sad, and his heart sorrowed over his people's sinfulness, wars, bloodshed and contentions. Alma had declared the word, or had sent others to declare it, in every city. But now the people's hearts were growing hard, and they were offended by the strictness of the word. Alma gathered his sons, Helaman, Shiblon and Corianton, to give each of them instructions pertaining to righteousness.

36 - Alma instructs his son Helaman...

I, Mormon, now include an account of Alma's instructions, taken from his own record:

"Listen my son, Helaman, for I promise you that if you keep God's commandments, you will prosper in the land. Remember our fathers' captivity. They were in bondage and no one could deliver them except the God of Abraham, Isaac and Jacob. And He surely delivered them from their afflictions. You are still young, so I plead with you to listen to me and learn. I know that all those who put their trust in God will be supported in their trials, troubles and afflictions, and will be lifted up at the last day. I would not want you to think that I know this by my carnal and temporal mind, for this knowledge is spiritual—from God. If I had not been born of God, I would not know these things. Through His holy angel, God made these things known to me, and not because I was worthy. For I went about with Mosiah's sons, trying to destroy God's church. And God sent His holy angel to stop us.

"The angel spoke to us with a voice of thunder. The earth shook beneath our feet and we fell down, fearing the Lord. Then the angel said, 'Get up,' and I stood up and saw him. He said to me, 'You may destroy yourself, but stop trying to destroy God's church!' After the angel left, I could not speak or move for three days and nights. The angel said more things to me that I did not hear, but Mosiah's sons heard them, for when the angel said, 'You may destroy yourself, but stop trying to destroy God's church,' I was struck with such great fear of being destroyed that I fainted. I was tortured with eternal torment, for my soul could remember all my sins in the greatest detail. I remembered everything I had done and was tormented with the pains of hell. I clearly saw that I had rebelled against my God and had not kept His holy commandments. I had murdered many of his children by leading them away to destruction. My sins were so great that the very thought of coming into the presence of my God struck my soul with inexpressible horror.

"I remember wishing, 'If only I could be banished and become extinct, both body and soul, so that I would not have to stand in the presence of my God to be judged for my deeds.' For three days and nights I was tortured with the pains of a damned soul. During this torment, as I remembered my many sins, I also remembered my father's prophecies to the people about the coming of Jesus Christ, the Son of God, to atone for the sins of the world. As my mind caught hold of this thought, I cried within my heart, 'Oh Jesus, Thou Son of God, have mercy on me, for I am in the middle of great bitterness, surrounded by the everlasting chains of death.'

"As soon as I thought this, I could no longer remember my pains, for the memory of my sins no longer tortured me. And oh, what joy, and what marvelous light I saw! My soul was filled with as much joy as it had been with pain! My son, nothing could have ever been so exquisite and so bitter as my pain! And on the other hand, nothing could ever be so exquisite and so sweet as my joy was at that moment! Like our forefather, Lehi, I thought I saw God sitting upon his throne, surrounded by countless hosts of angels who were singing and praising their God, and my soul longed to be there with them. My limbs received their strength again, and I stood on my feet and witnessed to the people that I had been born of God. Ever since then, I have never stopped working to bring souls to repentance—to bring them to taste the great joy that I had tasted, that they might also be born of God and be filled with the Holy Ghost.

"Now my son, the Lord gives me great joy in the fruit of my labors. Because of the word that He has given me, many have been born of God, have tasted the joy that I have, and have been given understanding. They know the things that I have told you, and their knowledge also comes from God. I have been supported under every kind of trial, trouble and affliction. God has delivered me from prison, from bonds, and from death. I still put all my trust in Him, for He will yet deliver me. I know He will raise me up at the last day to live with Him in glory. I will praise Him forever, for He brought our forefathers out of Egypt and commanded the Red Sea to swallow up the Egyptians. He also led our forefathers by His power into the promised land, and He delivered them out of captivity many times.

"He also brought our forefathers out of Jerusalem, and He delivered them out of bondage many times by His everlasting power, even until today. I have always remembered our forefathers' captivity, and so should you. But this is not all, my son. You should know, as I do, that if you keep God's commandments, you will prosper in the land. Otherwise, you will be cut off from His presence according to His word."

37 - Alma instructs his son Helaman...

Alma continued, "My son, Helaman, I command you to take the records that have been entrusted to me. I also command you to keep a record of this people, as I have done, upon Nephi's large plates. Preserve all these sacred things (Laban's sword, the Liahona, the interpreters) as I have, for these things are kept for a wise purpose. These brass plates contain the records of the holy scriptures and the genealogy of our forefathers back to Adam and Eve. Our forefathers prophesied that the brass plates would be handed down from one generation to another. They will be preserved by the hand of the Lord until they are read by all people in every nation. All people will read them in their own language and come to know the mysteries contained in them. The brass plates, and all other plates that contain holy writings, will be preserved, and will always retain their brightness.

"You may think that I am foolish to say these things, but I know that by small and simple things great things are brought to pass. At many times, small things confound the wisdom of the world. This is how the Lord God works, using very small means to bring about His great and eternal purposes, confounding the wise while bringing His salvation to many souls.

"God has shown His wisdom in preserving these things (the records of the holy scriptures), for they have reminded this people of their forefathers and have given them a knowledge of their God. The words engraved on them have convinced many of their sinful ways, bringing them to repentance and the salvation of their souls. If it were not for these records, Ammon and his brethren could not have convinced thousands of Lamanites that their forefathers' traditions were false. The words of these records brought them to repentance—to the knowledge of the Lord their God, so they may rejoice in Jesus Christ, their Redeemer.

"Because of these plates, who knows how many more thousands of Lamanites will be converted, or how many thousands of our stubborn fellow Nephites will be brought to know their Redeemer? Now these mysteries are not yet fully made known to me, so I will not speculate any further. It is enough to say that these plates will be preserved for wise purposes known by God. For He counsels in wisdom over all His works. His paths are straight and His course is one eternal round (a continuing cycle). Oh remember, remember, my son, Helaman, how strict God's commandments are. He has said, 'If you keep my commandments, you will prosper in the land. Otherwise, you will be cut off from my presence.' Remember, God has trusted you with the sacred things that He will preserve for His wise purposes, to show His power to future generations.

"I tell you by the spirit of prophecy, that if you transgress God's commandments, these sacred things will be taken from you by His power, and you will be delivered to Satan, who will then do with you as he pleases. But if you keep God's commandments, and always ask the Lord what to do with these sacred things, then no power of earth or hell can take them from you, for God is powerful in fulfilling all His words. He will fulfill all His promises to you, just as He fulfilled the promises He made to our forefathers. He promised them that He would preserve these sacred things for His wise purposes—to show His power to future generations.

"He has already fulfilled one wise purpose by restoring thousands of Lamanites to the knowledge of the truth. He has shown the Lamanites His power and will show His power to their descendants, in order to preserve them. This is why I command you, Helaman, to be diligent in fulfilling all my words, and to be diligent in keeping God's commandments as they are written. Keep these interpreters and these twenty-four gold plates so that the existence of the Jaredites' mysteries, secret works of darkness, murder, robbery, plunder and wickedness may be made known to our people. For when the Lord saw His people beginning to work in darkness, to commit secret murders and abominations, He said, 'If they do not repent, they will be destroyed off the face of the earth. I will prepare for my servant, Gazelem, a stone that will shine and bring what is in darkness into the light. Then my people who serve me will know that their brethren practiced secret works of darkness.'

"And now, my son Helaman, these interpreters were prepared to fulfill God's word, which is: 'I will bring all their secret works of darkness into the light, and unless they repent, I will sweep them off the face of the earth, and then bring a knowledge of all their secret sins to every nation that will live in this land.'

"Now we see that the Jaredites did not repent, and that is why they have been destroyed. So far, God's word has been fulfilled, for their secret abominations have been brought out of darkness and made known to us. And now my son, I command you to keep all their oaths, covenants, agreements, and secret abominations, as well as their signs and wonders, hidden from our people. For if our people were to use them, they would fall into darkness and be destroyed. For there is a curse upon all this land, that when they are fully ripe, destruction will come upon all the workers of darkness, according to God's power. And I do not wish for this people to be destroyed. So keep these secret plans, oaths and covenants away from this people, and only tell them about the wickedness, murders and abominations of those who have gone before them. Teach them to abhor these things and that all the people on the face of this land were once destroyed because of such things.

"For the Jaredites murdered all of the Lord's prophets who told them of their sinfulness. And the murdered prophets cried to the Lord their God for vengeance upon their murderers. Then God's judgments came upon these workers of darkness and secret combinations.

"This land is forever cursed to those who work in darkness and secret combinations, even to their destruction, unless they repent before they are fully ripe. Remember my words, Helaman. Do not give those secret plans to our people, but teach them an everlasting hatred against sin and iniquity. Preach repentance and faith in the Lord Jesus Christ. Teach them to humble themselves, to become meek and lowly in heart, and to resist every temptation of the devil by their faith in the Lord Jesus Christ. Teach them to never be weary of good works, but to be meek and lowly in heart, for such will find rest to their souls.

"Remember all these things, my son. Learn to be wise—to keep God's commandments—while you are still young. Pray to God for all your support. Wherever you go, let all that you do be for the Lord. Let all your thoughts and the affections of your heart be toward the Lord forever. Counsel with Him in all that you do, and He will direct you for good. At night, pray to the Lord, that He may watch over you in your sleep. And when you arise in the morning, let your heart be full of thanks to God. If you do these things, you will be lifted up to Him at the last day.

"And now, I want to tell you about the Liahona that the Lord made, which means, 'A compass.' No mortal could make anything like the Liahona. It was made to show our forefathers which way to go in the wilderness. It worked according to their faith in God, and its spindles pointed the way they should go. Day by day, this and many other miracles were shown to them. Even though these miracles were performed in small ways, our forefathers were shown God's marvelous power. When they forgot to use their faith and diligence, those marvelous works stopped, and they did not progress in their journey. When they transgressed, they did not travel in a straight course, which caused them to suffer from hunger and thirst. I want you to understand, my son, that a lack of faith in this temporal thing, the Liahona, is a symbol of a lack of faith in spiritual things. For it is just as easy to follow Christ's words, which point a straight course toward eternal bliss, as it was for our forefathers to follow the directions of this compass, which pointed a straight course for them toward the promised land. This Liahona was an example for us. For just as surely as it brought our forefathers to this promised land, Christ's words will carry us beyond this vale of sorrow into a far better land of promise.

"Oh my son, let us not be careless or take things too lightly because the way is easy, as it was for our forefathers. All they had to do was look and they would live. So it is with us. The way is prepared, and if we will look to Christ, we will live forever with Him.

"And now, my son, see that you take care of these sacred things. See that you look to God and live. Go among this people and declare the word. Be careful and serious minded. Farewell, my son."

38 - Alma instructs his son Shiblon...

"Listen my son, Shiblon. I will tell you what I told Helaman, that if you keep God's commandments, you will prosper in the land. Otherwise, you will be cut off from His presence. I trust that I will have great joy in you because of your steadiness and faithfulness to God. I hope that when you are older you will continue looking to the Lord your God by keeping His commandments, for whoever continues in righteousness throughout his life is blessed. I have had great joy in you already because of your faithfulness, diligence, patience and long-suffering among the Zoramites. I know you were in prison and had rocks thrown at you for preaching. You have suffered all this with patience because the Lord was with you. And you know it was the Lord who delivered you. Remember, if you put your trust in God, you will be delivered out of your trials, troubles and afflictions, and you will be exalted on the day of judgment.

"Now, my son, do not think that I know this on my own, for it is God's Spirit in me that makes these things known to me. For if I had not been born of God, I would not have known these things. But in His great mercy, the Lord sent His angel to tell me to stop the work of destruction among His people. I saw the angel face to face, and he spoke to me. His voice was like thunder, and it shook the earth beneath my feet. For three days and nights I was in the most bitter pain and anguish of soul. Only after I cried out to the Lord Jesus Christ for mercy did I receive a remission of my sins and peace to my soul. My son, I tell you this so that you may learn wisdom from me, that there is no other way or means that can save anyone other than Christ. He is the life and light of the world. He is the word of truth and righteousness.

"Continue to teach the word and be diligent and temperate in all things. Do not be lifted up in pride, boasting in your own wisdom or strength. Be bold, but not overbearing. Control your passions so that you may be filled with love. Do not be idle. Do not pray like the Zoramites, for you have seen how they pray to be heard by others and to be praised for their wisdom. Do not say, 'Oh God, I thank Thee that we are better than our brethren,' but rather say, 'Oh Lord, forgive my unworthiness and remember my brethren in mercy.' Acknowledge your unworthiness before God at all times.

"May the Lord bless your soul and receive you at the last day into His kingdom, to sit down in peace. Now go my son, and teach the word to this people. Be serious minded. Farewell, my son."

39 - Alma instructs his son Corianton...

"And now my son, Corianton, I have more to say to you than to your brother, for you have not followed his good example—his faithfulness and diligence in keeping God's commandments. You have not listened to my words as your brother did, when we were among the Zoramites. I speak against your boasting in your own strength and wisdom.

"This is not all, my son. You did what was grievous to me. You left the ministry and went to the land of Siron, near the Lamanite border, after the harlot, Isabel. She stole away many hearts, but that is no excuse for you, my son. You should have attended to the ministry with which you were entrusted.

"My son, what you did is a very serious sin in the Lord's sight—even the worst sin, except for murder or denying the Holy Ghost. For if you deny the Holy Ghost after it once has had a place in you, and you know that you deny it, this sin is unpardonable. And anyone who murders against the light and knowledge of God is not easily forgiven. And now, my son, I would to God that you had not been guilty of so great a crime. I would not dwell upon your crimes, to harrow up your soul, if it were not for your good. But you cannot hide your crimes from God. And unless you repent, they will stand as a testimony against you at the last day.

"I advise you to repent and forsake your sins, and no longer seek after the lust of your eyes, but deny yourself these things. Unless you do this, you can never inherit God's kingdom. Oh remember, and take upon yourself the responsibility to repent.

"I command you to counsel with your older brothers in whatever you do, for you are young, and still need their counsel. Do not let yourself be led away by any vain or foolish thing. Do not let the devil lead away your heart again after those wicked harlots. What a great sin you have brought upon the Zoramites, for when they saw your conduct, they would not believe my words.

"The Spirit of the Lord says to me, 'Command your children to do good, or they may lead away the hearts of many people to destruction.' This is why I command you, my son, in the fear of God, to stop your sinfulness. Turn to the Lord with all your mind, might and strength. Stop leading others to sin. Go back to them and admit to them your faults and wrong-doing. Do not seek riches or the vain things of this world, for you cannot carry them with you.

"And now, my son, I will speak to you about the coming of Christ. He will surely come to take away the sins of the world. He comes to declare glad news of salvation to His people. This was the ministry to which you were called—to declare this glad news to our people, that salvation might come to them, and that they may prepare their children to hear the word when Christ comes. I will explain this subject to you, for you wonder why these things need to be known so far ahead of time. Is not a soul just as precious to God now as it will be when He comes? Is it not just as important for the plan of redemption to be known by this people as it will be for their children? Yes, and it is just as easy for the Lord to send His angel to declare this glad news to us as it will be for Him to send His angel to declare it to our children.

40 - Alma instructs his son Corianton...

"Now my son, Corianton, I perceive that you are worried about how the resurrection works, so let me explain it to you. People will not be resurrected until after Christ comes, for only He brings to pass the resurrection of the dead. Now I will explain a mystery to you. There are many mysteries known only by God, so I have prayed intently about the resurrection, to gain my own knowledge of it from Him.

"There is a time appointed, known only by God, when all people will come forth from the dead. It does not matter if there is a first, second, or third time when people come forth from the dead, for God knows all these things. It is sufficient to know that all will rise.

"There is a period between the time people die and when they are resurrected. I have prayed and asked, 'What happens to people's spirits after they die, and before they are resurrected?'

"Again, it does not matter if people are resurrected at different times, for they do not all die at the same time. Everything that happens may as well occur in one day to God, for time is only measured by people on earth. So a time is appointed for all people to rise from the dead, and there is a period of time between death and the resurrection. When the time comes to rise, all will know that God knows their appointed time to rise. It has been made known to me by an angel, that just as soon as their bodies die, the spirits of all men and women are taken home to God, who gave them life. This is the case for both the good and the evil.

"The righteous spirits are received into a state of happiness, called paradise—a state of rest and peace, where they rest from all their trouble, care and sorrow. The spirits of the wicked will be sent into outer darkness. There will be weeping, wailing and clenching of teeth over their own sinfulness—being led captive by the will of the devil. They are evil, having no part of the Lord's Spirit because they chose evil works rather than good, and the devil's spirit entered them. The wicked remain in this dark state, fearfully waiting for God's fiery anger to come upon them, while the righteous remain in paradise until the time of their resurrection.

"Some people think that this state of happiness or misery after death is a first resurrection. I admit that it could be called a resurrection—the raising of the spirit to a consigned state of happiness or misery. Others believe the first resurrection is when everyone who lived before Christ is resurrected along with Him. Perhaps this is true, but in any case, the first resurrection is certainly more than the spirit being assigned to a state of happiness or misery.

"The first resurrection is the reuniting of spirits with their bodies, from Adam and

Eve's time to the resurrection of Christ. I do not know whether or not the spirits of the wicked and the righteous are resurrected all at once. It is enough to say that those who have died, from the time of Adam to the resurrection of Christ, will be resurrected before those who live after Christ's resurrection. I do not say they will all be resurrected along with Christ, for it is my opinion that the righteous who lived before Christ will be resurrected with Him when He ascends into heaven. Whether they will be resurrected at that time or not, I do not know. I only know that there is a time between death and the resurrection—a state of happiness or misery—for all spirits, while they wait, according to God's appointed time, to be reunited with their bodies—to be brought to stand before God and judged according to their works.

"This brings about the restoration of those things mentioned by the prophets. The soul will be restored to the body—to every limb and joint. Not even a hair of the head will be lost, for every part of the body will be restored perfectly. My son, this is the restoration of which the prophets have spoken. At that time, the righteous will shine forth in God's kingdom. But an awful death comes upon the wicked, who die as to things having to do with righteousness, being unclean. And since no unclean thing can inherit God's kingdom, they are cast out and must taste the fruits of their labors, or their works, which have been evil—and their fruit will be bitter.

41 - Alma instructs his son Corianton...

"My son, Corianton, because some people have not read the scriptures, they have gone far astray, and do not understand the plan of restoration. I perceive that you have been worried about this, so I will explain it to you. God's justice requires everything to be properly restored to its own order, according to the power and resurrection of Christ,—that each spirit be restored to its body and that each part of each body be restored to itself.

"God's justice also requires us to be judged according to our works. If our works were good in this life, and the desires of our hearts were good, then at the last day we will be restored to what is good. If our works were evil, then we will be restored to what is evil. This is how all things will be restored to their proper order. First, every imperfect mortal body becomes immortal and perfect. Then every immortal body is joined to its spirit—resurrected—to receive endless happiness and inherit God's kingdom, or to receive endless misery and inherit the devil's kingdom. One is raised to happiness and good according to his desires, while the other is raised to evil according to his desires, for those who desired evil during their lives will have their reward of evil when they die.

"All who repent of their sins, desiring righteousness until the end of their days, will be rewarded with righteousness. All these are redeemed by the Lord—taken out of and delivered from an endless night of darkness. This is how we will stand or fall, being able to judge for ourselves whether to do good or evil. God's decrees are unalterable, and the way is prepared for the righteous to be saved.

"My son, do not risk one more offense against your God upon these points of doctrine, which you have already risked by sinning. Do not think that because I have spoken about a restoration that you will be restored from sin to happiness, for wickedness cannot make anyone happy. My son, all men and women are in a carnal, natural state, bound by sins, and full of bitterness. They are without God in the world, going against His nature—the nature of happiness.

"The word restoration does not mean to take something in a natural state and change it to an unnatural state, opposite to its nature. Restoration means bringing back evil to what is evil, carnal to what is carnal, and devilish to what is devilish. It means bringing goodness back to what is good, righteousness to what is righteous, justice back to what is just, and mercy to what is merciful. Knowing this plan, see that you are merciful to your brethren, my son. Deal justly, judge righteously, and do good continually. If you do all these things, then you will receive your reward, and have mercy, justice, righteousness and good restored to you. For what you send out will return and be restored to you. This is how the plan of restoration fully condemns, rather than justifies, the sinner.

42 - Alma instructs his son Corianton...

Alma continued, "My son, Corianton, I perceive that there is still more that worries you because you do not understand how God's justice punishes the sinner. You are thinking that it is not fair for a sinner to be consigned to a state of misery, so I will explain this to you.

"The Lord God sent our first parents out of the east end of the Garden of Eden to till the earth. Then He placed an angel, wielding a flaming sword, to guard the tree of life.

"At that time, (by eating of the fruit of the tree of knowledge of good and evil), Adam and Eve had become like God, knowing good from evil. If they had eaten of the fruit of the tree of life, they would have become immortal and would have lived forever in their sins.

"But instead, Adam and Eve became mortal—subject to death. The time of their mortality became a time of probation—a time for them to repent and learn to serve God. According to God's word, if they had eaten of the fruit of the tree of life before being sent out of the garden, they would not have had a time to repent. Then God's word would have been void, and the great plan of salvation would have been frustrated.

"But men and women were appointed to die. So just as they were cut off from the tree of life, they would be cut off from the face of the earth. In this natural state, they and their children were lost and fallen from God forever, being cut off from His presence, both temporally and spiritually. This is how we became beings who follow after our own will. In their fallen state, it was not necessary for Adam and Eve to be spared from a temporal death, for that would have destroyed the great plan of happiness. But since their souls were immortal, and their fall had cut them off from the Lord's presence, it was essential for them to be spiritually reclaimed. And since they had become carnal, sensual and devilish by nature, their probationary state became a time for them to prepare and improve.

"Remember my son, if it were not for the plan of redemption, then as soon as we die, our souls would be miserable, being cut off from the Lord's presence forever. Adam and Eve had no way to save themselves from their fallen state—a state they brought upon themselves and their descendants by disobeying God. Without an atonement, mercy alone could not have redeemed Adam and Eve, for mercy could only redeem them after they repented and relied on the atonement. Otherwise, mercy would have destroyed justice (which cannot be destroyed), and God would have ceased to be God.

"Now we see that Adam, Eve and all their descendants were in the grasp of God's justice, which required them be cut off from His presence forever. But the plan of mercy could save them if an atonement were made. This is why God Himself atones for the sins of the world—to bring about the plan of mercy—to appease the demands of justice, that God might be a perfect, just and merciful God. Now, there would be no need for men and women to repent unless their eternal happiness were threatened by an eternal punishment, for the life of the soul is eternal. People can only repent after they sin, which is to break a law that requires the sinner to be punished. These punishments are affixed to just laws, and breaking just laws bring feelings of guilt. For example, if there was no law that said a murderer would be put to death, then potential murderers would have no fear of death.

"With no laws against sin, there would be no fear of sinning. And with no laws, justice and mercy would have no purpose, and there could be no misery nor happiness. This is why laws are given to man by God. Punishments are given by justice while repentance is granted by mercy. Otherwise, everyone would be punished, for without perfect justice, God would cease to be God.

"But God lives, and because of His atonement, His mercy claims those who repent. His atonement also makes possible the resurrection, which brings us all back into His presence, to be judged by our works, according to the law and justice (the application of the law).

"For justice exercises all its demands and mercy claims all who are worthy of it. This is why only those who truly repent will be saved from spiritual death. Do you think that mercy can rob justice? No, not even one bit. If so, God would cease to be God, for His justice brings about His great, eternal purposes, which were prepared before the world was created. Through His justice, all people are resurrected, and either redeemed from their sins or condemned in their sins.

"Remember my son, that all who come may drink the waters of life freely. Those who will not come are not forced, but when they are resurrected at the last day, their works will be restored to them. If they wanted to do evil, and did not repent during their mortal life, then evil will be restored to them by God's justice. My son, do not let these things trouble you any longer. Only let your sins trouble you until they bring you to repentance. Do not make the smallest excuse for your sins, for doing this denies God's justice. Instead, let a realization of God's justice, and His mercy and patience fill your heart and bring you to the depths of humility. Oh my son, you are called of God to preach the word to this people. Now go do this in truth and in soberness. May you bring souls to repentance, that the great plan of mercy may claim them, and you. May God grant this according to my words. Amen."

43 - The wicked Zoramites create war...

After Alma had spoken to his sons, they went to declare the word among the people. Alma could not rest, and he, too, went out to declare the word. Alma and his sons preached the truth according to the spirit of prophecy and revelation—according to the holy order of God, by which they were called.

Now I, Mormon, return to an account of the wars between the Nephites and the Lamanites during 74 BC.

The wicked Zoramites had become Lamanites, and they prepared to fight the Nephites. Seeing this, the Nephites gathered their armies in the land of Jershon. Then thousands of Lamanites came into the Zoramite land of Antionum, led by Zerahemnah. Since the Amalekites and Zoramites were of a more wicked and murderous disposition, Zerahemnah appointed them to be chief captains over the Lamanites. He did this to keep the Lamanites' hatred toward the Nephites strong. Zerahemnah wanted to use the Lamanites' anger for his own designs—to conquer the Nephites and make them his slaves. But all the Nephites wanted was to protect their lands, houses, wives and children from their enemies. They also wanted to preserve their rights, privileges and liberty to worship God according to their desires. They knew that if they fell to the Lamanites, then all those who worshiped the true and living God in spirit and in truth would be killed. The Nephites knew of the Lamanites' hatred toward them and toward the people of Anti-Nephi-Lehi, or Ammon's people—those who would not take up arms, having made a covenant which they refused to break.

If Ammon's people were to fall into the Lamanites' hands, they would all certainly die, so the Nephites had given them protection and lands for their inheritance. Ammon's people gave much of what they had to support the Nephite armies, which were compelled to fight the Lamanites alone. Yet the Lamanites were joined by the Nephite dissenters—the Amalekites, Zoramites and the descendants of Noah's wicked priests (the Amulonites).

The Lamanites and the dissenters were almost as numerous as the Nephites, who had no choice but to fight their brethren. As the Lamanites gathered in the land of Antionum, the Nephite army was prepared to meet them in Jershon. The chief captain over the entire Nephite army was Moroni, age twenty-five. He and his army met the Lamanites at the Jershon border, armed with swords, scimitars and all types of weapons.

The Lamanites saw Moroni's army wearing breastplates, arm-shields, helmets and thick clothing. Zerahemnah's army did not have such protection. They only had swords, scimitars, bows, arrows, stones and slings, and only wore loin cloths, except for the Zoramites and Amalekites.

Because the Nephites were so well protected, the Lamanites were afraid to attack them, even though they greatly outnumbered them. So the Lamanites did not dare come to the Jershon border. They left the land of Antionum and went into the wilderness, going around the Nephite army, near the head of the Sidon River, to take the land of Manti. They thought that Moroni's army would not know where they had gone.

As soon as they went into the wilderness, Moroni sent spies to watch their camp. Moroni also knew of Alma's prophecies, so he sent men to ask Alma to find out from the Lord where his army should go to defend themselves against the Lamanites.

The word of the Lord came to Alma, who informed Moroni's men that the Lamanite army was marching around them into the wilderness, heading toward the land of Manti, to attack their weaker fortifications. Upon receiving this message, Moroni left part of his army in Jershon and took the other part into the land of Manti. Moroni had all the people in Manti gather to battle against the Lamanites—to defend their lands, country, rights and liberties.

Moroni hid part of his army in a valley near the west bank of the Sidon River, and then sent out spies to discover when the Lamanites would come. He knew it was the Lamanites' intention to kill their brethren, or to make them slaves and establish a kingdom for themselves over all the land. He also knew the Nephites only wanted to defend their lands, liberty and church. This is why Moroni did not feel it was wrong to use spies to find out which way the Lamanites were heading.

Moroni used the strategy of dividing his army, hiding part of them in a valley on the east side of the Sidon River, just south of Riplah Hill. He kept the rest hidden in the valley near the west bank of the Sidon River, which ran down toward the Manti border. Having placed his armies according to his desire, Moroni was prepared to meet the Lamanites.

Then, coming from the north side of Riplah Hill, the Lamanite army passed by the hill, and came into the valley where part of Moroni's army was hiding. As they passed through the valley and began to cross the Sidon River, part of Moroni's army, led by Lehi, attacked the Lamanites from behind.

When the Lamanites saw the Nephites coming from behind, they turned and fought Lehi's army. Men on both sides died, but it was more dreadful for the Lamanites. Their bare skin was exposed to the heavy blows of the Nephite swords and scimitars, which brought death at almost every stroke.

A Nephite fell only now and then, having lost too much blood from sword wounds. Their more vital parts were protected by their breastplates, arm-shields and helmets, so it was mostly the Nephites who carried on the work of death among the Lamanites. Seeing this slaughter, the Lamanites became frightened and started to run toward the Sidon River. Lehi and his men chased them into the river and then waited on the bank while the Lamanites crossed over to the west side.

Then Moroni and his army met the Lamanites in the valley on the west side of the river and began to kill them. The Lamanites ran toward the land of Manti, but were again met by Moroni's army. Then the Lamanites fought with more strength and courage than they had ever fought before, even from their beginnings. They were inspired by Zerahemnah and their Zoramite and Amalekite chief captains and leaders. They fought with fierce anger, like dragons, killing many Nephites by slicing many of their helmets in half, by piercing many of their breastplates, and by cutting off many of their arms.

But the Nephites were inspired by a better cause. They were not fighting for kingship or power, but for their homes, liberties, wives, children, church and rites of worship.

They were doing what they felt was their duty to God, for the Lord had said to them and their fathers, "If you are not guilty of the first or second offense, you must not allow yourselves to be killed by your enemies. You will defend your families even if you must kill."

When Moroni's men saw the Lamanites' fierce anger, they were about to run from them. But seeing the situation, Moroni sent word among them to inspire their hearts—to remind them that they were fighting for their lands, their liberty, and their freedom from bondage!

After hearing this, the Nephites turned on the Lamanites, crying with one voice to the Lord their God for their liberty and freedom from bondage. They began to stand against the Lamanites with power during the same hour they had cried to the Lord for their freedom, and they drove many Lamanites into the Sidon River.

The Lamanites outnumbered the Nephites two to one, yet the Lamanites were rounded into one group in the valley near the west bank of the Sidon River. They were surrounded by Moroni's army on the west and by Lehi's army on the east side of the river.

When Zerahemnah's army realized their precarious situation, they were struck with terror. Seeing this, Moroni commanded his men to stop killing them.

44 - Moroni demands an oath...

Then Moroni said to Zerahemnah, "You know that you are in our hands, but we do not want to kill you and become men of bloodshed. We have not come to battle to kill you, or to make you our slaves, but this is exactly why you have come against us. You are angry with us because of our religion.

"But now you see that the Lord is with us and has delivered you into our hands. I want you to understand that this is done because of our religion and our faith in Christ, which you now realize you cannot destroy.

"You must now realize that this is the true faith of God, and that He will support and preserve us as long as we are faithful to Him. The Lord will never allow us to be destroyed unless we fall into transgression and deny our faith.

"And now, Zerahemnah, I command you, in the name of that all-powerful God who has strengthened our arms so that we have gained power over you— by our faith, religion, rites of worship, church and sacred support, which we owe to our wives and children—by that liberty which binds us to our lands and our country—by the maintenance of God's sacred word, to which we owe all our happiness, and by all that is most dear to us—

"I command you, by all the desires that you have for life, to give up your weapons! If you do this, and go your way, and do not come to war against us again, then we will spare your lives. Otherwise, I will command my men to kill you. Then we will see who will have power over this people, and who will be brought into bondage."

When Zerahemnah heard this, he came forward and delivered up his sword, scimitar and bow to Moroni, and said, "These are our weapons of war. We will deliver them up to you, but we will not make such an oath to you—an oath that we know we and our children will break. Take our weapons and allow us to depart into the wilderness. Otherwise we will keep our swords, and perish or conquer.

"We are not of your faith, and we do not believe that a God delivered us into your hands. We believe that your cunning, your breastplates and shields have preserved you from our swords."

When Zerahemnah finished speaking, Moroni gave him back his sword and other weapons, and said, "We will end the conflict, for I cannot recall my words. As the Lord lives, you will not leave here without making an oath that you will not return to war. Now as you are in our hands, we will spill your blood upon the ground, or you will submit to the conditions that I have made."

Upon hearing this, Zerahemnah was so angry with Moroni that he rushed forward to kill him. But as he raised his sword, one of Moroni's soldiers struck it, breaking it off near the handle. Then the soldier struck Zerahemnah, cutting off his scalp, which fell to the ground. And Zerahemnah withdrew into the midst of his soldiers.

Then Moroni's soldier put Zerahemnah's scalp on the point of his sword, held it up high, and shouted, "Even as your chief's scalp has fallen to the earth, so will all of you fall, unless you give up your weapons and depart with a covenant of peace."

Many who heard this and saw the scalp on the sword were struck with fear. They came forward, threw down their weapons at Moroni's feet, and entered into a covenant of peace. Those who entered into a covenant were allowed to depart into the wilderness. Now in great pain, Zerahemnah was very angry. He stirred up the rest of his soldiers to fight even more powerfully against the Nephites.

Seeing this stubbornness, Moroni became angry and commanded his people to kill those who had kept their swords. The Lamanites' bare skin and heads were exposed to the Nephites' sharp swords. They were pierced and stricken, and quickly fell before the Nephites, being swept down as Moroni's soldier had foretold.

When Zerahemnah finally realized that they were all about to be destroyed, he cried out loudly to Moroni, promising that if they were spared, he and his people would covenant never again to come to war against them. Moroni commanded his men to stop the killing and to take away the remaining Lamanites' weapons. After they had all entered into a covenant of peace, they were allowed to depart into the wilderness.

So many of the Lamanites had died that they were not counted, and the losses of both Nephites and Lamanites were very great. The dead were thrown into the Sidon River, which carried the bodies out to the depths of the sea.

Then Moroni's army returned to their houses and lands. This is how 74 BC, the eighteenth year of the judges' reign over the Nephites, ended. This is the end of what Alma wrote on Nephi's large plates.

45 - War ends and Alma questions Helaman...

The Nephites were very happy because the Lord had delivered them from their enemies again. They thanked the Lord their God, fasted and prayed often, and worshiped Him with great joy. In 73 BC, the nineteenth year of judges' reign, Alma visited his son, Helaman, and asked, "Do you believe what I said about the records that have been kept?" Helaman answered, "Yes, I believe." Alma then asked, "Do you believe in Jesus Christ, who will come?" "Yes, I believe all the words you have spoken," answered Helaman. Alma asked, "Will you keep my commandments?" Helaman answered, "Yes, I will keep your commandments with all my heart." Then Alma said, "You are blessed, and the Lord will prosper you in this land. I have a prophecy to tell you, but do not tell it to anyone, for it must not be known until it is fulfilled. For now, only write it down. This is the prophecy: I perceive that this very people, the Nephites, (according to the spirit of revelation in me), will falter in unbelief 400 years after Jesus Christ shows Himself to them. At that time, they will have wars, pestilences, drought and bloodshed—even until they become extinct! This will happen after they receive great light and knowledge, for not even four generations will pass before they become unbelieving, and work in darkness, and become full of all types of sinfulness. When that great day comes, the time is near when our descendants will no longer be counted with the Nephites. Our Nephite descendants who survive that great and dreadful day will be counted with the Lamanites, and will become like them, except for a few—the Lord's disciples, all of whom the Lamanites will hunt down and kill. And because of great sinfulness, this prophecy will be fulfilled."

After Alma said this to Helaman, he blessed him, and also his other sons. Then Alma blessed the earth for the sake of the righteous. He said, "The Lord God says, 'This land will be cursed to every nation, tribe, tongue and people—even to destruction, who become fully ripe in wickedness.' It will be as I have said, for this is God's cursing and blessing upon the land. The reason for this curse is that the Lord cannot allow any degree of sin to be acceptable in His sight."

After blessing the earth, Alma blessed those in the church who would stand firm in the faith from that time forward. Then Alma left the land of Zarahemla and went toward the land of Melek. He was never heard of again, and we know nothing of his death or burial.

We know that he was a righteous man. Among the church members, it was widely believed that Alma was taken up by the Spirit, or buried by the hand of the Lord, like Moses.

In the beginning of 73 BC, Alma's son Helaman went among the people to declare God's word to them. Because of their wars with the Lamanites, and because of the many little dissensions and disturbances that had been among the people, it became necessary for God's word to be declared, and for the church to be regulated.

Helaman and his brothers established the church once again, appointing priests and teachers in every city throughout all the Nephite lands. But after the church was established, a dissension arose among those who refused to listen to Helaman or his brethren. They grew proud, lifting themselves up because of their great riches. They grew rich in their own eyes, and would not listen to God's words nor walk uprightly before Him.

46 - Church members led away by flattery...

Those who would not listen to Helaman and his brothers gathered against them, and were determined to kill them. The leader of these angry apostates was Amalickiah, a large, strong man. Amalickiah wanted to be king, and his followers also wanted him to be king. Most of the lower judges of the land had become angry apostates, desiring more and more power. They had been led along by Amalickiah's flattering words, who promised them ruling positions over the people if they helped him to become king. This is how Amalickiah led the dissensions in spite of the preaching of Helaman and his brethren, who as high priests, took great care of the church. Many church members believed in Amalickiah's flattery and left the church. Because of this situation, the Nephite affairs became very precarious and unstable, even though they had just been victorious over the Lamanites, and had greatly rejoiced in being delivered by the Lord.

From this we learn just how quickly people forget the Lord their God and return to sin, being led away by the evil one. We also learn how only one man can cause great wickedness among the people. For Amalickiah led many hearts away by his cunning plans and flattering words, seeking to destroy God's church and the foundation of liberty—a blessing that God had sent upon the land for the sake of the righteous.

When Moroni, chief commander of the Nephite army, heard about these dissensions, he was very angry with Amalickiah. He tore off a piece of his coat to make a flag, and on it he wrote, "In memory of our God, our religion, our freedom, our peace, our wives and our children." Then he fastened the flag to the end of a pole. After putting on his helmet, breastplate, shields and armor, Moroni took his flag, which he called The Title of Liberty, and bowed himself to the earth. He prayed mightily to his God for the blessings of liberty to rest upon his brethren, as long as a band of Christians was left in the land. All the true believers of Christ, who belonged to God's church, were called Christians by the non-believers.

Those who belonged to the church, who truly believed in Christ, were faithful to Him. They gladly took on the name Christians because they believed in Christ who would come.

Moroni prayed for the Christians' cause and for freedom in the land to be favored. After he had poured out his soul to God, he named all the land that was south of Desolation, both the northern and southern parts, "A chosen land, the land of liberty." Then Moroni said, "Surely God will not allow us, who are despised because we take the name of Christ upon us, to be trodden down and destroyed, until we bring it upon ourselves by our own transgressions."

Then Moroni went among the people, holding his flag in the air for all to see its message. He shouted, "Whoever would maintain this title upon the land, come forward in the strength of the Lord and enter into a covenant to maintain your rights and religion, that the Lord God may bless you!" When he had proclaimed this, the people came running, wearing their armor and tearing their coats as a covenant that they would not forsake the Lord their God. In other words, if they transgressed God's commandments, and became ashamed to be called Christians, then the Lord would justly tear them, as they had torn their coats.

As they threw their coats at Moroni's feet, they said, "We covenant with our God that we will be destroyed like our brethren in the northern land (the Jaredites) if we fall into transgression. God may throw us at the feet of our enemies, as we have thrown our coats, to be trampled under foot, if we ever fall into transgression." Then Moroni said, "We are descendants of Jacob (Israel), the father of Joseph of old, whose coat was torn into many pieces by his brothers. Now let us remember to keep God's commandments, or our coats will be torn by our brethren, and we will be thrown into prison, sold or killed. Let us preserve our liberty as descendants of Joseph of old. Let us remember the words of his father, Israel, who before his death, saw that a remnant of his son's coat had been preserved. He said, 'Even as this remnant of my son's coat has been preserved, a remnant of my son's descendants will be preserved by God's hand, to be taken to Himself. The rest of Joseph's descendants will perish, just as the rest of Joseph's coat has perished. This brings sorrow to my soul, but my soul has joy in my son, Joseph, because of the part of his descendants that will be taken to God.'"

Moroni then speculated, "Perhaps the remnant of Joseph's descendants that will perish, like his coat, are those who have dissented from us. Surely we will be part of the destroyed remnant if we do not stand firm in the faith of Christ."

After saying this, Moroni went out himself, and also sent letters to all parts of the land where there were dissensions. In this way, he gathered all who wanted to maintain their liberty by standing against Amalickiah and his dissenters, called Amalickiahites.

When Amalickiah saw that Moroni's people outnumbered his followers, and that his followers also had doubts about the justice of their cause, he was afraid that they would not prevail. So he took his faithful followers and headed toward the land of Nephi to join the Lamanites.

Moroni did not want the Lamanites to gain any more strength. He knew that he had to bring back Amalickiah and his followers and put Amalickiah to death. Otherwise, they would stir up the Lamanites to become angry and to battle against them in order to obtain their own purposes. Moroni knew he had to take his army, who had entered into a covenant to keep the peace, and stop Amalickiah in the wilderness. Moroni acted on this, and marched his army into the wilderness to head off Amalickiah's army. Upon seeing Moroni's army, Amalickiah ran away with a few of his men. The rest of his army fell into Moroni's hands and were taken back to the land of Zarahemla.

Moroni had been given authority over the Nephite army by the chief judges, who in turn had been elected by the people. With this authority, Moroni had every Amalickiahite put to death who would not enter into a covenant to support the cause of freedom and maintain a free government. Only a few would not enter this covenant of freedom. Moroni ordered The Title of Liberty to be raised up on every tower in all the land, thereby planting a standard of liberty among the Nephites. They had peace in the land until the end of 73 BC.

Helaman and the high priests were able to maintain order in the church for four years, during which they had peace and rejoicing. Many went out of the world rejoicing, firmly believing that their souls were redeemed by the Lord Jesus Christ.

Some died from the seasonal fevers, but not many, for they were healed by the excellent qualities of the plants and roots that God had prepared to remove the causes of their diseases.

Note: Another herbal recommendation is found in D&C 42:43.

Many died of old age, and we must suppose that those who died in the faith of Christ are happy with Him

47 - *Amalickiah gains power...*

Now we will return to our record of Amalickiah and of those who ran into the wilderness with him. They joined the Lamanites in the land of Nephi, and as Moroni had predicted, they made the Lamanites angry with the Nephites. The Lamanite king sent a message throughout all his land, telling his people to prepare for war against the Nephites. When the Lamanites heard this message, they were very afraid to displease the king, yet they were also afraid to fight the Nephites. Most of them decided not to obey the king's command.

This made the king very angry. He gave Amalickiah command of those who would fight and told him to force the other Lamanites to fight. This is exactly what Amalickiah wanted the Lamanite king to do, for he was cunning and had an evil plan to take the king's throne and become king himself.

As commander of part of the Lamanite army, Amalickiah had a plan to gain the support of the Lamanites who had refused to obey the king's orders. He and his army went to Onidah, a place where the weapons were kept. All the rebelling Lamanites had gone there, thinking that Amalickiah's army was coming to kill them.

The rebels had appointed Lehonti as their own king, and were determined not to be forced to fight the Nephites. They prepared to defend themselves from the top of Mt. Antipas.

Amalickiah had no intention of fighting the rebels as the king had commanded him to do. He wanted to gain favor with all the Lamanite men, and thereby obtain an army to take the king's throne and take control of the kingdom.

Amalickiah had his army camp in the valley near Mt. Antipas. By night, Amalickiah sent a secret embassy to the top of Mt. Antipas, asking the rebels' leader, King Lehonti, to come down and talk with him. Lehonti would not dare go down, so Amalickiah sent another message to him, again asking him to come down. Lehonti refused again, and also a third time. Seeing that Lehonti would not come down, Amalickiah went up near Lehonti's camp and sent his fourth message to him, asking him to come down, and to bring his guards with him. Lehonti finally came down with his guards. Amalickiah told Lehonti that if he brought his army down that night and surrounded the men under his command, he would deliver them into Lehonti's hands, providing that he, Amalickiah, would be made second in command.

Lehonti came down with his men and surrounded Amalickiah's army before they awoke. When the men saw that they were surrounded, they begged Amalickiah to allow them to join their brethren, and not be destroyed. This was exactly what Amalickiah wanted them to do. He delivered his men, contrary to the commands of the Lamanite king, as part of his plan to dethrone him.

Now according to Lamanite custom, if their chief leader was killed, the second in command was made chief leader. So Amalickiah had a servant give small doses of poison to Lehonti, until he died. Amalickiah was appointed to be their leader and chief commander. Then he marched with his armies to the land of Nephi—to the capital city of Nephi. The king came out to meet him with his guards, thinking that Amalickiah had fulfilled his commands by gathering this great army to go against the Nephites. As the king came out to meet him, Amalickiah sent his servants ahead. They bowed before the king, as if to reverence him because of his greatness.

The king held out his hand to raise them. This custom—a token of peace—had been taken from the Nephites. As the king raised the first servant, that servant stabbed him in the heart, and the king fell dead. Frightened, the king's servants ran away, and Amalickiah's servants shouted, "The king's own servants have stabbed him and have run away. Come and see!" Amalickiah commanded his army to go and see what had happened to the king. When they found the king dead, Amalickiah pretended to be angry, and said, "Whoever loved the king, let them chase his servants and kill them."

Then all those who loved the king chased the king's servants. When the servants saw an army pursuing them, they were frightened again and ran into the wilderness. They went into the land of Zarahemla and joined Ammon's people. The Lamanite army returned, having pursued the servants in vain. This is how Amalickiah, by his fraud, gained the confidence of the people.

The next day he entered the city of Nephi with his armies and took possession of it. Amalickiah sent an embassy to the queen informing her that the king had been murdered by his servants, and that he had chased them with his army but had not caught them. When the queen received this message, she sent a message to Amalickiah, asking him to spare the people of the city. She also wanted him to come to her with witnesses to testify of the king's death. Amalickiah brought the same servant who had stabbed the king, and the others who were with him, and went to the queen. They all testified to her that the king was killed by his own servants, whose guilt was proven by the fact that they had run away. The queen was satisfied with their story.

Then Amalickiah sought the favor of the queen and married her. This is how by his fraud, and by the assistance of his cunning servants, he obtained the kingdom. He was acknowledged as the king throughout all the land, among all the Lamanites, which included Lemuelites, Ishmaelites and all the Nephite dissenters since the days of Nephi.

Now these dissenters had been taught about the Lord. But it is strange to relate that not long after they dissented, they became more stubborn, unrepentant, wild, wicked and ferocious than the Lamanites. They embraced the Lamanites' false traditions, and gave way to all types of sin, completely forgetting the Lord their God.

48 - Amalickiah seeks for total power...

Just as soon as Amalickiah had obtained the kingdom, he began to inspire the Lamanites to hate the Nephites. He appointed men to speak from their towers against the Nephites.

By the end of 73 BC, having accomplished his plans so far, Amalickiah sought to reign over all the people, Nephite and Lamanite.

After blinding their minds and making them angry, he gathered a numerous host of Lamanites to battle against the Nephites. Amalickiah was determined (knowing how numerous his people were) to overpower the Nephites and bring them into bondage.

He appointed Zoramites as chief captains, for they were the most acquainted with the Nephite strongholds and the weakest parts of their cities. The chief captains led the Lamanite armies into the wilderness toward the land of Zarahemla.

While Amalickiah had been obtaining power by fraud and deceit, Moroni had been preparing his people to be faithful to the Lord their God. He had also been strengthening the Nephite armies by ordering them to build small forts, to pile up banks of dirt around them to enclose his armies, and to build stone walls around their cities and the borders of all their lands.

Moroni placed the greatest number of men in the cities with the weakest fortifications. He was preparing to support their liberty, lands, wives, children and peace, so they might live to serve the Lord their God and maintain what their enemies called, "the Christians' cause."

Moroni was strong and mighty. He had a perfect understanding and did not delight in bloodshed. His soul rejoiced in the liberty and freedom of his country. His heart swelled with thanksgiving to his God for the many privileges and blessings that He had bestowed upon his people, and he worked hard for their welfare and safety. He was firm in the faith of Christ, and he had sworn an oath to defend his people, their rights, country and religion, even to the loss of his own blood.

The Nephites were taught to defend themselves against their enemies, shedding blood if necessary. They were also taught never to begin an offense, and only to raise the sword against an aggressor in defense of their lives. They believed that if they were faithful in keeping God's commandments, He would prosper them in the land and warn them to run or to prepare for war according to their danger.

They also believed that God would tell them where to go to defend themselves against their enemies, and that by doing so, He would deliver them. This was Moroni's belief. His heart did not glory in the victories of warfare, but rather in doing good, in preserving his people, in keeping God's commandments, and in resisting sinfulness.

If all men had been, or would be, like Moroni, the very powers of hell would have been shaken forever, and the devil would have never had power over anyone's heart. Moroni was like Ammon, and also like Mosiah's other sons. He was also like Alma and his sons, for they were all men of God.

Helaman and his brethren's service to the Nephites was just as important as Moroni's service, for they preached God's word and baptized unto repentance all those who would listen to the gospel. Because of their words, the people humbled themselves. They were highly favored of the Lord and were free from internal wars and contentions for four years. But as I said, toward the end of 73 BC, in spite of their peace among themselves, they were reluctantly compelled to fight their brethren, the Lamanites.

Even though they were very reluctant to fight, their wars with the Lamanites lasted for many years. They were sorry to take up arms because they did not delight in war. They were sorry to be the means of sending so many of their brethren out of this world to an eternal world, unprepared to meet their God.

But they could not lay down their own lives and allow their wives and children to be massacred by the barbaric cruelty of those who had once been their brethren but who had left their church. They could not allow the Lamanites to rejoice in killing them as long as any of them kept God's commandments, for the Lord's promise was that if they kept His commandments, they would prosper in the land.

49 - An inspired system of defense...

On the tenth day of the eleventh month of 73 BC, the Lamanite armies were seen approaching the land of Ammonihah. That city of Ammonihah had been partly rebuilt, and Moroni had stationed an army near its border. They had piled up banks of dirt around the city, which protected them from stones and arrows—the principal Lamanite weapons.

Because the Lamanites had once destroyed Ammonihah, they thought they could easily destroy it again, not knowing that they had been allowed to destroy it before because the people there had been so wicked.

The Lamanites were greatly disappointed, for the bank of dirt around the city was so high that they could not hit the Nephites with their stones and arrows. The only way they could come in was through a single entrance. The Zoramite chief captains were very surprised by the Nephites' wisdom in preparing their places of security. They had thought their great numbers would allow them to easily conquer Ammonihah again. They had also prepared themselves with shields, breastplates and thick clothing. They thought they would be able to overpower the Nephites, and kill and capture them as they pleased. But to their complete astonishment, the Nephites were prepared for them in a way never before known among Lehi's descendants, having prepared for battle according to Moroni's instructions.

If King Amalickiah had come out of the land of Nephi at the head of his army, perhaps he would have ordered the Lamanites to attack the city of Ammonihah, for he did not care how many Lamanites died in battle.

But Amalickiah had not come to battle, and the Zoramite chief captains dared not attack the city of Ammonihah. Moroni had changed the Nephites' tactics, and the Lamanites were disappointed in their desire to conquer because of the Nephite strongholds. The Lamanites retreated into the wilderness and marched toward the land of Noah, thinking it was the next best place to attack the Nephites.

They did not know that Moroni had fortified every city in all the land, so they marched with firm determination. Their chief captains came forward and took an oath that they would destroy the people in the next city.

Upon arriving, they were astonished to see the city of Noah, once a very weak place, now a stronger fortification than Ammonihah! This had been done according to Moroni's wisdom. He knew the Lamanites would be frightened upon seeing the city of Ammonihah, and then would come to the city of Noah, which had once been the weakest city in the land.

Lehi, whose army had fought the Lamanites in the valley east of the Sidon River, was appointed by Moroni to be chief captain over the men in the city of Noah. When the Lamanites learned that Lehi commanded the city, they were disappointed again, for they were very much afraid of Lehi. But their chief captains had sworn with an oath to attack the city, so they advanced their armies.

The only way the Lamanites could penetrate the fort was through the entrance, for the bank of dirt was too high, and the ditch was too deep, except at the front entrance. From the top of the bank, the Nephites were ready to shoot arrows and sling rocks at anyone attempting to climb up to enter their fort by any way other than the entrance. Within the entrance, the Nephites had placed their strongest men, armed with swords and slings, to strike down any who attempted to come through. When the Lamanite captains ordered their armies to attack the entrance, they were driven back again and again with an immense slaughter.

When they realized that they could not get through the pass, they started to dig down the dirt banks to make a pass for their armies. As they did this, they were swept off by Nephite stones and arrows. The Lamanites tried to fill up the ditches by pulling down the dirt, but instead the ditches were partly filled with their dead and wounded bodies.

The Nephites had complete power over their enemies, who continued to make attempts to take their stronghold until all their chief captains were dead. Over 1,000 Lamanites were killed, but not a single Nephite was killed.

The Nephites had been protected by their shields, breastplates and helmets. However, about fifty Nephites had been wounded in their legs, some very severely, having been exposed to Lamanite arrows through the pass. After their chief captains had all been killed, the Lamanites ran away into the wilderness. They returned to the land of Nephi and told their king, Amalickiah, a Nephite by birth, about their great loss. He was very angry with his people for not obtaining his desire to subject the Nephites with the yoke of bondage. He cursed God and cursed Moroni, swearing with an oath that he would drink Moroni's blood.

On the other hand, the Nephites thanked the Lord their God because of His matchless power in delivering them from the hands of their enemies. This is how 73 BC ended. The Nephites enjoyed continual peace and great prosperity in the church, for they had diligently obeyed God's word that had been declared to them by Alma's sons, Helaman, Shiblon, and Corianton, by Ammon and his brethren, and by all who had been ordained by the holy order of God, who had been baptized unto repentance and sent forth to preach among them.

50 - Nephites drive out the Lamanites...

It was now 72 BC, and Moroni continued to have his people pile up banks of dirt around all the Nephite cities. On top of these ridges surrounding the cities, walls of timber were built as high as a man. And sharpened stakes were attached to the tops of these strong, high walls of timber. Moroni also had secure towers built from which the Nephites could see over their walls and still be safe from Lamanite stones and arrows. The towers were positioned so that stones could be slung down upon any who would attempt to approach the city walls. This is how Moroni had his people build strongholds in every city in all their lands.

After doing this, Moroni took his armies into the eastern wilderness and drove all the Lamanites there back into their own lands, which were south of the land of Zarahemla. The border of the Lamanite lands ran directly from the east sea to the west sea. After driving all the Lamanites out of the eastern wilderness, which was north of the Lamanite lands, he allowed his people in the land of Zarahemla to occupy the eastern wilderness all the way to the eastern seashore.

Then Moroni placed armies on their southern borders and had them build fortifications. By doing this, the Lamanite strongholds from the eastern wilderness to the west were cut off.

The border between the Nephites and Lamanites, which ran from west to east, south of Zarahemla, was now completely controlled by the Nephites. The Nephites possessed all the northern land and also all the land north of the land of Bountiful.

Moroni's armies grew larger every day because the men felt assured of protection within all the fortifications. Moroni and his armies weakened the Lamanites and cut them off from the Nephite lands in the north.

Then the Nephites began to build a city named Moroni. It was on the south, near the eastern seashore, and bordered the Lamanite land. The Nephites also began to build a city named Nephihah located between the city of Moroni and the city of Aaron, which joined their borders. The construction of many cities in the north began that year. One of these cities, named Lehi, was located near the eastern seashore.

This is how 72 BC ended. During the following year, the twenty-first year of the judges' reign, the Nephites continued to be prosperous. They were a very prosperous and rich people, quickly populating and growing strong in the land.

From this we see the Lord's mercy and justice in fulfilling all His words to His people. At this time, these words that He spoke to father Lehi were verified: "You and your children are blessed, and they will continue to be blessed if they keep my commandments. But remember, if they will not keep my commandments, they will be cut off from my presence."

From this period of Nephite history we learn that these promises were verified. For it was not the Lord, but their internal quarreling, contention, murders, plundering, idolatry, sexual impurity and other great sins that brought on the Nephite wars and destruction.

Those among them who were faithful in keeping the Lord's commandments were delivered at all times, while thousands of their wicked brethren were consigned to bondage or death, or to falter in unbelief and mix with the Lamanites. There was never a happier time among the Nephites since the days of Nephi than in the days of Moroni in 71 BC.

The years 70 and 69 BC were also peaceful for the Nephites.

Sixty-eight BC was a peaceful year except for some internal disputes that arose over the lands of Lehi and Morianton, which bordered the land of Lehi. The people who possessed the land of Morianton claimed part of the land of Lehi. This caused some serious fighting, for the people of Morianton took up swords against their brethren and were determined to kill them. But the people in the land of Lehi ran to Moroni's camp and begged for his assistance, for they were not in the wrong.

When the people of Morianton, led by Morianton, heard that the people of Lehi had run to Moroni's camp, they were very afraid that Moroni's army would come and destroy them. So Morianton planned with his people to run to the northern land, a land covered with large lakes, and take possession of it. This plan would have been carried out and caused great sorrow had it not been for Morianton's bad temper. He was angry with one of his maid servants and beat her very badly. She ran over to Moroni's camp and told him what Morianton had done to her, and that he was planning to run away into the northern land. Moroni was afraid that the people in Bountiful would listen to Morianton and unite with him, taking control of the northern land and jeopardizing his people's freedom. Because of this threat to their freedom, Moroni sent an army to head off Morianton and prevent his people from going into the northern land.

Moroni's men headed them off at the border of the land of Desolation, near the narrow pass that led to the northern land, with a sea on the west and the east. The Nephite army that Moroni sent was led by a man named Teancum. He killed Morianton during the battle which broke out (for Morianton's flattery had made his people stubborn enough to take up the sword). Teancum took Morianton's people as prisoners and returned to Moroni's camp. This is how 68 BC ended—the twenty-fourth year of the judges' reign over the Nephites.

After Morianton's people were brought back, and after they covenanted to keep the peace, they were restored to the land of Morianton. They became united with Lehi's people, who were also restored to their lands. That same year, the second chief judge, Nephihah, died. He had filled the judgment-seat with perfect uprightness before God. However, he had refused to take possession of the plates and sacred things, so Alma had conferred them upon his son, Helaman.

Nephihah's son, Pahoran, was appointed to fill the judgment-seat as chief judge and governor over the people. With an oath and sacred ordinance, Pahoran covenanted to judge righteously, to keep the peace and freedom of the people, to allow them their sacred privileges to worship the Lord their God, to support and maintain the cause of God all his days, and to bring the wicked to justice according to their crimes. He began his reign toward the end of 68 BC.

51 - Freeman vs. Kingman...

Sixty-seven BC began with peace in the Nephite lands. But soon the people started to have internal political disputes, for a few people wanted to change parts of the law. Pahoran ignored those who had sent him their petitions and would not allow the law to be changed.

Those who wanted the law to be changed were angry with him and wanted him to give up the judgment-seat. They caused some heated arguing, but no bloodshed. Those who wanted to get rid of Pahoran were called Kingmen, for they wanted to overthrow the free government and establish a king over the land.

Pahoran's supporters called themselves Freemen. They covenanted to maintain their rights and the privileges of their religion by a free government. The matter was settled by a vote, and the majority was in favor of the Freemen. Pahoran retained the judgment-seat, over which the people of liberty rejoiced. The Kingmen were silenced and dared not oppose, but were obliged to maintain the cause of freedom. Those in favor of kings were of high birth (descendants of Nephite kings) and they wanted to be kings themselves. They were supported by those who wanted power and authority over the people.

This was a critical time for the Nephites to be having internal contentions, for Amalickiah had stirred up the hearts of the Lamanites to come against the Nephites again. He was gathering soldiers from all parts of his land and diligently arming them, for he had made an oath to drink Moroni's blood.

We will see that Amalickiah's oath was foolish, and yet he prepared his armies to go to battle against the Nephites. His armies were not as great as they had once been, because thousands of his men had been killed by the Nephites. But in spite of their great losses, Amalickiah gathered such a great army that he was not afraid to come to the land of Zarahemla.

In 67 BC, just as the Nephites had settled the matter concerning Pahoran, Amalickiah led his Lamanite army toward the land of the Nephites. When the Kingmen heard that the Lamanites were coming to battle against them, they were glad in their hearts and refused to take up arms. When Moroni saw this, and saw that the Lamanites were marching toward their borders, his soul was filled with anger toward the Kingmen. He was angry because they had become so stubborn after he had worked so hard to preserve their liberty.

Moroni sent a petition to Pahoran, the chief judge and governor of the land, which voiced Moroni's and the people's desire. He asked to be given the power to compel the Kingmen to defend their country or be put to death. Moroni's first priority was to put an end to the internal disputes and dissensions among the Nephites, which had caused all their previous destruction. And according to the voice of the people, Moroni was granted the power to compel the Kingmen.

Then Moroni commanded his army to go against the Kingmen and pull down their pride and nobility, leveling them to the earth unless they took up arms to support the cause of liberty. As the Kingmen lifted their weapons against Moroni's army, they were leveled to the earth. Four thousand dissenters were killed by the sword, and their leaders who had not been killed were put into prison. There was no time for their trials, for the Lamanites were coming.

Rather than be killed, the rest of the Kingmen were compelled to raise The Title of Liberty upon their towers, and in their cities, and to take up arms in defense of their country.

This is how Moroni put an end to those Kingmen and to the stubbornness and pride of those who professed noble blood. They were brought down to humble themselves like their brethren, and to fight valiantly to maintain their freedom from bondage.

While Moroni was dealing with these internal contentions and making regulations to prepare for war, the Lamanites came into the land of Moroni near the eastern seashore. The Nephites in the city of Moroni were not strong, so Amalickiah killed many of them and drove them out. Amalickiah took possession of the city and all of its fortifications. Those who ran out of the city of Moroni came to the city of Nephihah. The people in that city, and also in the city of Lehi, gathered and made preparations to battle the Lamanites.

Amalickiah had not attacked with all of his men. He had left many of them in Moroni to maintain and defend it while he marched on to other cities. He took many east coast cities, including Nephihah, Lehi, Morianton, Omner, Gid, and Mulek. By Amalickiah's cunning, and with his numberless hosts, he took the strongly fortified cities for the Lamanites. Then he and his army marched north to the borders of the land Bountiful, driving the Nephites before them and killing many. Then he met Teancum's army.

Teancum headed off Amalickiah, preventing his army's advance into the northern lands, just as he had previously headed off Morianton's rebellion. Teancum's men were great warriors. Each of them was stronger than any Lamanite and more skillful in warfare. They distressed and killed the Lamanites until nightfall. Then Teancum and his men pitched their tents inside the land of Bountiful while Amalickiah's men pitched their tents near the beach.

That night, on the eve of the new year, Teancum and his servant went into Amalickiah's camp. The whole army was asleep, worn out from fighting during the heat of the day.

Teancum sneaked into Amalickiah's tent and put a javelin through his heart, killing him instantly so that he did not wake his servants. Then Teancum went back to his camp, woke his men and told them what he had done. They made themselves ready for the Lamanites in case they had awakened and were coming to attack them. This is how 67 BC ended.

52 - Teancum and Moroni fight separately...

On the first day of 66 BC, the Lamanites awoke and found Amalickiah dead in his tent. They also saw Teancum's army, ready for another day of battle. All of this frightened them, and they retreated into the city of Mulek, seeking protection from within its fortifications. Then Amalickiah's brother, Ammoron, was appointed king over the Lamanites. He commanded his people to maintain the cities they had taken at the cost of so many of their men.

When Teancum saw their determination to maintain the cities they had taken, and saw their enormous numbers, he decided not to attack them in their forts. He kept his men nearby, making preparations for war and building their own protective walls. Teancum's men continued to make their preparations while they waited for Moroni to send reinforcements.

Moroni sent orders for Teancum to take prisoners as a ransom for the many Nephite prisoners taken by the Lamanites. He also sent orders to fortify the land of Bountiful and secure the narrow pass that led into the northern land. Otherwise, the Lamanites would obtain that pass and have power to torment them on every side.

Moroni wrote to Teancum, telling him to be faithful in maintaining that part of the land while he, Moroni, did everything in his power to regain their cities and fortify the cities that had not fallen to the Lamanites. Moroni wrote, "I would have come to your assistance, but the Lamanites are upon us in the borders near the west sea. I must go against them, so I cannot come to your assistance at this time."

King Ammoron left the land of Zarahemla, and told the Lamanite queen that Amalickiah had been killed. Then he gathered a large number of men and marched against the Nephites near the west sea. King Ammoron wanted to harass the Nephites and draw away part of their forces to the west sea while his forces in the conquered cities harassed the Nephites near the east sea, to take possession of as much land as they could. Because of Ammoron's tactics, the Nephites were in a dangerous position by the end of 66 BC.

In 65 BC, Moroni had established armies to protect the southern and western borders. Then he began his march toward the land of Bountiful to assist Teancum's army in retaking their east coast cities. Teancum had received orders to attack the city of Mulek and retake it if possible. As he prepared to attack Mulek, he realized that it would be impossible to overpower its fortifications. So he gave up his plans and went back to the city of Bountiful to wait for Moroni's reinforcements. Toward the end of 65 BC, Moroni and his army arrived in the land of Bountiful.

In the beginning of 64 BC, Moroni, Teancum and many chief captains held a war council to decide how to draw the Lamanites out of their stronghold. They decided to send an embassy to Jacob, the leader of the Lamanite army in the city of Mulek. They asked him to come out with his armies and meet them upon the plains between the two cities. But when Jacob, who was a Zoramite, received their message, he refused to come out with his army. With no hope of meeting them on fair grounds, Moroni made a plan to lure the Lamanites out of their strongholds. He sent Teancum with a small number of men to the beach on the east side of Mulek. That night, Moroni and his army went into the wilderness on the west side of the city. The next day, when the Lamanite guards saw Teancum and his men, they ran and told Jacob. Then the Lamanite army came out against Teancum's men, thinking they could easily destroy them because of their small numbers. But Teancum and his men ran north along the coast. When the Lamanites saw this, they became over-confident and chased them vigorously. While Teancum was leading away the Lamanites, who were pursuing them in vain, part of Moroni's army took possession of Mulek, and all the Lamanites in Mulek who would not give up their weapons were killed.

Meanwhile, Moroni and the rest of his army marched out to meet the Lamanites that would return from pursuing Teancum. As the Lamanites chased Teancum, they came close to the city of Bountiful and met Lehi and his small army, who had been left to protect that city.

When the Lamanite chief captains saw Lehi coming with his army, they panicked and ran back toward the city of Mulek. They were afraid of being overtaken before they could get back to the safety of Mulek, for they were tired and Lehi's men were fresh.

The Lamanites did not know they were heading straight toward part of Moroni's army. All they feared were Lehi and his men, (who did not want to overtake them until they had met Moroni's army).

The Lamanites had not retreated far when they were surrounded by Nephites—Lehi on the north and Moroni on the south, all fresh and full of strength. The Lamanites were very tired, having marched long and hard. Moroni commanded his men to attack them until they gave up their weapons. Their leader, Jacob, a Zoramite, had an unconquerable spirit. He led the Lamanites to battle with great fury against Moroni. Jacob was determined to kill Moroni's men and cut his way back to Mulek, but Moroni and his men were more powerful. Both sides fought with great fury. Moroni was wounded and many Nephites and Lamanites were killed, including Jacob. Then from behind, Lehi and his strong men attacked with such fury that the Lamanites in the rear gave up their weapons. The rest of them were so confused, they did not know which way to go or strike. Seeing their confusion, Moroni shouted, "If you will give up your weapons, we will not kill you." Upon hearing this, the Lamanites' remaining chief captains threw down their weapons at Moroni's feet and commanded their men to do the same. Many would not, so their weapons were taken from them and their hands were tied. Then they were forced to march with their brethren to the land of Bountiful. The number of prisoners taken was greater than the number of those who had been killed on both sides. Moroni placed guards over the Lamanite prisoners and forced them to bury all the dead Nephites and Lamanites.

53 - Nephites prepare amidst dissent...

Moroni gave Lehi command of the city of Mulek. Lehi had been with Moroni in nearly all his battles. He and Moroni were much alike, and they rejoiced in one another's safety. They loved each other and the Nephites loved them.

When the Lamanites finished burying the dead, they were marched back into the land of Bountiful. Moroni ordered Teancum to force them to dig a ditch around the city of Bountiful. On the city side of the ditch, the Lamanites were forced to build a strong, high retaining wall of timber. After this was done, Bountiful became a great stronghold, and the Nephites guarded the Lamanite prisoners within its walls. Moroni had to make the Lamanites work because it required fewer men to guard them while they worked, and he needed most of his forces to attack the Lamanites.

Moroni had gained a victory over a great Lamanite army, had regained the city of Mulek—a great Lamanite stronghold, and he had built a stronghold in Bountiful to retain his prisoners. He did not attempt to battle with the Lamanites again that year, but instead had his men prepare for war by making fortifications and growing food, which kept their women, children and armies from suffering.

And now, while Moroni went to settle more internal dissensions, the Lamanite army took possession of a number of cities in the southern land near the west sea. And because of their own sinfulness, dissensions and intrigue, the Nephites were again placed in the most dangerous of circumstances.

Now I, Mormon, have something to say about Ammon's people (the Anti-Nephi-Lehies), who in the beginning were Lamanites, but were converted to the Lord by His power and word. Ever since they had come to the land of Zarahemla, they had been protected by the Nephites. Because of their oath never to kill again, they had not taken up arms against their Lamanite brethren. And because of their oath, they would have been killed if Ammon and the other Nephites had not had pity on them and a great love for them.

And because of their love for them, the Nephites had brought them into the land of Zarahemla and had protected them.

But when Ammon's people saw the danger, and the many afflictions and tribulations that the Nephites bore for them, they were moved with compassion and wanted to take up arms to help defend their country. They were about to break their oath, but were convinced not to by Helaman and his brethren. Helaman was afraid that if they took up arms they would lose their souls. Those who had entered this covenant had been compelled to watch their brethren go through afflictions and dangerous circumstances, while they could do nothing to help them.

But they had many sons who had not entered into this covenant. The sons who were able, gathered together and took up arms. They called themselves Nephites and entered into a covenant to fight for the Nephites, to protect the land with their lives and never give up their liberty. Two thousand young men made this covenant and took up their weapons to defend their country.

Before this time, Ammon's people had not been a burden to the Nephites, yet they could not help them fight. But now, at this time of Nephite dissent, they were a great help to the Nephite cause. Their sons took up their weapons, and they asked Helaman to be their leader. They were all young men, all valiant, courageous, full of energy and strength. They were also true to all with which they were entrusted. They were serious minded, for they had been taught to keep God's commandments and to walk uprightly before Him.

Helaman marched at the head of his 2,000 young soldiers in the cause to support the people in the southern border near the western sea. And this is how 64 BC ended.

54 - Moroni's reply to Ammoron's letter...

In the beginning of 63 BC, Ammoron, the Lamanite king, sent a message to Moroni requesting an exchange of prisoners. Moroni was happy with this request, for he needed the provisions being used to support the Lamanite prisoners for his own people. He also wanted to increase the size of his army.

The Lamanites had taken many women, children and men as prisoners, but Moroni had only taken Lamanite men as prisoners. He had a strategy to get back many of his captured people. He wrote a letter and gave it to Ammoron's servant, who had delivered Ammoron's message to him. The letter read:

"Ammoron, I have written to you about this war that you have waged against my people, or rather that your brother has waged against them, which you are still determined to carry on after his death. The sword of God's almighty wrath hangs over you unless you repent and take your armies back to the land of your possession, the land of Nephi. I would tell you more about these things if you were capable of responding to them. I would tell you about the awful hell that has received your brother, and that awaits you unless you repent by giving up your murderous ways, and take your armies back to your own lands. But since you have rejected these things once before, and have fought against the Lord's people, I expect you to do it again.

"We are prepared to receive you, and unless you withdraw, you will pull down the wrath of that God, whom you have rejected, upon you, even to your utter destruction. For as the Lord lives, our armies will come upon you if you do not withdraw. You will soon be visited with death, for we will retain our cities and lands, and we will maintain our religion and the cause of our God.

"I may be writing to you about these things in vain, for I think that you are a child of hell. I will end my letter by telling you that I will not exchange prisoners unless you deliver up a man with his wife and children for one prisoner. If you will not do this, I will come against you with my armies. I will even arm our women and children. We will follow you into your own land, the land of our first inheritance, and give you battle until you are destroyed off the face of the earth!

"My people and I are very angry, for you have sought to murder us while we have only sought to defend ourselves. If you seek to destroy us anymore, we will seek to destroy you and take the land of our first inheritance. This is the end of my letter. I am Moroni, the leader of the Nephite armies."

Upon reading Moroni's letter, Ammoron became angry. He wrote another letter to Moroni, which read:

"I am Ammoron, the king of the Lamanites. I am the brother of Amalickiah, whom you have murdered. I will avenge his blood upon you by coming upon you with my armies, for I do not fear your threats. Your forefathers wronged their brothers, robbing them of their right to govern when it rightly belonged to them. If you will lay down your weapons and subject yourselves to be governed by those to whom the government rightly belongs, then I will tell my people to lay down their weapons and this war will end.

"You have threatened me and my people, but we do not fear you. However, I will gladly exchange prisoners according to your request, to preserve my food for my men of war. We will wage an eternal war, and either subject the Nephites to our authority or make them eternally extinct.

"And as for that God whom you say we have rejected, we do not know such a being, and neither do you. If there is such a thing, he made us as well as you.

And if there is a devil and a hell, he will send you there to live with my brother, whom you have murdered, and whom you have hinted has gone to such a place. But these things do not even matter.

"I am Ammoron, a descendant of Zoram, whom your forefathers forced out of Jerusalem. I am a bold Lamanite, and this war has been waged to avenge the wrong-doings of your forefathers upon ours, and to obtain our rights to the government. This is the end of my letter to you, Moroni."

55 - Angry, Moroni makes a plan...

When Moroni received Ammoron's second letter, he became angrier than before, knowing that Ammoron, a Zoramite/Nephite dissenter, was perfectly aware of his own fraud—aware that his own reasons for waging war against the Nephites were not just. Moroni exclaimed, "We will not exchange prisoners with Ammoron unless he withdraws his armies, as I stated to him in my letter, for I will not give him more men than he already has. I know where the Lamanites guard our people, whom they have taken prisoner. Because Ammoron will not do what I have asked him, I will give him what I said I would. I will seek their death until they beg for peace."

Then Moroni searched among his men to find a descendant of Laman. A pure Lamanite was found, named Laman. He was one of the Lamanite king's servants who had run away after Amalickiah's servant had stabbed the king. Moroni sent Laman and a few of his men to the city of Gid, where the Nephite prisoners were being held.

At night, Laman walked up to the men guarding the Nephites. When they saw him coming they called out, but Laman shouted, "No need to fear, I'm a Lamanite. We escaped from the Nephites as they slept, and we took their wine with us."

When the Lamanites heard this, they received Laman with joy, saying, "Give us some wine! We're glad you brought it, for we are weary." But Laman replied, "Let's save it until we go and fight the Nephites." This only made the Lamanites want it more. They said, "We're so weary, so let's drink it now! We'll get more wine in our rations to strengthen us when we fight the Nephites." Laman replied, "Do as you wish."

Then they drank freely. The wine had been prepared extra strong, and it was good tasting, so the Lamanites drank it even more freely, and all became very drunk. After they had all passed out, Laman returned to Moroni and told him what had happened.

Things were going according Moroni's plan, and he prepared his men with weapons and went to the city of Gid. While the Lamanites were in a deep, drunken sleep, he and his men threw weapons in to the prisoners. The Nephite women and even all the children who were able to use a weapon were armed. All this was done in complete silence.

Even if they had awakened the Lamanites, they could have easily killed them, for they were all drunk. But this was not Moroni's intention. He did not delight in murder or bloodshed, but in saving his people from destruction. He had obtained his desire to arm the prisoners, giving them the power to take back their city from within. He had his men step back from the drunken guards and surround them.

In the morning, when the Lamanites awoke, they saw that they were surrounded by Nephites, and that their prisoners were armed from within the city walls. Realizing that the Nephites now had power over them, they did not fight. Their chief captains demanded their weapons, brought them to the feet of the Nephites, and pled for mercy. This is what Moroni wanted. He took them as prisoners of war, and then took possession of the city. He had liberated the Nephite prisoners, and many of them joined and strengthened his army.

Moroni put the Lamanite prisoners to work strengthening the fortifications around the city of Gid. After Gid was fortified, Moroni sent his prisoners to Bountiful, which was guarded by a very large Nephite force. In spite of the Lamanites' plots, the Nephites kept and protected all their prisoners and maintained the advantage in all the places they had retaken. The Nephites began to be victorious by reclaiming their rights and privileges.

Many times the Lamanites tried to surround them at night, but during these attempts, many Lamanite prisoners were killed. Many times the Lamanite armies tried to give their wine to the Nephites, to poison them or make them drunk. But the Nephites remembered the Lord their God during their time of affliction, and they could not be tricked. They did not drink wine from the Lamanites until first giving some of it to Lamanite prisoners. The Nephites were careful not to be poisoned by the Lamanites' wine, for if it would poison a Lamanite, it would poison a Nephite.

Soon it became necessary for Moroni to prepare to attack the city of Morianton, for the Lamanites had fortified that city and had made it into a great stronghold. The Lamanites were continually bringing new forces, supplies and provisions into Morianton. And this is how 63 BC ended.

56 - Helaman reports to Moroni...

On the second day of 62 BC, Moroni received a letter from Helaman, informing him of the affairs of the people in the Zarahemla area. The letter read:

"My dearly beloved brother in the Lord (as well as in the tribulations of warfare, for we have also had our share of warfare in this part of the land). I will tell you about the 2,000 sons of the people that Ammon brought out of the land of Nephi, who as you know, are descendants of Laman, the oldest son of father Lehi.

"I do not need to tell you about the traditions and unbelief of the Lamanites, for you already know of them. I am writing to tell you about these 2,000 young men, who took up their weapons and made me their leader, and came to the defense of their country.

"You know about the covenant that their fathers made not to take up weapons against their brethren. Four years ago, in 66 BC, when their fathers saw the afflictions we were suffering on their behalf, they were about to break their covenant and take up weapons to defend us. But I would not let them do this, thinking that God would strengthen us and keep us from suffering too much.

"Then something happened that has given me great joy! I marched at the head of those 2,000 young men to the city of Judea to assist Antipus, whom you had appointed as the leader in that city. I joined my 2,000 sons (for they are worthy to be called sons) with Antipus' army. This made Antipus very happy, for his army had been greatly reduced by the Lamanites, which gives us cause to mourn. Our only consolation is knowing that our men have died in the cause of their country and their God, and are now in a state of happiness.

"The Lamanites have taken many chief captains as prisoners, for they kill everyone else. If those prisoners are still alive, we think they are being held in the land of Nephi. These are the cities that the Lamanites have conquered by killing so many of our valiant men: Manti, Zeezrom, Cumeni and Antiparah. When I arrived at Judea, these four cities had already been conquered, and I found Antipus and his men working with all their strength to fortify the city. They had become depressed in body and spirit, for they fought valiantly during the day and worked at night to maintain their cities. They had suffered greatly with every type of affliction. Antipus and his men were determined to hold out in Judea or die, so you can imagine how glad they were to see those sons of mine coming to their assistance.

"When the Lamanites saw that Antipus' army had been reinforced, their leader, Ammoron, ordered his men not to attack Judea. This is how we were favored and spared by the Lord, for if they had attacked us then in our weakness, they might have destroyed our small army.

"Instead of attacking us, Ammoron commanded his Lamanite army to maintain the cities that they had already taken. By the end of 66 BC, we had completed our fortification of Judea, and we wanted the Lamanites to come against us. We had no desire to attack them in their strongholds. We kept our spies out to watch their movements so that they would not be able to pass by us during the day or night, and go northward to attack our other cities. We knew that our northern cities were not strong enough to withstand them. If they tried to pass near us, our plan was to attack them from behind while others met them in the front. We were disappointed not to have had the chance to do this.

"The Lamanites, fearing that they would not be strong enough against us out in the open, did not dare pass by us. Nor did they dare march out against the city of Zarahemla, or cross the Sidon River toward Nephihah. They were determined to use their forces to maintain the cities they had taken."

"In the second month of this year, many provisions came to us from the fathers of my 2,000 sons. We also received an additional 2,000 men from Zarahemla. Now we had a total of 10,000 men and provisions for them and their wives and children.

"Seeing our forces and provisions increasing daily, the Lamanites began to be afraid, so they tried to cut off our supplies and reinforcements. When they began to do this, we knew the Lamanites were growing uneasy, so we planned a strategy. Antipus ordered me to march out with my young sons as if we were carrying supplies to a neighboring city.

"We were to pass by the conquered city of Antiparah pretending to be carrying supplies to the next city near the coast.

"After my little army left Judea and came near the city of Antiparah, Antipus and part of his army left Judea and followed us. Antiparah was where the strongest, most numerous Lamanite army was stationed. After their spies told them that we had passed nearby their city, carrying supplies, the entire Lamanite army came out after us, thinking they could easily kill us and take the supplies. We ran from them heading north, and led away the most powerful Lamanite army. By the time they saw Antipus following them, we had led them too far from Antiparah for them to return to it safely. So the Lamanite army chased us vigorously, marching in a straight course to catch and kill us before Antipus caught up to them, for they did not want to be surrounded.

"When Antipus saw our danger, he hurried his army. When night came, we camped, for the Lamanites had not caught up to us, nor had Antipus caught up to them. Before dawn, the Lamanites were coming after us. We were not strong enough to fight such a great army, nor would I allow my sons to be caught by them, so we quickly marched into the wilderness. The Lamanites did not turn to the left or the right, fearing that they would be surrounded. And I would not turn to the left or the right for fear of being overtaken. Again we marched until nightfall. And again, the next morning we saw the Lamanites coming closer to us, and we ran. They chased us for a short time and then stopped. This was the morning of the third day of the seventh month of the year.

"We did not know if Antipus had overtaken them or not, but I said to my men, 'Maybe the Lamanites want us to attack them so that they can catch us in their snare. What do you say, my sons, will you go against them in battle?'

"My beloved brother, Moroni, I had never seen such great courage, even among the bravest Nephites. Because I called them my sons (for they were all very young), they said to me, 'Father, our God is with us, and He will not allow us to fall. Let us go to battle, for we would not kill our brothers if they would leave us alone. Let us go before they overpower Antipus and his army.' They had never fought before, yet they did not fear death. They thought more of the liberty of their fathers than they did of their own lives. Their mothers had taught them that if they did not doubt, God would deliver them. They repeated their mothers' words to me and then said, 'We do not doubt that our mothers know this.'

"I went against the Lamanites with my 2,000 young men. By then, the armies of Antipus had caught up to the Lamanites, and a terrible battle had begun. Because they had marched long and hard to catch up to the Lamanite army, the army of Antipus was tired, and they were about to be beaten. If my 2,000 young men and I had not come to their assistance, they would all have certainly been killed.

"Antipus and many of his leaders had already been killed, and without their leaders, the army had become confused. The Lamanites were boldly chasing them when we attacked the Lamanites from behind. We killed so many Lamanites so quickly that their entire army turned away from the army of Antipus and turned upon us. Then the army of Antipus came upon the Lamanites from behind and started to kill them. By surrounding and killing them quickly, we terrified the great Lamanite army so completely that they gave up their weapons and surrendered. Then I counted my young men who had fought with me, fearing that many of them had been killed. But to my great joy, not a single one of them had fallen! They had fought as if they had the strength of God! Never were men known to have fought with such miraculous strength, frightening the enemy so completely. We had no place to guard our prisoners, so we sent them to the land of Zarahemla with some of Antipus' men. Then we marched back to Judea."

57 - Helaman's letter to Moroni continues:

"Then I received a letter from the Lamanite king, Ammoron, stating that if I would give up our prisoners of war, he would give up the city of Antiparah. I sent a reply to the king, saying that we were strong enough to take Antiparah by force, so we would only give up our prisoners in exchange for theirs. After Ammoron rejected my letter, being unwilling to exchange prisoners, we prepared to attack Antiparah. But before we had the chance to attack, the Lamanites abandoned Antiparah and ran away to other cities they had taken, hoping to fortify them. By now 64 BC had come to an end.

"In the beginning of 63 BC, we received 6,000 additional soldiers and supplies from Zarahemla. Sixty additional sons of the Ammonites also came to join their brethren, my little band of 2,000. Now we were a strong and well-supplied force, and we wanted to wage a battle with the Lamanite army holding the city of Cumeni.

"One night, prior to the time the Lamanites were to receive a supply of provisions, part of our strong force surrounded the city. We camped around the city for many nights, posting guards and sleeping on our swords. Many nights, the Lamanites attacked us, but their attacks were in vain.

"When those bringing the provisions finally arrived, we intercepted them with thei provisions. In spite of having their provisions cut off, the Lamanites were determined to maintain the city. We sent the Lamanites that we had intercepted as prisoners to the land of Zarahemla, and their provisions to Judea. After a few days, the Lamanites in the city of Cumeni began to lose hope, so they gave up the city and surrendered to us. At that time, we had so many prisoners that even with our large force it was all we could do to control them, and we had to kill many of them. They would break out in great numbers, fighting with stones, clubs and whatever they could find. We had to kill nearly 2,000 of them after they had surrendered as prisoners of war. It became necessary to kill them or guard them, sword in hand, down to the land of Zarahemla. Even though we had intercepted the Lamanites' provisions, we barely had enough food for our own people. Under these critical circumstances, we had to decide what to do with so many prisoners of war.

"We were determined to get the prisoners to the land of Zarahemla, so we selected part of our men to take the prisoners there.

"The next day our men returned to us without the prisoners. We did not have time to ask what had happened, for the Lamanites were upon us. The Lamanite king, Ammoron, had sent a new supply of provisions along with a numerous army. The men we had sent out with the prisoners had arrived just in time to save us.

"Before they had arrived, my little band of 2,060 had been fighting the Lamanites most desperately. My young men were firm in battle, giving death to all who opposed them. While the rest of our army were about to give in to the Lamanites, my 2,060 were firm and fearless. They obeyed every command with exactness. They were protected according to their faith, and I remembered the words that they said their mothers had taught them.

"It was my sons, and the part of our army that had returned, to whom we owe this great victory, for it was they who beat the Lamanites and drove them back to the city of Manti. We retained the city of Cumeni and were spared, although we suffered great losses.

"After the Lamanites fled, I immediately gave orders for my wounded men to be taken from among the dead and their wounds dressed. About 200 of my 2,060 had fainted for the loss of blood. But by the goodness of God, and to the great astonishment and joy of our whole army, not one of them had been killed! However, all of them had received many wounds.

"Their preservation was astonishing to our whole army, for over 1,000 Nephites had been killed. We credit this to God's miraculous power, shown because of their great faith in what they had been taught to believe—that there was a just God, and that all who did not doubt would be saved by His marvelous power.

"Now this is the kind of faith these young men have. Their minds are firm and they put their trust in God continually.

"After we had taken care of our wounded men, and had buried our dead and the many dead Lamanites, we asked Gid what had happened to the prisoners that he and his men had been taking to Zarahemla. Gid was the chief captain over the band that had been appointed to guard them. He reported:

"'As we started out toward the land of Zarahemla with our prisoners, our spies came running to us. They cried out, "The Lamanite army is marching toward Cumeni. They will fall upon them and destroy our people!" When our prisoners heard this, they took courage and rose up in rebellion against us. We tried to contain them, but they ran in a group against our swords. Most of them were killed, but the rest broke through and escaped. We could not catch them, so we quickly marched toward Cumeni, hoping to arrive in time to assist you, Helaman. Now we have been delivered from our enemies again, and blessed is the name of our God, for it is He that has delivered us!'

"When I, Helaman, heard this report, I was filled with great joy because of God's goodness in preserving us, that we might not all perish. And I trust that the souls of those who have died have entered into His rest."

58 - Helaman's letter to Moroni continues:

"Our next goal was to retake the city of Manti. We could not lure the Lamanites out of their strongholds again, for they remembered what we had done before. The Lamanites were so much more numerous than we that we did not dare attack them. Instead, we had our men maintain the cities which we had retaken, and waited for more reinforcements and provisions from Zarahemla.

"I had sent an embassy to our chief judge and governor in Zarahemla, requesting more provisions and soldiers, and then waited to receive our provisions. If we had received provisions and more soldiers sooner, it would not have helped us much, for every day the Lamanites received many soldiers and provisions.

"On occasion, the Lamanites rushed out against us, and tried using their own strategies to destroy us. This was frustrating to us, for we could not attack them in their retreats and strongholds. We waited many months for our provisions and almost starved to death. But our food finally arrived, along with 2,000 men, and this is all the assistance we have received to defend ourselves and our country from an innumerable enemy.

"We did not know why more reinforcements were not sent, and we became sorrowful and afraid that God's judgments would overthrow our land and completely destroy us. We poured out our souls in prayer to God, asking Him to deliver us from our enemies and give us the strength to hold our cities, lands and possessions for the support of our people.

"By speaking peace to our souls, the Lord our God assured us that He would deliver us. He gave us great faith in Him, through which we hoped for deliverance. We took courage with the small force we had received, and became determined to conquer our enemies, and to maintain our lands, possessions, wives, children, and our cause of liberty.

"We marched in all our strength against the Lamanites who had taken the city of Manti. First we pitched our tents near the city on the wilderness side. The next day, when the Lamanites saw us near the city, they sent out spies to see how large our army was. When they discovered that our small army threatened to cut off their supplies, they prepared to come out, thinking they could easily kill us with their large army. "Knowing the Lamanites were preparing to come out of the city, I ordered Gid and Teomner each to take a small group of men and hide in the wilderness. Gid's group hid on the right, and Teomner's on the left. I stayed with the rest of my army in our camp and waited for the Lamanites to come out.

"When the numerous Lamanite army came out and were about to attack us with their swords, our men ran away into the wilderness. The Lamanites wanted very much to kill us, so they ran after us very quickly. We ran between the places where Gid and Teomner were hiding. After the Lamanites had passed by Gid and Teomner, they rose up from their hiding places and prevented the Lamanite spies from returning to the city. Then they ran to the city, killed the Lamanite guards, and took possession of it. Gid and Teomner were able to do this with only a few men because the Lamanites had allowed their entire army, except for a few guards, to be led away into the wilderness.

"Meanwhile, after traveling for a long time in the wilderness, we headed toward Zarahemla. When the Lamanites realized where we were headed, they became very afraid and began to return through the wilderness. By then it was dark, so the Lamanites set up camp for the night. Their chief captains thought that our whole army had been on the march and were tired, so they did not worry about the safety of Manti.

"That night, rather than sleep we went around the Lamanites and headed back to Manti by another route. In the morning, we arrived at the city ahead of the Lamanites. This was our strategy to take back Manti without much bloodshed.

"As the Lamanite army came near the city, they saw us prepared to meet them. They were very astonished, and so afraid that they ran away into the wilderness. All the Lamanites ran out of this part of the land, taking many women and children as prisoners. All the cities that had been taken by the Lamanites are now back in our possession. Our men, women and children are returning to their homes, except for those who were taken prisoner and carried off by the Lamanites. Our armies are too small to maintain so many cities and possessions, but we trust in our God, who has given us victory over our cities and lands. And we do not know why the government does not send us more reinforcements.

"Moroni, for all we know, your army has been unsuccessful, and has needed the forces in your part of the land. If this is the case, we do not wish to complain. But if this is not the case, we feel there must have been some unrest in the government, for we know many more reinforcements could have been sent. It does not matter, for we trust in God to deliver us in spite of our small numbers.

"This year, 63 BC, is coming to an end, and we have regained our lands that the Lamanites have abandoned. And those sons of Ammon's people, of whom I have so highly spoken, are now with me in the city of Manti. The Lord has supported them and has kept them from falling by the sword, for not even one soul has been killed. They have received many wounds, but they stand firm in that liberty with which God has made them free. They are strict to remember the Lord their God from day to day. They continually keep His statutes, judgments and commandments, and their faith is strong in the prophecies of that which is to come.

"Now my beloved brother, Moroni, may the Lord our God, who has redeemed us and made us free, keep you continually in His presence. May He favor this people so that you may have success in regaining what the Lamanites have taken from us. This is the end of my letter. I am Helaman, Alma's son."

59 - Without support, Nephite city falls...

Moroni received Helaman's letter in 62 BC, the thirtieth year of the judges' reign over the Nephites. Moroni was very happy to learn that Helaman and his people had been successful in regaining their lands. He announced this news to all the people in his region so that they would also rejoice. He immediately sent a letter to Pahoran, requesting troops to help Helaman more easily maintain the Nephite cities that his army had so miraculously regained. After sending this letter, Moroni again made plans to obtain the rest of their possessions and cities from the Lamanites.

The Nephites from the cities of Moroni, Lehi and Morianton had found refuge in Nephihah, but as Moroni was making battle plans, the Lamanites attacked Nephihah.

The Lamanites who had run away from Helaman's army in the Manti region had joined the Lamanite army which made this attack. The numerous Lamanite army grew larger every day. Feeling strong and confident, Ammoron, the Lamanite king, commanded his army to attack Nephihah, and they began to kill the Nephites with a great slaughter. But many Nephites escaped and joined Moroni's army.

Moroni thought that men would be sent to Nephihah from their capital, Zarahemla, to assist the people in maintaining that city. Moroni assumed that the government knew, as he did, that it was easier to keep a city from falling than to retake it. This is why Moroni kept his forces in the cities that he had retaken.

When Moroni learned that Nephihah was lost, he was very sorry. He began to wonder if they, too, would fall because of the wickedness of their people in Zarahemla. All of Moroni's chief captains felt the same way. Because the Lamanites were having success over them, they wondered what was happening with the people in Zarahemla, and doubted their personal righteousness. Moroni became angry with the government officials because of their apparent indifference to the freedom of their country. He wrote another letter to Pahoran, the governor of the land in Zarahemla, which read:

60 - Moroni's angry letter to Pahoran...

"This letter is directed to Pahoran, the chief judge and governor of the land, and also to those who have been chosen by this people to govern and manage the affairs of this war.

"I condemn you, for you know that you were appointed to gather armies and send them out against the Lamanites in whatever areas they were attacking us. Helaman and his men, and my men and I have suffered greatly with hunger, thirst, fatigue, and all types of afflictions. If this is all we had suffered, we would not doubt or complain. But thousands of our people have fallen by the sword who might not have fallen if you had not neglected us, but had sent us support. We want to know why you have neglected us for so long. Can you just sit upon your thrones in a thoughtless stupor while your enemies are spreading the work of death around you, murdering thousands of your brethren? You might have saved thousands, who looked to you for protection, who trusted you to support them by sending them armies.

"But this is not all. You have withheld your provisions from them, so that many men have fought and bled out their lives while desiring only the welfare of this people. They defended their country while they were nearly starving, because of your great neglect.

"And now, my beloved brethren—for you ought to be beloved, you should have been more diligent in supporting the welfare and freedom of this people. You have neglected them so much that the blood of thousands will come upon your heads for vengeance, for God has witnessed all their cries and suffering. Do you think you can just sit upon your thrones doing nothing, and that God will deliver you because of His great goodness? If you think this, you do so in vain. Do you think that so many of your brethren have been killed because of their wickedness? If you do, you are mistaken, for many have fallen by the sword to your condemnation.

"The Lord allows the righteous to be killed so that His justice and judgment can come upon the wicked. So do not think the righteous are lost because they are dead, for they have entered into the rest of the Lord their God. I am very afraid that God's judgments will come upon this people because of our government's great slothfulness and neglect of those who have been killed. For if the head of our government had not become wicked, we could have withstood our enemies, and they would not have gained any power over us. If those Kingmen had not desired power over their fellow men, and had not raised their swords to us, but instead had been true to the cause of our freedom, uniting with us, then we would have gone against our enemies in the strength of the Lord, and we would have fulfilled His word by dispersing them.

"But now the Lamanites are coming upon us and are taking possession of our lands. They are murdering our women and children, and carrying them away captive, causing them to suffer all types of afflictions. All this is happening because of the great wickedness of those Kingmen, who only want power and authority. But why should I say this? For all we know, you yourselves are seeking for power and authority as traitors to your country. Have you neglected us because you feel safe in the heart of our country, surrounded by security? Is this why you have not sent us food and reinforcements to strengthen our armies? Have you forgotten the commandments of the Lord your God? Have you forgotten the captivity of our forefathers, and how many times we have been delivered out of the hands of our enemies?

"Do you think the Lord will deliver us while you sit upon your thrones, not using the means He has provided for us? Will you do nothing, surrounded by tens of thousands who also do nothing, while thousands who fight to maintain the borders of the land fall by the sword, wounded and bleeding? Do you think that God will see you as guiltless while you sit and watch? No, He will not. Remember, God has said that the inner vessel will be cleansed first, and then the outer vessel. Unless you repent of what you have done, and begin to be up and doing, sending food and men to us, and also to Helaman, it will be necessary for us to stop fighting the Lamanites until we first cleanse the inner vessel, even you, the great head of our government.

"Unless you respond to this letter and show me the true spirit of freedom, sending reinforcements and food, I will leave part of my Freemen here to maintain this part of our land. I will leave the strength and blessings of God upon them so that no other power can operate against them. I will do this because of their great faith and patience in their tribulations. Then I will come to you, and if even a spark of desire for freedom remains among you, I will stir up a revolt among you until those who desire to usurp power and authority are extinct. I do not fear your power or authority, but only God's. According to His commandments, I take up my sword to defend the cause of my country, for it is because of your sinfulness that we have suffered so much loss. Unless you begin to defend your country and your little ones right now, the sword of justice hangs over you, and it will utterly destroy you. I wait for your assistance. If you do not administer to our relief, I will come against you in the land of Zarahemla and strike you with the sword, for the Lord will not allow you to live and grow strong in your iniquities, to destroy His righteous people.

"Do you think the Lord will spare you in your love of glory and the vain things of the world, and destroy the Lamanites, who hate us because of their traditions? You know when you are breaking God's laws and trampling them under your feet. This is why the Lord has said to me, 'If those whom you have appointed as governors do not repent of their sins and iniquities, you will go up to battle against them.'

"I, Moroni, will be constrained to do just that, according to the covenant that I have made to keep the commandments of my God. So rather than have me come against you, you should adhere to the word of God and quickly send provisions and men to us, and to Helaman. If you will not do this, I will come against you quickly, for God will allow us to kill you and take your food before He will allow us to die of starvation. Now see that you fulfill God's word.

"I am Moroni, your chief captain. I do not seek for power, but to pull it down. I do not seek for the honors of the world, but the glory of my God, and the freedom and welfare of my country. This is the end of my letter."

61 - Pahoran's reply letter to Moroni...

Soon after Moroni had sent his letter to Pahoran, he received this reply:

"Moroni, I have no joy in your great afflictions, for they grieve my soul. But a great number of people here do rejoice in your afflictions, for they have risen up in rebellion against me and my people, the Freemen. Your great suffering has been caused by those who have taken the judgment-seat from me. By using great flattery, they have led away the hearts of many people, which will be the cause of sore affliction among us. They have withheld our provisions and have prevented our Freemen from coming to you. They have driven me out, and I have escaped to the land of Gideon with as many men as I could get.

"I have sent a proclamation, calling people to arms throughout this part of the land. They are coming to us daily, armed to defend their country and freedom, and to avenge our wrongs. Because of this, those who have risen up in rebellion against us are afraid to come out of Zarahemla and fight us. They have taken over the city and have appointed Pachus to be their own king.

"Pachus has written to the Lamanite king, making an alliance with him. He has agreed with the Lamanite king to maintain Zarahemla, making it easier for the Lamanites to conquer the rest of our lands. In return, Pachus will be made king over our people if we are conquered by the Lamanites. You rebuked me in your letter, but I am not angry. I rejoice in the greatness of your heart. I, Pahoran, also do not seek for power. I desire to regain my judgment-seat to preserve the rights and liberty of my people. My soul stands fast in that liberty with which God has made us free. We will resist wickedness even if we must shed blood. We would not kill the Lamanites if they would stay in their own land, nor would we kill our own brethren if they would not rise up in rebellion against us with swords.

"We would subject ourselves to the yoke of bondage if God's justice required us to do so. But He does not require us to subject ourselves to our enemies. He requires that we trust in Him to deliver us.

"My beloved brother, Moroni, let us resist evil, and whatever evil we cannot resist with our words, such as rebellions and dissensions, let us resist them with our swords, that we may retain our freedom, that we may rejoice in the great privilege of our church and in the cause of our Redeemer and God. Come to us quickly with a few of your men. Leave the rest under the command of Lehi and Teancum. Let them fight in that part of the land according to the Spirit of God in them—the Spirit of freedom. I have sent a few provisions so that your men will not starve before you can come to me.

"As you come, gather more men along the way. Then according to our faith, in the strength of our God we will go quickly against those dissenters. We will take back the city of Zarahemla, obtain more food to send to Lehi and Teancum, and put an end to this great iniquity.

"After reading your letter, Moroni, I was very happy, for I was not sure if my plans to go against our brethren was a just cause. But now I know it is a just cause, for as you said, unless they repent, the Lord has commanded you to go against them. Be sure to strengthen Lehi and Teancum in the Lord. Tell them, and all those who stand firm for their liberty, that God will deliver them. This is the end of my letter to you, my beloved brother, Moroni."

62 - Moroni sets Zarahemla in order..

Upon receiving this letter, Moroni took courage and was filled with great joy because of Pahoran's faithfulness. He was glad to know that Pahoran was not a traitor to the cause of freedom for his country. However, Moroni was very sorry because of the sinfulness of the people who had driven Pahoran from the judgment-seat, rebelling against their God and country.

Moroni took a small number of men and marched toward the land of Gideon, leaving Lehi and Teancum in command over the rest of his army. He raised The Title of Liberty in every place he entered, adding whomever he could to his forces while marching toward Gideon. Thousands rallied to his flag, taking up swords to defend their freedom. After Moroni gathered all the men he could, he arrived in the land of Gideon and united his forces with Pahoran's. Together, their army was much stronger than the Kingmen's army.

Moroni's and Pahoran's armies met the Kingmen's army in the city of Zarahemla. During the battle Pachus was killed, and his men were taken prisoner. Then Pahoran was restored to his judgment-seat.

All of Pachus' men and the Kingmen received their trial and were executed according to the law. It was necessary for this strict law to be observed in order to preserve the safety of their country. This is why all those who denied the freedom of others were quickly executed according to the law. By the end of 62 BC, Moroni and Pahoran had restored peace in the land of Zarahemla by destroying all those who were not true to the cause of freedom.

In the beginning of 61 BC, Moroni quickly sent provisions and 6,000 men to assist Helaman in preserving his part of the land. Moroni also sent provisions with 6,000 men to Lehi's and Teancum's armies. Then he and Pahoran left many men in the land of Zarahemla and took a large army to Nephihah, determined to overthrow the Lamanites in that city. During their march, they attacked a large Lamanite army, killing many and capturing the rest. They also captured their provisions and weapons. Moroni told the 4,000 captured Lamanites that they must enter into a covenant never to take up their weapons of war against the Nephites again. After they entered into this covenant, they were sent to live with Ammon's people.

Then Moroni and Pahoran's army came near Nephihah, camping in the plains near the city. Moroni wanted the Lamanites to come out and fight them in the plains. Seeing their large army, and also knowing the Nephites were very courageous, the Lamanites dared not come out against them. That night, Moroni climbed on top of the wall to see where the Lamanites were camping inside the city. He saw their camp on the east side, near the entrance, and they were all asleep. Moroni returned to his army and told them to quickly prepare strong ropes and ladders.

Then Moroni and his men climbed on top of the west wall, away from the Lamanites' camp, and climbed down into the city, using their strong ropes and ladders. In the morning they were all within the city walls. When the Lamanites awoke and saw Moroni's army in the city, they were so afraid that they began to run out of the entrance. Moroni ordered his men to attack them. Many were killed and many more were surrounded and taken as prisoners. The rest escaped into the land of Moroni, near the eastern shore.

This is how Moroni and Pahoran regained Nephihah without losing a single Nephite. The Lamanite prisoners wanted to join Ammon's people and become free, so they were granted their freedom according to their desires. All the prisoners joined Ammon's people. They worked hard tilling the ground and raising all types of grain, flocks and herds. This is how the Nephites were relieved from the great burden of keeping prisoners.

In regaining the city, Moroni had set many Nephite prisoners free. He had also reduced the Lamanite forces by the number of those who had made a covenant of peace. Thus strengthened, Moroni's army marched toward the land of Lehi.

When the Lamanites in the land of Lehi saw Moroni's army coming, they were again frightened and ran away. Moroni and his army chased them from city to city, until they were met by Lehi and Teancum. The Lamanites ran from them, down the coast, until they came to the land of Moroni. The entire Lamanite army, including their king, Ammoron, gathered there.

Moroni's, Lehi's and Teancum's armies camped near the southern and eastern borders of the land of Moroni, near the wilderness, surrounding the Lamanites. The Nephites and Lamanites were tired, having made a long journey, so they both camped for the night. The Nephites did not decide on any night-time strategy, except for Teancum. He was very angry with Ammoron, knowing that he and his brother, Amalickiah, had been the cause of this long war and so much bloodshed and famine. So Teancum went out that night, lowered himself over the city wall and went looking for Ammoron in the Lamanite camp. Teancum found him sleeping and stabbed him near the heart with a javelin. Yet Ammoron cried out and awoke his servants before he died, and the servants chased Teancum and killed him.

When Lehi and Moroni heard Teancum was dead, they were very sorry, for he was a man who had fought valiantly for his country. He had been a true friend of liberty and had suffered many great afflictions. But now he was dead and had gone the way of all the earth.

The next morning, Moroni's army attacked the Lamanites, killing them with a great slaughter, and the Lamanites were driven out of the land. This is how 61 BC ended, and the Nephites had been experiencing wars, bloodshed, famine and affliction for many years. There had been murders, contentions, dissensions, and all types of iniquity among the Nephites, but for the sake of the righteous, and because of their prayers, the Nephites had been spared.

Because the war had lasted for so many years, many people had hardened their hearts. Others, because of their afflictions, had softened their hearts, humbling themselves before God in the depths of humility.

After Moroni had fortified the most vulnerable parts of the land, he returned to the city of Zarahemla. Helaman returned to the place of his inheritance, and peace was once again established among the Nephites. Moroni retired from the army and went to his own house to live out the rest of his life in peace. He gave the command of his armies to his son, Moronihah.

Pahoran returned to his judgment-seat, and Helaman took up preaching the word of God to the people again. Because there had been so much war and contention, it had become necessary to regulate the affairs of the church again. Helaman and his brethren declared the word of God with great power, convincing many people of their wickedness, and many repented of their sins and were baptized to the Lord their God. A church of God was established once again throughout the land, regulations were made concerning the law, and judges and chief judges were chosen.

The Nephites began to prosper again, populating the land and growing rich. Even though they became rich, they did not become proud. They were not slow to remember the Lord their God, and they greatly humbled themselves before Him. They remembered the great things the Lord had done for them in delivering them from death, captivity and all types of afflictions. They prayed to the Lord their God, so much that He blessed them according to His word. And in 57 BC, Helaman died.

63 - More than 20,000 Nephites go north...

In the beginning of 56 BC, Shiblon took charge of the sacred things that Alma had given to Helaman. Shiblon was a just man who did good continually. He kept the commandments of the Lord his God, like his brother, Helaman.

By the end of 56 BC, Moroni had died. In 55 BC, 5,400 men took their families out of the land of Zarahemla and traveled to the northern land. One man, named Hagoth, was very curious and adventurous. He built a very large ship and launched it into the western sea.

By the end of 55 BC, many Nephite men, women and children had boarded this ship, which sailed north, carrying many provisions.

In 54 BC, Hagoth built other ships. The first ship returned, and many more people boarded the ship with many provisions, and the ship sailed north a second time. They were never heard of again, and we think they were drowned in the depths of the sea. Ane one other ship sailed to a destination not known to us.

In 54 BC, many people went to the northern land. In 53 BC, Shiblon died, and Corianton was gone, having boarded a ship to deliver provisions to the people who had gone to the northern land.

Before he died, Shiblon gave those sacred things to Helaman's son, Helaman.

Now all the engravings on the plates held by Helaman were published and distributed among the people throughout the land. Only those parts of the record that Alma had commanded not to go forth were not published. Those things were to be kept sacred and handed down from one generation to another.

In the same year that Helaman had been given the sacred things, some dissenters had gone to the Lamanites and had stirred them up again to be angry with the Nephites. That year, the Lamanites came with a numerous army to war against the army of Moronihah, but the army was beaten, driven back to their own lands, suffering great losses.

This is how 53 BC ended. This is the end of the account of Alma, and of his sons, Helaman and Shiblon.

1 - A secret band of killers...

At the beginning of 52 BC, the fortieth year of the judges' reign, the Nephites began to have serious problems again, for Pahoran had died, and three of his sons, Pahoran, Paanchi and Pacumeni, were fighting over the judgment-seat. Pahoran had many sons, but only these three wanted the judgment-seat, and they caused three divisions among the people. The majority of the people voted for Pahoran to be the chief judge and governor over the Nephites. Although he was disappointed, Pacumeni accepted the voice of the people, but Paanchi and those that wanted him to be governor were angry. Paanchi was about to convince his followers to rise up in rebellion against their brethren, when he was taken and tried according to the voice of the people. He was condemned to death for attempting to destroy the people's liberty.

When Paanchi's followers heard that he was condemned to die, they became very angry. They sent out Kishkumen, who murdered Pahoran as he sat on the judgment-seat. Pahoran's servants chased Kishkumen, but he ran so quickly that he could not be caught.

Kishkumen went back to those who had sent him. Together they all entered into a secret covenant, vowing by their everlasting Maker, that they would not tell anyone that Kishkumen had murdered Pahoran. Because of this covenant, and because he was in disguise when he murdered Pahoran, Kishkumen was not suspected among the Nephites.

Kishkumen and his band, who had covenanted with him, mixed with the people in a way that they could not all be found. But those who were found were condemned to death.

Now being the rightful heir, and according to the voice of the people, Pacumeni was appointed as chief judge and governor over the people. All this happened in 52 BC.

In 51 BC, the Lamanites gathered a countless number of soldiers and armed them with swords, scimitars, bows, arrows, helmets, breastplates and shields. Then they came down to fight the Nephites again. This time they were led by Coriantumr, a descendant of Zarahemla, a large, strong man as well as a Nephite traitor.

King Tubaloth, son of Ammoron, was the Lamanite king. He appointed Coriantumr to lead his army, thinking that Coriantumr was so strong and wise that he could beat the Nephites. And King Tubaloth stirred up his army to march to

Zarahemla to fight the Nephites.

Because the Nephites had so much contention in their government, they had not kept enough guards in the land of Zarahemla. They never thought the Lamanites would dare come to their capital and attack their great city. But Coriantumr led so many into their city so quickly that there was no time for the Nephites to gather their army. Coriantumr killed the guards at the city entrance. Then his entire army marched into the city, killing all who opposed, and they captured the entire city. Pacumeni, the chief judge, tried to run out of the city, but Coriantumr struck him against the city wall and killed him.

After Coriantumr conquered Zarahemla, the strongest hold in all the land, he became very bold. He did not stay long in Zarahemla, but marched with a large army toward the city of Bountiful, determined to conquer all the northern lands. Coriantumr thought that the army he had destroyed was the greatest Nephite army in all the land, so he marched out quickly against the Nephites, giving them no time to gather, except into small groups. By doing this, he cut them down to the earth. Even though many Nephites had been killed in Zarahemla, Moronihah had a great advantage over Coriantumr because Coriantumr's army was now in the center part of the land.

Moronihah never thought the Lamanites would come in to the center of the land. He thought they would attack the outer cities as they had in the past. This is why he had placed his strongest armies in the outer areas. But under the command of a Nephite traitor, the Lamanites had not been afraid to come into the center of the land. They had taken Zarahemla, and they were taking more cities and strongholds, killing many men, women and children.

When Moronihah heard about this, he immediately sent Lehi with an army to head off Coriantumr's army before they reached Bountiful. Lehi's army met them and began to force them back to Zarahemla. Moronihah met them in their retreat, and a great, bloody battle ensued. Many Lamanites were killed, and Coriantumr was found among the dead. The Lamanites were surrounded and taken as prisoners because Coriantumr had led them right into the hands of the Nephites.

Now Moronihah again took possession of Zarahemla and sent the captured Lamanites out of the land in peace. This is how the year 51 BC ended.

2 - Kishkumen killed, Gadianton escapes...

In 50 BC, the forty-second year of the judges' reign, Moronihah had established peace once again between the Nephites and the Lamanites. But there was no living heir to fill the judgment-seat, so the people started to argue about who would fill it.

Helaman's son, Helaman, was elected to fill the judgment-seat. Now Kishkumen, who had murdered Pahoran, waited for his chance to kill Helaman. His secret band had entered a covenant with him to keep his wickedness secret. This system of secret covenants came from a man named Gadianton. He was an expert with words, and his craft was to carry on secret works of murder and robbery. And so he became the leader of Kishkumen's band.

Gadianton had flattered Kishkumen and his band, promising them positions of power and authority if they would place him in the judgment-seat. This is why Kishkumen sought Helaman's life.

One of Helaman's servants had been out that night, disguised as one of Gadianton's followers. He had learned of the plot to kill Helaman and waited for Kishkumen to come.

Kishkumen came and the disguised servant gave him the secret sign. Kishkumen told the servant, "Take me to the judgment-seat so that I may kill Helaman." Helaman's servant knew Kishkumen's desires and the desires of his band—to secretly conspire in order to murder, rob and gain power. Knowing this, Helaman's servant said to Kishkumen, "Let us go to the judgment-seat." Kishkumen was very pleased to hear this, thinking that he would accomplish his plan. But as they went to the judgment-seat, the servant stabbed Kishkumen in the heart, and he died without a sound. Then the servant ran and told Helaman everything that had happened.

Helaman sent men out to capture this band of robbers and secret murderers so that they might be executed according to the law. But Helaman's men could not find the secret band, for when Kishkumen had not returned, Gadianton was afraid for his life. He had led his band out of the land, by a secret way, into the wilderness.

I, Mormon, will tell you more about Gadianton later. This is how 50 BC ended. By the end of this book, you will see how those who followed Gadianton's evil system were responsible for the overthrow and destruction of nearly all the Nephites. I do not mean by the end of my account of the book of Helaman, but by the end of my account of the book of Nephi (end of 4 Nephi, page 313)—the book to which I have referred while making this particular account of Nephite history.

3 - More Nephites go north...

In 49 BC, the Nephites only had a few disputes among themselves, caused by some prideful church members. However, these disputes were settled by the end of the year.

There was peace during 48 and 47 BC, but during 46 BC, there were many disputes among the Nephites. Many left the land of Zarahemla and went to inherit the northern land.

They traveled a great distance, and they found large bodies of water and many rivers. They spread out over all parts of the land, going wherever they could to find timber, to parts of the land that had not been desolated by the many people (Jaredites) who had lived there before.

The land was not really desolate, it was only without timber. It was called desolate because of the great destruction of the people who had once lived there. Because there was not very much timber, the people became expert in working cement, and they built and lived in cement houses. The people who had migrated to the north populated the land. Soon they spread over all the land—from the southern to the northern land, from the southern to the northern sea, and from the western to the eastern sea.

The people in the northern land lived in tents and cement houses. They were careful to let the young trees grow, so that they would eventually have timber to build houses, cities, temples and churches. Because timber was so scarce in the northern land, it was shipped from the south. With shipping, the people in the northern land were able to build many cities, both of wood and cement. Many of Ammon's people, who were Lamanites by birth, also went north. Many of our people have kept records concerning them, which records are very extensive.

I, Mormon, cannot include in my book even one percent of these records—the Lamanite and Nephite history—their wars, preaching, prophecies, their shipping, their building of ships, temples, synagogues and sanctuaries, their righteousness and their wickedness—murders, robbery, plunder, immorality, etc. There are many books and records of every kind, mostly kept by Nephites. They have handed down the records from one generation to another, even until they have fallen into sin. The Nephites have been murdered, plundered and hunted across the land—even until they have mixed with the Lamanites and are no longer called Nephites. For they have become Lamanites and are wicked and ferocious. Now I will continue with my particular account:

Many Nephites had migrated north after having internal disputes, great contentions and wars throughout 46 BC There were still many disputes during 45 and 44 BC, but Helaman continued to judge with justice and equity. He kept God's statutes, judgments and commandments, always doing what was right. Because of his righteousness, Helaman prospered in the land, as had his father, Helaman. Helaman had two sons. The oldest was Nephi and the youngest, Lehi. Helaman taught them to obey the Lord.

Some of the wars and contentions among the Nephites began to stop toward the end of 44 BC, the forty-eighth year of the judges' reign over the Nephites. In 43 BC, there was continual peace established in the land, except for the secret combinations that Gadianton, the robber, had established in the more populated areas. But the government leaders did not know of those secret combinations. This is why Gadianton and his followers were not detected and destroyed. The church prospered with converts in 43 BC, for thousands joined the church and were baptized unto repentance. There was such a great conversion, and so many blessings were poured out upon the people, that even the high priests and teachers were completely amazed. The Lord's work prospered, for tens of thousands were baptized and united with God's church.

In this way we can see that the Lord is merciful to all who will call upon His holy name in the sincerity of their hearts. We see that the gate of heaven is open to all who will believe in the name of Jesus Christ, the Son of God. We see that those who accept the word of God, which is quick and powerful to destroy all the devil's cunning plans, will be led, as a man or woman of Christ, in a straight and narrow course, to cross over that everlasting gulf of misery prepared for the wicked. Their immortal souls will end up at the right hand of God in the kingdom of heaven, to sit down with Abraham, Isaac, Jacob, and with all our holy forefathers, never to leave again.

Forty-three BC was a year of continual rejoicing in the land of Zarahemla and in all the surrounding regions, even in all the land populated by Nephites. This peace and great joy continued during 43 and 42 BC. In 41 BC, there was still peace, though it was somewhat disturbed by pride in the hearts of those who professed to belong to God's church. Those who truly belonged to God's church were not proud. The Nephites who lifted themselves up in pride above many of their brothers and sisters persecuted the more humble ones, causing them to suffer and wade through great affliction. This was a great evil in the church. But the most humble people prayed and fasted often. Their humility grew stronger and stronger, and their faith in Christ grew more and more, filling their souls with joy and comfort. Their hearts were purified and sanctified because they allowed God to change the desires of their hearts.

Forty BC ended in peace, except for the great pride that had taken hold of the people's hearts. They had become very proud because they were rich and prosperous, and they became more wealthy and proud each day.

Helaman died in 39 BC, the fifty-third year of the judges' reign. Helaman's oldest son, Nephi, began to reign in his place. Nephi was a just and equitable judge who kept God's commandments and walked in the ways of his father.

4 - Pride within the church causes loss...

In 38 BC, many Nephites left the church because of the fighting from within. There was much bloodshed among the people, and the rebellious Nephites were either killed or driven out of the land. They went to the Lamanite king and tried to convince the Lamanites to make war against the Nephites. But the Lamanites were very afraid and would not listen to the Nephite dissenters. But in 36 BC, the dissenters finally convinced the Lamanites to fight the Nephites, and they spent all that year preparing for war.

In 35 BC, the Lamanites and the Nephite dissenters attacked the Nephites. By 34 BC, they conquered the land of Zarahemla and all the lands up to the land of Bountiful. Moronihah's armies and the Nephites were driven north to the land of Bountiful.

There the Nephites made fortifications against the Lamanites. They made these fortifications from the west sea to the east sea (a distance of a day's journey for a Nephite). They stationed their armies along these lines of fortification.

During 34 and 33 BC, the Nephite dissenters and the large Lamanite army had taken over all the Nephite lands in the south. But in 32 BC, Moronihah and his armies regained many cities. After another year of fighting, in 31 BC, the Nephites had regained half of their possessions.

All the Nephite losses, including the loss of many lands and possessions, and the great loss of life among them, happened because of the wicked practices among them, upheld by many who claimed to be members of God's church. The pride of those who were very rich, who did not give food and clothing to the poor, but oppressed them, was responsible for this destruction. The proud were unkind to the poor. They made fun of sacred things and denied prophecy and revelation. They murdered, stole, lied, plundered and committed adultery. They also fought among themselves for power, and many of them defected to the Lamanites. Because of their great wickedness and boasting, they were left to their own strength. They were not protected, but were attacked and killed.

They were driven out by the Lamanites until they had lost nearly all their lands.

Moronihah had preached many things to the people because of their sinfulness. Nephi and Lehi, Helaman's sons, had also preached many things. They had prophesied to the Nephites about their sins, and about what would happen to them if they did not repent.

As the people repented, they immediately began to prosper. When Moronihah saw that they had repented, he led them from city to city until they had regained half of their property and lands. This is how 31 BC ended. After yet another year of fighting, Moronihah and his armies could not regain any more land. There were so many Lamanites, that it was all Moronihah's army could do to maintain what they had retaken.

The Nephites became very frightened for their lives, and began to remember Alma's prophecies and Mosiah's words. They realized that they had been stubborn and had ignored God's commandments. They knew that they had ignored the laws that Mosiah had left for them—laws that the Lord had commanded him to give to the people. They realized that their laws had become corrupt and that they had become a wicked people like the Lamanites. Because of their sins, the church as a whole began to lose its strength, for some church members stopped believing in the spirit of prophecy and revelation. This is why God's judgments were staring them in the face.

They finally realized just how weak they really were—that they had become like the Lamanites. The Spirit of the Lord no longer saved them in their battles. It had left them because the Spirit of the Lord does not dwell in unholy temples. Once the Spirit had left them, the Lord stopped saving them by His miraculous and matchless power. They had fallen into a state of unbelief and awful wickedness. They saw that they were out-numbered by the Lamanites, and they realized that unless they looked to and held on to the Lord their God, they would certainly be destroyed. They saw that man for man, the Lamanites were just as strong as they were. Because they had fallen into this great transgression, they had become weak in just a few years.

5 - Helaman teaches his sons...

And in that same year, 30 BC, Nephi gave up the judgment-seat to Cezoram.

The laws had been established by the voice of the people, but the majority of the people had chosen evil. Because of this, the Nephites were becoming ripe for destruction, having corrupted their laws.

This was not all. They had become too stubborn to be governed by just laws, which were written for a righteous people. In their fallen condition, just laws could only condemn them. Nephi had grown weary of the people's sinfulness, so he gave up the judgment-seat to preach God's word for the rest of his life. Nephi's brother, Lehi, also went and did the same. They both remembered these words, which their father, Helaman, had spoken: "My sons, I hope you remember to keep God's commandments and teach them to the people. I named you both after our forefathers who came out of Jerusalem, hoping you would remember their good works.

"I hope you will both do good so it may be said and written of you, as it has been said and written of our forefathers. Now, my sons, do not boast of your good works. Do them to have that precious gift of eternal life—a gift which we believe has been given to our forefathers. My sons, remember King Benjamin's words—that there is no other way for anyone to be saved other than through the atoning blood of Jesus Christ, who will come to redeem the world. Also remember the words that Amulek spoke to Zeezrom while in the city of Ammonihah. Amulek said the Lord will surely come to redeem His people, not in their sins, but from their sins. The Father has given Jesus Christ the power to redeem us from our sins through our repentance. This is why He sends angels to us to teach us how to repent. Always remember, my sons, that you must build your foundation upon the rock of our Redeemer, who is Christ, the Son of God. If you trust in Him, then you cannot fall, and the devil's temptations will not overpower you and drag you down to a condition of endless torment."

Helaman taught his sons many other things, some of which are written, and some of which are not. Nephi and Lehi remembered their father's words and kept God's commandments. They went out to teach the Nephites, beginning in the city of Bountiful. From there they went to Gid, and from Gid to Mulek. They continued to go from city to city until they had gone into every Nephite city in the southern land. Then they went to the land of Zarahemla to teach the Lamanites. They taught with great power, confounding many Nephite dissenters, who came forward and confessed their sins. Those who repented were baptized, after which they immediately returned to the Nephites to try to repair the damage they had done.

As Nephi and Lehi preached, God gave them great power and authority and told them what to teach. While in Zarahemla, they astonished the Lamanites with their teaching, and convinced 8,000 of them to repent of their forefathers' wicked traditions.

Then Nephi and Lehi went from Zarahemla to the land of Nephi. There they were captured by Lamanite soldiers and thrown into prison—the same prison that Ammon and his brethren had been put into by Limhi's servants.

After they had been in prison for many days without food, the Lamanites went into the prison with the intention of taking them out and killing them. The Lamanites saw Nephi and Lehi surrounded with what appeared to be fire. Not a single Lamanite dared touch them, for they were afraid of being burned, yet Nephi and Lehi stood among the flames unharmed.

When they realized they were safe from the fire and from the Lamanites, Nephi and Lehi became courageous—for the Lamanites just stood there in complete amazement. Nephi and Lehi said to them, "Don't be afraid, for it is God who shows you this marvelous thing. It is He who prevents you from harming us."

Then a great earthquake began, and it seemed as if the prison walls would collapse at any moment, but they did not. Everyone was overshadowed by a dark cloud, and an awful, sobering fear came over the Lamanites and the Nephite dissenters. Then a voice was heard coming from above the dark cloud, saying, "Repent ye, repent ye, and seek no more to destroy my servants, whom I have sent to declare good tidings." This voice was not loud, like thunder. It was a calm voice of perfect mildness, like a whisper. However, it pierced everyone to their very souls. Then another earthquake began and shook the prison walls, and the dark cloud remained. Again, the calm, whisper-like voice spoke from above, "Repent ye, repent ye, for the kingdom of heaven is at hand. Seek no more to destroy my servants." Then the earth shook again and the prison walls trembled. A third time the voice came, saying such marvelous words that they cannot be uttered by man, and the earth shook as if it were about to split open and devour them!

The Lamanites were surrounded by darkness, and they were so afraid, they could not move. One of them, Aminadab, a Nephite by birth, had once belonged to God's church, but had left it. Aminadab turned and saw Nephi and Lehi's faces through the dark cloud. Their faces shone very brightly, like the faces of angels, and they were looking up into heaven, talking to some being. Then he shouted to the multitude, "Look over there!" And the people were given the power to turn and see Nephi and Lehi's faces. They asked Aminadab, "What do all these things mean, and with whom are Nephi and Lehi speaking?"

Aminadab answered, "They are speaking with the angels of God." Then the Lamanites asked, "What can we do to make this darkness go away?" Aminadab replied, "You must repent and cry to the voice until you have faith in Christ, of whom Alma, Amulek and Zeezrom spoke. After you do this, the darkness will leave."

So they all cried out to the voice of Him who had shaken the earth, pleading with God until the dark cloud was taken away. When they looked around, they saw that the darkness was gone. But now they were surrounded by a pillar of fire. Nephi and Lehi stood in the middle of the people, also surrounded by fire. The fire did not burn anyone, nor did it burn the prison walls, but every soul was filled with glory and unspeakable joy. Then God's Holy Spirit came down from heaven and entered their hearts, filling them with what seemed to be fire. It enabled them to speak marvelous words. Then a pleasant voice came to them, like a whisper, and said, "Peace, peace be unto you, because of your faith in my Well Beloved, who was prepared from the beginning of the world."

Upon hearing this, they looked up to see where the voice was coming from. They saw the heavens open, and angels came down out of heaven and spoke to them. About 300 souls saw and heard these things. They were told to go their way, and not to wonder or doubt. These 300 Lamanites went and told other people what had happened, testifying throughout the entire land of what they had seen and heard. Most of the Lamanites who were told of this great event believed it, and all who believed put away their weapons and hatred of the Nephites. They gave up their forefathers' false traditions, and they gave the Nephites back their land.

6 - A short lived peace...

By the end of 30 BC, the sixty-second year of the judges' reign, most of the Lamanites had become a righteous people—more righteous than the Nephites—because of their great faith. Many Nephites had become hardened, unrepentant and very wicked. They had rejected God's word and all the preaching and prophesying that had come to them.

However, the people of the church were overjoyed by the conversion of the Lamanites. They fellowshipped them and with great joy established God's church among them.

Many Lamanites came down to the land of Zarahemla and told the Nephites of their conversion, calling them back to the faith. They preached with great power and authority, bringing many Nephites to the depths of humility, and convinced them to become humble followers of God and the Lamb.

At the end of 29 BC, many Lamanites went north to preach, as did Nephi and Lehi. There was peace in all the land, and the Nephites traveled freely without any fear among the Nephites and Lamanites. The Lamanites also traveled freely—buying, selling and profiting as they wished. Everyone became rich together, having plenty of gold, silver and other precious metals that were found both in the southern and northern lands.

The southern land had been named after Lehi, and the northern land after Mulek, for they were the first inhabitants of those lands, and they had been brought there by the Lord.

There was plenty of gold, silver and precious ore to be found in all the lands, and many Nephites and Lamanites became very skilled in the art of refining and metal working. This is how they became very rich. They also raised plenty of grain in the north and south. Soon they became a populous, strong people. They raised many flocks, herds and fatlings, and their women spun and wove all types of cloth and fine linen.

Their peace continued throughout 28 and 27 BC. The people were filled with joy and peace as they listened to the many prophecies of what was to come. But in 26 BC, Cezoram was murdered by an unknown assassin while sitting upon the judgment-seat. That same year, his son, who had been appointed by the people to take his father's place, was also murdered. As the next year began, the people began to grow very wicked again. The Lord had blessed them with so many riches of the world that they began to set their hearts upon them, and they began to war with one another. They sought for more and more wealth in order to put themselves above their neighbors. They committed secret murders, robbed and plundered in order to obtain more wealth and power.

Those who did these things were part of the band that had been formed by Kishkumen and Gadianton. At this time, there were many members of this secret band, even among the Nephites. However, most of the band was made up of wicked Lamanites, and they were called Gadianton's robbers and murderers. They had murdered the chief judge, Cezoram, and also his son, yet they had not been found. When the Lamanites discovered that there were robbers among them, they were very sorrowful and did everything in their power to destroy them off the face of the earth. But Satan had taken hold of the hearts of most of the Nephites, who united with those bands of robbers. They entered covenants and oaths to protect and preserve one another in whatever difficult circumstances they might be placed. This is how they escaped justice and did not suffer for their murder, plunder and theft.

All of the bands had secret signs and words to distinguish a brother who had entered into the covenant. Once identified, regardless of what crime he had committed, an evil brother would not be hurt by another brother of his own band who had taken this covenant.

This is how they were able to get away with murder, theft, immorality and all types of wickedness, contrary to the laws of their country and their God.

If any brother that belonged to their band revealed their wickedness to the outside world, he was tried and punished, not by the laws of the land, but according to their wicked laws given to them by Gadianton and Kishkumen. These evil secret oaths and covenants were the same ones that Alma had commanded his son not to describe to the world. For if they were known among the people, they would bring them all down to destruction. These secret oaths and covenants did not come to Gadianton from the records that were delivered to Helaman. They were put into Gadianton's heart by that same being who enticed our first parents to eat of the forbidden fruit—by that same being who plotted with Cain that if he would murder his brother, Abel, it would not be known to the world. He plotted with Cain and his followers from that time forward. It was that same being who had inspired people to build a tower high enough to get to heaven. Then he inspired those people, who came to this land from the tower, to spread the works of darkness over the land until he had dragged them down to an entire destruction and everlasting hell. It was that same being who had inspired Gadianton to continue the work of darkness and secret murder. He has done this from Adam and Eve's day even until now. He is the author of all sin, carrying on his works of darkness and secret murder, handing down their plots, oaths, covenants and plans from generation to generation as he takes hold of the people's hearts. He had a great hold on the Nephites' hearts, and they became very wicked. Most of them turned away from righteousness and trampled God's commandments. They turned to their own ways and built up for themselves idols of gold and silver.

All these sins came to them in only a few years, and most of them had come in 25 BC. Their sinfulness continued to grow during 24 BC, to the great sorrow and lamentation of the righteous. From this history we see that the Nephites began to lose their power and faith, while at the same time, the Lamanites began to spiritually grow in the knowledge of their God. For they kept His statutes and commandments, and walked in truth and uprightness before Him. We also see that the Lord's Spirit began to leave the Nephites because of sin and pride.

The Lord began to pour out His Spirit upon the Lamanites because of their willingness to believe in His words. The Lamanites hunted the band of Gadianton's robbers. They preached God's word among its most wicked members until the band of robbers was completely dissolved from among the Lamanites. But on the other hand, the Nephites built up and supported the robbers. At first, only the most wicked Nephites built up these bands. Then, over a period of time, the Gadianton system seduced most of the righteous—those who belonged to God's church—until they not only believed in the Gadianton system, but actively participated in its wickedness and in reaping its benefits.

This is how the wicked system gained complete control of the government, putting down God's poor, meek and humble followers. We know that these people were in an awful state, ripening for an everlasting destruction. This is how 24 BC ended—the sixty-eighth year of the judges' reign over the Nephites.

7 - *Nephi laments and preaches...*

By 23 BC, Helaman's son, Nephi, returned to Zarahemla from the northern land. He had been preaching God's word to the people there, prophesying many things to them.

But they had rejected all his words, so he could not stay among them, and he returned to his native land. Nephi had seen the people in a state of awful wickedness. Those Gadianton robbers had taken over the judgment-seats. He saw God's commandments being laid aside in their judgments as they denied the people justice. He saw Gadianton robbers sitting in his judgment-seat, condemning the righteous because of their righteousness and letting the guilty go free because of their money. The Gadiantons did this to gain riches and to be re-elected at the head of the government, ruling and doing as they wished while the world praised them. They also did this so that they could more easily get away with adultery, theft, murder or anything else they wanted.

This great iniquity had come upon the Nephites in only a few years. When Nephi saw all this, his heart was swollen with sorrow, and he exclaimed in the agony of his soul, "How I wish that I could have lived when my father Nephi first came from Jerusalem, so that I could have enjoyed the promised land with him. His people were teachable, firm to keep God's commandments, and slow to sin. They were quick to listen to the Lord's words.

"If I could have lived in those days, then my soul would have had joy in the righteousness of my brethren. But I must live in these days, and my soul is filled with sorrow because of my brethren's wickedness."

Nephi had raised his voice while on the top his garden tower—a tower that was near the highway that led to the main Zarahemla marketplace. As some men were passing by, they saw Nephi upon his tower pouring out his soul to God. Since Nephi was well-known, the men ran and told the people what they had seen, and a crowd came to find out why Nephi was mourning.

When Nephi arose and saw the crowd, he said to them, "Have you gathered so that I may tell you of your sinfulness? Yes, you are here because I have been pouring out my soul to my God because of your iniquities! You have gathered to wonder, and you should wonder because the devil has taken such a great hold on your hearts. How could you have given way to the enticing of the devil, who seeks to hurl your souls down to an everlasting misery and endless woe? Oh repent, for why will you allow yourselves to die spiritually? Turn to the Lord your God now, for His Spirit has already left you. This has happened because you have hardened your hearts and will not listen to the Good Shepherd's voice. You have provoked His anger against you.

"Now instead of gathering you together, He will scatter you, and you will become food for dogs and wild animals, unless you repent. How could have you forgotten your God in the very day that He has delivered you? You have done these things to get gold and silver, and to be praised by others. You have set your hearts on riches and the vain things of this world. To get them, you murder, plunder, steal and bear false witness against your neighbors. Because you do this, a curse will come upon you unless you repent. This city, and other great cities in this region, will be conquered, and you will have no place in them, for the Lord will not give you the strength to defend your cities as He has in the past. He says, 'I will not show my strength to the wicked, but only to those who repent and listen to my words.' My brethren, it will be better for the Lamanites than for you unless you repent. They are more righteous than you, for they have not sinned against the great knowledge that you have.

Note: Sinning against gospel knowledge is much more offensive to God than not accepting the gospel. In each prophecy about those with the gospel—Alma's prophecy to the Nephites of Ammonihah in 82 BC (Alma 9:23-24), Nephi's prophecy to the Nephites around 20 BC (Helaman 7:23-24), Samuel's prophecy to the Nephites in 6 BC (Helaman 15:12-17), and Christ's 34 AD prophecy to the latter-day Gentiles (3 Nephi 16:10-15), when those with gospel light and knowledge "sin against" it, the Lamanites fare much better than the "offenders," who are either trodden down or completely destroyed.

"This is why the Lord will be merciful to them by sparing their lives and allowing them to have many descendants, long after you are extinct! You are cursed for joining that secret Gadianton band! You are cursed for being so proud of your great prosperity, and finally, you are cursed because of your wicked deeds. If you do not repent, your lands will be taken away and you will be destroyed off the face of the earth! All this is not just my opinion, for the Lord God has made these things known to me. And I testify that they will surely happen."

8 - Nephi confronts corrupt judges...

Hearing Nephi, some of the Gadianton judges became angry. They cried out to the people, "Why don't you seize this man and bring him forward to be condemned for his crime?

"Why do you do nothing when you have seen and heard this man revile against us and our law?" Nephi had spoken about their corrupt laws. He had also said many other things, but nothing contrary to God's commandments. Those judges were angry because Nephi had spoken so plainly to them about their secret works of darkness. But they dared not lay their hands upon him, fearing that the people might cry out against them. This is why they cried to the people, "Why do you allow this man to revile against us? He condemns our people to destruction, saying that our great cities will be taken from us and that we will have no place in them. We know this is impossible because we are so powerful. Our cities are so great that our enemies could never overpower us."

The judges stirred up some of the people to become angry with Nephi, and the people started to argue among themselves. Some said, "Leave this man alone. He is a good man, and what he says will surely come to pass unless we repent. We know that all the judgments of which he has testified will come upon us because he has correctly testified of our many sins. If he were not a prophet, he could not have testified of our sins so accurately."

The judges were too afraid to lay their hands on Nephi, and he continued to speak, having gained favor with some of the people. Nephi said, "Have you not read that God gave power to one man, even Moses, to strike the waters of the Red Sea? After the waters parted, and after our forefathers, the Israelites, walked through on dry ground, the waters closed up over the Egyptian armies. If God gave this much power to one man, then why should you argue whether or not He has given me the power to know of the judgments that will come upon you unless you repent? But rather than repent, you will deny my words. You also deny all of our forefathers' words. You deny the words of Moses, who had great power given to him, and who spoke about the coming of the Messiah. Didn't Moses testify that the Son of God would come? As Moses lifted up the brass snake in the wilderness, the Messiah will also be lifted up. Just as those who looked upon that snake lived, all who humbly look to the Son of God with faith will have eternal life.

"All the holy prophets since Adam have also testified of the Son of God. Abraham saw His coming and was filled with gladness and joy. Like many before him, Abraham was called to the order of the Son of God (Melchizedek priesthood), so that thousands of years beforehand, his people would know that the Son of God was coming to redeem them. And since Abraham, there have been many prophets who have continued to testify of these things. Because Zenos testified so boldly, he was killed. Zenock, Ezias, Isaiah and Jeremiah all testified that the Son of God would come. Jeremiah also testified that Jerusalem would be destroyed. And you know that Jerusalem was destroyed. You also know that Zedekiah's sons were killed, except Mulek, whose descendants are now among us. And there is more—

"Our forefather, Lehi, was driven out of Jerusalem because he testified of these things. Nephi and almost all of our forefathers have also testified of these things, even down to this time. They have testified of Christ's coming, looking forward and rejoicing in it.

"Our forefathers are now with Christ. He showed Himself to them while they lived and redeemed them spiritually. Because they knew He would yet redeem them physically through the resurrection, they praised Him. Seeing that you know these things, if you deny them, you are liars, and you reject the many witnesses from heaven and earth that testify that these things are true. Even now you have rejected the truth, rebelling against your holy God. Instead of securing a place for yourselves in heaven, where no unclean being may enter, you are inviting God's anger on judgment day. You are becoming ripe for an eternal destruction because of your immorality, murder and sinfulness. Unless you repent, this destruction will soon come to you. This destruction is very near, for as I speak, your judge has been murdered by his brother who wants the judgment-seat for himself. These two brothers both belong to your secret band, which Gadianton organized as he was inspired by the devil who seeks to destroy everyone's soul."

9 - Nephi, falsely accused, exposes murderer...

When Nephi said this, five men ran to the judgment-seat. As they ran, they said to each other, "Now we will know for sure if God has really commanded Nephi to prophesy such incredible things to us. We do not believe that he is a prophet, but if what Nephi said about the chief judge is true, then we will believe his other words."

The five men quickly ran to the judgment-seat and found the chief judge lying in his blood. They were so astonished that they fell down, for they never thought they would actually see what Nephi had prophesied. Now they knew Nephi was truly a prophet. They were so afraid of God's judgments upon the people that they trembled and fainted. The judge had been secretly stabbed by his brother, who had run away in disguise. Being the first ones to discover the dead judge, his servants had gone out to tell the people of the murder. The people came to the judgment-seat and were surprised to find the five men lying on the ground. The people did not know anything about the other crowd gathered at Nephi's garden, so they said, "These men have killed the judge, and God has struck them down so they would not escape!" They tied up the men and carried them off to prison. Then a proclamation was sent throughout the land that the judge had been killed and that his murderers had been captured.

The next day, the people assembled to mourn and fast at the great chief judge's funeral. The corrupt judges who had heard Nephi in his garden were also there. They asked the people where the five men were, whom they had sent. The people answered, "We do not know anything about five men who were sent by the judges, but we have put five murderers in prison." The judges called for the five men, and they were the five who had been sent. The judges asked them what had happened. The men reported: "We ran to the judgment-seat, and when we saw that everything of which Nephi had testified was true, we were so shocked that we fainted. When we recovered, we were bound and put into prison. We do not know who killed the chief judge. All we know is that when we went to the judgment-seat as you asked us, we found the judge murdered, just as Nephi said he would be!"

Then the judges explained the matter to the people, accusing Nephi of conspiring with someone to kill the judge. They said, "He told us about this murder, attempting to trick us into converting to his faith, and to get us to believe that he is a great man—a chosen prophet of God. We will question him, and he will confess his guilt and tell us who murdered the judge." The people untied the five men, but still held them as suspects. These men defended Nephi by arguing with and confounding the judges. But the judges still took Nephi and bound him. They questioned him, trying to trap him with his words. They wanted to trick him into confessing so that they could legally execute him. They said to him, "You have conspired with someone to kill the judge. If you will confess and tell us who killed the judge, we will give you money and spare your life." Nephi replied, "Oh you fools with unclean hearts. You blind, stubborn people. Do you know how long the Lord your God will tolerate your sins? You should start to howl and mourn because of the great destruction that awaits you if you do not repent. You accuse me of conspiring with someone to murder Seezoram, our chief judge. I testified to you about his murder in order to witness to you that I know about the wickedness among you. Because of this, you now accuse me of conspiring to murder. Because I showed you this sign, you are angry with me and want to put me to death. Now let us see if you will still seek my life after I show you another sign. And this is the other sign:

"Go to the house of Seantum, Seezoram's brother. Ask him, 'Has Nephi, the pretended prophet, who prophesies so much evil about our people, conspired with you to murder your brother, Seezoram?' He will say, 'No, I have not conspired with Nephi.' Then ask him if he murdered his brother. He will be afraid and not know what to say. Then he will act surprised, denying everything, and declare his innocence. Then examine his cloak and you will find blood on it. Ask him where the blood came from. Ask him if it is the blood of his brother. Then he will turn pale and shake as if he were about to die. Then say to him, 'Because you are so afraid and pale, we know you are guilty.' He will become even more afraid and confess that he murdered his brother. He will tell you that

I, Nephi, could only have known these things through the power of God. Then you will know that I am an honest man and have been sent to you from God."

The people did as Nephi told them. Nephi's words were true, for Seantum denied the murder and then confessed just as Nephi said he would. Seantum was convicted of murder, and Nephi and the five men were set free.

Some of the Nephites believed Nephi's testimony and were converted. Others believed the testimony of the five men who had been converted while in prison. Some said, "Nephi is a prophet!" Others said, "He is a god, for only a god could know all things, telling us our thoughts and who murdered our chief judge."

10 - God blesses Nephi...

Then the people went their separate ways, leaving Nephi standing alone. He walked toward his home thinking of what the Lord had shown him. He was very sorry because of the Nephite wickedness, for they participated in all types of secret works of darkness, murder and theft.

As Nephi was sorrowing, the Lord's voice said to him, "Nephi, you are blessed for what you have done. I have seen how dedicated you have been in telling my words to this people. You have not been afraid of them or of losing your life. You have only wanted to do my will and keep my commandments. Because you have been so dedicated to me, I will bless you forever. I will make your faith, words and actions mighty. Whatever you say will be done, for I know that you will not ask for anything that is against my will. I, God, tell you in the presence of my angels that you will have power over this people. You will smite the earth with drought, pestilence and destruction according to their wickedness. I give you my power among this people. Whomever you bless will be blessed forever, and whomever you curse will be cursed forever. If you command a temple to split in two, it will be done. If you command a mountain to fall down and become a smooth valley, it will be done. If you say that God will smite this people, then I will. And now I command you to tell this people that the Lord God, who is Almighty, has said, 'Unless you repent, you will be destroyed.'"

As soon as the Lord's voice had come to Nephi, he went to the many groups of people scattered throughout the land, telling them what the Lord had told him—that if they did not repent, they would be destroyed. Even after seeing Nephi's great miracle—telling of their chief judge's murderer, they were still too proud and stubborn to listen. Nephi repeated the Lord's warning to the people wherever he went, but the people just became angry with him and tried to throw him into prison. So much of God's power was with Nephi that the Spirit carried him away from the crowds that wanted to put him into prison, and he freely walked away from them. Nephi went from crowd to crowd in the Spirit, telling them God's word, until he had personally told or had sent His word among all of them. But no one would listen. Instead, they began to again fight among themselves, killing each other with swords. This is how 21 BC ended—the seventy-first year of the judges' reign over the Nephites.

11 - Nephi asks for a drought to begin, and to end...

By 20 BC, the Nephites were fighting with one another throughout all their lands, and it was the secret band of robbers who were responsible for this destruction and wickedness.

Their wars continued throughout 19 BC. In that year Nephi prayed, "Oh Lord, do not allow this people to destroy themselves by the sword. Instead, let there be a drought to stir them to remember Thee, and perhaps they will repent and return to Thee."

Then there was a great drought in the land among all the Nephites. It continued throughout 18 BC, forcing the Nephites to stop fighting. During 17 BC, the third year of drought, no grain could be grown by the Nephites or Lamanites. And in the more wicked parts of the land, thousands of people died of starvation. When the people realized that they were all about to die of starvation, they began to remember the Lord their God by remembering Nephi's words. They begged their chief judges and leaders to tell Nephi, "We know you are a man of God, so pray to the Lord our God to end this drought, or else everything you have said about our destruction will happen."

The judges asked Nephi to pray for the people. Seeing the people humble themselves and repent, Nephi prayed, "Look how this people repent, oh Lord. They have destroyed Gadianton's band and have buried the band's secret plans in the earth. Now, oh Lord, because of their humility, please turn away Thine anger, and let it be appeased by the destruction of those wicked men who have already died. Oh Lord, will Thou turn away Thy fierce anger and end this drought? Oh Lord, will Thou hear me and do according to my words, sending rain so that the earth may bring forth her fruit and grain again? Oh Lord, Thou did listen to my words when I said, 'Let there be a drought.' I know that Thou will hear my words now, for Thou said, 'If these people repent, I will spare them.' Thou sees that they have repented because of the drought, pestilence and destruction that has come to them. And now, oh Lord, will Thou turn away Thine anger and see if they will serve Thee again? If they do serve Thee, oh Lord, Thou can bless them according to Thy words."

By 16 BC, the Lord had turned away His anger from the people. He caused rain to fall, and the earth brought forth her fruit and grain once again. The people rejoiced, glorifying God, and they stopped trying to destroy Nephi. They considered him to be a great prophet, a man of God, with great power and authority given to him from God. And Nephi's brother, Lehi, was just as righteous.

The Nephites started to prosper in the land again and rebuilt their cities. They multiplied and spread out, covering the whole face of the land from the north to the south, and from the western to the eastern seas. Throughout the year 16 BC, there was peace. Fifteen BC was also a peaceful year, and the church spread throughout the land. Most of the people, both Nephites and Lamanites, belonged to the church and enjoyed great peace. The year 14 BC was also peaceful, except for a few disagreements about some of the doctrine given by the prophets.

In 13 BC, there was much debating and arguing over church doctrine. But Nephi, Lehi and many of their brethren who knew the true points of doctrine, having many revelations daily, preached to the people. Because of their preaching, many arguments were ended.

However, by 12 BC, there were many Nephite dissenters, who called themselves Lamanites. They persuaded the Lamanites to attack the Nephites. The Lamanites and the dissenters came out of their hiding places to murder and plunder and then retreated back into the mountains, the wilderness, and secret places. Each day their numbers grew as more Nephite dissenters joined them. In only a few years there was again a large band of robbers. They studied all the secret plans of Gadianton in order to become Gadianton robbers. These robbers brought havoc and destruction among the Nephites and Lamanites.

Soon it became critical to destroy these robbers, and a strong army was sent into the wilderness and mountains to search for and destroy the robbers, but the army was driven back into their own lands. This is how 12 BC ended—the eightieth year of the judges' reign over the Nephites.

In the beginning of 11 BC, the army again went out against this band of robbers, killing many of them, but not without great losses of their own. They were forced to retreat out of the wilderness and mountains, for there were too many robbers there. By the end of the year, the robbers were so numerous and strong that they resisted the entire combined Nephite and Lamanite armies. They continued to terrorize all the people in the land. They destroyed cities, killed many people, and carried away many women and children into the wilderness.

This great evil had come upon the people because of their sins, and again they were stirred to remember the Lord their God. As 11 BC ended, they were beginning to remember Him, but just a year later they started to forget their God again. In 10 and 9 BC, they were very sinful, with no desire to repent. By 7 BC, their pride and wickedness had grown stronger than ever, and they were once again ripening for destruction by the end of that year.

12 - The Nephite apostasy...

From all this we learn just how false and unsteady people's hearts are. We learn that the Lord, in His great, infinite goodness, blesses and prospers those who trust in Him.

We learn that at the very moment the Lord gives temporal blessings to His people, they forget Him, because their prosperity makes their lives so easy. For it was the Lord who fed them, making their crops grow and herds increase. It was the Lord who gave them their gold, silver and precious things, and inspired every kind of art. The Lord saved their lives by delivering them from their enemies, who were softened and did not declare war on them. The Lord did everything to insure the welfare and happiness of His people, but instead of thanking Him, the people considered His words to be worthless.

We also learn that unless the Lord afflicts His people with death, terror, famine and all types of pestilence, they will not remember Him. Oh how foolish, vain, evil and devilish are the people. How quick they are to sin—listening to the evil one and setting their hearts upon the vain things of the world—and how slow they are to do good!

How quickly they lift themselves up in pride, boasting and sinning in every way, and how slowly they remember the Lord their God. How slow they are to listen to His counsel and walk in wisdom's paths! So many people do not want the Lord their God, their Creator, to rule and reign over them. Even though He extends His great goodness and mercy to them, they consider His counsel to be worthless, and they will not let Him be their guide. Oh how great is the nothingness of people, who are less obedient than the dust of the earth. For the dust moves when the everlasting God commands it. At His voice the hills and mountains tremble and quake. By the power of His voice they are broken up and become a smooth valley. By the power of His voice the whole earth shakes, even to the center. If He says to the earth, "Move," it moves. And if He says, "Stop, and make this day longer," the earth obeys. It stops and the sun appears to stand still—for it is the earth that moves, and not the sun. If the everlasting God commands the ocean to dry up, it is done. If He says to a mountain, "Rise up, fall over here and bury this city," then it is done.

If a sinful man hides his treasure in the earth, and the Lord curses it, then that treasure is cursed. If the Lord says, "You are cursed, and nobody will ever find you," then it is so. If the Lord says to a man, "Because of your sins you will be cursed forever," then that man is cursed forever. If He says, "Because of your sins you will be cut off from my presence," then he will be cut off. And the Lord will say this to the sinful—those who will not repent and who cannot be saved. People are told to repent, that they may be saved and return to God's presence.

This is the salvation and blessing of those who listen to His voice. May God grant, in His great fullness, the chance for His children to repent and do good works, that they may be restored by grace, because of their gracious works.

I, Mormon, would hope that everyone will be saved. But we read that at the great and last day, some will be cast off from the Lord's presence. Some will be consigned to a state of endless misery, fulfilling these words: "Those who have done good will progress forever, and those who have done evil will be damned."

13 - Samuel warns the Nephites...

The Nephites were still wicked in 6 BC, while the Lamanites kept God's commandments according to the law of Moses. During that year, a Lamanite named Samuel came into the land of Zarahemla and began to preach to the people. For many days he preached repentance, but the people threw him out. Because he had been rejected, Samuel was about to return to his own land, but the Lord's voice told him to go back and prophesy the things that would come into his heart.

The people would not let Samuel come back into the city, so he climbed on top of the city wall, held out his arm, and shouted, "I, Samuel, a Lamanite, speak the Lord's words that He puts into my heart. His words are: 'The sword of justice hangs over the Nephite people. In less than 400 years this sword will fall upon them. Heavy destruction will surely come upon them, and nothing can stop it unless they repent and show faith in the Lord Jesus Christ, who will surely come into the world and suffer many things, and will be slain for His people.'

"An angel of the Lord told me this. He brought glad news to my soul and I was sent to bring it to you, but you would not receive me. This is why the Lord has told me to tell you: 'Because you Nephites are so hard in your hearts, if you do not repent, I will take my word and my Spirit away from you. I will not protect you any longer, and I will turn the hearts of your brethren against you. In less than 400 years you will be extinct, for I will visit you with the sword, drought and pestilence. I will visit you in my fierce anger, and four generations from now your enemies will witness the entire destruction of your people. This will surely happen unless you repent.'

"I, Samuel, tell you that if you will repent and return to the Lord your God, He will turn away His anger. For He said, 'Whoever repents and turns to me is blessed, but whoever does not repent will be cursed. This great city of Zarahemla has already been cursed. It has only been spared because of the righteous who live here. I, the Lord, see that most of the people in Zarahemla will harden their hearts against me.'

"I, the Lord, will save those who repent. If it were not for the righteous people in this great city, I would have already rained down fire from heaven and destroyed it. But for the sake of the righteous this city has been spared. When the times comes that you drive the righteous out, then your city will be ready for destruction. The city of Gideon is also cursed because of its wickedness and great sins. All the Nephite cities in this region are cursed for their great wickedness. Because of their wickedness, a curse will come upon the land, and when you bury treasure in the earth, you will not find it again. Only the righteous, who hide their treasure unto me, will be able to find it again. It is my will that people consecrate their treasure for my purposes. Anyone who does not do this is not righteous, but is cursed along with his treasure. The Nephites will hide their treasures before running from their invading enemies. They will do this because their hearts are set upon riches. But because they do not hide their treasures unto me, they and their treasure will be cursed, and they will be killed by their enemies.'"

Samuel continued, "The Lord says you are cursed along with your riches because you have set your hearts upon them, and because you have ignored the words of Him who gave them to you. You only remember your riches. Your hearts are not grateful to the Lord. They swell with great pride as you boast, envy, argue, plot, persecute, murder and commit all types of sins. This is why the Lord God curses the land and your riches. You are cursed even now because you have thrown out the prophets. You have mocked them, thrown rocks at them, and killed them, just as wicked people did anciently.

"You tell one another that if you had lived long ago, you would not have killed the prophets like the ancients did. But you are worse than those who lived long ago! For as the Lord lives, if a prophet comes among you and tells you the Lord's words which testify of your sins, then you are angry with him. You throw him out and plot his death. You say he is a false prophet, a sinner, and of the devil. You do this because he testifies of your evil acts.

"But you listen to those who say, 'What you are doing is not wrong. You will not suffer. Be proud of yourselves. Do whatever you like.' You make these men famous and give them your money. They begin to wear expensive clothes and tell you how wonderful you are, and how great your future will be, so you find no fault in them.

"Oh you wicked, perverse generation. You hard, stubborn people. How long do you think the Lord will tolerate what you do? How long will you be led by foolish and blind guides, choosing darkness rather than light? The Lord is already angry with you, and has cursed the land because of your sinfulness. Soon your riches will be cursed. When you are poor, you will not be able to find them. In your poverty, you will cry to the Lord in vain, 'But your cries will be in vain, for it will be too late, and nothing can stop your destruction,' says the Lord of Hosts.

"You will cry and moan, saying, 'If only we had repented and had not killed the prophets. If only we had remembered the Lord our God when He gave us our riches, then we would not have lost them. Now when we put down a tool, the next day it is gone. When we need our swords for battle, they are taken from us. Our buried treasures have eluded us because of the curse on the land. If only we had repented when the Lord warned us, for now the land is cursed and we cannot keep anything.'

"In the days ahead, you will also say, 'We are surrounded by demons—by the angels of him who has sought to destroy our souls, and our sins are great. Oh Lord, can Thou not turn Thine anger away from us?'

"But in those days ahead, your days of probation will be over. You will have put off the day of your salvation until it is everlastingly too late, and your destruction will be certain.

"All your lives you have been trying to get what you can never have—happiness in doing wrong. You can never be happy while being wicked because this goes against the nature of righteousness. If only you people would listen to my words! I pray that the Lord's anger will be turned away from you—that you will repent and be saved."

14 - Samuel prophesies of the signs of Christ...

This Lamanite prophet, Samuel, said many other things to the people, but not all his words can be written in this book. Here are more of his words:

"I will give you a sign, which will happen in five years, when the Son of God comes to redeem all who believe in Him. There will be great lights in heaven during the night before He comes. That night there will be no darkness, for it will seem like day.

"This will be your sign: You will see the sun set and rise as usual, but the night before His birth will not be dark. You will have one day, one night, and one day without darkness.

"You will also see a new star in the sky. This is not all, for you will see many signs and wonders in the sky and be so amazed that you will fall to the earth. And everyone who believes in the Son of God will have everlasting life. This is what the Lord's angel told me to tell you. The angel commanded me to prophesy these things to you. He told me to cry to this people, 'Repent and prepare the way of the Lord!'

"Because I am a Lamanite, and because I told you the Lord's harsh words, you threw me out of your city. Now you are angry with me again and want to kill me. But you will hear me now, for I have climbed on top of this wall to tell you of God's judgments that await you because of your sins, and how you may yet repent of them. I came to tell you of the coming of Jesus Christ, the Son of God, the Father of heaven and earth, the Creator of all things from the beginning, and also of the signs of His coming so that perhaps you will believe in Him. If you believe in Him, you will repent of all your sins and have them taken from you through His merits.

"I give you another sign—the sign of His death, for He must surely die so that salvation and the resurrection may come. After men and women are resurrected, they will again be brought into the presence of the Lord. His death and resurrection will redeem all people from the first death of their spirit and body. The first death came upon Adam and Eve and upon all their descendants when they were sent out from the Lord's presence, out of the garden into a world in which their bodies had to die. Because they were no longer in the Lord's presence, they were considered to be dead to spiritual things. This condition for them, and now for us, is called the first death. The resurrection of Christ redeems all people from this first death of the body and spirit by bringing them back into the Lord's presence. The resurrection of Christ also allows us to repent and not suffer a second death, or a spiritual death, which is to be cut off from the Lord's presence again after we are judged. Therefore, I call upon all of you to repent! Otherwise, you will suffer a second death for knowing these things and not doing them.

"On the day that Christ dies, the sun will be darkened and refuse to give its light. The moon and the stars will do the same, so that no light will be upon the face of this land. This complete darkness will continue for three days, beginning from the time Christ dies and continuing until He rises again. And when His spirit leaves His body, there will be thunder and lightning for many hours as the earth shakes and trembles. Massive rocks, both on the surface of the earth and below it, will be broken up. The entire face of the earth will be broken up, above and below. There will be great storms, and many mountains will become valleys, while many valleys will become very high mountains. Many highways will be broken up, and many cities will become desolate. Graves will be opened, and resurrected saints will appear to many.

"The angel told me that this thunder and lightning will last for many hours. He said that after these great destructions, darkness will cover the whole earth for three days. The angel told me that before Christ is born, many people will see even greater signs than these. This will prepare them to believe in Christ when the signs of His birth are given—so that whoever believes might be saved, and whoever will not believe will be given a righteous judgment. If the unbelievers receive condemnation, they will have brought it upon themselves.

"And now, remember my brothers and sisters, that those who die in their sins can only blame themselves, for God has given you the knowledge and the freedom to act for yourselves—the knowledge to know good from evil, and the freedom to choose life or death. You may do good and have good restored to you, or you may choose evil and be restored to evil.

15 - Nephites are cursed and the Lamanites blessed...

My brothers and sisters, unless you repent, your houses will be destroyed. Your nursing women with small children will have a great reason to mourn, for there will be no place for them to hide. Your pregnant women will not be able to run, and will be trampled and left to die. "You, the Nephites, will be cursed unless you repent when you see all these signs and wonders. For you have been the chosen people of the Lord, and He has chastised you because He loves you. The Lord hated what the Lamanites did according to their false traditions. But salvation has come to them through the preaching of your people. The Lord has spared them so that they would have time to be converted to the truth. Most of the Lamanites are now righteous, and they keep God's commandments, statutes and judgments according to the law of Moses. Most of them are doing everything they can to help their brethren know the truth. And because of their efforts, many of their brethren are converted each day. You have seen that after coming to know the truth, the Lamanites' testimonies are firm. After realizing their false traditions, they believe the holy scriptures and prophecies written therein. You have seen the change that has come upon their hearts as they have been led by the prophecies to repent with faith in the Lord. You know that those Lamanites who have done this are firm in their faith in Christ, who has made them free.

"You know that they have buried their weapons, being afraid to sin again by fighting. They would rather be killed than fight, because of their faith in Christ. Because of their strong faith, the Lord will bless them and extend their lives, even though they were once terrible sinners. But even if they did not believe in the Lord, He would still let them live in the land until they are converted in the latter days. Our forefathers, the prophet Zenos, and many other prophets spoke about this latter-day conversion of the Lamanites.

"The Lord's promises are made to the Lamanites in the last days, because in spite of the many difficulties they will have—being driven like cattle over the land, being hunted, killed and scattered with no safe place to go—the Lord will show mercy on them. According to prophecy, they will once again know their Redeemer, their Great and True Shepherd, and be numbered among His people.

"It will be better for them than for you unless you repent, for if the Lamanites had seen the mighty works that you have seen, they would not stay ignorant under the curse of their forefathers' false traditions, and they would never again falter in unbelief. The Lord says, 'I will not completely destroy the Lamanites, but in the day of my wisdom I will cause them to return to me again. Now if the Nephites will not repent and do my will, as surely as I live, I will completely destroy them. I will do this if they will not believe and obey me after I have done so many mighty works among them.'"

16 - Some Nephites repent...

Many people heard Samuel, a Lamanite, as he spoke from the city walls. The ones who believed him went looking for Nephi. When they found him, they confessed their sins to him and asked him to baptize them unto the Lord.

But those who did not believe Samuel threw rocks at him as he stood on the wall. Many shot arrows at him, but the Lord's Spirit was with Samuel, so they could not hit him.

When they realized that they could not hit him, many more believed and went to Nephi to be baptized. Nephi baptized, prophesied, preached and cried repentance to the people. He showed them signs and wonders and performed miracles among them so they would know that Christ would soon come.

Nephi told them about things that would soon happen, so that when they did happen, the people would believe, remembering that they had been prophesied. But most of the people did not believe Samuel. After realizing that they could not kill him, they called out to their captains, "Bind this man, for he is possessed with a devil. Because the devil's power is in him, we cannot hit him with rocks and arrows. So catch him, bind him, and take him away."

As the captains started to come after Samuel, he jumped off the wall and ran out of their lands. He went back to his own country and began to preach and prophesy among his own people, and the Nephites never heard of him again. This is how the year 6 BC ended. By the end of 5 BC, most of the Nephites were still full of pride and wickedness, while only a few repented and kept God's commandments.

This condition did not change throughout 4 BC,—the eighty-eighth year of the judges' reign over the Nephites. The following year was the same, except that most of the people were even more hardened, doing things that were more and more contrary to God's commandments. But in 2 BC, two years before Christ was to be born, great signs and wonders were given to the people, and the prophets' words began to be fulfilled.

Angels appeared to wise men, bringing them glad news of great joy. In this way, the scriptures were beginning to be fulfilled.

But in spite of all these things, only the most believing Nephites and Lamanites were not hardened. Nearly all the people in the land depended on their own strength and wisdom. They said, "With so many predictions, of course they have guessed some things right. But we know that all the great and marvelous works that they have predicted cannot occur."

They began to reason and debate among themselves, saying, "It is not reasonable for such a being as a Christ to come. For if He will come as the Son of God, the Father of heaven and earth, as it has been spoken, then why will He not show Himself to us as well as to those in Jerusalem? Why will He not come into this land and show Himself, as they say He will in Jerusalem?

"We know this is only a wicked tradition, handed down to us by our forefathers to make us believe in some great and marvelous thing that will happen, not among us, but in some far away land that we know nothing about. This wicked tradition was designed to keep us in ignorance, for we cannot see with our own eyes if these traditions are true or not. Those who teach us, using these wicked traditions, do it by the cunning and mysterious arts of the evil one, working this great mystery that we cannot understand. They do this to keep us down—to be servants to their words and to them, for we depend on them to teach us the word. If we let them, they would keep us in ignorance all our lives."

Now the people imagined in their hearts many other things like this, which were foolish and vain. They were very disturbed, for Satan stirred them up to sin constantly. Satan spread rumors and contentions all over the land to harden the people's hearts against good and against that which was to come.

By the beginning of 1 BC, in spite of all the signs, wonders and miracles that the Lord's people had performed, Satan had taken a great hold upon the hearts of nearly all the people in the land. This is the end of Helaman's book, according to the record that he and his sons made.

1 - Signs of Christ's birth are given...

The year was 1 BC when Lachoneus was the chief judge and governor over the land. Helaman's son, Nephi, had left Zarahemla, putting his oldest son, Nephi, in charge of the brass plates, all the records that had been kept, and all those sacred things that had been handed down for 600 years. After Nephi left, no one heard of him again, and his son, Nephi, continued to keep a record of the people.

In the beginning of the ninety-second year of the judges' reign (1 AD), more prophecies were fulfilled, for greater signs and miracles began to be seen among the people.

But some said the time was past for Samuel's words to be fulfilled. They began to celebrate over their brethren, saying, "The time is past and Samuel's words are not fulfilled, so your joy and faith in those things has been in vain."

They made a great uproar throughout the land, causing sorrow among the believers, who thought that perhaps the promised signs might not come. But they continued to watch for the day, the night, and the day that would be like one long day, so that their faith would not be in vain.

Then the unbelievers set a date when all those who believed in those traditions would be killed unless Samuel's signs came to pass. When Nephi heard this wicked plan, his heart became full of sorrow. He went out and bowed himself down upon the earth and cried mightily to his God on behalf of his people—those who were about to be killed because of their faith in their forefathers' words.

After Nephi had cried mightily to the Lord all that day, the Lord's voice said to him, "Lift up your head and be of good cheer, for the time has come. Tonight the sign will be given, and tomorrow I will come into the world, to show the world that I will fulfill all that I have told my holy prophets to say. I will come to my own, to fulfill all things that I have made known to the people from the beginning of the world, and to do the will of both the Father and the Son—of the Father because of me, and of the Son because of my flesh."

These words that came to Nephi were fulfilled, for after the sun went down, it did not get dark, and the people were astonished. Many who had not believed the prophets fell to the earth as if they were dead, for they knew that their great plan of destruction for those who believed the prophets had been frustrated. They knew the Son of God would soon appear.

All the people from the west to the east, both in the northern and southern lands, were so astonished that they fell to the earth. They knew the prophets had testified of these things for many years and that the sign had come. They were afraid because of their sins and unbelief.

There was no darkness all that night. It was as light as mid-day. The sun rose in the morning as usual, and everyone knew it was the day that the Lord would be born.

All things happened down to the last detail according to the prophets' words. Even a new star appeared. From this time on, Satan sent lies among the people to harden their hearts against believing in the signs and wonders they had seen. In spite of these lies, most of the people believed and were converted to the Lord.

Nephi and many others went among the people, baptizing them unto repentance, which took away their sins. And the people began to have peace in the land again. There was no contention, except for some arguing among a few who had begun to preach, who were trying to prove by the scriptures that it was not necessary to continue to observe the law of Moses. They were mistaken in this preaching because they did not understand the scriptures. But soon they were convinced of their error and confessed their faults, for it was made known to them that the law was not yet fulfilled, and that it must be fulfilled down to the last detail.

The year 1 AD passed, bringing good news to the people, for the signs came according to the words of all the holy prophets. Two AD was also a peaceful year, except for the strife caused by the Gadianton robbers. They lived in the mountains, infesting the land. Their hiding places in the mountains were so hard to attack that the people could not overpower them. So the Gadiantons continued to commit many murders among the people.

In 3 AD, they began to increase their numbers greatly because so many Nephite dissenters joined them. This caused much sorrow among the Nephites who stayed in their lands.

This also caused many Lamanites to sorrow, for many of their young men and women were led away by some of the Gadiantons who were Zoramites. These young Lamanites were seduced into joining the Gadiantons through lies and flattery. Because their rising generation was becoming wicked, the Lamanites began to decrease in faith and righteousness.

2 - Signs are explained away...

By 4 AD, the people started to forget the signs and wonders they had heard from heaven, and they were less and less impressed by new signs. They became more stubborn and blind to the truth, no longer believing what they had seen and heard. The people made up excuses to account for the great wonders they had witnessed, saying that they were made up by men and by the devil's power to deceive them. This is how Satan got possession of the people's hearts once again, leading them away to believe that Christ was a product of foolish and vain imaginations.

As the people became more and more wicked, they did not believe that any more signs and wonders would be given. Satan continued to lead away the people and tempted them to do more wicked things. This continued through the year 9 AD. And now a hundred years had passed since the days of Mosiah, king of the Nephites. Six hundred and nine years had passed since Lehi had left Jerusalem, and nine years had passed since the sign of Christ's birth had been given. (The Nephites had begun to count their years from the time that Christ was born). Now Nephi was in charge of all the plates and sacred things. His father, Nephi, did not return to Zarahemla, and could not be found anywhere in the land.

In spite of all the preaching and prophesying among them, the people remained wicked throughout the years 10 and 11 AD. By the year 13 AD, wars broke out everywhere because there were so many Gadianton robbers killing people and destroying their cities.

All the Lamanite converts united with the Nephites, and they were compelled to take up arms to defend their women and children, and their rights to live and worship freely.

Before 13 AD was over, the Nephites' situation became desperate, for they were threatened with utter destruction.

The Lamanite converts who had united with the Nephites were considered to be Nephites. Their curse was taken from them, and their skin became lighter, like the Nephites'. Their children also became very fair, and were also called Nephites. By 14 AD, the fighting was terrible, but the Nephites managed to drive the robbers back into their hiding places in the mountains.

In 15 AD, the Gadiantons again came against the Nephites. The Nephites in general had become wicked, and had so many arguments and dissensions, that they lost their battles, and the robbers gained more power over them. By the end of 15 AD, the Nephites were suffering greatly, and the sword of destruction hung over them because of their sinful ways.

3 - Nephites fight the Gadianton robbers...

In 16 AD, Lachoneus, the governor of the land, received the following letter from Giddianhi, the Gadianton leader, or governor.

"Lachoneus, most noble and chief governor of the land, I write this letter to praise your people's determination to maintain what they think are their rights. You put up a good fight, as if you were supported by a god, while defending what you call your liberty, property and country.

"It is a pity, most noble Lachoneus, that you should be so foolish and vain as to think you can stand against so many brave and well armed men, who anxiously wait for my command to destroy you.

"I know of their unconquerable spirit and eternal hatred toward you for the many wrongs you have committed against them. I have proven my men in battle and know that if I were to command them to attack, you would be completely destroyed. Because I know you are determined to fight for what you believe to be right, and because I respect your noble spirit, I have written this letter for your sake. I would rather see you give up your cities, lands and possessions to my people than see you be destroyed. We do not want you to be our slaves, but our brethren. Surrender to us, and become acquainted with our secret works, and we will share what we have with you. I swear to you with an oath, that if you will do this, you will not be destroyed. But if you will not do this, I swear to you with an oath that next month I will command my armies to attack, and not stop killing until you are extinct! I am Giddianhi, governor of the secret society of Gadianton—a good society with good works—ancient works that have been handed down to us. I write this letter to you, Lachoneus, hoping that you will give up your lands and possessions, without a fight, to my people—those who have left you because you have kept their right to govern from them. Unless you do this, I will avenge them."

As Lachoneus read this letter, he was shocked at Giddianhi's boldness in demanding that the Nephites give up their land, and in threatening to destroy them to avenge their defectors, who had only wronged themselves by becoming Gadiantons. Lachoneus was a just man and could not be frightened by the threats and demands of a robber, so he ignored Giddianhi's letter. Lachoneus had his people pray to the Lord for strength to defend themselves against the robbers' attack. He sent a proclamation among all the people to gather their women, children, flocks, herds and all their belongings into one place.

He told the Nephites that after they had gathered, they should build very strong fortifications around themselves, which were to be guarded day and night by their Nephite and Lamanite armies.

In his proclamation, Lachoneus said, "As the Lord lives, unless you repent of all your sins, and pray to the Lord, you will not be delivered from the Gadianton robbers."

Lachoneus' prophecies were so great and marvelous that fear came over all the people. They exerted themselves with all their might to do what Lachoneus had told them.

Lachoneus appointed chief captains to command the Nephite armies during the robbers' imminent attack. Gidgiddoni was appointed to be the chief commander of the entire Nephite army. Except for when they were completely wicked, it was the Nephite custom to appoint someone with the spirit of revelation and prophecy as the leader over all their chief captains. This is why Gidgiddoni, who was a great prophet, was appointed commander. Their chief judge, Lachoneus, was also a prophet.

Then the people said to Gidgiddoni, "Pray to the Lord, and ask Him to let us go into the mountains and wilderness to destroy the robbers in their own lands." But Gidgiddoni replied, "The Lord forbids this, for if we were to go against the robbers, He would deliver us into their hands. We will gather and prepare in the center of our lands, and gather our armies. Then we will wait for them to come out against us. If we do this, as the Lord lives, He will deliver the robbers into our hands."

Toward the end of 17 AD, the proclamation of Lachoneus had gone throughout all the land. Tens of thousands of Nephites gathered their horses, chariots, flocks, herds, grain and all their belongings to the gathering place where they would defend themselves against their enemies. The land of Zarahemla, the land between Zarahemla and Bountiful, up to the land of Desolation, was to be the gathering place.

Several thousand Lamanites, who were now called Nephites, also gathered to this land. Lachoneus had them gather in the southern land because the northern land had a great curse upon it. They fortified themselves against their enemies, and lived together in this one large area. They feared Lachoneus' words enough to repent of all their sins. They prayed to the Lord their God to deliver them when their enemies would attack. And the Nephites were very sorrowful because of their Gadianton enemies.

Now Gidgiddoni had them make all types of weapons, armor and shields.

4 - Nephites defeat the robbers...

Toward the end of 18 AD, the Gadianton armies began to come down from the hills and mountains and out of their secret places and wilderness strongholds, taking possession of the lands in the north and south that had been deserted by the Nephites.

The Gadiantons found that there were no more wild animals to be hunted in these deserted lands. They could only find game in the wilderness, so they could not survive in the abandoned Nephite cities. The Nephites had left their lands desolate by gathering their flocks, herds and all their belongings into one area. By doing this, the Nephites kept the robbers from stealing their food. The only way the robbers could get food from the Nephites was to fight them out in the open. The Nephites' plan was to destroy the robbers by holding out against them in one large group, for they had gathered a seven year's supply of food and provisions.

Within the next year, 19 AD, Giddianhi and his people were in great need of food. They could only survive by stealing and killing, so they had to attack the Nephites. The robbers did not dare spread out over the land to raise their own grain, for fear of being attacked by the Nephites.

During the sixth month of 19 AD the robbers made their attack. They looked terrifying, for they had shaved their heads and had painted themselves with blood. They also wore armor, helmets, and lamb-skin loin cloths. When the Nephite armies saw Giddianhi's army, they fell to the earth and prayed to the Lord to deliver them from their enemies. When Giddianhi's army saw this, they began to shout with joy, thinking that the Nephites had fallen in fear of them.

But they were soon disappointed, for the Nephites did not fear them. They feared their God instead, and were asking for His protection. As Giddianhi's army rushed upon them, the Nephites were prepared to meet them in the strength of the Lord. This battle resulted in the greatest slaughter ever known since the time of Lehi. In spite of Giddianhi's oaths and threats, the Nephites beat the robbers. Gidgiddoni commanded his armies to chase the robbers as far as the borders of the wilderness, and that they should not spare any that fell into their hands by the way. This is exactly what the Nephites did.

Giddianhi, who had stood and fought with boldness, was pursued as he fled. Because he was so tired from fighting, he was overtaken and killed. Then the Nephite army returned to their place of security, and the robbers did not attack them again for over a year.

In 21 AD, the robbers surrounded the Nephites, thinking they could cut them off from their lands and force them to surrender. The robbers had appointed a new leader, Zemnarihah, who had ordered this siege. The Nephites had the advantage, because it was impossible for the robbers to lay siege long enough to have any effect on their food supply. Meanwhile, the robbers had no grain, but only the meat they could hunt in the wilderness. Soon wild game became scarce, and the robbers were about to starve to death. The Nephites continually went out against the weak robbers day and night, killing tens of thousands of them. Because of this, Zemnarihah's people wanted to end their siege. So Zemnarihah withdrew and had his armies march to the most northern part of the land. Gidgiddoni was aware of Zemnarihah's plan, and knowing that the robbers had been weakened, he sent out his army at night to cut off their retreat. In the morning, the robbers were met by Nephite armies ahead of them and behind them, leaving them no place of retreat. Several thousand robbers surrendered, and those who did not surrender were killed.

Their leader, Zemnarihah, was taken to a tree and hung. When Zemnarihah was dead, the Nephites cut down the tree and shouted, "May the Lord preserve His people in righteousness and holiness of heart. And as this man has fallen to the earth, may the Lord cut down all who seek to kill the righteous with their power and secret combinations."

The Nephites rejoiced and cried again with one voice, "May the God of Abraham, Isaac and Jacob protect this people in righteousness, as long as they call upon Him for protection." Together they sang praises to their God for the great thing He had done for them in preserving them from falling into the hands of their enemies. They cried, "Hosanna to the Most High God! Blessed be the name of the Lord God Almighty, the Most High God!"

5 - Covenants fulfilled when understood...

Their hearts were swollen, and they cried with joy because of the great goodness of God in delivering them out of the hands of their enemies. They knew they had been delivered from an everlasting destruction because of their repentance and humility.

Not a single Nephite doubted the words of all the holy prophets, but knew they would all be fulfilled. They knew that Christ must have come because of the many signs they had seen, and they gave up all their sins and served God diligently both day and night.

For the next three years, the Nephites preached God's word to all the robbers they had taken as prisoners. The robbers who repented and made a covenant not to murder anymore were set free. Those who would not repent, who continued to desire secret murders and threaten their brethren, were condemned and punished according to the law. This is how the Nephites put an end to all those wicked, secret combinations.

Many things happened that were great and marvelous, but they cannot all be written in this book. Not even one percent of what took place during this twenty-five year period (from 1 AD to 26 AD) was written by Nephi in his book. But there are other records which contain the history of everything the people did. From these records, Nephi made a shorter version, which is true. And I have made this record of these things by referring to Nephi's shorter record.

I, Mormon, make this record on plates that I have made with my own hands. Like my father, I was named after the land of Mormon, the land where Alma first established the church among the Nephites after their transgressions under King Noah. I am a disciple of Jesus Christ, the Son of God. I have been called by Him to declare His word among His people, that they might have everlasting life.

Because the prayers of the holy ones who have gone before me must be fulfilled according to their faith, it has become necessary for me, according to God's will, to make a record of the Nephites. This is a small record of what has taken place from the time Lehi left Jerusalem in 600 BC until the present time (about 380 AD). I have begun making my record from the accounts of those who have lived before, and I will finish it with an account of what I have seen myself. I know this record is just and true, but there are many things that we cannot write because of the nature of our language.

Now I will review the history of my people: I, Mormon, am a pure descendant of Lehi. I have reason to bless my God and Savior Jesus Christ, who brought our forefathers out of the land of Jerusalem. He has given me and my people great knowledge unto the salvation of our souls.

Surely He has blessed the house of Jacob (Israel) and has been merciful to the descendants of Joseph of old. When Lehi's descendants have kept His commandments, He has blessed and prospered them according to His word. As surely as the Lord lives, He will bring many of Joseph's descendants to a knowledge of the Lord their God and gather them together from all over the earth. In His own due time, His covenant with all of Israel's descendants will be fulfilled, as they come to understand the covenant itself.

Note: Other references to this covenant—2 Nephi 29:13-14 and 3 Nephi 21:7.

When they understand this covenant, they will know their Redeemer, who is Jesus Christ, the Son of God. And after they come to know Christ they will be gathered in from all over the earth to their own lands, from where they have been dispersed. And as the Lord lives, so will it be. Amen.

6 - Those with the gospel seek for power...

Now I will continue the Nephite history. All the Nephite families took their flocks, horses, cattle and all their possessions, and returned to their own lands in 26 AD. They had not eaten all their grain, so they took it back with them. They also took their gold, silver and precious things to their own lands and homes in the northern and southern lands.

They gave lands to the robbers who had repented, yet who still wanted to be called Lamanites. By doing this, all the people were able to work the land and feed themselves, and they established peace.

By 27 AD, the Nephites prospered greatly. There was great order in the land, and they made fair and just laws. As long as the people did not become sinful, there was nothing to keep them from continual prosperity. This great peace was established by Gidgiddoni, by Lachoneus, the judge, and by the appointed leaders.

Many new cities were built and many old ones repaired. Many highways and roads were built to connect the cities and lands, and peace continued throughout 28 AD.

But in 29 AD, some disputes started among the more proud people, who boasted because of their riches and greatly persecuted those who had less.

There were many merchants, lawyers and officers in the land. The people began to be distinguished into upper and lower classes according to their wealth and education. The rich received more opportunities for learning, while the poor were denied an education.

Yet, while some people were lifted up in pride, others were very humble. Some fought, while others refused to fight, even while being persecuted and afflicted.

As this great inequality spread throughout the land, the church began to break up. In just one year the church was broken up, except among a few converted Lamanites, who would not depart from the true faith and who diligently kept the Lord's commandments.

This sinful condition was caused by Satan's great power, which increased as the people yielded to his temptations, seeking power, authority, riches and the vain things of the world. Satan led them away to commit all types of sins, so their peace lasted only a few years.

By 30 AD, the people were being completely controlled by the devil's desires, for they were in a state of awful wickedness. These people did not sin ignorantly, for they had been taught God's will. They chose to willfully rebel against God.

In 30 AD, Lachoneus, son of Lachoneus, filled his father's position as governor of the people. That year, men began to be inspired from heaven and were sent forth to stand among the people all over the land, preaching and testifying boldly of the people's sins. They testified about the redemption and resurrection, which the Lord would bring to pass for His people after His death and suffering.

Many people (mostly the chief judges, those who had been high priests and lawyers, and those who were lawyers) became very angry with those who testified, but the wicked men could not condemn anyone to death without the governor's signature.

However, many of those who boldly testified of Christ were secretly put to death by the judges. The governor did not know about these murders until a complaint came to him against the corrupt judges.

Then the corrupt judges were brought before the governor to be judged for their crimes, according to the law that had been given by the people. But the corrupt judges' friends and relatives conspired with nearly every lawyer and high priest. Together, they made a covenant—even that same covenant given by them of old, administered by the devil, to combine against all righteousness.

They secretly combined against the Lord's people, entering into a covenant to destroy them and to assist those guilty of murder to escape the grasp of justice. They defied the laws of their country, covenanting with one another to kill the governor, to destroy liberty, and to establish a king over the land, so that instead of being free, the people would be subject to kings.

7 - *Wicked tribes prevail, and Nephi is hated...*

The conspirators were not successful in establishing a king over the land, but in that same year, 30 AD, they murdered the chief judge of the land as he sat on the judgment seat.

The rest of the people divided into tribes according to families, relatives and friends, but these tribes were not unified. This is how the government was destroyed.

Each tribe appointed a chief, and every man in each tribe had a large family, many relatives and friends. This is how many large tribes were established.

There were no wars as yet among the tribes, but all this degeneration was the result of the people yielding to Satan's power. The government regulations had been destroyed because of the secret combinations of the friends and relatives of those who had murdered the prophets. Because there was so much contention in the land, nearly all the righteous people had become wicked, and only a few remained righteous. All this happened in less than six years.

Then this secret combination, which had brought on such great iniquity, assembled and selected a man named Jacob to be their king. Jacob had been one of the main voices against the prophets who testified of Jesus. This secret combination of wicked people was not as numerous as the people of the tribes. Although each tribal leader established his own laws, and the tribes were enemies with one another, they were united in their hatred of Jacob's secret band.

Knowing this, Jacob commanded his people to go to the most northern parts of the land to build a kingdom. Jacob promised his people that soon many more dissenters would join them and make them strong enough to conquer the tribes.

By the end of 30 AD, Jacob's people had gone north. They had gone so quickly that the tribes were not able to cut off their escape. In 31 AD, the various tribes agreed not to go to war with one another. However, they continued to keep their own separate laws. They all established very strict laws not to trespass against one another. By doing this, they had some peace in the land. Still, their hearts were turned away from the Lord, and they stoned the prophets and ran them out of their lands.

Nephi had been visited by angels. He had heard the Lord's voice and had been given the power to know of Christ's ministry. He had also seen the people's quick return from righteousness to wickedness. Being grieved for the hardness of their hearts and blindness of their minds, Nephi went among the people in 31 AD, boldly testifying of repentance, and of the remission of sins through faith in the Lord Jesus Christ.

Nephi said and did many things among his people, ministering with power and great authority. All that Nephi did cannot be written in this book. To write only part of what he did would not be enough, so that history is not written here.

The people hated Nephi because his powerful witness was too great for them to deny. Nephi had such great faith in the Lord Jesus Christ that angels visited him each day. He cast out devils in the name of Jesus, and he even raised his brother, Timothy, who had been stoned to death by the people. As the people saw Nephi do this and many other miracles in the name of Jesus, they became more angry with him for being so powerful.

By the end of 31 AD, there were few converts to the Lord, but those who were converted testified to the people that they had been visited by the power and Spirit of God, which was in Jesus Christ, in whom they believed. Those who had devils cast out of them and who were healed from sickness also testified that the Spirit of God had come upon them, and they showed signs and performed miracles among the people.

In the beginning of 33 AD, Nephi continued to preach repentance and remission of sins. He ordained men to baptize, and all those who repented were baptized by them. (Now, I want to remind you that those who were baptized were immersed in water). Their baptisms were a witness and a testimony before God that they had repented and had received a remission of their sins.

8 - The greatest destruction ever known...

We know Nephi's record is true, for he was a just man. He performed many miracles in the name of Jesus, and no man could do a miracle in the name of Jesus unless he was completely cleansed from sin.

According to Nephi, if he has made no mistake in the reckoning of our time, the year was 33 AD when the people began to earnestly look for the sign that Samuel had given—that there would be three days of complete darkness. Yet the people started to doubt, argueing with one another in spite of the many signs that had been given. On the fourth day of the first month in 34 AD, a terrible tempest arose like no other that had ever been known. There was thunder and intense lightening, and the whole earth shook as if it were about to break apart. The city of Zarahemla caught fire, and the city of Moroni sank into the ocean, and its inhabitants were drowned. A great mountain rose up and covered the city of Moronihah. There was great and terrible destruction in the southern land, but even greater and more terrible destruction in the northern land. The whole face of the land was changed by tempests and tornadoes, thunder and lightning, and great earthquakes. Highways were broken up, level roads were ruined, and many smooth places were made rough. Many great and notable cities were either sunk, burned or leveled by earthquakes, and all the inhabitants thereof were killed. The cities that did remain were heavily damaged, and many people in them died. Some people were carried away and lost in tornadoes. All the land became deformed because of the tempests, thunder, lightning and earthquakes, and rocks were broken up all over the land. This terrible destruction lasted for three hours, and then the earth became calm, and covered in darkness.

The darkness was so thick, people could feel it. No light could be made by candles, torches or fires, even when the people tried to light very fine, dry wood. There was no light from the sun, moon or stars because the mist of darkness over the land was so great. This darkness lasted for three days. During this time, there was great and continual mourning, howling and weeping among all the people because of the darkness and great destruction that had come upon them. In one place they cried, "If only we had repented before this great and terrible day. Then our brethren would have been spared instead of being burned in the great city of Zarahemla."

In another place the people mourned and cried, "If only we had repented before this great and terrible day, and our people had not killed, stoned or exiled the prophets. Then our mothers, our fair daughters, and our children would have been spared instead of being buried in the great city of Moronihah."

9 - The voice of Christ is heard...

And then a voice was heard by all the people, which said, "All people on earth are greatly cursed if they will not repent. The devil now laughs, and his angels rejoice over the fair sons and daughters of my people who have been killed, and who have fallen because of their sinfulness. I have burned that great city of Zarahemla along with its inhabitants. I have sunk that great city of Moroni in the depths of the ocean, and its inhabitants have drowned. I have covered that great city of Moronihah, and its inhabitants, with earth to hide their wickedness and sins from before my face—*that the blood of the prophets and saints will not come to me anymore against them.* I have caused the city of Gilgal to be buried in the earth along with its inhabitants. I have caused the waters to come and cover the cities of Onihah, Mocum and Jerusalem with their inhabitants, to hide their wickedness and sins from before my face—*that the blood of the prophets and saints will not come to me anymore against them.* I have sunk the cities of Gadiandi, Gadiomnah, Jacob and Gimgimno into the earth, and have made hills and valleys in their places. The inhabitants thereof have been buried up in the depths of the earth to hide their wickedness and sins from before my face—*that the blood of the prophets and saints will not come to me anymore against them.* I have caused that great city of Jacobugath, inhabited by Jacob's people, to be burned, for their sins and wickedness were above all the wickedness of the whole earth—even their secret murders and combinations. They destroyed the peace of my people and the government of the land. I destroyed them with fire to hide them from before my face—*that the blood of the prophets and saints will not come to me against them anymore.* I have also burned the cities of Laman, Josh, Gad and Kishkumen along with their inhabitants, because of their wickedness in casting out the prophets and stoning those whom I sent to tell them of their wickedness.

"Because they cast them all out, and there was not one righteous person among them, I sent down fire to destroy them, that their great wickedness might be hid from before my face—*that the blood of the prophets and saints whom I sent among them might not cry to me from the ground against them.* I have caused many great destructions to come upon this land, and upon this people because of their wickedness. Oh, all of you who are spared because you were more righteous than they, will you not return to me now, repent of your sins and be converted, that I may heal you? If you will come to me, you will have eternal life, for my arms of mercy are extended toward you. Whoever will come, I will receive, and blessed are those who come to me.

"Behold, I am Jesus Christ, the Son of God. I created the heavens and the earth, and all things that are in them. I was with the Father from the beginning. I am in the Father, and the Father in me, and by me the Father has glorified His name. I came to my own people and was rejected by them. And now the scriptures of my coming are fulfilled. All those who receive me will become God's sons and daughters, for redemption comes by me, and I have fulfilled the law of Moses. I am the light and life of the world. I am Alpha and Omega—the beginning and the end.

"You will no longer make blood sacrifices or burnt offerings to me, for I will no longer accept them. You will offer as a sacrifice to me a broken heart and contrite spirit, after which I will baptize you with fire and the Holy Ghost, even as I baptized the Lamanites. Because of their faith in me at the time of their conversion, they were baptized with fire and the Holy Ghost, although they did not know it. I have come to the world to redeem it from sin. Therefore, I will receive those who repent and come to me as little children, for of such is the kingdom of God. For such I have laid down my life and have taken it up again. Therefore, repent. Come to me from the ends of the earth and be saved."

10 - The voice of Christ is heard again...

After all the people in the land heard this voice, they were so astonished that they stopped mourning the loss of their family members who had died in the destruction, and it was quiet for many hours.

Then the voice was heard again by all the people, saying, "Oh you people of those great fallen cities, who are descendants of Jacob—the house of Israel, how often have I gathered and nourished you, as a hen gathers her chickens under her wings. And how often I would have gathered you, oh house of Israel in Jerusalem, as well as those who have died here, but you would not come. Oh people of the house of Israel, whom I have spared, how often will I yet gather you, as a hen gathers her chickens under her wings, if you will repent and return to me with full purpose of heart. But if you will not return to me, your cities will become desolate until the covenants made with your forefathers are fulfilled."

After the people heard this, they began again to weep and cry aloud over the loss of their family members and friends. But after three days of this despair, the morning sun finally broke the darkness, and the earth stopped trembling and breaking up with dreadful groaning and loud noises. As the earth settled and became still again, the mourning, weeping and wailing of the people turned to joy. They praised and gave thanks to the Lord Jesus Christ, their Redeemer.

The scriptures, or words of the prophets, had been fulfilled. The more righteous part of the people had been saved—those who had received the prophets and saints instead of killing them. The more righteous were not sunk and buried in the earth. They were not drowned in the sea or burned. They were not crushed by falling buildings, carried away in tornadoes, nor suffocated by thick, dark smoke.

Mormon comments: As you read this, ask yourself whether or not all this death and destruction fulfilled the prophecies of the many holy prophets, who were killed for testifying that these things would happen at Christ's coming. Zenos and Zenock testified about these things, and particularly about us, their descendants. Our forefather, Jacob (Israel), also testified about us, the descendants of his son, Joseph of old. And Joseph's prophecies are written on the brass plates that our forefather, Lehi, brought out of Jerusalem. I, Mormon, will show you that by the end of 34 AD, the Nephites and converted Lamanites who had been spared had been shown great things and had received great blessings, for soon after Christ went up into heaven from Jerusalem, He came down and showed Himself to them. He showed Himself and ministered to them. I will now continue this account, which includes His ministry to these people:

11 - Christ appears soon after the destruction...

A great multitude had gathered around the temple in Bountiful. They were marveling and wondering, showing each other the great and marvelous changes that had been made over the entire landscape. They were also talking about Jesus Christ, of whose death these signs had been given.

As they were speaking, they heard a voice from heaven. They looked around, not understanding the voice. It was not harsh or loud, but calm. Although it was a calm voice, it made their entire bodies quake as it penetrated them to the very center of their souls. They all heard the voice a second time, but still did not understand it. A third time they heard the voice, and they looked intently toward heaven from where it came. Only after looking upward did they understand the voice, which said, "Behold my Beloved Son, in whom I am well pleased, in whom I have glorified my name. Hear Him."

As they understood, they looked up again and saw a Man dressed in a white robe, descending out of heaven. He came down and stood among them. All eyes were upon Him, and no one dared speak, for they thought He was an angel. He held out His hands and said, "Behold, I am Jesus Christ, whom the prophets testified would come into the world. I am the light and life of the world. I have drunk out of that bitter cup that the Father has given me. I have glorified the Father in taking upon me the sins of the world, in which I have suffered the will of the Father in all things from the beginning."

After Jesus said this, the whole multitude fell to the earth, remembering that it had been prophesied that Christ would show Himself to them after going up into heaven from Jerusalem. Then the Lord said, "Arise and come to me, that you may put your hands into my side, and feel the prints of the nails in my hands and feet, that you may know that I am the God of Israel, and the God of the whole earth, and have been slain for the sins of the world."

One by one, the multitude put their hands into His side and felt the prints of the nails in His hands and feet. They all knew and witnessed that it was He, of whom the prophets had written, who would come. After they had all witnessed for themselves, they cried out with one voice, "Hosanna! Blessed be the name of the Most High God!" And they fell down at Jesus' feet and worshiped Him.

Then Jesus asked Nephi to come forward. Nephi came forward, bowed himself before the Lord and kissed His feet. The Lord commanded Nephi to rise, and then said to him, "I give you power to baptize this people after I ascend into heaven again."

The Lord called eleven others and also gave them power to baptize. He said to them, "This is how you will baptize, and there will be no disputes among you: Those who repent through your words and desire to be baptized will go down into the water, and you will baptize them in my name. Calling them by name, you will say, 'Having authority given me of Jesus Christ, I baptize you in the name of the Father, and of the Son, and of the Holy Ghost. Amen.' Then you will immerse them in the water and bring them out again. This is how you will baptize in my name, without disputes, for you must be unified, as the Father, the Son, and the Holy Ghost are unified.

"There must be no more disputes about how to baptize, as there have been in the past. There also must not be anymore arguments about the points of my doctrine. For whoever has the spirit of contention is not of me, but of the devil, the father of contention. He stirs up people to become angry and fight with one another. My doctrine, which the Father has given me, is that such things should be done away. I bear record of the Father, the Father bears record of me, and the Holy Ghost bears record of us both. I bear record that the Father commands all people everywhere to repent and believe in me.

"Those who believe in me and are baptized will be saved to inherit God's kingdom. Those who do not believe in me and are not baptized will be damned. This is my doctrine, and I bear record of it from the Father. The Father will bear record of me to those who believe in Him, and in me, by visiting them with fire and with the Holy Ghost. Just as the Father bears record of me, the Holy Ghost will bear record of the Father and of me. This is because the Father, and I, and the Holy Ghost are one. I repeat, you must repent, become like a little child, and be baptized in my name. Otherwise, you cannot receive these things and inherit God's kingdom.

"This is my doctrine. Those who build upon my doctrine build upon my rock, and the gates of hell will not prevail against them. Those who declare more or less than this, and call it my doctrine, are inspired by the devil. They are not built upon my rock but upon sand. When trials and temptations come, they will fall, and the gates of hell will be opened to receive them.

12 - Christ teaches His new law...

"Now, declare the words which I have spoken, to the ends of the earth."

After Jesus said these words to Nephi and the twelve others, He held out His hand to the multitude and cried, "You are blessed if you follow these twelve whom I have chosen from among you to minister to you and be your servants. I have given them the power to baptize you with water, after which I will baptize you with fire and the Holy Ghost. You are blessed if you believe in me and are baptized after you have seen me, and know that I am.

"Those who will believe your testimony—that you have seen me and know that I am, who humble themselves and are baptized, will be more blessed, for they will be visited with fire and with the Holy Ghost, and they will receive a remission of their sins.

"Blessed are the poor in spirit who come to me, for they will inherit the kingdom of heaven. Blessed are all who mourn, for they will be comforted. Blessed are the meek, for they will inherit the earth. Blessed are all who hunger and thirst for righteousness, for they will be filled with the Holy Ghost. Blessed are the merciful, for they will obtain mercy. Blessed are the pure in heart, for they will see God. Blessed are the peacemakers, for they will be called the children of God.

"Blessed are all who are persecuted for my name's sake, for they will inherit the kingdom of heaven. You are blessed when others revile, persecute and lie about you because of your devotion to me. You will have great joy in your heavenly reward, which will be great. Remember that the prophets who lived before you were persecuted in the same way. I give you the responsibility to become the salt of the earth.

Note: Becoming the salt is a result of making covenants. See D&C 101:39-40.

But remember, if the salt of the earth loses its flavor, then it is only good to be thrown out and trampled under foot. I tell you to be a light to the people. A city built on a hill is seen by all. You do not hide a lit candle, you put it on a candlestick, so that it may light your house. In this same manner, let your light shine before all people, that they may see your good works and glorify your Heavenly Father. Do not think that I have come to destroy the law or the words of the prophets. I have not come to destroy the law, but to fulfill it, and I have fulfilled it in every detail. I gave you the law and my Father's commandments, that you would believe in me, repent of your sins, and come to me with a broken heart and contrite spirit. You have the commandments before you now, and the law is fulfilled. Therefore, come to me and be saved, for unless you keep my commandments that I have now given, you will not enter the kingdom of heaven.

"You have heard that it was said by them of old, and it is also written in your scriptures, that you shall not kill, and that those who kill will be in danger of God's judgment. But I say that those who are angry with their brother or sister are in danger of God's judgment. Those who feel contempt for another by saying such things as 'You are worthless' will be in danger of God's council. Those who demean another by saying such things as 'You fool' will be in danger of spiritual torment. If you come to me, or even want to come to me, and you remember that someone has bad feelings toward you, go to that person and make amends first. Then sincerely come to me, and I will receive you. Quickly agree with your enemy while you are in his way, or else he may catch you at any time and put you into prison, and you will not be released until you have paid all his fines. And how can you pay even a penny while in prison?

"It is written by them of old, 'Do not commit adultery.' But I say that those who lust have already committed adultery in their hearts. I give you a commandment not to allow any lustful thoughts to enter your heart. It is better for you to deny yourselves these things, taking up your cross, than to forfeit living in God's presence forever. It has been written by them of old, 'A man can divorce his wife by simply giving her written notice.' But I say, if a man divorces his wife without good cause, then God will not honor that divorce. It is also written, 'Do not forswear yourself, but perform your oaths to the Lord.' But I say, swear not at all, not by heaven—His throne, nor by the earth—His footstool. Do not swear by your head, for you yourself cannot control what must be. Let your communication be as simple as the words 'Yes' and 'No,' for too many words often result in evil.

"It is written, 'Others must pay for harming you by being harmed in the same manner.' But I say, do not contend with evil people. If they offend you, do not respond by offending them. If someone sues you for your coat, give it to him, and give him a blanket as well. If someone forces you to go a mile with him, go two miles. Give to those who ask of you, and do not turn away those who would borrow from you.

"It is also written, 'Love your neighbor and hate your enemy.' But I say, love your enemies. Bless those who curse you. Do good to those who hate you. Pray for those who use and persecute you. By doing this, you will become the children of your Heavenly Father, for He makes His sun rise upon both the evil and the good. By fulfilling all the old laws (through the atonement)—by making all things new, I have made it possible for you to become perfect, even as I, and your Heavenly Father, are perfect."

13 - Christ teaches His gospel...

Jesus continued speaking to the multitude; "Give to the poor because you want to, for if you give just to appear good to others, then your Heavenly Father will not reward you. When you give to the poor, do not call attention to yourself as the hypocrites do in order to be praised, for they have their reward. When you give to others, do it secretly. If you give secretly, then your Heavenly Father, who sees you in secret, will reward you openly. When you pray, do not pray like the hypocrites, who love to pray in front of others, for they have their reward. Go into your room and close the door. Then pray to your Heavenly Father in secret and He will reward you openly. When you pray, do not repeat insincere phrases, for this is how the heathens pray, thinking that God will hear them better if they use many words. You do not need to use many words, for your Heavenly Father already knows what you need before you ask Him. Here is an example of a sincere prayer: Our Father who art in Heaven, hallowed be Thy name. Thy will be done on earth as it is in heaven. Forgive us our debts as we forgive our debtors. Lead us from temptation and deliver us from evil, for Thine is the kingdom, and the power, and the glory forever. Amen.

"If you forgive others who have hurt you, your Heavenly Father will forgive you of your sins. But if you refuse to forgive others, your Heavenly Father will refuse to forgive you.

"When you fast, do not fast like the hypocrites, who make long, sad faces in order to look humble to others. They have their reward. When you fast, hold your head up and be cheerful. Do not let others know you are fasting by act-ing weak and tired. Instead, present your fast only to your Heavenly Father, and He, who sees you in secret, will reward you openly.

"Do not collect earthly treasures. They can easily be lost or stolen, and all things rust and decay. Instead, save up treasures in heaven, where things do not decay and are not lost or stolen, for where your treasure is, there will your heart be also.

"The light of the body is the eye. If your eye is upon God, and you are dedicated to serving Him, then your whole soul will be full of light. If your eye is focused on evil, and you are not dedicated to serving God, then your whole soul will be full of great darkness! You cannot serve two opposing masters, for you will hate one and love the other. For example, if you love God, you will hate worldliness, and if you love worldliness, you will hate God, for no one can serve God and the world at the same time."

When Jesus finished speaking to the Nephites, He turned to His twelve disciples and said, "Remember my words, for you will be teaching them again to the people. Do not worry about your life—your food, drink and clothing, for your life is more than just your food, and your body is more than just your clothing. Look at the birds. They do not worry about having enough food, and your Heavenly Father feeds them. Are you not more valuable to God than they? And by worrying about your food, can you extend your life one day? And why worry about having adequate clothing? Consider how the lilies of the field grow. They do not concern themselves with their appearance, yet even King Solomon in his glorious attire was never as beautiful as they. If God clothes the short-lived flowers, He will also clothe you, if you have faith in Him. Knowing this, do not worry about your needs. Your Heavenly Father knows you have need of food, clothing and many other things. If you show your faith by seeking the kingdom of God and His righteousness above all else, then He will provide you with all these things. Do not worry about what will happen tomorrow, for tomorrow will take care of itself. Be more concerned about the temptations you must overcome today."

14 - Christ teaches His gospel...

After speaking to His disciples, Jesus turned to the multitude again, and said, "Do not judge others, for God will judge you in the same way that you judge others. Why notice your brother's or sister's little faults while ignoring your own, larger ones? Why do you try to solve their problems before solving your own? Do not be a hypocrite. Correct your own faults first, then you will be better able to help others correct theirs. Do not give holy things to wicked people, for they will mock and reject them and then try to destroy you.

"Ask, and it will be given to you. Seek, and you will find. Knock, and it will be opened to you. What man among you, if his son asks him for bread, will give him a stone? Or if his son asks for a fish, will he give him a snake? If you, in a natural, evil state, are able to give good things to your children, then how much more will your Heavenly Father give good things to those who ask Him?

"All the good things you want others to do for you are the very things you should do for them. This is the law given to the prophets.

"Many people travel the wide road and go through the wide gate to destruction. But you should go through the narrow gate. Yet because the road and gate to eternal life are narrow, few find it.

"Beware of false prophets, who seem righteous, but seek to destroy good. You can detect them if their works do not lead you to me. A righteous person brings to pass good works, but a wicked person only does evil. All who do evil (lead others away from Christ) will be cut down and burned at my coming.

"Again, by their works you will know them.

"Only those who do the will of their Heavenly Father will enter His kingdom. On judgment day, many will say to me, 'Lord, Lord, we have prophesied, cast out devils, and we have done many wonderful works in Thy name.' Then I will say to them, 'I never knew you. Leave me, you evil-doers.'

"Those who hear my words and obey them are like the wise man who built his house on solid rock. When it rained and floods came, and when strong winds blew, his house stood because it was built on rock.

"And those who hear my words and do not obey them are like the foolish man who built his house on sand. When it rained and the floods came, and when strong winds blew, his house fell with a great crash."

15 - Christ teaches His new law...

Jesus continued to speak to the multitude: "Now you have heard what I told the people in Jerusalem before ascending to my Father. At the last day, I will raise up those who have remembered my teachings and have done what I have commanded them."

Jesus then perceived that some of the people were wondering what was going to happen to the law of Moses, for they did not understand what He had meant when He said, "Old things have passed away and all things have become new." So Jesus said, "Here is how old things have passed away and how all things have become new. The law that was given to Moses is fulfilled. I gave the law to Moses after covenanting with Israel and his descendants. I came to fulfill the law, and I have fulfilled it. This is why the law of Moses now comes to an end. I have not done away with the prophets, for all the prophets' words that are not yet fulfilled soon will be. Because I said that old things have passed away, I do not mean that the prophecies of things to come will not be fulfilled. The covenant I made with Israel and his descendants is not completely fulfilled yet, but the law that I gave to Moses is fulfilled and has come to an end in me.

"Behold, I am the law and the light. Look to me, continue in righteousness throughout your life, and you will live, for unto such I will give eternal life. Keep my commandments that I have given you. This is the law given to the prophets, who truly testified of me."

Jesus then turned to the twelve whom He had chosen, and said, "You are my disciples, a light to this people who are descendants of Joseph, who was sold into Egypt. The Father has given this land to you as an inheritance. The Father did not command me to tell the descendants of Judah (the Jews) in Jerusalem about this land, inherited by you, the descendants of Joseph.

"I also was never commanded to tell the Jews about the other tribes, descended from Israel's other sons, who were led away from Judah's rule. I was only commanded to say to the Jews, 'I have other sheep which are not of this fold. I must gather them, and they will hear my voice, and there will be one fold and one shepherd.' Because the Jews were so stubborn and unbelieving, they could not understand my words. This is why the Father commanded me not to tell them more about you. But the Father has commanded me to tell you that you were separated from Judah's descendants, who know nothing about you because of their wickedness.

"The Father has also separated the other tribes from Judah's descendants, and the Jews also know nothing of them. You are the other sheep of whom I spoke, but the Jews thought I was telling them about the Gentiles, not knowing that they would convert the Gentiles through their preaching. The Jews did not understand that the Gentiles will not at any time hear my voice directly, but only through the Holy Ghost. But both hear my voice and see me, and you are my sheep, numbered among those given to me by the Father."

16 - The Jews to gather after accepting Christ...

"I have other sheep, other tribes and nations who neither live here nor in Jerusalem. They have not yet heard my voice nor have seen me, but I will show myself to them because the Father has commanded me to go to them. They will hear me and be numbered among my sheep, and there will be one fold and one shepherd.

"I command you to write down what I am saying, for if my people in Jerusalem do not ask the Father in my name, and receive a knowledge of you by the Holy Ghost, and also a knowledge of the other tribes, then your record of me (*The Book of Mormon*, including the sealed portion) will come forth through the Gentiles (the Latter-day Saints) to their descendants (the latter-day Jews), scattered all over the earth. And through the fullness of the Gentiles in the last days, these records will bring the knowledge of me, their Redeemer, to many of them. After they receive this knowledge, then I will gather them from all over the earth and fulfill the Father's covenant that He made to all of Israel's descendants.

> **Note:** The Latter-day Saints are referred to as Gentiles (1 Ne 15:17-18, 2 Ne 25:17-18, 30:3-10, Ether 4:6-7). The phrase "fullness of the Gentiles" means the Latter-day Saint Gentiles bringing the "fullness of the gospel," or "greater things" to the house of Israel, which will contribute to convincing them to accept Christ as their Redeemer (1 Ne 15:13-14 and 3 Ne 26:8-9).

"The Gentiles are blessed because of their testimony of me through the Holy Ghost, who witnesses to them of me and the Father. The Father said, 'Because the Gentiles will believe in me, and because you will not, oh house of Israel, in the last days the gospel will come to the Gentiles first. But cursed are the unbelieving Gentiles, for even though the Father will show mercy on the Gentiles, and allow them to conquer, afflict and kill Israel's descendants because of His judgments upon the house of Israel (Native Americans), He commanded me to tell you this: 'When the Gentiles sin against my gospel, and reject its fullness, when through their pride, they lift themselves above all nations and people of the earth, when they are full of lying, deceit, mischief, hypocrisy, murder, priestcraft, immorality and secret abominations, then I will take the fullness of my gospel from among them.

Note: The Savior warns the latter-day Gentiles in like manner three times (3 Ne 16:10-15, 20:27-28, 21:11-14).

"'And I will remember the covenant that I made to Israel's descendants by bringing my gospel to them (a great latter-day Lamanite conversion).

Note: This great Lamanite conversion is described in 1 Ne 15:14-16, 2 Ne 30:4-5, and 3 Ne 26:8-9.

"'The Gentiles will no longer have power over them, and they will come to know the fullness of my gospel. But if the Gentiles repent and come back to me,' says the Father, 'They will be numbered among my people of the house of Israel, and I will protect them from being trampled by my people. But if the Gentiles sin against my gospel, rejecting its fullness, and do not repent and come to me, then I will allow my people to go among them and conquer them. For the Gentiles will be like salt that has lost its flavor, and is good for nothing but to be thrown out and trodden under the feet of my people—the house of Israel.'

"I have been commanded by the Father to give this land to the house of Israel and their descendants as an inheritance. When this land is given back to Israel's descendants, then these words, spoken by Isaiah, will be fulfilled:

"'Your watchmen will lift up their voices and sing together, for they will have understanding when the Lord again brings Zion.

"'Be joyful and sing together, house of Israel, once scattered, for the Lord has comforted His people and redeemed Jerusalem. The Lord has shown His great power in view of all people in all nations, and they will witness His salvation.'"

17 - Christ heals, prays and blesses children...

After speaking these words, Jesus looked over the multitude, and said, "I must go now. I perceive that you do not understand all my words. Go to your homes and think about these things. Ask the Father, in my name, to give you understanding, and prepare your minds for tomorrow, when I will come to you again. Now I will go to the Father, and also show myself to the lost tribes of Israel. They are not lost to the Father, for He knows where He has taken them."

After Jesus said this, He looked over the multitude, who were in tears, looking at Him as if they would ask Him to stay a little longer. Then Jesus said to them, "I am filled with compassion toward you. Have you any who are sick, lame, blind, deaf, or who suffer in any way? Bring them here, and I will heal them, for I have compassion and mercy upon you. I perceive that you want me to show you the same things that I showed your brethren in Jerusalem, and I see that you have enough faith for me to heal you."

Then the multitude brought their sick and afflicted to Jesus, and He healed them one by one. Those who were healed, and those who were well, all bowed at His feet and worshiped Him. As many others who were able to get through the crowd came and kissed His feet and bathed them with their tears of joy.

Then Jesus asked them to bring their children to Him. The people set their children down around Jesus, and then stepped back until all the children had been brought to Him. Then Jesus told the multitude to kneel upon the ground. Jesus groaned, and said, "Father, I am troubled because of the wickedness of the people of the house of Israel." Then He knelt on the earth and prayed to the Father. The things He prayed cannot be written, but the multitude heard His words, and this much was written: "Never before has anyone seen or heard such great and marvelous things as we saw and heard when Jesus spoke to the Father. For human language cannot describe, and human hearts cannot conceive of the joy that filled our souls when we heard Him pray to the Father for us."

When Jesus finished praying, He stood up, but the multitude was too overcome with joy to stand. Jesus invited them to stand, and after they stood, He said, "You are blessed because of your faith. And now my joy is full."

Then Jesus wept, and He took their children, one by one, blessed them, and prayed to the Father for them. Then He wept again and said to the multitude, "Behold your little ones."

Then the multitude saw the heavens open, and angels descending as if surrounded with fire. They came down and surrounded the little ones with fire, and taught them. The multitude, consisting of about 2,500 people, saw and heard these things, and bore record that what they saw and heard was true.

18 - Christ introduces the sacrament...

Then Jesus told His disciples to bring some bread and wine. While they were gone, He told the multitude to sit upon the ground. After the disciples returned with bread and wine, Jesus broke the bread, blessed it, and gave some of it to His disciples to eat. After they were filled, Jesus told them to give bread to the multitude.

After the multitude had eaten and were filled, Jesus said to His disciples, "I will ordain one of you, giving him the power to break bread, bless it, and give it to the people of my church—to all who believe and are baptized in my name. Do this often, even as I have done, in remembrance of my body that I now show you. Do this as a testimony to the Father that you will always remember me. If you always remember me, my Spirit will always be with you."

Then Jesus told His disciples to drink of the wine, and then give it to the multitude to drink. The disciples and the multitude drank, and were all filled. Then Jesus said to His disciples, "You are blessed because of what you have done, for this fulfills my commandments and witnesses to the Father that you are willing to obey them. Always do this, giving the wine to those who repent and are baptized in my name, in remembrance of my blood that I have shed for you, witnessing to the Father that you will always remember me. If you always remember me, my Spirit will always be with you.

"I give you a commandment to do these things. If you obey it, you will be blessed for building upon my rock. But if one of you does more or less than these things, he is not built upon my rock, but upon sand. He will fall, and the gates of hell will open to receive him. You are blessed and kept from hell if you keep my commandments that the Father has told me to give you. You must watch and pray always, or you will be tempted by the devil and become his captives. As I have prayed among you, pray in my church—among my people who repent and are baptized in my name. I am the light and have set an example for you."

After Jesus said these things to His disciples, He turned to the multitude and said, "You must watch and pray always. Otherwise, you will be tempted by Satan, who wants to have power over you. Therefore, you must always pray to the Father in my name. Whatever you ask the Father, if it is right and if you believe that you will receive, it will be given to you.

"Pray with your families to the Father, always in my name, and they will be blessed. Meet together often as my church. Do not forbid anyone from meeting with you, but invite all to come. If they come, pray for them in my name to the Father. Hold up your light that it may shine to the world. I am the light you should hold up—the things you have seen me do. You have seen me pray to the Father, and you see that I have not sent any of you away, but I have commanded each of you to come to me—to feel and see. You must do likewise, inviting those in the world to come to me. And those who do not keep this commandment will be led by the devil's temptations."

After saying this to the multitude, Jesus turned to His disciples again, and said, "Before I go to my Father to fulfill other commandments that He has given me, I give you one other commandment: Do not allow anyone, whom you know to be unworthy, to eat the bread or drink the wine that you will minister to my people.

"Whoever eats and drinks these emblems of my flesh and blood unworthy, eats and drinks damnation to his soul. Do not tell an unworthy man to leave your meeting, but care for him and pray for him. If he repents and is baptized in my name, then receive him and give him the bread and wine. But if he does not repent, he will not be numbered among the sheep of my flock, for he might destroy them. (For I know my sheep, and they are numbered.) Even though he is not baptized and numbered among my sheep, you will continue to invite him to your meetings, for he may yet repent and come to me with full purpose of heart, and I will heal him, and you will have assisted me in saving him. Do as I have commanded and you will not come under condemnation, for cursed are those whom the Father condemns.

"I give you, my disciples, these commandments because of the disputes that have been among you. You will be blessed if you have no disputes among you. Now I go to the Father, because it is necessary for your benefit." Then Jesus touched each of His disciples as He spoke to them individually. Later, the disciples bore record that Jesus gave them the power to give the Holy Ghost And I, Mormon, will show you later that their record is true. After Jesus touched His disciples, a cloud came over the multitude, preventing them from seeing Him, and only His disciples saw Him ascend into heaven.

19 - Teaching, baptism, Holy Ghost, prayer...

After Jesus ascended into heaven, the multitude dispersed and went home with their families. The multitude who had seen Jesus, immediately told everyone who had not been with them that Jesus had spoken to them, and that He would show Himself again the next day.

All that night the people spread the word to many others who had not seen Jesus. Those who were told traveled all night so they could be where Jesus would show Himself the next day. By morning, a very large multitude had gathered. The twelve disciples whom Jesus had chosen stood in the middle of the multitude. They were Nephi, his brother, Timothy, whom he had raised from the dead, Timothy's son, Jonas, Mathoni and his brother, Mathonihah, Kumen, Kumenonhi, Jeremiah, Shemnon, Jonas, Zedekiah and Isaiah.

Because the multitude was so large, the disciples divided them into twelve groups. Each of the twelve groups was instructed by a disciple to kneel and pray to the Father in the name of Jesus. Each disciple also prayed in the same manner and taught his group of people. After the disciples had taught the very same words that Jesus had spoken to them, they knelt again and prayed. They all prayed for what they desired most—the gift of the Holy Ghost. After they had all prayed, they led the people down to the edge of the water.

First, Nephi went down into the water and was baptized. Then Nephi baptized the eleven other disciples. After the twelve had all been baptized, the Holy Ghost fell upon them, and they were filled with fire and the Holy Ghost. The twelve were surrounded with what appeared to be fire, which came down from heaven, and angels also came down and spoke to the twelve, and the large multitude witnessed all of this.

As the angels were teaching the disciples, Jesus came and stood in the middle of the large multitude and began speaking to them. Jesus told the multitude and His disciples to kneel upon the ground. He told His disciples to pray, and they began to pray to Jesus, calling Him their Lord and God.

Jesus went a short distance from them, knelt on the ground and prayed, "Father, I thank Thee that Thou has given the Holy Ghost to these whom I have chosen. Because of their belief in me, I have chosen them out of the world. Father, I pray Thee that Thou will give the Holy Ghost to all who believe their words. Father, Thou has given them the Holy Ghost because they believe in me, and Thou sees that they believe in me, and they pray to me because I am with them. I pray for my disciples and also for those who will believe in their words, that they may believe in me, that I may be in them as Thou, Father, art in me, that we may be one."

After Jesus prayed, He went over to His disciples, who were still praying to Him. They were not repeating the same words, for the Holy Ghost gave them their words and the desire to continue praying. Jesus blessed them as they prayed, and His smile and His light shone upon them. The disciples became as white and pure as Jesus' light.

Nothing on earth could be as white and pure as this light. Jesus told them to keep praying. Then went a short way off again, knelt and prayed, "Father, I thank Thee that Thou has purified the twelve whom I have chosen because of their faith, and I pray for my disciples, and for those who will believe their words, that they all may be purified in me, through their faith. I do not pray for the world, but only for those whom Thou has given me out of the world, because of their faith, that they may be purified in me, that I may be in them as Thou art in me, that we may be one, that I may be glorified in them."

Then Jesus came back over to His disciples who were still praying to Him. He smiled upon them again, and they were as bright as He. Then Jesus went off a third time to pray. And it is impossible for humans to speak or write the marvelous words that Jesus prayed. Yet the large multitude heard, and their hearts were open so they understood His words. After Jesus finished praying, He went to His disciples, and said, "I have never seen such great faith among all the Jews. Because of their unbelief, I could not show them such great miracles. None of the Jews saw or heard such great things as you have seen and heard."

20 - Latter-day gathering and covenant fulfillment...

Jesus told the multitude and His disciples to stop praying, but to continue to pray in their hearts. He told them to stand, and then He broke bread again, blessed it, and gave it to His disciples to eat. After they had eaten, He told them to break bread and give it to the multitude. Then Jesus gave His disciples wine to drink and told them to give it to the multitude. None of the disciples nor anyone in the multitude had brought bread or wine, but Jesus truly gave them bread and wine. Jesus said to them, "Whoever eats and drinks of these emblems eats and drinks in remembrance of me (my body and my blood), and his soul will never hunger nor thirst, but will be filled." After the multitude had partaken of the emblems, they were filled with the Spirit, and they shouted with one voice, giving glory to Jesus.

Then Jesus said, "Now I will finish the commandment that the Father gave to me concerning this people, who are a part of the house of Israel. Do you remember my telling you that Isaiah's words would be fulfilled? They are written, and you have them, so read and study them. When Isaiah's words are fulfilled, the covenant that the Father made with the house of Israel will also be fulfilled. The scattered parts of the house of Israel will be gathered together from all over the earth. They will all be brought to a knowledge of the Lord their God, who has redeemed them. The Father has commanded me to give you this land for your inheritance. If the Gentiles do not repent after receiving my blessings, and after scattering my people, then your descendants, who are a part of the house of Jacob (Israel), will go in among the Gentiles. They will be few among many, but they will destroy the Gentiles, their enemies. They will destroy them as a young lion might destroy flocks of sheep when there is no one to come and rescue them.

"I will gather my people together like one who brings in the wheat to the threshing floor, and I will make my people, with whom the Father has covenanted, very strong against the Gentiles—strong as iron, strong as brass. They will destroy many people and beat them into pieces. And the Gentiles' wealth will be consecrated to the Lord. I am He who will do it. The Father says, 'The sword of my justice will hang over the Gentiles at that day. Unless they repent, it will fall upon them, even upon all the Gentile nations. When these nations fall, I will establish my people, oh house of Israel. I will establish the house of Israel in this land in order to fulfill the covenant that I made with your father, Jacob (Israel). This land will be a New Jerusalem and the powers of heaven will be among this people. Even I will be among them.'

"Behold, I am the one of whom Moses spoke, saying, 'The Lord your God will raise up a prophet. You must listen to Him, for those who will not listen to Him will be destroyed.' All the prophets have testified of me. You are the children of the prophets, of the house of Israel, and of the covenant that the Father made with your forefathers. For He said to Abraham, 'Through your descendants all the nations of the earth will be blessed.' Because you are children of the covenant, the Father raised me up and sent me to you first, that I may turn you from your sins.

"After you and your descendants have been blessed, then the Father's covenant to Abraham will be fulfilled, and all nations will be blessed with the gospel. The Gentiles will have the Holy Ghost, and they will be blessed, and made mightier than any other people. Then the Gentiles will scatter my people, oh house of Israel, for the Father said, 'The Gentiles will be a scourge to the Lamanites upon this land. But after the Gentiles receive the fullness of my gospel, if they then harden their hearts against me, then I will return their sins back upon them.

"'I will remember the covenant that I made with my people and will gather them together in my own due time. I will give them the land of their forefathers—the land of Jerusalem (and the New Jerusalem)—as an inheritance forever.' The time will come when the fullness of my gospel will be preached to my people. Then they will believe that I am Jesus Christ, the Son of God, and they will pray to the Father in my name. Then their leaders will sing together, for they will all understand the truth together. And the Father will gather the house of Israel and give them Jerusalem as their inheritance. Then the house of Israel (the Lamanite tribes, the lost tribes, the Jews, and those adopted in) will all sing together with joy, for the Father will comfort His people and redeem the Old and New Jerusalems.

The Father will show His power as all nations watch, and they will yet see the Father's salvation. And the Father and I are one. Then these, Isaiah's words, will be fulfilled: 'Oh Zion, awake, awake again, oh Jerusalem, the holy city. For no longer will the wicked or the unclean be among you. Shake the dust off yourself, come and sit down, oh Jerusalem (Jews). Loose the cords from around your neck, oh captive daughter of Zion (Lamanites of the New Jerusalem). You sold yourselves for nothing, and will be redeemed without money.' And in the day that my people are redeemed, they will know the name of the one who redeems them (Jesus Christ).

"The house of Israel will say, 'How beautiful among all the nations are the feet of him who brings good news and peace, who brings salvation to us, who says to those in

Zion, "Your God is King!'" They will shout, 'Leave your corrupt towns and cities. Stay unspotted from the world! But do not leave in a hurry or in fear, for the Lord will protect you with His divine and complete protection.'

The Savior continued, "My servant will be wise and esteemed highly by all, for many will be very surprised when he survives a great physical ordeal. He will purge many nations, for many kings will take notice, will see his mighty miracles, and will listen to the truths that he will teach.

Note: This servant who is protected is mentioned in 3 Ne 21:10, 2 Ne7:7-9 and 20:24-25.

"The Father has commanded me to tell you that all these things will surely happen. After these things happen, the covenant that the Father made with His people will be fulfilled, and Jerusalem will be inhabited again with my people, for it is the land of their inheritance."

21 - Christ speaks of latter-day Israel...

Christ continued to speak to the multitude, "I will give your descendants this sign, which will tell them that they are about to be gathered in from their long dispersion, and I will again establish my Zion.This is the sign: My words (written in *The Book of Mormon*) will come from the Father to the Gentiles. Then the Gentiles will know that they have scattered your descendants (Native Americans—a remnant of the house of Jacob). And they will bring your descendants *The Book of Mormon*. By bringing forth this book, the Father will begin to fulfill His covenants with His people, the house of Israel. As He fulfills this covenant, the Father will show His power to all the Gentiles, that they might become humble and repent, come to me and be baptized, know my gospel, and be included with my people.

"When your descendants begin to know the truth of *The Book of Mormon*, their mighty conversions will be another sign to them. By this second sign, they will know that the Father's work has already begun—a work that will soon completely fulfill His covenant with the house of Israel. In that day, for my sake, the Father will do a work that will be great and marvelous among the Gentiles and their kings, who will be humbled, seeing and considering things that they had never known before. Yet many will not believe the truth, even though a man (servant) will declare it to them.

Note: *The Book of Mormon* is the sign of the beginning of the Father's powerful work (Ether 4:17, 3 Ne 29:1-8). This power is the Lord's setting His hand a second time to recover Israel, showing Himself to them in power and great glory, and destroying their enemies (2 Ne 6:14). This power will enable His new scriptures to be read throughout the world, to bless those who believe them and curse those who contest them (1 Ne 14:7, 2 Ne 27:11, Ether 4:8-11). Finally, this power will redeem Zion as a man, like Moses, whom the Lord raises up, leads latter-day Israel to their lands of inheritance (D&C 103:15-18, 113:5-6, 2 Ne 3:24). More scripture will come through the sanctified Gentiles to the house of Israel (Ether 4:6-7, 3 Ne 26:8-9, 1 Ne 14:1, 2 Ne 28:30). "Great and marvelous" works are yet to come (Ether 4:15). This "servant" will present the new scripture to Gentile kings, who will listen intently (3 Ne 20:45). Then the believing of the house of Israel will be restored to their lands of inheritance, assisted by the wealthy, believing Gentiles (2 Ne 10:7-9, 3 Ne 20:45-46).

"Those who reject the truth will persecute my servant, but his life will be in my hands. So even though they will hurt him, I will heal him to show them that my wisdom is greater than the devil's cunning. As Moses said it would be done, the Father will give my servant the power to bring forth my words to the Gentiles.

Note: The Father will give Christ's servant the power to bring forth the greater portion of His words, which He spoke to the Nephites, which are written on the plates of Nephi (3 Ne 23:4, 26:6-10). The vision of Jared's brother, engraved on Mormon's plates by Moroni, will also come forth (2 Ne 27:10, Ether 3:28, 4:4-6). The brass plates will also come forth and be read by all nations (1 Ne 5:17-19, Alma 37:3-4).

Those who reject these words will be cut off from my covenant people.

Note: As all these scriptures come forth to all nations, they will become the means of mass conversion and condemnation as the Lord fulfills His covenant with the house of Israel (1 Ne 14:7, 22:8-12, D&C 1:12-15, 3 Ne 16:10-15, 29:4-9).

The Savior continues speaking: "And my people who are Jacob's descendants will be among the Gentiles, like a young lion among a flock of sheep. They will tread the unbelieving Gentiles down and tear them to pieces, and no one will be able to save them. Jacob's descendants will fight their enemies, the Gentiles, and cut them off. The Gentiles will be cursed unless they repent, 'For in that day,' says the Father, 'I will cut off their means of transportation, and also cut off their cities and places of defense. I will rid them of their spiritualists and material images that they will make for themselves. I will destroy their places of idol worship and their cities.' Then all the Gentiles' lying, deception, envy, strife, priestcraft and prostitution will be done away, because the Father has said, 'Whoever will not repent and come to my Beloved Son at that day will be cut off from my people.' I, the Lord, will execute vengeance and fury upon them, even as upon the heathen, such as they have never known! But if they will repent, listen to my words, and humble themselves, I will establish my church among them. Then they will enter the covenant and be numbered among Jacob's descendants, to whom I have given this land for their inheritance.

"Then the Gentiles will assist my people, Jacob's descendants, who are scattered over the land, to gather together and build a city that will be called the New Jerusalem. The power of heaven will come down and I will be among them. Then the Father's work will begin among all my dispersed people—including the lost tribes that the Father led out of Jerusalem—that they may come to me and call upon the Father in my name.

"And the Father's work will begin as He prepares the way in all nations for His people to be gathered home to their lands of inheritance. They will come from all nations, but not in haste, because 'I will go before them,' says the Father, 'And I will also be behind them.'

22 - Jesus quotes Isaiah...

"When Isaiah's prophecies of Israel's descendants are fulfilled, these words will go forth: 'Sing and shout for joy, for although you were once barren and desolate, you will have more children than the Gentiles (as numerous as the sands upon the seashore). You will build large homes and many cities across the face of the land as your children inherit the Gentiles' wealth and inhabit their desolate cities. Do not be afraid, oh house of Israel, for you will forget the shame, confusion and humiliation of your earlier widowhood. I, your maker and husband, am the Lord of Hosts—your Redeemer—the Holy One of Israel—the God of the whole earth. I will again call Israel—a young wife, who was left and refused, who grieved in spirit. In a little wrath I left you alone for a small moment, but I will gather you together, and with everlasting kindness I will have great mercy on you. As I have sworn not to flood the earth again, so I will swear not to be angry with you again, oh house of Israel. Though the mountains depart and the hills be removed, my kindness will not depart from you, nor will the covenant of my peace be removed.

"'Oh you who have been afflicted and tossed with tempests, and have not been comforted! I will lay your foundations with sapphires, make your windows of agate, your gates of rubies, and surround your lands with beautiful stones. All your children will be taught of me and have great peace, for you will be established in righteousness, far from terror, oppression and fear. Your enemies will surely gather against you, but they will fall, for I have created all men, and your enemies are in my hands. Therefore, no weapon that your enemies create will harm you, for you will condemn those who speak out against you. This is the heritage of my servants, and their righteousness is of me.'

23 - Jesus commands study of Isaiah...

"I, Jesus Christ, command you to diligently search Isaiah's words, for they are great. Surely Isaiah spoke of all things having to do with my people—Israel and his descendants. This is why Isaiah also speaks to the Gentiles. Everything he has written has come to pass, or will yet come to pass. Because Isaiah's prophecies will all come to pass, listen to my words and write them down. Then according to the Father's will, my words will come to the Gentiles. Whoever responds to my words by repenting and being baptized will be saved. Therefore, search the words of the prophets in the scriptures, for many of them testify of these things."

After Jesus had explained all the scriptures He had given them, He said, "There are other scriptures that should be written, that you have not written." Jesus said to Nephi, "Bring the record that you have kept." Nephi brought the records to Jesus and laid them before Him. As Jesus looked at the records, He said, "I commanded my servant, Samuel, the Lamanite, to testify to this people, that on the day the Father would glorify His name in me, many saints would arise from the dead, and appear and minister to many. Was this not so?"

His disciples answered, "Yes, Lord, Samuel did prophesy according to Thy words, and they were all fulfilled." Then Jesus asked them, "How is it that you have not written that many saints did arise, appear and minister to many?" Nephi remembered that these things had not been written. Jesus commanded that they were to be written, and so it was done.

After Jesus explained all their scriptures to them, He commanded them to teach His explanations to one another.

24 - Christ commands teaching and writing...

Then Jesus commanded them to write as He repeated the words that the Father had given to Malachi. After they were written, Jesus explained them. And these are the words that the Father said to Malachi: "I will send my messenger, and He will prepare the way before me. The Lord, whom you seek, even the messenger of the covenant, in whom you delight, will suddenly come to His temple.

"And who will survive the day of His coming? For He is like a refiner's fire and will come to cleanse the earth. He will purify Levi's sons, purging them as gold and silver, that they may offer a righteous offering to the Lord. Then Judah's and Jerusalem's offerings will again be pleasant to the Lord, as they once were in days of old.

"I will come to judge, being a swift witness against the spiritualists, adulterers, and false swearers, against those who oppress by withholding wages, who oppress the widows, who turn away strangers, and who have no fear of me. I am the Lord and do not change. Therefore, according to my promises, you, the descendants of Jacob, will not be consumed.

"But even from the days of your forefathers you have strayed from my ordinances. Return unto me, and I will return unto you. But you ask, 'How do we return unto the Lord?'

"You would not think of robbing God, yet you have robbed me. But you ask, 'How have we robbed Thee?' You have robbed me by not paying your tithes and offerings. Because of this, the whole nation of Israel is cursed. So bring all the tithed items into my storehouse, that it may be full. Prove me and see whether or not I will open the windows of heaven and pour out so many blessings upon you that you will not have enough room to receive them all. And I will rebuke the devil for your sake, and he will not be able to destroy your prosperity. All nations will call you blessed, for your lands will be delightful.

"In the past your words have been strong against me. But you ask, 'How have we spoken against Thee?' You have said, 'It is useless to serve God, for how do we profit by keeping His ordinances—by mournfully walking before the Lord of Hosts? Look how happy the proud are, how successful the wicked, and how those who tempt God escape His judgment.' Then those who feared the Lord, speaking of Him often, were heard by Him, and a book of remembrance was written about them. The Lord of Hosts said, 'They will be mine in the day that I make up my jewels—when I support my people as a man supports his own son who serves him. Then you will return to me and know the righteous from the wicked, and see who has served God and who has not.

25 - Christ quotes Malachi...

"'The day comes that will burn like an oven. In that day all the proud—all who do wickedly, will burn like kindling, like stubble in a field. But for you who fear me, the Son of Righteousness will arise with healing in His wings, and you will be safe and cared for like calves in a stall. Then you will tread down the wicked, who will be ashes under your feet.

"'Remember to observe the statutes and judgments that I gave to my servant, Moses, while in Horeb, for all of Israel.

"'I will send the prophet Elijah to you before the great and dreadful day of the Lord. Elijah will turn the hearts of the forefathers to their children and the hearts of the children to their forefathers. Otherwise, I would curse the whole earth.'"

26 - Christ explains all things...

Jesus explained everything to the multitude—great things and small things. He said, "The Father commanded me to repeat these scriptures to you so that you would have them to give to future generations." Christ explained all things, from the beginning until the time, when He will come in His glory—when the elements will melt with fervent heat—when the earth will be wrapped together like a scroll—when the heavens and the earth will pass away. Christ also explained everything that would happen before that great and last day, when all people will stand before God to be judged by their good or evil works. Those who do good will receive a resurrection of everlasting life, and those who do evil will receive a resurrection of damnation. This will be done according to the mercy, justice and holiness of Christ, who was prepared before the world was created.

This book that I, Mormon, am writing cannot contain even one percent of what Jesus taught the people, but Nephi's plates contain most of what He taught (the greater things).

I have written these words (the lesser things) with the hope that they will again be brought to this people (the Lamanites) through the Gentiles, according to the words of Jesus.

If the Lamanites and Gentiles prove their faith by believing these lesser things (in *The Book of Mormon*), then the greater things will be shown to them (all of Christ's words). But if they will not believe these things, the greater things will be withheld from them, to their condemnation.

I was about to write the greater things, all of which are engraved on Nephi's plates, but the Lord commanded me not to, saying, "I will try the faith of my people." On my plates, I have written only what the Lord has commanded me to write. And now I, Mormon, end my comments and write more of what I have been commanded to write.

The Lord taught the people for three days. (After this, He showed Himself to them often, breaking and blessing bread, and giving it to them.) And He taught and ministered to their children, enabling them to say great and marvelous things to their fathers, even greater things than He had revealed to the people. For on the second day, Christ came again and healed all their sick, lame, blind, and deaf, and raised a man from the dead. Then He ascended to the Father again. And it was on the next day, the third day, that the multitude saw and heard those children. Even babes opened their mouths and spoke things too marvelous to be written.

The disciples whom Jesus had chosen began to baptize and teach all who came to them, and all who were baptized in the name of Jesus were filled with the Holy Ghost. Many of them saw and heard unspeakable things—things not lawful to be written.

They taught and ministered to one another. They had all things in common, and everyone dealt fairly with one another, doing everything that Jesus had commanded them to do.

Those who were baptized in the name of Jesus formed the church of Christ.

27 - Christ's church: His name and doctrine...

As the disciples were journeying, preaching and baptizing in the name of Jesus, they were united in mighty prayer and fasting. And Jesus showed Himself to them again, for they had been praying to the Father in His name. Standing among them, He asked, "What do you desire of me?"

They answered, "Lord, tell us what to name this church, for there are disputations among the people on this matter." The Lord replied, "Why do the people dispute over this? Have they not read the scriptures that say you must take the name of Christ upon yourself? For you will be called by my name at the last day. Those who take my name upon themselves and continue in righteousness throughout their lives will be saved at the last day. Whatever you do, do it in my name. Call the church by my name, and call upon the Father in my name to bless the church for my sake. And how can it be my church unless it is called by my name? If a church is called by Moses' name, then it is Moses' church. If it is called by the name of a man, then it is the church of a man. But if it is called by my name, then it is my church, if it is built upon my gospel. You are built upon my gospel. So call upon the Father in my name for the sake of the church and He will hear you. If a church is built upon my gospel, then the Father will show His own works within it. If a church is not built upon my gospel, but upon the works of men, or the devil, its members will have joy in their works for awhile, but eventually the end will come. Then they will be cut down and thrown into the fire, from where there is no return. For their works will follow them, and because of their works, they will be cut down. Therefore, remember what I have told you.

"I have given you my gospel, which is this—I came into the world to do the will of my Father, who sent me. My Father sent me to be lifted up on the cross, that I may draw all people to me. As I have been lifted up by the people, so shall the people be lifted up by the Father, to stand before me and be judged by their works, whether they be good or evil.

"Those who repent and are baptized in my name will be filled with the Holy Ghost. Those who continue in righteousness throughout their lives will be guiltless before my Father when I stand to judge the world. Because of the Father's justice, those who do not continue in righteousness throughout their lives will be cut down and thrown into the fire, from which they cannot return. This is the message that the Father has given to all people. And because He does not lie, He will fulfill all His words.

"No unclean thing can enter His kingdom. Only those whose robes have been washed clean through my blood, who by faith repent of all their sins and continue in righteousness, will enter His kingdom. This is my commandment to all: Repent, come to me, and be baptized in my name, that you may be sanctified by receiving the Holy Ghost—that you may stand spotless before me at the last day.

"This is my gospel. In my church, do what you have seen me do. And if you do these things, you are blessed, for you will be lifted up at the last day. Write what you have seen and heard, except for the things which are forbidden to be written.

Also write the works of this people, who will be judged by your records, for your records will make their works known. All things are written by the Father, and the world will be judged by what is written in all these books.

"You, my disciples, will be the judges of this people, according to the gift of fair judgment that I will give you. Because of this gift, what kind of men should you be? Even as I am. Now I will go to the Father, and whatever you ask of Him in my name will be given to you. Ask, and you will receive. Knock, and it will be opened to you.

"Because of you and this generation, my joy is great, and is full. Even the Father and all the holy angels rejoice over this generation, for none of them who live now will be lost. But I sorrow over the fourth generation from this time, for they will be led away captive by the devil, even as the son of perdition was led away. They will sell me for silver, gold and the temporary things of this world. When they do this, I will visit them, turning their works upon their own heads.

"Enter through the narrow gate and straight way that leads to life, which few people find. Because the gate that leads to death is wide, many go through it, and travel the broad way until night comes, when no work can be done."

28 - The disciples are granted their desires...

After saying these things to His disciples, Jesus asked each of them, one by one, "What is it that you desire of me after I have gone to the Father?" Nine of the disciples answered, "I desire that after I have lived to an old age, my ministry will come to an end, and I will quickly come to Thee in Thy kingdom." Jesus' response to each of them was, "You are blessed for desiring this, so when you are seventy-two years old, you will come to me in my kingdom and rest with me."

Then Jesus turned to the remaining three disciples and asked them, "What is it that you desire of me after I have gone to the Father?" They sorrowed, not daring to ask Him for what they wanted, thinking that it was too great a request. Jesus said to them, "I know your thoughts. You desire what John, my beloved, who was with me in my ministry before I was lifted up by the Jews, desired of me. You are more blessed, for you will never experience death. You will live to see all of the Father's work among His children, even until all things are fulfilled according to His will, when I come in my glory with the powers of heaven. You will never endure the pains of death, for when I come in my glory you will be changed in an instant from mortal to immortal beings. Then you will be blessed in my Father's kingdom. Again I say, you will not have pain as mortals, nor sorrow, except over the sins of the world. I will do all this because your desire is to bring souls to me in this world.

"Because of this, you will have a fullness of joy—just as my Father has given me. You will sit down in His kingdom and be like me, for I am like the Father, and we are one. The Holy Ghost bears record of the Father and me, and the Father gives the Holy Ghost to His children because of me."

After saying this, Jesus touched each of the nine disciples with His finger. Then He departed into heaven with the remaining three. They were caught up into heaven, seeing and hearing unspeakable things—and the power to even speak about what they had seen and heard was not given to them.

At the time they were caught up, the three disciples could not tell if they were in or out of their bodies, for it seemed as if their bodies had become immortal, enabling them to see the things of God. Afterward, when they spoke to the people on earth, they did not tell them of what they had seen and heard, for they had been commanded not to. Whether or not they were mortal or immortal from that day on, I do not know. But I do know, according to the record, that these three disciples went throughout the land, speaking to all the people. They united the believers with the church by baptizing them and giving them the Holy Ghost.

These disciples were thrown into prison by those who did not belong to the church, but the prisons broke apart and fell down. They were thrown into pits, but they struck the earth with God's word, and by His power they were delivered out of the pits. Because of this, the unbelievers could not dig pits deep enough to hold them. Three times they were thrown into a very hot fire and received no harm. Twice they were thrown into a den of wild beasts, but they played with the beasts like children playing with lambs, and received no harm.

These three disciples went among all the Nephites, preaching the gospel of Christ to everyone in the land, converting them to the Lord and uniting them with the church of Christ. This is how the people of that generation were blessed according to Jesus' words.

And now I, Mormon, make an end of speaking about these things for a time. I was about to write the names of those three disciples who will never die, but the Lord forbade me so that their identity would remain hidden from the world. However, I have seen them, and they have spoken to me. They will also be among the Gentiles and the Jews, but they will not be known by them.

When the Lord sees fit in His wisdom, they will minister to all the scattered tribes of Israel, and to all nations, bringing many souls to Jesus. They will fulfill their desires as they use God's convincing power within them. They are like God's angels, and if they pray to the Father in the name of Jesus, they can show themselves to whomever they desire. Great and marvelous works will be performed by them before that great day to come, when all people must surely stand before the judgment-seat of Christ.

There will even be a great and marvelous work performed by them among the Gentiles before that judgment day. If you had all the scriptures that gave an account of all the marvelous works of Christ, then you, too would know that these things must surely come.

And cursed are those who reject the words of Jesus and the words of His chosen servants, for they will be rejected by Him at the last day. It would be better for them if they were never born, for they will not be able to escape the justice of an offended God and be saved after rejecting His words.

Earlier I wrote that I did not know whether or not the three disciples had become immortal after going up into heaven. Since then, I have asked the Lord, and He has shown me that their bodies were changed. Otherwise, they would have died like other men. Their change was not the same kind of change that will come upon everyone at the last day, but because of it, Satan has no power to tempt them. They are sanctified in the flesh and are holy. This is why the powers of the earth cannot hold them. They will remain in this condition until Christ's judgment day, when they will receive a greater change, and will be received into the Father's kingdom, never to leave again.

29 - The Gentiles are warned again...

In the latter days, when the Lord sees fit in His wisdom to bring my words (*The Book of Mormon*) to the Gentiles, then you will know that His covenant with Israel's descendants—their restoration to their lands of inheritance—is beginning to be fulfilled.

You will also know that the Lord's words spoken by all the holy prophets will soon be fulfilled. Then you Gentiles will no longer need to say, "The Lord delays His coming to Israel's descendants." You will no longer need to think that the scriptures were written in vain, for the Lord will remember His covenant to His people of the house of Israel.

When you read my words, I warn you to no longer ignore the Lord's work, for the sword of His justice is in His right hand, and in the last days, if you reject His work, He will cause this sword to soon overtake you, just as it has overtaken all my people.

Cursed are those who reject the Lord by denying Christ and His works! Cursed are those who deny the Lord's revelations, who will say, "The Lord no longer works by revelation, prophecy, gifts, tongues, healing or by the power of the Holy Ghost!" Cursed are those who will say, in order to get money, that Christ cannot do miracles for them, for they will become like the son of perdition, for whom there was no mercy, according to the word of Christ!

Note: Like Judas, those who have the gospel and prefer to seek money over Christ's power sell their souls for nothing, and their fate is worse than all else (2 Ne 9:27, 3 Ne 20:28, Mormon 8:38-41).

You Gentiles must no longer despise the Jews and make fun of them, nor of any other of Israel's descendants, for the Lord will remember His covenant to them and do what He promised for them. Therefore, do not think you can turn the Lord's hand and somehow prevent His judgments from coming upon you as He fulfills His covenant to Israel's descendants.

30 - Another warning...

Listen, oh you Gentiles, and hear the words of Jesus Christ, the Son of the living God, that He has commanded me to write about you, "Turn from your wicked ways, all you Gentiles. Repent of your evil-doing—lying, deception, sexual impurity, idol worship, secret abominations, murder, priestcraft, envy and strife. Come to me and be baptized in my name, that you may receive a remission of your sins and be filled with the Holy Ghost, that you may be numbered with my people who are of the house of Israel."

Amidst blessings, pride returns...

By the end of 35 AD, the disciples of Jesus had formed a church of Christ in all the surrounding lands. All who came to them and truly repented of their sins were baptized in the name of Jesus and given the Holy Ghost.

By 36 AD, all the people in the land, both Nephite and Lamanite, were converted to the Lord. There was no contention among them, and they all dealt fairly with one another. They had all things in common, so there were none who were rich, poor or in debt. They all freely enjoyed their heavenly gifts.

Throughout 37 AD, there was continued peace in the land. There were great and marvelous works performed by the disciples of Jesus. They healed the sick, raised the dead, and caused the lame to walk. They gave the blind their sight and the deaf their hearing. They did all these things in the name of Jesus. The Lord continued to prosper them greatly for the next twenty-two years. They began to build cities where cities had been burned. They rebuilt the great city of Zarahemla, but the many cities that had been sunk and covered with water could not be rebuilt. The Nephites and converted Lamanites quickly became strong and numerous, and they were very fair and delightful. They married, were given in marriage, and were blessed according to the multitude of promises that the Lord had made to them. They no longer performed the ordinances of the law of Moses. They obeyed the commandments they had received from the Lord their God. They fasted and prayed, and met together often to pray and hear the word of the Lord. There was no contention among all the people in the land, and mighty miracles were performed by the disciples of Jesus. By 100 AD, all the disciples of Jesus had gone to the paradise of God, except for the three who would never die. Other disciples had been ordained to replace those who had died. And many of that generation had also passed away. There was no contention in the land because the love of God was in the people's hearts. There was no envy, strife, immorality, lying, murder or any kind of sinfulness. There were no robbers, murderers, Lamanites, or any kind of -ites.

And surely there could not be a happier people among all of God's creations. They were one—the children of Christ, and were heirs to God's kingdom. How blessed they were! For the Lord blessed them in all they did through the year 110 AD. By then, the first generation from Christ had all passed away, and still there was no contention anywhere in the land.

After Nephi died (having kept this record upon Nephi's plates), his son Amos kept the record in his place. Amos kept the record on Nephi's plates for eighty-four years, and there was still peace in the land, except for a small group of people who had revolted from the church, taking on themselves the name "Lamanite." This is how there began to be Lamanites again in the land. Amos died in 194 AD, and his son, Amos, kept the record in his place, continuing to write on Nephi's plates. By 200 AD, the second generation had all passed away, except for a few.

And now I, Mormon, want you to know that the people had multiplied and spread out over the entire face of the land. They had become very rich because of their prosperity in Christ.

By 201 AD, some of them started to lift themselves above others in their pride. They wore expensive clothes, fine pearls, and all kinds of fine things of the world. From that time on they stopped having their goods and substance in common. They started to divide themselves into classes, and they built churches to get gain, denying the true church of Christ.

By 210 AD, they had established many churches in the land. Each church claimed to know Christ, yet they denied most of His gospel. Each church received all kinds of wicked people and administered the bread and wine to the unworthy. This church multiplied quickly as Satan took hold of their hearts. Another church was established that denied the Christ. This church persecuted Christ's true church because of their humility and belief in Him. This false church despised the humble believers because many miracles were performed among them. It exercised power and authority over the disciples of Jesus, who were still among the people. Members of this false church threw the three disciples in prison, but by the power of God's word in them, the prison walls fell, and they went out and continued to perform mighty miracles.

Even after seeing all these miracles, the people hardened their hearts and tried to kill the disciples, just as the Jews in Jerusalem had sought to kill Jesus because of His words. The wicked threw the three disciples into hot fires and into dens full of wild beasts, but the disciples were not harmed.

No matter what the disciples did or said, the people were hardened, being led by many priests and false prophets to build up their churches and to do all kinds of sinful things. These wicked apostates even beat the true believers of Jesus, but the believers did not fight back. This is how the Nephites became increasingly wicked from year to year, until 230 years had passed since the birth of Christ.

By 231 AD, there was a great division among the people. One group called themselves Nephites. They were the true believers of Christ, and among them were Jacobites, Josephites, Zoramites and the three disciples of Jesus. Those who sinned against the gospel were called Lamanites, Lemuelites and Ishmaelites. They did not sin ignorantly, but they willfully rebelled against the gospel of Christ. They taught their children not to believe and to hate the children of God, even as their forefathers had done from the beginning.

By 244 AD, the wicked people had become much more numerous than God's people. They continued to build up churches for themselves, adorning them with all kinds of precious things. This continued throughout the year 260 AD.

And once again, the wicked began to build up the secret oaths and combinations of Gadianton. Because of their many riches, even those who had called themselves Nephites began to be proud in their hearts. They soon became vain like their brethren, the Lamanites. From this time forward, the disciples began to sorrow for the sins of the world.

By 300 AD, both the Nephites and Lamanites had become very wicked. The robbers of Gadianton spread over the entire land. They collected an abundance of gold and silver, and did all kinds of business with one another. Only the three disciples of Jesus remained righteous.

Amos died in 305 AD, and his brother, Ammaron, kept the record in his place.

In 320 AD, Ammaron was told by the Holy Ghost to hide all the sacred records that had been handed down from generation to generation. He hid them up unto the Lord so they would come to Israel's descendants, according to the prophecies and the Lord's promises. This is the end of Ammaron's record.

1 - Mormon's early years (chapters 1-9)....

And now I, Mormon, make a record of what I have both seen and heard, and I call it the *Book of Mormon*.

Note: Mormon wrote chapters 1-7 before he was killed, and his son Moroni wrote chapters 8 and 9.

When I was about ten years old, I had already begun to learn the ways of my people. At that time, Ammaron came to me, and said, "I have noticed that you are a serious minded child, quick to observe and learn. So remember what you now observe among this people. And when you are about twenty-four years old, go to Shim Hill in the land of Antum. In that hill, I have deposited all the Nephite records unto the Lord. Take out only Nephi's plates, leaving the rest alone. Then engrave everything that you have observed about this people onto those plates." I remembered what Ammaron told me to do.

I, Mormon, am a descendant of Nephi. My father's name was also Mormon. When I was eleven years old, my father took me south to Zarahemla. The whole land had become covered with buildings, and the people were almost as numerous as the sands of the sea. A war broke out between the Nephites (which included Jacobites, Josephites and Zoramites) and the Lamanites (which included Lemuelites and Ishmaelites). The war was fought near the Sidon waters in the land of Zarahemla.

The Nephite army, with more than 30,000 men, beat the Lamanites in many battles that year, killing many of them. After the Lamanites retreated, there was peace for about four years. So much wickedness prevailed throughout the whole land that the Lord took away His beloved disciples along with their healing and miracles. From then on, there were no gifts from the Lord, for the Holy Ghost did not come upon anyone because of the wickedness and unbelief.

When I was fifteen, because I was a serious young man, the Lord visited me, and I tasted and knew of Jesus' goodness. But when I attempted to preach to my people, my mouth was shut. I was forbidden to preach because my people had willfully rebelled against their God. I stayed among them, but said nothing about God because their hearts were so hard. The land was also cursed because of their hardened hearts. The Gadianton robbers among the Lamanites infested the land so much that the Nephites buried their treasure to keep it from being stolen. But their treasure became elusive, for the Lord's curse was upon the land, and the Nephites could not find their buried treasures. There was also sorcery, witchcraft and magic, for the power of the evil one was over the entire land. This condition fulfilled all of Abinadi's and Samuel's words.

2 - At age 16, Mormon leads an army...

Another war broke out between the Nephites and the Lamanites in 325 AD. Though young, I was strong, so the Nephites appointed me to lead their armies. In the year 326 AD, at age sixteen, I led the Nephite army against the Lamanites. In 327 AD, the Lamanites came upon us with such great power that they frightened my army, and we retreated to the north. We came to the city of Angola, took possession of it, and prepared to defend ourselves against the Lamanites. We fortified the city with all our strength, but the Lamanites still drove us out. They also drove us out of the land of David, and we marched to the land of Joshua, near the western seashore. We gathered our people as quickly as possible into one body. But the land was filled with robbers and Lamanites. In spite of the great destruction that hung over my people, they would not repent of their evil doings. Blood and carnage spread throughout all the land among both the Nephites and Lamanites. All the people in the land were in a constant cycle of warfare. The Lamanite king, Aaron, came against us with an army of 44,000. I withstood him with my army of 42,000, and their army ran before us. By the time this war ended, it was 330 AD.

The Nephites began to repent and cry out, as it had been prophesied by Samuel. No one could keep his own property because of the thieves, robbers, murderers, magic arts and witchcraft in the land. This caused great mourning and lamentation all over the land, especially among the Nephites. When I, Mormon, saw their sorrow before the Lord, my heart began to rejoice, for I knew of the Lord's mercy and long-suffering. I thought He would be merciful to them, and that they would again become a righteous people. But my joy was vain, for their sorrowing did not bring them to repentance. Theirs was the sorrowing of the damned, for the Lord no longer allowed them to take pleasure in sin. They did not come to Jesus with broken hearts, for they were not truly sorry for their sins. They cursed God and wished to die, yet they fought with the sword for their lives.

My sorrow returned as I realized that their day of grace had passed, both temporally and spiritually, for I saw thousands of them cut down in open rebellion against their God and heaped up like manure over the land. I had witnessed all this by the end of 344 AD.

In 345 AD, the Nephites were chased by the Lamanites to the land of Jashon, near Antum—the land where Ammaron had deposited the records unto the Lord. About eleven years earlier, I had gone to Shim Hill and had taken the plates of Nephi, and I had engraved on them according to Ammaron's instructions.

Upon Nephi's plates, I made a complete account of all the Nephites' wickedness and sins that I had seen in my youth. But on these, my own plates, I did not make a full record of their wickedness, for I have seen nothing but wickedness ever since I have been old enough to understand the ways of men.

My life has been cursed, and my heart has been filled with sorrow because of their wickedness. Yet I know that I will be resurrected at the last day.

During 345 AD, we, the Nephites, were again hunted and driven north to the land of Shem. We fortified the city of Shem and gathered as many people as possible, hoping to save them from destruction.

In 346 AD, the Lamanites came upon us again. Using great energy, I urged my people to stand boldly before them and fight for their wives, children and homes. My words aroused them enough to keep them from running away from the Lamanites, and they stood boldly against them.

Our army of 30,000 fought the Lamanite army of 50,000 so firmly that they ran from us. We chased them, met them again, and beat them. But the Lord's strength was not with us, for His Spirit was not in us, and we had become weak like our brethren, the Lamanites.

My heart sorrowed because of my people's great calamity, but we went against the Lamanites and Gadianton robbers again and again until, by 349 AD, we had retaken our lands of inheritance.

In 350 AD, we made a treaty with the Lamanites and Gadianton robbers to divide our lands of inheritance. The Lamanites gave us the northern land, all the way to the narrow passage that led into the southern land, and we gave them all the southern land.

3 - Another chance to repent...

The Lamanites did not come to battle again for ten years. During that time, I employed my people, the Nephites, in preparing their lands and preparing weapons for the time of battle.

Then the Lord told to me to cry to this people, "Repent and come to me. Be baptized and build up my church again. If you do this, you will be spared."

I told this to my people, but it was in vain. My people did not realize that it was the Lord their God who had spared them and given them a chance to repent, so they hardened their hearts against Him.

Three hundred and sixty years after the coming of Christ, the Lamanite king sent a letter to me, telling me that he and his people were preparing to come to battle against us again.

I had my people gather in the city of Desolation, which was on the border near the narrow pass that led to the southern land. We placed all our armies in Desolation to stop the Lamanite army from taking possession of our lands. In 361 AD, the Lamanites came to Desolation to battle against us, but we beat them, and they returned to their own lands.

The following year they came again, and we beat them again, killing a great number of them, and we threw their bodies into the sea. Because of this victory, my people began to boast of their own strength.

They swore by the heavens and by the throne of God that they would avenge the blood of their brethren who had been killed, and that they would go to battle against their enemies and cut them off the face of the land.

When they had done this, I, Mormon, utterly refused to continue being their commander and leader. Before this, I had led them to battle many times, in spite of their wickedness. I had loved them with all my heart because of God's love in me. My soul had been poured out in prayer to my God all day long for them, but I prayed without faith in them, for their hearts were hard. The Lord had delivered them out of the hands of their enemies three times, and they still would not repent.

Our Lord and Savior Jesus Christ had forbidden them to swear by heaven or by the throne of God. And because they did this, swearing that they would avenge themselves of the blood of their brethren, the Lord's voice said to me, "Vengeance is mine, and I will repay. Because this people will not repent after I have delivered them, they will be cut off the face of the earth."

This is why I refused to go against my enemies again. I did what the Lord commanded me, and I became a witness to the world of what I saw and heard—things shown to me by the Spirit, which had testified of things to come.

This is why I now write to you, the Gentiles, and also to the house of Israel. When the work of the Father begins, you, the members of the house of Israel, will be preparing to return to the lands of your inheritance.

I write to the people of the earth, who will be judged by the twelve apostles whom Jesus chose in Jerusalem. I also write to the descendants of this people (the Lamanites), who will be judged by the twelve disciples whom Jesus chose in this land. And those disciples will be judged by the twelve apostles of Jerusalem.

The Spirit shows these things to me. I write to all of you so you will know that you must all stand before the judgment-seat of Christ. Every soul who belongs to the family of Adam and Eve must stand to be judged by his or her works, whether they be good or evil.

I also write to help you believe the gospel of Jesus Christ that will be among you, and I write so that the Jews—the covenant people of the Lord—will have another witness, besides Him whom they saw and heard, that Jesus, whom they killed, is the very Christ and God. I wish I could persuade all the people of the earth to repent and prepare to stand before His judgment-seat.

4 - Mormon witnesses evil, leads army...

In 363 AD, the Nephite armies went out of the city of Desolation to battle the Lamanites, but they were driven back. While they were still weary, they were attacked by a fresh Lamanite army. After a sore battle, the Lamanites took the city of Desolation, killing many Nephites and taking many prisoners. Those who were not killed or captured ran to the nearby city of Teancum, which was on the western seashore near Desolation.

The Nephite army lost many men because they attacked the Lamanites. If they had stayed in the city of Desolation, the Lamanites would not have overpowered them. It was in reality, God's judgments that overpowered the Nephites, for He allows the wicked to create war, and thereby punish the wicked.

The Lamanites began to prepare for war again. In 364 AD, the Lamanites attacked the city of Teancum, to try to take that city, too.

But the Lamanites were driven back by the Nephites, who again boasted of their own strength. With confidence in their own might, the Nephites regained the city of Desolation.

Thousands of Nephites and Lamanites were killed during these struggles. By 366 AD, the Nephites still had not repented, and the Lamanites attacked them again.

It is impossible to speak, or to write a perfect description, of the horrible scene of blood and carnage among the Nephites and the

Lamanites. Every heart was so hard that they all delighted in constant bloodshed. The Lord told me that there had never been such great wickedness among all of Lehi's descendants, or among all the house of Israel, as there was among this people.

Because they greatly outnumbered the Nephites, the Lamanites conquered Desolation a second time. Then they marched against the city of Teancum and drove out the Nephites. They captured many women and children and offered them up as sacrifices to their idol gods.

In 367 AD, the Nephites went against the Lamanites in great anger, for the Lamanites had sacrificed their women and children. They beat the Lamanites a second time and drove them out of their lands. This time the Lamanites did not come back for eight years. When they did come back, they came in all their power—with an army too numerous to be counted.

From this time on, the Nephites never overpowered the Lamanites again, but began to be swept off the earth like the morning dew before the sun.

The Lamanites attacked Desolation a third time and beat the Nephites in a very sore battle. The Nephites ran to the city of Boaz and stood very boldly against the Lamanites, who had to attack them twice before beating them. The Nephites were again driven and slaughtered, and again their women and children were sacrificed to idol gods. The Nephites ran, taking with them all the inhabitants of their towns and villages.

As I, Mormon, realized that the Lamanites were about to overthrow the land, I went to Shim Hill and took out all the records that Ammaron had hidden unto the Lord.

5 - Covenants remembered through this book...

Then I went among the Nephites, breaking the oath I had made to no longer help them. They again gave me the command of their armies, and looked to me as if I could deliver them from their afflictions. But I had no hope for them, knowing that the Lord's judgments were upon them. They would not repent, but struggled for their lives without calling upon that Being who created them.

The Lamanites attacked us in the city of Jordan, but we drove them back. They came again, and we again held them off. Other cities were also maintained by the Nephites. These strongholds cut the Lamanites off from the northern lands, preventing them from destroying our people in the north.

By the end of 379 AD, the Lamanites had killed all the Nephites who had not gathered into the strongholds, and had burned their towns, villages and cities.

In 380 AD, the Lamanites attacked us again, and we stood against them boldly. But it was all in vain, for they were so numerous that they tread down the Nephites. We ran again before the Lamanites. Those who ran faster than the Lamanites escaped, and all others were swept down.

And now, I, Mormon, do not want to horrify you by describing this awful scene of blood and carnage that was laid before me, but I know that this history must be made known. I also know that all things that are hidden must be made known to all people.

I know that the descendants of this people (Native Americans), and the Gentiles, who will scatter them and consider them to be worthless, will have this history. Knowing this, I write this limited account of what I have seen. I do not make a full account because of what I have been commanded, and so that you would not have too much sorrow over this people's wickedness.

I write to their descendants, and also to the Gentiles who care for the house of Israel, who realize and know from where their blessings come. They will sorrow over the destruction of this people, wishing they had repented and had been held in the arms of Jesus.

These records are written to Israel's descendants, for God knows that my people, who are wicked, cannot preserve these records. This is why I have been commanded to hide them unto the Lord, and I know they will all come forth in His own due time.

This record will go to the unbelieving Jews to persuade them that Jesus is the Christ, the Son of the living God—that through His most Beloved Son, the Father may bring about His great, eternal purposes, and fulfill His covenant to restore the Jews and all of the house of Israel to the lands that He has given them as an inheritance.

This record will also help my people's descendants to more fully believe His gospel, which will come to them from the Gentiles. Before this, my people's descendants will be scattered by the Gentiles. They will have become a dark, filthy and loathsome people, more than any who have lived among us, or among the Lamanites. This condition will be the result of their unbelief and idolatry.

The Lord's Spirit has already left this people. They are without Christ and God in this world, and they are driven about like chaff in the wind. Once they were a delightful people with Christ as their shepherd, and they were led by God the Father. But now they are led by Satan, like a ship being tossed on the waves without a sail, anchor or rudder.

The Lord will give their blessings to the Gentiles, who will possess this land. After the Gentiles have scattered my people's descendants, the Lord will remember the covenant that He made with Abraham, and with all the house of Israel. He will also remember the prayers of the righteous, who have prayed for their descendants.

And then, oh you Gentiles, how can you stand before God's power without repenting of your evil ways? Don't you know that you are in God's hands—that He has all power, and at His great command the earth will be rolled together like a scroll?

Therefore, repent and humble yourselves before Him. Otherwise, He will come out in justice against you, and a remnant of Jacob's descendants will go in among you, like a lion, and tear you to pieces, and no one will be able to save you.

6 - Mormon's last battle...

Now I, Mormon, will finish engraving the record of the destruction of my people, for the Nephite people fought one last battle with the Lamanites.

I wrote a letter to the Lamanite king, asking him to allow us to gather our people to the land of Cumorah, near Cumorah Hill, where we could battle them. The Lamanite king allowed this, so we marched to the land of Cumorah and pitched our tents around Cumorah Hill. This land was full of lakes, rivers and springs, and here we hoped to gain advantage over the Lamanites.

We gathered all our people to Cumorah in 384 AD. At age seventy-four, I knew this was my people's last struggle. The Lord had commanded me not to allow the sacred records that had been handed down by our forefathers to fall into Lamanite hands, for they would destroy them. This is why I made this record from Nephi's plates. I hid all the other plates in Cumorah Hill. The only plates I have not hidden are these, which I have given to my son Moroni. My people, along with their wives and children, watched the great Lamanite army marching toward them, and waited to receive them with that awful fear of death that fills the hearts of the wicked. As the Lamanites came, every one of us was terrified because of their great numbers. They attacked my people with swords, bows and arrows, axes and all other types of weapons.

My 10,000 men were cut down, and I fell wounded among them, so the Lamanites passed over me and did not put an end to my life.

The next morning, from the top of Cumorah Hill, my son Moroni and I, and twenty-three other survivors saw my 10,000 soldiers that I had led into battle, and they were all dead.

We also saw Moroni's 10,000 dead. We saw Gidgiddonah's 10,000 dead, and he had fallen among them. We saw Lamah, Gilgal, Limhah, Jeneum, Cumenihah, Moronihah, Antionum, Shiblom, Shem and Josh, who had each fallen with their 10,000.

There were ten more leaders who had fallen by the sword, each with their 10,000. In addition to these men (230,000 dead), all my people (probably more than a million, not including the dead of the Lamanites) had been killed, except for the twenty-four who were with me, a few who had escaped to the south, and a few who had deserted to the Lamanites. Everywhere lay the flesh, bones and blood of the dead, who had been left by the Lamanites to decompose and return to their mother earth.

My soul was torn with anguish over my people, and I cried, "Oh you fair ones, how could have you departed from the Lord's ways, rejecting Jesus, who stood with open arms to receive you! If only you had not rejected Him, then you would not have fallen. But you have fallen, and I mourn your loss. Oh you fair sons, daughters, fathers and mothers, how could you have fallen! But you are gone, and my sorrow cannot bring you back.

"Soon the day will come when your mortal bodies will be made immortal. Then you will stand before the judgment-seat of Christ to be judged according to your works. If you are somehow found righteous, you will be blessed with your forefathers. Oh that you had repented before this great destruction. But you are gone, and knowing your condition, the Eternal Father of heaven will deal with you according to His justice and mercy."

7 - A message to the latter-day Lamanites...

Now I write to the descendants of this people who are spared (the latter-day Lamanites), if God will give them my words, that they may know of their forefathers.

I want you to know that you are of the house of Israel, and that you must repent or you cannot be saved. You must put down your weapons and not delight in bloodshed. Do not take up your weapons again unless God commands you. You must learn of your forefathers and repent of all your sins, believing in Jesus Christ—that He is the Son of God who was killed by the Jews. He rose again by the power of the Father and gained victory over the grave. He brings about the resurrection so that we may stand before His judgment-seat. He has redeemed the world. This redemption brings the gift of living with God forever to those who are found guiltless before Him on judgment day. With the choirs above, those who are given this gift will sing endless praises to the Father, the Son, and the Holy Ghost, who are as one God. So repent and be baptized in the name of Jesus, embracing the gospel of Christ that will be presented to you. The Gentiles will bring you this gospel, found in this record (The Book of Mormon), and also found in the record that the Jews will give to the Gentiles (The Holy Bible).

The Holy Bible will be written to persuade you to believe the gospel of Christ. If you believe its messages, you will also believe the messages of *The Book of Mormon.* Then you will come to know about the marvelous works which were done by God's power among your forefathers. You will also know that you are descendants of Jacob, numbered among the people of the first covenant. If you believe in Christ and are baptized, first with water, and then with fire and with the Holy Ghost, following the example of our Savior, then it will be well with you on judgment day. Amen.

8 - Moroni finishes his father's book...

Now I, Moroni, finish the record of my father, Mormon. There are only a few things that he told me to write.

After the tremendous battle at Cumorah, the Nephites who had escaped to the south were all hunted and killed by the Lamanites. My father was also killed by them. Only I remain to write the sad tale of my people's destruction, for they are all gone. I, alone, fulfill my father's commandment, not knowing if the Lamanites will kill me, too. I will write and then hide these records in the earth. After I do this, it does not matter where I go.

My father made this record and wrote its purpose. I would also write the purpose if I had room on the plates, but I do not. And I have no ore, for I am alone. All my friends and relatives have been killed in battle, and I do not know where to go, nor how long the Lord will allow me to live.

Four hundred years have passed since the coming of our Lord and Savior. The Lamanites have hunted down my people in every city until they have become extinct. It has been a great and marvelous destruction. The Lord's hand has done this. The

Lamanites are now at war with one another, and on the whole face of this land, there is one continual round of murder and bloodshed.

I will write no more about the Lamanites, for only Lamanites and robbers are left.

There is no one left who knows the true God, except Jesus' three disciples. The Lord would not allow them to stay with us because of the people's wickedness, and nobody knows where they are. But my father and I have seen them, for they have visited us.

Whoever receives this record and does not condemn it because of its imperfections will know greater things than these.

Note: Greater things are mentioned in 2 Ne 28:30, 3 Ne 26:8-10, and Ether 4:6-8.

If it were possible, I would make all things known to you. This is all I will say about our people. I am the son of Mormon, who was a descendant of Nephi. I am the one who hides this record unto the Lord. These gold plates themselves are of no worth to anyone, for no one will be allowed to have them to sell for money. However, the messages written on these plates are of great worth, and whoever brings them to light will be blessed by the Lord.

Only those who work to glorify God, and for the welfare of the ancient and long-dispersed covenant people of the Lord, will have the power to bring these records to light. He who will bring them to light is blessed according to God's word. By His power, these records will come out of the earth, shining out of darkness, and will come unto the knowledge of the people.

If this record has faults, they are the faults of men. We do not know of any faults (historically or doctrinally), but God knows all things. Whoever condemns this record is in danger of spiritual destruction. Whoever says, "Show me a sign that this is true, or you will die," is doing what the Lord forbids. For whoever judges rashly will be judged in the same manner. All will be paid according to their works. So whoever destroys others will be destroyed by the Lord. The Lord says in the scriptures, "Do not kill or judge, for judgment and vengeance are mine, and I will repay."

Those who fight the Lord's work and His covenant people—the house of Israel, saying, "We will destroy the Lord's work, and the Lord will not remember the covenant that He made to the house of Israel," will be in danger of being cut down and burned. For the Lord's eternal purposes will continue until all His promises are fulfilled.

Study all of Isaiah's prophecies, for I cannot write them all.

The saints who have gone before me, who have possessed this land, will cry from the dust to the Lord. As the Lord lives, He will remember the covenant that He made with them. The Lord has heard their prayers, made in behalf of their descendants. He knows of their faith, for in His name they moved mountains and caused earthquakes. By the power of His word they caused prisons to collapse. Fire, wild animals and poisonous snakes could not hurt them. They prayed for the man whom the Lord would allow to bring forth these records.

They will come forth because the Lord said they would. By His hand, they will come out of the earth, and no one can stop it. These records will come at a time when people will say that miracles are over. They will come forth as one speaking from the dead. These records will come forth when the blood of the saints will cry to the Lord for justice to be brought upon secret combinations and works of darkness. They will come at a time when God's power is denied, when churches are defiled (having once been holy), and when church leaders and teachers are lifted up in the pride of their hearts so much that they will envy members of their own church. All these records will come when fires, storms and volcanoes will occur in foreign lands. There will also be wars and earthquakes in various places. All these records will go throughout the earth when great pollutions are upon it—murder, robbery, lying, deception, prostitution and every other type of sin.

Note: In the scriptures, the words "pollute, polluted, and pollutions" were never intended to refer to a physical state. One of Moroni's main commissions was to describe the spiritual degeneration of the last days, and to warn us accordingly. An isolated description of urban environmental conditions would not only be an inconsistent use of the word "pollutions," but irrelevant to the purpose of his record. Note the singular meaning of the words "pollutions" and "polluted," in Mormon 8:38, 1 Ne 8:33 and Mosiah 25:11.

Many will say, "Do whatever you like. It doesn't matter, for the Lord will support you in the end." Cursed are such, for they are controlled by their sins and are full of bitterness.

These records will come in a day when people will build up churches and say, "Come to me, and for money you will be forgiven of your sins." Oh you wicked, perverse, stubborn people. Why have you built up churches for yourselves to make money? Why have you distorted God's holy word, damning yourselves? Look to God's revelations, for the time will come when all of these things will be fulfilled. The Lord has shown me the great and marvelous things that will occur at the time when these records will come forth to you.

I speak to you as if you were present, for Jesus Christ has shown you to me, and I know your works. I know that except for a few of you, you are all proud, wearing fine clothes, envying, contending with and persecuting one another. Every single one of your churches has become polluted because of your pride. You love money and the things you own. You love fine clothing and decorating your churches more than you love the poor, the needy, the sick and afflicted among you.

Oh you polluted, hypocritical teachers who sell yourselves for nothing. Why have you polluted God's holy church? Why are you ashamed to take the name of Christ upon yourselves? Why do you value the world's praise more than endless happiness? Why do you wear those beautiful things that have no life of their own, while ignoring the hungry, the needy, the ill-clothed, the sick and the oppressed who pass by you?

Why do you build up and uphold secret combinations in order to profit yourselves, and allow the widows and orphans to mourn as their dead fathers and husbands cry to the Lord for vengeance upon your heads?

Note: Regarding "building up and supporting secret combinations", see Ezra T. Benson, ENSIGN, Jan. 1988, p. 5, par. 1. Compare this quote with the verbage and context of Helaman 6:38.

The sword of vengeance hangs over you, and the time soon comes when the Lord will avenge the blood of the saints upon you, for He will not allow their cries to go unanswered.

9 - Moroni questions latter-day people...

And now I, Moroni, speak about those whom I saw, who will not believe in Christ.

Will you believe in Christ when He comes on that great day when the earth is rolled together like a scroll, and when the elements will melt with fervent heat? And when you are brought to stand before the Lamb of God, will you then say there is no God? Will you deny Christ while in His presence? Do you think you could live with Him, aware of your own guilt? Do you think you could be happy living with that holy Being when your soul is racked with guilt for having abused His laws? You would be more miserable living with a holy and just God, being aware of your filthiness, than you would living with the damned souls of hell. For when you realize how exposed your soul is before God in His glory, and realize the holiness of Jesus Christ, your soul will be filled with a flame of unquenchable fire.

Turn to the Lord, you who are unbelievers. Cry mightily to the Father, in the name of Jesus, that perhaps you may be found spotless—spiritually pure, fair and white, having been cleansed by the blood of the Lamb at that great and last day.

Again, I speak to you who deny God's power, who say there are no more revelations, prophecies, and other gifts, such as healing, or the speaking and understanding of foreign or unknown languages. Whoever denies these things does not know the gospel of Christ and has not read the scriptures. Or if he has read the scriptures, he does not understand them. For do we not read that God is unchangeable forever? If you have imagined that He varies, then you have imagined a god that is not a God of miracles. But I will show you a God of miracles—the God of Abraham, Isaac and Jacob, the same God who created the heavens, the earth, and everything in them. He created Adam and Eve, who fell from the garden. Because they fell, Jesus Christ came, who is the Father and the Son. Because of Jesus Christ, all people will be resurrected (redeemed from the death of the body).

Because of the resurrection, when the trumpet will sound at the great and last day, everyone will be brought back into the Lord's presence to be judged. Whoever was happy, being righteous on earth, will still be happy in his righteousness. And whoever was unhappy, being wicked on earth, will remain unhappy, and will still be wicked.

To those who have imagined a god who cannot do miracles, I ask, have all the miracles I have mentioned come to an end? No, for God has not stopped being a God of miracles.

Are not the things that God has done marvelous to our eyes? Yes, and who can comprehend His marvelous works? Who can say that the creation of the heavens, of the earth, and of Adam and Eve, all from the dust and by His word, are not miracles? Who can say that Jesus Christ and His disciples did not do many mighty miracles? If there were miracles then, how can God stop being a God of miracles when He is an unchangeable being? He has not changed, for He continues to be a God of miracles.

The reason He stops doing miracles among people is that they lose faith, turn from the right way, and they grow in ignorance of the God they should be trusting.

If one believes in Christ, doubting nothing, then whatever he asks the Father in the name of Christ will be given to him. This promise is to every person on the earth. For the multitude heard Jesus Christ, the Son of God, say to His three disciples who will never die, "Go into all the world and preach the gospel to every soul. Those who believe and are baptized will be saved, but those who do not believe will be damned. These signs will follow those who believe: In my name they will cast out devils and speak in new languages. They will hold deadly serpents and consume poisoned drink and suffer no harm. They will lay their hands on the sick and heal them. To all who believe in my name, doubting nothing, I will confirm all my words, no matter where they live on earth."

Now, who can stand up against the Lord's works? Who can deny His words? Who will rise up against the almighty power of the Lord? Who will despise Christ's children and their works? All of you who despise the Lord's works will be amazed and then perish. Do not despise revelation, but rather, listen to the Lord's words. Ask the Father, in the name of Jesus, for whatever you need. Do not doubt, but believe, and begin to come to the Lord with all your heart, working out your own salvation with fear and trembling before Him.

Be wise in the days of your probation. Strip yourselves of all uncleanness. Do not ask for something to fulfill your selfish desires. Ask with determined faith that you will not give in to any temptation, but that you will serve the true and living God. Do not be baptized or take the sacrament of Christ unworthy. Do it in the name of Jesus Christ, the Son of the living God. If you do this, and continue in righteousness throughout your life, you will live in God's kingdom.

I speak to you as if I were speaking from the dead, for I know you will have my words after I am gone. Do not condemn me, my father Mormon or others because of our imperfections. But rather give thanks to God for showing you our imperfections so that you may learn to be more wise than our people have been.

We have written this record according to our knowledge, in the characters we call reformed Egyptian. This language has been handed down and changed by us, according to our way of speaking. If our plates had been large enough, we would have written in Hebrew, which we have also changed over the years. If we had the space to write in Hebrew, our record would not have the writing imperfections it now has.

The Lord knows what we have written, and also that no other people know our reformed Egyptian language. This is why He has prepared a way for it to be interpreted. We write these things to rid our robes of our brethren's blood, who have lived in unbelief. We want our brethren (the Lamanites) to know about Christ again. According to the prayers of the saints who have lived in this land, and according to their faith in Jesus Christ, may God the Father remember the covenant He made with Israel's descendants and bless them forever. Amen.

1 - The Jaredite history begins around 2,200 BC...

Now I, Moroni, will begin engraving my account of those ancient people who lived for about 1,600 years in the northern lands before annihilating themselves. I take my account from the twenty-four gold plates called the Book of Ether, found by Limhi's men.

I know that the Jews have the first part of this record already—the part about the creation of the world, and of Adam and Eve and their descendants, until the time of the great tower. Therefore, I will not write that part. But that account is on these twenty-four plates, and whoever finds them will be given the power to read the full account.

I will begin with the genealogy of these people, from the time of the tower, until the time they destroyed themselves during Ether's day.

Ether, who wrote this record, was a descendant of Coriantor, son of Moron, whose direct line of genealogy (going backwards) is as follows: Ethem, son of Ahah, son of Seth.

Before Seth were Shiblon, Com, Coriantum, Amnigaddah, and Aaron, a descendant of Heth, son of Hearthom, son of Lib. Before Lib were Kish, Corom, Levi, Kim, and Morianton, a descendant of Riplakish. Before Riplakish were Shez, Heth, Com, Coriantum, Emer, Omer, Shule, Kib, Orihah and Jared.

Jared and his brother, their families, and other families, came from the great tower in 2200 BC, when the Lord confused the language of the people, and vowed in His wrath to scatter them over all the face of the earth.

Jared's brother was a large, strong man, highly favored by the Lord. Jared asked his brother to ask the Lord not to confuse their language. Jared's brother did as his brother asked, and the Lord had compassion on Jared and his brother and did not confuse their language.

Then Jared said to his brother, "Pray again to the Lord, asking Him to turn away His anger from our friends, so that their language will not be confused either." Jared's brother did this, and their friends' and families' language was not confused. Then Jared asked his brother to ask the Lord whether or not they were going to be driven out of the land, and if they were to be driven out, where they should go. Jared wondered if the Lord would take them to a new land—perhaps more choice than any other. He told his brother, "If we are to be led to a choice land, let us be faithful to the Lord so that we may receive it for our inheritance."

Jared's brother prayed to the Lord as Jared had asked him. The Lord heard Jared's brother and had compassion on him. He said, "Gather your flocks together, both male and female of every kind. Also gather all types of seeds. Gather your family, Jared's family, and your friends' families. Lead them all down into the valley to the north. I will meet you there and will go before you into a land that is more choice than any other. In that choice land, I will bless you and your descendants and raise up a great nation, and none will be greater in all the earth. I will do this because you have prayed to me so diligently."

2 - A choice land is promised...

Jared, his brother, their families, and their friends' families went into the valley in the north named Nimrod (named after the mighty hunter), taking all their flocks with them. They set snares to catch live birds and made containers in which to carry live fish. They also took beehives and all types of seeds with them.

Upon arriving in Nimrod, the Lord came down and talked with Jared's brother. The Lord was in a cloud, and Jared's brother could not see Him. The Lord commanded them to go into an area of the wilderness where no man had ever been. Then the Lord went before them and talked with them as He stood in a cloud, and He directed them which way to go.

As they traveled, they came to many bodies of water. They crossed these small seas on barges that they made, and they were directed continually by the Lord's hand. The Lord told them not to stop after crossing the small seas in the wilderness. He wanted them to continue toward the promised land, which was more choice than all others, and which He had saved for a righteous people.

The Lord vowed in His wrath to Jared's brother that all who possessed this land of promise forevermore would serve Him, the true and only God, or be swept off the land.

Moroni comments: Now we can understand God's decrees over this land, that it is a land of promise, and that any nation who possesses it will serve God or be swept off when the fullness of His wrath comes upon them. This is God's everlasting law—that the people are swept off the land as soon as they are ripe in their sins.

This warning is for you, oh Gentiles, so you will know God's decrees. Repent, and do not continue in your sinfulness, bringing down the fullness of God's wrath upon you as the people in this land have done before. Whatever nation lives here will be free from the bondage of all other nations under heaven, if they serve the God of the land, who is Jesus Christ, who has been shown to you through our records. Now I, Moroni, continue my record.

The Lord brought Jared and his brethren to that great sea which divides the continents. They camped on the seashore in tents for four years, and they named the place Moriancumer. After four years, the Lord came to Jared's brother again, standing in a cloud, and He talked with him for three hours. He also chastened him because he had forgotten to call upon the Lord.

Note: Note that the Lord did not chastise Jared's brother for three hours.

Jared's brother repented of the evil he had done and prayed to the Lord for his brethren. The Lord said to him, "I will forgive you and your brethren of their sins, but do not sin anymore. Remember that my Spirit will not always be with you if you sin. If you become fully ripe in sin, then you will be cut off from my presence. This is my law upon the choice land that I will give to you for your inheritance. Now build more barges like the ones you built before."

As before, Jared's brother, along with many of his brethren, built the barges according to the Lord's instructions. They were small and light, and floated like water fowl, for they were extremely water-tight. The bottom and the sides were shaped like a dish with peaked ends. The top was water-tight, too, and was also shaped like a dish. Each barge was as long as a tree and had a water tight door.

Jared's brother prayed, "Oh Lord, we have made the barges according to Thy directions. But Lord, there is no light inside. And how will we steer them? And they are so air-tight, we will not be able to breathe inside them." The Lord replied to Jared's brother, "Make a hole in the top and also in the bottom. When you need air, unplug the top hole. If the waves come in, then plug up the hole." Jared's brother did as he was instructed. Then he prayed again, "Oh Lord, I have made the holes as Thou has told me. But we still have no light inside. Must we cross this great ocean in darkness?" The Lord replied, "What would you like me to do to give you light inside your barges? You cannot have windows, for they would break, and you cannot make fires on your barges. Your barges will be like whales under mountainous waves. But I will bring you up to the surface again, commanding the wind, rain and ocean to deliver you up. You cannot cross this great ocean unless I prepare your barges to withstand the waves, wind and floods that will come. Knowing this, how do you want me to make light for you when your barges are underwater?"

3 - The faith of Jared's brother...

Jared's brother went and climbed a high mountain named Shelem and smelted sixteen small white stones from a rock (two stones for each of the eight barges), which were transparent, like glass. Then he carried the stones to the top of the mountain, and prayed, "Oh Lord, Thou said we would be surrounded by water. Now, oh Lord, do not be angry with me because of my weakness before Thee. We know Thou art holy and lives in the heavens. We are unworthy before Thee because of our fallen natures, and we do evil continually. But Thou, oh Lord, has given us a commandment to call upon Thee, saying we would receive from Thee according to our desires. Oh Lord, Thou has stricken us because of our iniquity, and has driven us in this wilderness for several years. But Thou has been merciful to us. Oh Lord, look upon me in pity, and turn away thy anger from this, thy people, and do not allow them to cross this raging deep in darkness. Look at these stones that I have smelted out of the rock.

"I know, oh Lord, that Thou has all power, and can do whatever Thou wilt for the benefit of man. So touch these stones, oh Lord, with thy finger, and prepare them that they may shine in the barges as we cross the sea. Oh Lord, Thou can do this. We know that Thou art able to show great power by things that look small according to our understanding."

After Jared's brother said this, the Lord put out His hand and touched the stones one by one with His finger. The veil was taken from the eyes of Jared's brother, and he saw the Lord's finger. Struck with fear, Jared's brother fell down before the Lord.

The Lord asked him, "Why have you fallen? Arise." Jared's brother answered, "I saw the finger of the Lord and feared that He would smite me, for I did not know that the Lord had flesh and blood." The Lord said to him, "Because of thy faith, thou has seen that I will take upon me flesh and blood. Never has man come before me with such great faith as thou has, for without such faith, you could not have seen my finger. Did you see more than my finger?" "No," answered Jared's brother, "Show Thyself to me." Then the Lord asked, "Will you believe my words?" Jared's brother responded, "Yes, Lord, I know Thou speaks the truth, for Thou art a God of truth, and cannot lie."

Then the Lord showed Himself, and said, "Because you know these things, you are redeemed from the fall and are brought back into my presence, and I show myself to you.

"I am the one prepared from the foundation of the world to redeem my people. I am Jesus Christ, the Father and the Son. Through me, all who will believe in my name will have eternal life and become my sons and daughters. I have never shown myself to man, whom I have created, for no man has believed in me as much as you have. Now you know that you were created after my own image. In the beginning, all men were created after my own image. This body you now see is the body of my spirit. I have created man in the image of my spirit, and as I now appear to you in the spirit, I will appear to my people in the flesh."

As I, Moroni, said earlier, I cannot make a complete account of the things written on these twenty-four plates. It is enough to say that Jesus showed Himself in the spirit and ministered to Jared's brother in the same manner that He showed Himself in the flesh to the Nephites. He did this and other great works so Jared's brother would know that He was God. After Jared's brother had seen Jesus' finger, he no longer had faith, but a perfect knowledge of the Lord. With this perfect knowledge of God, he could not be kept from within the veil, and he saw Jesus, who spoke directly to him, face to face.

The Lord said to Jared's brother, "You will not allow what you have seen and heard to go to the world until the time comes when I will glorify my name in the flesh. When you come to me, you will make a record of what you have seen and heard and seal it up so that no one can interpret it, for you will engrave your record in an unknown language. I will give you these two stones to seal up with your plates. The language that you will engrave has been confused, and in my own due time these stones will allow your engravings to be translated."

After saying this, the Lord showed Jared's brother all the inhabitants of the earth who had lived, and who would yet live. The Lord did not hold back anything that would happen from his sight. The Lord did this because He had said to Jared's brother, "If you believe in me, I can show you all things." Jared's brother knew the Lord could show him all things, and so the Lord could not withhold anything from him. The Lord said to Jared's brother, "Engrave these things on plates, then seal the plates along with the two stones, and do not show them to anyone. In my own due time, I will show them to all people."

4 - More to come to the sanctified...

The Lord commanded Jared's brother to go down the mountain, away from His presence, and engrave the things he had seen—things that were forbidden to come to the people until after He would be lifted up on the cross. King Mosiah withheld this translated record (from the twenty-four pure gold plates) so that they would not come to the world until after Christ had shown Himself to His people.

After Christ had shown Himself to His people, He commanded this record to be made known. And now, after knowing these great things, the Nephites have all fallen because of their unbelief. Only the Lamanites are left, and they have rejected the gospel of Christ, so I, Moroni, have been commanded to hide the record of Jared's brother in the earth. Before hiding it, I engraved this vision upon my plates, and there never have been greater things made known than what is revealed in this vision. Because these things are so great, the Lord commanded me to engrave them on my plates. He also commanded me to seal them up along with the interpreters (the two stones affixed to the ends of a bow).

The Lord told me, "The Gentiles will not have this record unless they repent of their sinfulness and become clean before the Lord. But when they exercise faith in me, even as Jared's brother did, which will make them sanctified in me, then I will show them what Jared's brother saw. Then I will unfold all my revelations to them, says Jesus Christ, the Son of God, the Father of heaven and earth. All who fight against the Lord's word and reject these things will be cursed, for I will not show greater things to them. At my command, the heavens are opened and are shut. At my word, the earth will shake, and at my command, the inhabitants of the earth will pass away, even by fire. Those who reject my words reject my disciples. You may use you own judgment now and say my words are not true, but at the last day you will know that it is I, Jesus Christ, who speaks the truth. Those who believe in me will be visited with the witness of my Spirit. They will know and bear record that these things are true, for they persuade all to do good. Anything that persuades people to do good comes from me. Those who will not believe my words will not believe me—that I am, neither will they believe the Father who sent me. For I am the Father, and I am the light, life and truth of the world.

"Come to me, oh Gentiles, and I will show you greater things—knowledge that has been hidden because of unbelief. Come to me, oh house of Israel, and the great things that the Father has laid up for you since the beginning of the world will be shown to you—things that have not yet come to you because of your unbelief. When you Gentiles tear down your veil of unbelief, which causes you to remain in your awful state of wickedness, then the great and marvelous things that have been hidden since the beginning of the world will be shown to you. And when you, oh house of Israel, call upon the Father in my name with a broken heart and contrite spirit—with true sorrow, then you will know that the Father has remembered the covenant He made to your forefathers. Then my revelations, written by my servant John, will come to pass as all people watch. When you read this (*The Book of Mormon*), know that the time is near when these things will happen, and that the Father's work has already begun in all the land. Therefore, repent, everyone from the ends of the earth. Come to me, believe in my gospel, and be baptized in my name, for those who believe and are baptized will be saved, and signs will follow them. But those who do not believe in me will be damned. Blessed are those who are found faithful to my name at the last day, for they will be lifted up to live in the kingdom prepared for them since the beginning of the world. And it is I, the Lord, who has spoken this. Amen."

5 - Moroni's message to Joseph Smith...

Now I, Moroni, have engraved what I have been commanded, according to my memory. I have told you what I have sealed up, so do not touch that part or attempt to translate it, for that is forbidden until God permits. You may be privileged to show the plates to those who will help bring forth this work. You will show them to three men by God's power, and they will know for sure that these things are true. By three witnesses these things will be established. Their witness and this work will stand as a testimony against the world at the last day. This work will be shown to you by God's power, and also by His word—of which the Father, the Son and the Holy Ghost bear record.

If the people of the world repent and come to the Father in the name of Jesus, they will be received into His kingdom. And if you feel that I, Moroni, have no authority over these things, you may judge this book accordingly. But regardless of how you judge, you will know that I do have authority when you see me—when we stand together before God at the last day. Amen.

6 - The Jaredite ocean voyage...

And now I, Moroni, continue with the record of Jared and his brother:

After the Lord touched the stones that had been taken to the top of the mountain, Jared's brother came down and put one stone in each end of the eight vessels. The Lord had caused the stones to shine, and they gave off light so that His people would not have to cross the ocean in darkness. After they had prepared all kinds of food for themselves and for their flocks, herds, and other animals and birds that they would carry with them, they boarded their vessels and set out to sea, commending themselves to the Lord their God.

Then the Lord caused a furious wind to blow toward the promised land, and they were tossed on the waves by the wind. Many times they were submerged under the mountainous waves that broke upon them. But their vessels were watertight, like Noah's ark, so they were not harmed. And when they were buried in the sea they cried out to the Lord, who brought them up to the surface again. The wind never stopped blowing toward the promised land while they were on the ocean. Jared's brother and his people sang praises to the Lord, thanking Him all day long. And when night came, they continued to praise the Lord.

Their vessels were too strong for any whale to break, and they had continual light as they were driven on the sea, whether above water or below. They were carried across the stormy water for 344 days. Finally they landed on the shore of the promised land. As they set their feet on dry ground, they bowed down and shed tears of joy before the Lord, for He had shown such tender mercy toward them. Then they spread out and began to plow the earth.

Jared had four sons, Jacom, Gilgah, Mahah and Orihah. Jared's brother also had sons and daughters. There were about twenty-two friends of Jared and his brother, who all had sons and daughters before they came to the promised land. These sons and daughters began to marry, and they were all taught from on high to walk humbly before the Lord.

Soon these people spread out over the land and farmed it, and their numbers greatly increased.

As Jared's brother grew old, he realized he would soon die, and he said to Jared, "Let us gather our people and ask them what they desire of us before we leave this life." Jared's brother had twenty-two children, and Jared had twelve (four sons and eight daughters).

After all their people had gathered, Jared and his brother counted them and asked them what they desired of them before they died. The people wanted them to anoint one of their sons to be a king over them. This was grievous to Jared's brother, who replied, "Surely this will lead to captivity." But Jared said to his brother, "Allow them to have a king." So Jared's brother said to the people, "Choose a king from among our sons." The people chose Pagag, the firstborn of Jared's brother, but he refused to be their king. The people wanted Jared's brother to force his son to be their king, but he would not. He commanded them to force no man to be their king.

One by one, each of Pagag's brothers also refused to be king. Then Jared's sons also refused, except for Orihah, who was anointed king over the people. He began to reign and the people began to prosper and become very rich. Soon Jared died, and also his brother. Orihah walked humbly before the Lord, teaching his people about the great things the Lord had done for his father and forefathers.

7 - *Chorihor rebels...*

King Orihah executed righteous judgment in the land throughout his very long life. He had eight daughters and twenty-three sons. In addition to these sons, Kib was born when Orihah was old. Kib reigned in place of his father, and had a son, Corihor. When Corihor was thirty-two years old, he rebelled against his father and went over to the land of Nehor to live. There he had many attractive sons and daughters who drew many people away to the land of Nehor.

After Corihor had gathered an army, he went to the land of Moron and captured King Kib, his father. This act fulfilled the words of Jared's brother (which he had spoken about 100 years earlier), that having a king would lead to captivity.

The land of Moron, where King Kib lived, was near the land which the Nephites later called Desolation. Kib lived in captivity under Corihor until he was very old. In his old age, Kib had a son and named him Shule. As Shule grew older, he was angry with his brother. Shule grew into a large, strong man and was also mighty in judgment. He went to Ephraim Hill and made steel swords from the ore he found there. Then he armed his followers and returned to the city of Nehor. Shule and his followers gave battle to his older brother, Corihor, and restored the kingdom to his very old father, Kib.

Because of Shule's deeds, Kib bestowed the kingdom upon him. Like Orihah, his grandfather, Shule executed righteous judgment in the land. His kingdom spread all over the land as the population of the people dramatically increased. Shule had many sons and daughters. Meanwhile, Corihor repented of the many things he had done wrong, so Shule gave him power in his kingdom.

Corihor also had many sons and daughters. Among Corihor's sons, there was one named Noah, who rebelled against his uncle Shule, and also against his father, Corihor. Noah drew away Cohor, his brother, all his other brethren, and many other people. Noah and his followers gave battle to King Shule and obtained the land of their first inheritance. Then Noah became a king over that part of the land. Seeking even more power, Noah again gave battle to King Shule and took him captive to Moron. Noah was about to kill his uncle Shule, but Shule's sons crept into Noah's house at night and killed him. Then they broke down the prison door, rescued their father, and returned him to his throne in his own kingdom. But Noah's son, Cohor, built up his father's kingdom in his place. However, he did not gain power over King Shule, whose people prospered and became very great.

Now the country had been divided into two kingdoms—the kingdom of Shule and the kingdom of Cohor.

When Cohor and his people attacked Shule's kingdom, his people were defeated and he was killed in battle. Then Cohor's son, Nimrod, gave up his father's kingdom to Shule. Nimrod gained favor in the eyes of his great-great-uncle, Shule, who bestowed great favors and freedom upon him. As Shule reigned, the Lord sent prophets among the people, who prophesied that the wickedness and idolatry of the people was bringing a curse upon the land, and that they would be destroyed if they did not repent. The people reviled against and mocked the prophets, but King Shule punished all who did this. He passed a law throughout the land that allowed the prophets to go wherever they desired, calling the people to repentance.

Because the people repented of their sins and idolatry, the Lord spared them, and they began to prosper again in the land. Then King Shule had more sons and daughters in his old age. There were no more wars in the days of Shule. He remained a righteous king by remembering the great things the Lord had done for his great-grandfather, Jared, in bringing him and his people across the ocean to the promised land.

8 - Wicked plans to gain power...

Shule's son, Omer was the next king. Omer had a son, Jared, who also had sons and daughters. Jared rebelled against his father and went to the land of Heth to live. There he flattered many people with his cunning words until he gained the support of half the kingdom. Jared formed an army and conquered his father, Omer, bringing him into captivity and forcing him to serve in the land of Heth.

Omer was in captivity half of his life. Two of Omer's sons, Esrom and Coriantumr, were very angry with their brother Jared, and they raised an army that attacked his army by night. After killing his army, they were about to kill Jared as well, but he pled with his brothers to spare him, and said that he would give the kingdom back to his father.

Even though his life had been spared, Jared was very sad over the loss of the kingdom, for he had set his heart on it and upon the world's glory.

Jared had a cunning daughter who was an expert in the ancient ways. Seeing the sorrow of her father, she devised a plan to get the kingdom back for him. She asked her father, "Why are you so sad? Have you not read the record that our forefathers brought with them across the ocean? In that record, there is an account about those of old, who by their secret plans obtained kingdoms and great glory! "Here is my plan: Invite Kimnor's son, Akish, to come to our house. I will dance for him. Because I am beautiful, I will please him, and he will desire me for his wife. If he asks you to give me to him to marry, say, 'I will give her to you if you bring me my father's head.'"

Now Akish was one of King Omer's friends, and he came to Jared's house as Jared had asked. Jared's daughter danced for Akish, and he asked Jared if he could marry her.

Jared replied to Akish, "I will give her to you, if you will bring me King Omer's head."

Akish then invited all his relatives to Jared's house for a meeting and said to them, "Will you swear to me that you will be faithful to me in doing what I will ask of you?" They all swore to Akish, by God, by the heavens, by the earth, and by their heads, that whoever would not help Akish would lose his head, and that whoever told anyone what Akish told them would die.

After they had all sworn allegiance to Akish, he administered the ancient oaths to them that had been handed down by those who had sought power, even from Cain, a murderer from the beginning. These oaths were preserved by the devil's power to keep the people in darkness, and to give power to those who wanted to murder, plunder and commit all kinds of wickedness. Jared's daughter had convinced her father to search out these ancient oaths, who in turn convinced Akish. So Akish administered them to his family and friends, leading them away by promising them great rewards for their assistance.

They formed a secret combination, as the ancient ones had, which is the most serious form of wickedness in God's sight. The Lord does not work in secret combinations, nor does He want His children to kill one another. He has forbidden these things from the beginning.

Now I, Moroni, will not write the details of their oaths and combinations, for it has been made known to me that all people have them, including the Lamanites. These secret combinations caused the destruction of these ancient people, the Jaredites. They have also caused the destruction of all my people, the Nephites. Any nation that builds up and upholds these secret combinations in order to get power and gain, spreading them all over the nation, will be destroyed. The Lord will not allow His saints, who will be murdered by members of these combinations, to continue to cry to Him without avenging them.

This is why this record of destruction will be shown to you Gentiles, to give you the chance to repent, that you may not allow these murderous combinations to get above you. If you do support and build up these secret combinations, then the work of destruction will come upon you as the Eternal God's sword of justice falls upon you, causing your overthrow.

The Lord commands you Gentiles to wake up and realize your awful situation when you see these secret combinations that will be among you. For judgments will fall upon those secret combinations, and upon those who build them up, because those who have been murdered by them will cry from the dust for vengeance. Those who build up secret combinations seek to overthrow freedom in all lands, nations, and countries, and to bring about the destruction of all people. They follow the instructions of the devil, the father of all lies, who by his lies has caused people to murder from the beginning of the world. He has hardened the people's hearts so they will cast out the prophets and kill them.

I, Moroni, have been commanded to write about these secret combinations so that evil may be done away—that the time may come when Satan may have no more power over people's hearts—that they may be persuaded to do good continually and come to the fountain of all righteousness and be saved.

9 - The struggle with the ancient plans...

Now I, Moroni, will continue my record: Because Akish, his friends and family secretly combined in their vain ambitions, they overthrew Omer's kingdom. But the Lord showed His mercy to Omer, and to those members of his family who were loyal, by warning him in a dream to get out of the land. Omer took his family and traveled for many days. They passed by Shim Hill and by the place where my people (the Nephites) were destroyed (Cumorah Hill). Then they traveled east, and camped by the seashore in a place called Ablom. Meanwhile, Jared was anointed king over the people by the hand of wickedness, and gave Akish his daughter for a wife. Then Akish wanted to kill Jared, his father-in-law. He employed those who had vowed to him with the oath of the ancients, and they obtained Jared's head as he sat on his throne listening to his people.

This wicked, secret society had corrupted all the people. This is why they were able to murder Jared in public and put Akish in power. Then Akish became jealous of his son and put him in prison, where he starved to death. Akish had another son named Nimrah, who was angry with his father for killing his brother. Nimrah gathered a small group of men, fled out of the land, and went to live with Omer.

Akish had other sons, who won the hearts of the people, even though they had vowed to their father to do all kinds of sinful things according to his desires. Akish's people wanted money just as much as Akish wanted power. So Akish's sons bribed the people with money, and thereby gained most of their support. Then a war broke out between Akish and his sons. This war lasted many years and destroyed all but thirty people in the kingdom, not including those who had fled to join Omer's people.

Then Omer was restored again to the land of his inheritance. As he grew old, he had a son named Emer, and anointed him to be the next king. Omer had seen many days of sorrow, but he enjoyed peace for the next two years. After Omer died, Emer reigned righteously as his father had.

The Lord began to take the curse off the land again, and the house of Emer prospered greatly under his reign. Sixty-two years later, Emer's people had become very strong and rich. They had all kinds of fruit, grain, silk, linen, gold, silver and precious things. They also had cattle, oxen, sheep, pigs, goats, and many other kinds of animals for food. They had horses and donkeys, and other types of animals that were very useful to them, including elephants.

The Lord poured out His blessings upon this land—a land more choice than any other. He commands those who live here to remember Him or else be destroyed when fully ripe in iniquity. "For upon such," says the Lord, "I will pour out the fullness of my wrath."

Emer judged righteously all his life. He had many sons and daughters. Among his sons was Coriantum, whom he anointed to reign in his place. Emer lived four more years, and enjoyed peace in the land. He even saw a vision of the Son of Righteousness, and did rejoice and glory in His day. Then he died in peace.

Coriantum walked in his father's steps, building many mighty cities and administering righteously to his people all his life. He had no children until after his wife died when he was 102. Then in his old age, Coriantum married a young woman who bore him sons and daughters. Coriantum lived to be 142 years old.

After Coriantum died, one of his sons, Com, reigned in his place. After reigning forty-nine years, Com had a son, Heth. Com also had other sons and daughters. As the years passed, the people spread out over all the land, and once again, a great wickedness emerged. Heth embraced those ancient secret plans in order to destroy Com, his father. He dethroned his father, killing him with his own sword, and he reigned in his place.

Then prophets came into the land again, crying repentance to the people—that they must prepare the way of the Lord or a great famine would destroy them. The people did not believe the prophets and threw them out. By King Heth's command, they threw other prophets into pits and left them to die.

Then a great famine came upon the land and people started to die quickly, for there was no rain. Poisonous snakes came into the land and killed many people. Their flocks began to run from the snakes toward the southern land, (later called Zarahemla by the Nephites).

Many of the flocks died on the way, but some did escape into the southern land.

The Lord caused the snakes to stop chasing the flocks, and to block the way, preventing the people from passing through. The people who attempted to pass were killed by the snakes. The people followed their animals southward and ate the ones that had died along the way. When the people realized they would soon starve to death, they began to repent of their sinfulness and cry to the Lord.

After they had humbled themselves sufficiently before the Lord, He sent rain. Again there was fruit in the northern land and in all the surrounding lands. The Lord had shown His power to the people by ending the famine.

10 - Generations of wickedness...

Heth and his entire household died in the famine. His only surviving descendant, Shez, began to build up the broken people. Shez remembered the destruction of his fathers and built up a righteous kingdom. He remembered what the Lord had done in bringing Jared and his brother across the ocean. He walked in the ways of the Lord, and he had sons and daughters. His oldest son, also named Shez, rebelled against him, but he was killed by a robber because of his great riches. His death brought peace again to his father. Shez built up many cities and the people began to spread out over all the land again. Shez lived to a very old age and had Riplakish, who reigned after he died.

Riplakish sinned in the Lord's sight by having many wives and mistresses. He also placed heavy taxes on his people in order to build many spacious buildings. He had a very beautiful throne, and he ordered many prisons to be built. Those who refused to pay his taxes, or could not pay them, were put into these prisons. Those in prison were made to work constantly, and anyone who refused to work was put to death. He had all his fine things and fine gold made by those in prison. The whole kingdom was afflicted by his immorality.

After reigning this way for forty-two years, the people rebelled against him, bringing war into the land once again. During this war, Riplakish was killed and his descendants were driven out of the land. After many years, Morianton, a descendant of Riplakish, gathered an army of outcasts and fought the people, gaining power over many cities. This war became very sore and lasted for many years. Eventually Morianton gained complete power and made himself king over all the land.

After this, Morianton gained the favor of the people by easing their burdens, and they anointed him king. Morianton did justice to the people, but not to himself because of his adultery, which cut him off from the Lord's presence. He built up many cities and the people became very rich under his reign, having many buildings, plenty of gold and silver, and an abundance of grain, flocks and herds.

Morianton lived a very long time and then had a son, Kim, who reigned for eight years prior to his father's death. Kim did not reign in righteousness, so he was not favored of the Lord. Kim's brother rebelled against him and brought him into captivity, where he remained for the rest of his life. Kim had sons and daughters in captivity. In his old age he had Levi and then he died. Levi served in captivity for forty-two years and then made war against his uncle, the king of the land, and obtained the kingdom for himself. Levi did what was right in the sight of the Lord and the people prospered in the land. He lived to a good old age and had sons and daughters. He anointed his son, Corom, to be the next king.

Corom also did what was good in the sight of the Lord all his life. He had many sons and daughters and also lived a long life. Kish then reigned in his place.

After Kish passed away, Lib reigned in his place. Lib also did what was good in the sight of the Lord. During Lib's lifetime the poisonous snakes were destroyed. Then the people went to the southern land again to hunt for food. The southern land was full of animals of the forest, and Lib became a great hunter. His people built a great city near the narrow neck, where the sea divides the land. Lib's people preserved the southern land as a game wilderness for hunting, while the whole northern land was covered with people. They were very industrious, buying and selling with one another in order to profit. They created great mounds of dirt as they dug for ore—gold, silver, iron, brass and copper, with which to make all kinds of fine things. They made silks, linen and all types of cloth. They made all types of tools for plowing, sowing, reaping, hoeing and thrashing, and tools to work their animals.

They made their weapons and many other things with very fine workmanship. No people were more blessed or prospered by the Lord than they. And they were in a land that was more choice than any other, for the Lord had spoken it. Lib lived for many years and had sons and daughters. His son, Hearthom, reigned in his place. After reigning twenty-four years, the kingdom was taken from Hearthom, and he served in captivity for the rest of his life.

These next four generations following Hearthom also lived in captivity throughout their lives: Heth, Aaron, Amnigaddah and Coriantum. Coriantum's son, Com, was born in captivity, but he drew away half the kingdom. Com reigned over that half of the kingdom for forty-two years and then went to battle against King Amgid for many years. Finally, Com gained power over the rest of the kingdom.

In the days of Com, robbers came into existence again. They adopted the old plans, administered the oaths of the ancient people and sought to destroy the kingdom. Com fought the robbers, but he did not prevail.

11 - Prophets are killed and the land is cursed...

Also in the days of Com, many prophets came and prophesied of the destruction of that great people unless they repented, turned to the Lord, and gave up their murders and wickedness. The people tried to kill the prophets, who fled to Com for protection. They prophesied many things to Com, and he was blessed during the rest of his life. He lived to a good old age, and then had a son, Shiblom, who reigned in his place.

Then Shiblom's brother, Seth, rebelled against him, and a great war broke out all over the land. Seth had all the prophets put to death who prophesied the destruction of the people. Then there was great calamity in all the land, for the prophets had testified that if the people did not repent, a great destruction like one never before known on earth would come, after which their bones would be piled up on the ground.

The people did not listen to the Lord's voice because of their wicked combinations, which caused war, famine and pestilences all over the land. A great destruction like no other did come during Shiblom's lifetime, but as the people began to repent, the Lord had mercy on them. Although Shiblom was killed, Seth was conquered and spent the rest of his life in captivity. Ahah, Seth's son, inherited the kingdom, but his life was short. He was very sinful and caused much bloodshed.

One of Ahah's descendants, Ethem, then obtained the kingdom and was also very sinful. In the days of Ethem, many prophets came again and prophesied to the people that the Lord would completely destroy them off the face of the earth if they did not repent. The people would not listen, so the prophets mourned and withdrew from among them. Ethem ruled wickedly all his life. His son, Moron, also reigned in wickedness.

Because of that secret combination that was built up to get power and gain, a very sinful man caused a rebellion and rose to power. He gave battle to Moron, overthrew half the kingdom and maintained it for many years. But Moron overthrew him and regained the entire kingdom.

Then another very powerful man arose, a descendant of Jared's brother. He overthrew the kingdom, and Moron lived in captivity the rest of his life. Moron's son, Coriantor, also lived in captivity his whole life. During Coriantor's lifetime, many prophets came and prophesied of great and marvelous things, again telling the people that unless they repented, the Lord would bring His judgments against them and completely destroy them.

The prophets said that by His power, the Lord would bring another people (the Mulekites and Nephites) to possess the land, just as He had brought their forefathers. But the people rejected all the words of the prophets because of their secret society. Coriantor had a son, Ether, and then he died, having lived in captivity all his life.

12 - Moroni expounds on faith...

Ether lived at the time that Coriantumr was king. Ether was one of the Lord's prophets. He was born in captivity, but he came forth prophesying, and could not be restrained, for the Spirit of the Lord was in him. Ether cried out from morning until evening, telling the people that if they did not believe in God and repent, they would be destroyed. He told the people that all things are fulfilled by faith—that anyone who believed in God would surely hope for a better world, even a place at the right hand of God, which hope comes of faith. Ether taught that faith is an anchor to people's souls, making them firm in always doing good works, and enabling them to be led by God while glorifying Him. Ether prophesied great and marvelous things, which the people did not believe because they could not see them.

Moroni comments: Because faith is hoping for things you cannot see, do not reject the prophets, for you will only receive a witness of the truth after you have proven your faith.

It was by faith that Christ showed Himself to our forefathers after rising from the dead. He showed Himself to them after they had shown faith in Him. Before this time, He did not show Himself to the world. He has glorified the Father by preparing a way for others to also obtain the heavenly gift of eternal life, through faith in Him. Because of Christ, the way is prepared that you may also have the hope of eternal life if you have faith in Him.

It was by faith in Christ that Melchizedek and many other high priests were called to the holy order of God. By faith in Christ, the law of Moses was given, and then fulfilled, for through the gift of His Son, God has prepared a more excellent way. If His children do not believe in Christ, God cannot do miracles among them. This is why He did not show Himself to them until after they showed their faith in Him.

Because of Alma and Amulek's faith in Christ, the prison fell to the earth. Because Helaman's two sons, Nephi and Lehi, had faith in Christ, a mighty change came over the Lamanites, and they were baptized with fire and with the Holy Ghost. Ammon's and his brethren's faith in Christ brought a great miracle among the Lamanites. All who have performed miracles before and after Christ have done them by faith in His power. After they showed their faith in Christ, the three disciples were promised that they would never die. No miracle was ever performed by anyone who did not first believe in the Son of God. There were many whose faith was so strong, even before Christ came, that they could not be kept outside the veil. They were glad to witness for themselves things they had only before seen with an eye of faith. This record tells us that Jared's brother was one of these people. Because his faith in God was so great, and because of what he said to the Lord through his faith, God could not hide His finger from him. After Jared's brother saw the Lord's finger, because of the promise he had obtained by faith, the Lord could not withhold anything from his sight. This is why the Lord showed him all things and could not keep him outside the veil.

It is by faith in Christ that my forefathers have obtained the promise that this record will come to their brethren (the Lamanites) through the Gentiles. This is why the Lord Jesus Christ has commanded me to make this record. But I, Moroni, said to Him, "Lord, the Gentiles will mock at our poor writing, for Thou has made our people powerful speakers because of our faith and the Holy Ghost that Thou has given to us, but Thou has not made our writing powerful. Thou has limited our writing skills because our hands are awkward. Thou has not made us powerful writers like Jared's brother, to whom Thou gave the gift of writing things as mighty as Thou art—even to the overpowering of those who read them. Thou has made our words powerful, but we cannot express them in writing. We see our weakness, and we stumble while engraving our words on plates. Because of this, I fear the Gentiles will not take our words seriously."

The Lord replied, "Fools mock, but they will mourn, and my grace is sufficient for the meek who will not take advantage of your weakness. To those who come to me, I will show them their weakness. I give people weaknesses to humble them. My grace is sufficient for all who humble themselves and have faith in me, for I will turn their weaknesses into strengths. I will show the Gentiles their weakness, and that faith, hope and charity will bring their souls to me—the fountain of all righteousness."

After I, Moroni, heard these words, I was comforted and said, "Oh Lord, Thy righteousness will be done, for I know that Thou works among Thy children according to their faith. For Jared's brother said to Mt. Zerin, 'Remove,' and it was removed. If he had not the faith, the mountain would not have been moved. This is how Thou showed Thyself to Thy disciples, for after they had faith and spoke in Thy name, Thou did show Thyself to them in great power. I also remember Thy speaking of preparing a house, even among the mansions of Thy Father, in which we may have an even more wonderful hope. We must hope or we cannot receive an inheritance in the place which Thou has prepared. I also remember Thou has said that Thou has loved the world, even unto the laying down of Thy life for the world, that Thou might take it up again in order to prepare a place for all people. I know that this love Thou has for everyone is charity. This is why we must also have charity (Christ's love) or we cannot inherit that place which Thou has prepared in the mansions of Thy Father. Because of what Thou has said, I know that if the Gentiles do not have charity, because of our weak writing, that Thou will take away the talent that they will have received, and give it to those who will have more."

I prayed to the Lord that He would give the Gentiles grace, that they might have charity. Then the Lord said to me, "If the Gentiles do not have charity, it will not affect you, for you have been faithful, and your robes will be made clean. Because you see your weakness, you will be made strong, and you will sit down in the place I have prepared for you in my Father's mansions."

Now I, Moroni, bid farewell to the Gentiles, and also to my brethren, the Lamanites, whom I love, until we meet before the judgment-seat of Christ, where all people will know that my robes are not spotted with your blood. At that time, you will know that I have seen Jesus, and that in plain humility He talked with me face to face, telling me these things in my own language, just as one man speaks to another. I have only engraved a few of the things He told me because of my weakness in writing. Now I urge you to seek this Jesus, of whom the prophets and apostles have written, that the grace of God the Father, and of the Lord Jesus Christ, and of the Holy Ghost, who bears record of them, may be and abide in you forever. Amen.

13 - A choice land is promised...

And now I, Moroni, finish my record about the destruction of the people of whom I have been writing. The people rejected all of Ether's words, who truly told them of all things from the beginning of mankind. Ether said that after the flood this land became a land more choice than any other, that the Lord would have all who live here serve Him. He said that this land is the place of the Lord's holy sanctuary, and of the New Jerusalem which will come down from heaven. Ether saw the days when Christ would come, and he spoke about a New Jerusalem in this land. He also spoke about the house of Israel, and the old Jerusalem, from where Lehi would come. Ether said that after Jerusalem would be destroyed, it would be built up again for the house of Israel and become a holy city of the Lord. He said the New Jerusalem will be built in this land for part of Joseph's descendants, as a symbol of the past. For as Joseph brought his father to the land of Egypt, saving him and his brothers from starvation, the Lord brought part of Joseph's descendants (Lehi, Ishmael and Mulek) out of Jerusalem, saving them from destruction.

Joseph's descendants (through Ephraim and Manasseh) will build a holy city to the Lord in this land, like the Jerusalem of old. This will be the land of their inheritance, and they will no longer be oppressed. There will be a new heaven and a new earth, and the New Jerusalem will come down from heaven (Enoch's city—Zion). And blessed are those who will live there, for their robes will be white through the blood of the Lamb, and they will be numbered among Joseph's descendants.

Then the Jerusalem of old will come. Its inhabitants will be blessed, for they will be washed in the blood of the Lamb. Those who were scattered will be gathered in from all over the earth, especially from the northern countries. They will participate in fulfilling the covenant that God made with their father, Abraham. When these things happen, then the scripture will be fulfilled that says, "The first will be last, and the last will be first."

I was about to write more of Ether's great and marvelous prophecies, but I was forbidden. The people of Ether's day considered his words to be worthless, and they threw him out from among them. He hid in a cave during the day, where he made the rest of his record. At night he went out and witnessed the judgments that came upon the people.

In that same year, a great war broke out. Several mighty men rose up, seeking to destroy Coriantumr, the king, by their secret plans. Coriantumr had studied the art of war and the cunning of the world, so he gave battle to those who tried to destroy him. Coriantumr, Cohor, Corihor and all the people in the land, including all their fair sons and daughters, refused to repent of their sins.

During the first year that Ether lived in a cave, many of Coriantumr's people were killed by those people who formed secret combinations to obtain the kingdom. Coriantumr's sons fought and suffered greatly. During the second year, the Lord's word came to Ether again, "Go and prophesy to Coriantumr, 'If you and all your household will repent, the Lord will give you your kingdom and spare the people. Otherwise, all of your household will be destroyed, except for you. Then you will live to see the fulfilling of the prophecy that another people will receive this land for their inheritance, and you will be buried by them.'"

Ether made this prophecy to Coriantumr, but he, his household, and all the people still refused to repent. The wars continued and the people tried to kill Ether, but he ran away and again hid in a cave.

Three years after Ether was rejected, a man named Shared defeated Coriantumr's army and brought him into captivity. A year later, Coriantumr's sons beat Shared's army and regained the kingdom for their father. Now there was war in all the land. Every man with his band fought for whatever he wanted. There were robbers and all types of wickedness everywhere.

Coriantumr was very angry with Shared and went against him with his armies. They both met in great anger in the valley of Gilgal, and the battle became very sore, lasting for three days. Coriantumr's army prevailed and chased Shared's army to the plains of Heshlon.

Shared's army fought again on the plains and beat Coriantumr's army, driving them back again to the valley of Gilgal. Again, the two armies fought in the valley, and Shared was killed. Coriantumr's thigh was wounded as he fought with Shared. This kept him from going to battle for two years. During this time, all the people in the land were killing one another without restraint.

14 - Millions die, Coriantumr fights on...

Because of the people's sinfulness, there was such a great curse on the land that if a man set down his tool or sword, the next day he could not find it. So no one would lend or borrow, and all the men constantly held onto their swords in defense of their property, their lives, and the lives of their wives and children.

Two years after Shared was killed, his brother, Gilead, led his army against Coriantumr's. Gilead's army was defeated and chased into the wilderness of Akish, where another sore battle claimed thousands of lives. Coriantumr surrounded Gilead's army, who marched out of the wilderness by night, killing part of Coriantumr's army who had become drunk. Then Gilead's army went to the land of Moron where Gilead took over Coriantumr's throne.

Coriantumr stayed with his army in the wilderness for two years, during which he received great strength to his army. Gilead also received great strength to his army because of his secret combinations, yet his own high priest murdered him as he sat on his throne. Then Lib, a member of the secret combination, murdered the high priest in a secret pass and obtained the kingdom for himself. Lib was a man of great physical strength, stronger than any other.

During the first year of Lib's reign, Coriantumr came to the land of Moron to give him battle. Coriantumr's arm was wounded as he fought with Lib, but Coriantumr's army pressed Lib's army to the seashore. Then Lib's army drove Coriantumr's army back through the wilderness of Akish and onto the plains of Agosh. As Coriantumr's army ran through that part of the land, they gathered people to help them fight. In the plains of Agosh, Coriantumr fought Lib again, striking him with his sword until he died. Then Lib's brother, Shiz, came against Coriantumr's army and the battle became so sore that Coriantumr and his army retreated. The army of Shiz chased Coriantumr's army and overthrew many cities. He killed women and children and burned the cities. A fearful cry went throughout the land, "Who can stand before Shiz's army? He sweeps the earth before him!"

The people began to gather together in armies throughout the land. Part of them joined Shiz, and the rest joined Coriantumr. The war was so great and lasted so long that the whole land was covered with dead bodies. And so swift was the war that none were left to bury the dead. The bodies of men, women and children covered the land, and the smell was so great it troubled the people day and night.

And Shiz continued to chase Coriantumr, having vowed to avenge the death of his brother. But the Lord had told Ether that Coriantumr would not be killed by the sword.

From this account of their terrible war, we see that the Lord did visit them in the fullness of His wrath, for their wickedness had prepared the way for their everlasting destruction.

Shiz and his army chased Coriantumr's army to the eastern seashore where they fought for three days. So terrible was the destruction among the armies of Shiz, that they ran to the land of Corihor, killing all the people along the way who would not join them.

Shiz and his army camped in the valley of Corihor, while Coriantumr's army camped in the valley of Shurr, near Comnor Hill. The next day, Coriantumr gathered his armies on top of the hill and sounded a trumpet to the armies of Shiz, inviting them to battle.

Shiz and his army came against Coriantumr twice and were driven back both times. The third time they came, the battle became very sore. Shiz gave Coriantumr many deep wounds, and after losing much blood, Coriantumr fainted and was carried away as if he were dead.

Now the loss of men, women and children on both sides was so great that Shiz commanded his people to stop chasing Coriantumr's army and to return to their camp.

And as Coriantumr recovered from his wounds, he remembered what Ether had told him. Seeing nearly two million families killed by the sword (perhaps more than eight million dead), Coriantumr began to sorrow in his heart. He began to repent of the evil he had done, remembering the words of all the prophets that had been fulfilled so far in every detail. His soul mourned and refused to be comforted. He wrote a letter to Shiz, saying, "If you will spare my people, I will give the kingdom to you."

Shiz wrote back to Coriantumr, "If you give yourself up so that I may kill you with my own sword, then I will spare your people." Coriantumr's people would not repent, and they were angry with Shiz. The people of Shiz were also angry with Coriantumr's people, so Shiz and his people came against them again. During the battle, when Coriantumr realized that his people were about to fall, he ran from the people of Shiz.

He and his people camped near the waters of Ripliancum, which means "to exceed all." The people of Shiz also camped nearby. The next day they went to battle. They fought a very sore battle in which Coriantumr was wounded again, and he fainted with the loss of blood.

The armies of Coriantumr pressed upon the armies of Shiz and beat them, causing them to run before them. They ran south and camped in a place called Ogath. Coriantumr's army camped near Ramah Hill—that same hill where my father, Mormon, hid the sacred records unto the Lord.

During the next four years, Ether watched as the people gathered and joined either of the opposing armies, and prepared for war. Even the women and children were armed with weapons and wore shields, breastplates and helmets. When all the people had joined one side or the other, they marched against one another to battle. They fought all that day, and neither side conquered. By nightfall they were tired and returned to their camps. They pierced the air with their howling and lamenting for those who had been killed.

The next day they went to battle again. That day was great and terrible, but still neither side conquered. When night came, they cried and howled again, mourning the loss of their people. Again, Coriantumr wrote to Shiz, begging him not to come again to battle, but to take the kingdom and spare the lives of the people.

But the Spirit of the Lord had left them, and Satan had full power over the people, who had given in to their pride and ignorance. So they went to battle again.

At the end of the third and fourth days of fighting, they slept on their swords, drunken with anger. By the end of the fifth day of fighting, only fifty-two of Coriantumr's people and sixty-nine of Shiz's people remained.

During the sixth day, they fought with all their might, using their swords and shields. By the end of the sixth day, thirty-two of Shiz's people and twenty-seven of Coriantumr's people remained. And they were all large, strong men. They ate, slept and prepared to die the next day. On the seventh day, they fought for three hours before fainting with the loss of blood. Coriantumr's men regained their strength and were about to escape when Shiz and his men arose. Shiz vowed in his wrath that he would kill Coriantumr or die by the sword.

Shiz and his men chased Coriantumr and his men and caught up with them the next day. All the men on both sides killed one another, except for Shiz and Coriantumr, and Shiz fainted from the loss of blood. After Coriantumr rested a little while by leaning on his sword, he cut off Shiz's head. Shiz raised up on his hands, struggling for breath, and then fell dead. Then Coriantumr fell down as if he, too were dead.

Then the Lord said to Ether, "Go forth." Ether went out and saw how the Lord's words had all been fulfilled. Then he finished his record and hid them in a way that they could easily be found. And they were found by Limhi's men.

I, Moroni, have not written even one percent of what Ether wrote, but these are the last words he wrote: "Whether the Lord will translate me or allow me to suffer in the flesh, it does not matter, as long as I am saved in God's kingdom. Amen."

1 - Moroni writes to latter-day Lamanites...

When I, Moroni, finished engraving my shorter version of Ether's record, I thought I would not be able to engrave more words. I thought by now I would have been killed by the Lamanites. But I have survived by hiding from them. Their wars among themselves are very fierce, and because of their hatred, they kill every Nephite that will not deny Christ. I will not deny Him, so I go wherever I can to save my life.

Since I am still alive, I will engrave a few more words that may perhaps be of worth to my brethren, the Lamanites, in some future day, according to the Lord's will. These are the words that Christ spoke to each of His twelve disciples as He laid His hands upon them:

2 - Christ's words: The gift of the Holy Ghost...

Calling them by name, He said, "You will call on the Father in my name in mighty prayer. After this, you will have the power to lay your hands upon others and in my name give them the Holy Ghost, for this is what my apostles do." Christ said these words to His disciples when He first appeared, and the multitude did not hear. But the disciples heard Christ, and the Holy Ghost fell upon all those on whom the disciples laid their hands.

3 - Ordination to offices...

This is how the disciples, who were called the elders of the church, ordained priests and teachers: After they had prayed to the Father in the name of Christ, they laid their hands upon them, and said, "In the name of Jesus Christ, I ordain you to be a priest (or teacher). I ordain you to preach repentance and remission of sins through Jesus Christ, by enduring to the end with faith in His name. Amen." This is how they ordained priests and teachers according to God's gifts and callings to men. They ordained them by the Holy Ghost's power which was in them.

4 - Sacrament prayer on bread...

This is how the elders and priests administered the sacrament of Christ to the church. They did it according to Christ's commandments, and so we know it is the true way. They knelt down with the church and prayed to the Father in Christ's name, saying, "Oh God, the Eternal Father, we ask Thee in the name of Thy Son, Jesus Christ, to bless and sanctify this bread to the souls of all those who partake of it; that they may eat in remembrance of the body of Thy Son, and witness unto Thee, Oh God, the Eternal Father, that they are willing to take upon them the name of Thy Son, and always remember Him, and keep His commandments which He has given them, that they may always have His Spirit to be with them. Amen."

5 - Sacrament prayer on wine...

This is the way they administered the wine. They took the cup, and said, "Oh God, the Eternal Father, we ask Thee, in the name of Thy Son, Jesus Christ, to bless and sanctify this wine to the souls of all those who drink of it, that they may do it in remembrance of the blood of Thy Son, which was shed for them; that they may witness unto Thee, Oh God, the Eternal Father, that they do always remember Him, that they may have His Spirit to be with them. Amen."

6 - Who was baptized...

Now I will write about baptism. Elders, priests and teachers were baptized only if they were found worthy. And they baptized only those who had a broken heart and contrite spirit, who were willing to do God's will, and who witnessed to the church that they had truly repented of all their sins.

Also, only those who were willing to take Christ's name upon themselves, having a determination to serve Him throughout their lives, were baptized. After being baptized, they were given the Holy Ghost to come upon them and cleanse them, and then they were numbered among the people of Christ's church. Their names were written down so that they would be remembered and taught by others with God's good word. This teaching helped them to do right, to be continually watchful by praying, and to rely only upon the merits of Christ—the author and finisher of their faith.

The church met together often to fast and pray, and to speak with one another about the welfare of their souls. They also took the bread and wine, in remembrance of the Lord Jesus. They were strict in seeing that there was no sinfulness among them. If anyone was found committing sin, three witnesses of the church testified against him before the elders. And if he did not repent and confess his sins, then his name was removed from the record of Christ's people. But if he did repent, and desired forgiveness with real intent, then he was forgiven. Their meetings were conducted by the church according to the workings of the Spirit. For when the Holy Ghost's power led them to preach, pray or sing, that is what they did.

7 - *Moroni's words...*

Now I, Moroni, will write a few of the words that my father Mormon spoke about faith, hope, and charity, for this is what he taught our people in their synagogue.

"I, Mormon, speak to you, my beloved brothers and sisters. I am allowed to speak to you now because of the grace of God the Father, and our Lord Jesus Christ, because of His holy will, and because of the gift of His calling to me. Because of this calling, I speak to you who are of the church, who are the peaceful followers of Christ. You have obtained enough hope by which you can enter into the Lord's rest, from now until the time when you will rest with Him in heaven.

"I believe this of you because you are at peace with all people. I remember God's word, that says by their works you will know them, for if their works are good, then they are good. God said that an evil person cannot do good, for if he offers a gift or prays to God without being sincere, he receives nothing, for his works are not considered to be righteous. If an evil man gives a gift, he can only do it with a grudge, so it is the same as if he had not given the gift, and he is still evil before God. It is the same when an evil person prays. If he prays without real intent of heart, he receives nothing, for God rejects such prayers. This is why evil people cannot do good nor give a good gift.

"A filthy fountain cannot bring forth good water, nor can a good fountain bring forth filthy water. Those who serve the devil cannot follow Christ and those who follow Christ cannot serve the devil. All good things come from God and all evil things come from the devil, for the devil is God's enemy and never stops fighting Him. The devil invites and entices us to sin and do evil continually. But whatever invites and entices us to do good continually, to love God and serve Him, is inspired of God. So take this warning, my beloved brothers and sisters, so that you do not mistake evil to be of God, or good to be of the devil. The way to judge good from evil is as plain as judging day from night, and you may have a perfect knowledge of what is good and what is evil.

"The Spirit of Christ is given to everyone so that they may know good from evil. Let me tell you how to use your gift in order to judge properly. Everything that invites you to do good and that persuades you to believe in Christ is sent by Christ's power as His gift. By this you may know with a perfect knowledge that it is of God. When something persuades you to do evil, to deny Christ and not serve God, by this you may know with a perfect knowledge that it is of the devil. For this is how the devil works. He does not persuade anyone to do good, not even one person, nor do his angels. And those who surrender their will to the devil cannot persuade anyone to do good.

"My brothers and sisters, now that you know of this light of Christ by which you may judge, be sure that you do not judge wrongfully. For you will be judged at the last day according to how you judged others on earth. I beg you to search diligently, using the light of Christ, so that you may know good from evil. If you embrace every good thing, and do not condemn it, then you will certainly become a child of Christ. And how do you embrace every good thing? Through faith.

"Because God knows all things, He sent His angels to His children to tell them of Christ's coming and that every good thing comes from Him. And God Himself told His prophets that Christ would come. There were many ways that God showed good things to His children, through their faith, all of which came from Christ. If there were no faith, people would be fallen, and good things could not come to them. Because of visiting angels, and by God's words, people began to have more faith in Christ, and with that faith they accepted every good thing. This is how people were saved before Christ came.

"After He came, people were also saved by faith in His name. By faith, they became the sons and daughters of God. As sure as Christ lives, He spoke these words to our fathers: 'Whatever you ask of the Father in my name, if it is good, and if you have faith that you will receive it, then it will be done for you.'

"My brothers and sisters, have miracles ended because Christ has gone into heaven, and has sat down on the right hand of God, to claim His rights of mercy upon all people? Christ answered the ends of the law, and He claims all who have faith in Him. Those who have faith in Him will hold on to every good thing. And so Christ pleads their cause as He lives eternally in the heavens. And because He has gone, have miracles ceased? No, they have not, nor have angels stopped visiting people. Angels are subject to Christ. According to His command, they show themselves to those who have strong faith and a firm mind in every form of godliness. The office of the angels' ministry is to call people to repentance, and to do the work that fulfills the Father's covenants. Angels also prepare the way of Christ by declaring His word to chosen servants, who in turn bear their testimonies of Him.

"By sending His angels, the Lord prepared a way for the rest of the people to have faith in Christ, and faith allows the Holy Ghost to have a place in their hearts, according to His power. This is how the Father brings to pass the fulfilling of the promises that He has made to all people (in the covenant to Abraham, that through his descendants all nations of the earth would be blessed).

"Christ has said, 'If you have faith in me, you will have the power to do whatever is necessary for my cause. Repent, all people of the earth. Come to me, be baptized in my name, and have faith in me, that you may be saved.'

"If what I have said is true, has the day of miracles ceased? No, for with great power and glory, at the last day, God will show you that these things are true. Have angels stopped appearing to people? Has God kept the Holy Ghost's power from them? Will He ever withhold this power as long as there is one person on Earth to be saved? No, for miracles come by faith. Angels appear and speak to people because of their faith. So if these things have stopped, it is because the people do not believe. Then they are cursed and everything they do is in vain. People cannot be saved according to Christ's words unless they have faith in His name. If miracles have stopped, then so has faith, and the people are in an awful situation, for Christ's redemption has no effect on them. But I judge better things of you, for you have faith in Christ because of your meekness. If you had no faith in Him, then you would not be fit to be numbered among the people of His church.

"And how can you have faith unless you have hope? And what do you hope for? You hope to be raised to eternal life through Christ's atonement and the power of His resurrection. You hope for this because of your faith in Him and in His promises. So if you have faith, you also have hope, for without faith there is no hope. And you cannot have faith and hope unless you are humble. If you are proud, your faith and hope are vain, for only the humble are acceptable before God. If you are humble and confess by the Holy Ghost's power that Jesus is the Christ, then you must have charity, for without charity you cannot do this, and you are nothing. For charity is patient, kind, and does not envy others. Charity is not boastful, selfish, or easily provoked. Charity thinks no evil and does not rejoice in sin, but rejoices in the truth. Charity accepts all challenges from God, believes and hopes in Him, and endures all His trials.

"If you do not have charity, you are nothing, because charity never fails. Hold on to charity, the greatest thing of all, for everything else will fail. But charity, Christ's pure love, will endure forever. On the last day, things will be well for those who have charity. Therefore, my beloved brothers and sisters, pray to the Father with all the energy of your heart, that you may be filled with this love—a love that He gives to all who are true followers of His Son, Jesus Christ. Pray that you may become the sons and daughters of God—that when He appears you will be like Him, for we will all see Him as He is. May we have this hope and be purified, even as He is pure. Amen."

8 - Mormon denounces infant baptism...

This is a letter that my father, Mormon, wrote to me, Moroni, soon after I was called to the ministry:

"My beloved son, Moroni, I rejoice greatly because your Lord Jesus Christ has remembered you and has called you to His ministry and holy work. I always remember you as I pray to God the Father in the name of His Holy Child, Jesus Christ. I pray that He will protect you through His infinite goodness and grace, because of your constant faith in His name throughout your life. I am very sorry that there have been arguments among the people you are teaching. You wrote and told me that there have been arguments among your people about the baptism of their little children. Now, my son, I want you to work hard to stop this great error of baptizing little children. This is why I am writing this letter.

"Just as soon as I read your letter, I asked the Lord about it. His word came to me by the Holy Ghost's power, saying, 'Listen to the words of Christ, your Redeemer, your Lord and your God. I did not come into the world to call the righteous to repentance, but rather the sinners. Those who are healthy do not need a doctor, only those who are sick. Children are completely alive in Christ and are not able to sin. Through me, the curse of Adam is taken from them and has no power over them. Also, the law of circumcision is done away because of me.'

"Moroni, this is how the Holy Ghost spoke God's word to me. Because of this, I know that it is solemn mockery before God to baptize little children. Teach repentance and baptism of those who are accountable and capable of committing sin. Teach parents to repent, to be baptized, and to humble themselves as their little ones. Tell them that if they do this, they will be saved with their children. Teach them that their little children do not need to repent or be baptized. Baptism is only for those who repent. Baptism fulfills the commandment to repent for all who are accountable, bringing them a remission of their sins.

"But little children are saved by Christ, and always have been. If this were not true, then God would be an unfair God, saving only those who have been baptized, for many little children have died without baptism! If little children could not be saved without baptism, there must be many little children in an endless hell, but we know this is not so. Whoever believes that little children need baptism is controlled by his sinfulness and is full of bitterness, having no faith, hope, or charity. Those who die with this belief will suffer in hell. It is awful wickedness to think that God saves one child because of baptism and that another goes to hell for not being baptized. Those who distort the Lord's ways in this manner will be cursed, for they will die spiritually unless they repent. I speak with boldness, having authority from God. I am not afraid of what anyone may do to me, for perfect love removes all fear. I am filled with charity—an everlasting love. All children are alike to me. I love them with a perfect love, and they are all saved. For I know that God is not an unfair god, and that He does not change His ways. Little children cannot repent, so it is awful wickedness to deny the pure mercies of God to them, for they are all alive in Him because of His mercy. Those who say that little children need baptism deny Christ's mercy, for they dismiss His atonement and the power of His redemption. Such people are cursed, and are in danger of spiritual death, hell, and an endless torment of soul. God has commanded me to speak boldly. Listen to me and be obedient, or my words will stand against you at the judgment-seat of Christ.

"All little children and all those without Christ's law are alive in Him. The power of His redemption saves all who have no law. They are not condemned, for with no law, they cannot repent. This is why baptizing those without the law is meaningless. To put trust in dead works, such as baptizing those with no law, is to deny Christ's mercy and the power of His Holy Spirit—it is mockery before God. Moroni, my son, this thing should not be done. Repentance and baptism are only for those who are under condemnation and the curse of a broken law.

"The first act of repentance is baptism, which is an act of faith toward fulfilling all the commandments. This brings the remission of sins, which in turn brings meekness and humility. The Holy Ghost, or Comforter, fills the humble with hope and perfect love. This perfect love remains with a person who diligently prays until the end, when all who have become saints will live with God.

"My son, I will write to you again soon unless I go out against the Lamanites. The pride of this Nephite nation will cause their destruction unless they repent soon. Pray for them, my son, that repentance may come to them. But I am afraid that the Spirit has already stopped working with them, and in this part of the land, they are trying to put down all the power and authority that comes from God. They are denying the Holy Ghost. After rejecting such great knowledge, my son, they must perish soon and fulfill the words of the prophets as well as the words of our Savior Himself. Farewell, my son, until I write or meet you again."

9 - Mormon describes deprivation...

Another letter from Mormon, to his son, Moroni:

"I now write again to you, my son, that you may know that I am still alive. But I write about something very sad. We have lost a great battle with the Lamanites. Archeantus, Luram and Emron have all fallen by the sword. We have lost a great number of our choicest men. I am afraid that the Lamanites will destroy all of our people, for they will not repent, and Satan never stops stirring them up to be angry with one another. I work with them constantly. When I speak God's word with sharpness, they become very angry with me. When I use no sharpness, they harden their hearts against God's word. I'm afraid the Lord's Spirit has stopped working with them. They are so angry that they seem to have no fear of death. They have lost their love for one another and continually want to kill and get revenge.

"And now, my beloved son, in spite of their hardness, let us continue to work diligently, for if we stop our work, we will be brought under condemnation. We have a purpose while we still live—to conquer the enemy of all righteousness. Then our souls will rest in God's kingdom.

"Now I must tell you about the suffering of our people. According to what Amoron has told me, the Lamanites have taken many men, women and children as prisoners from the tower of Sherrizah. They have killed the men and they feed their flesh to their wives and children, and give them only a little water. Though this is a great abomination, our people, the Nephites, in Moriantum, have done worse. They have captured many of the Lamanites' daughters, and after taking away that which was most dear and precious above all, which is chastity and virtue, they killed them in a most cruel manner, torturing them to death. After this, they ate their flesh like wild animals. They did this because of the hardness of their hearts, and as a token of bravery.

"Oh my beloved son, how can we expect a people like this—a people without civilization, who only a few years ago were a civil and delightful people, who now delight in so much abomination—to be spared from God's judgments? My heart cries, 'Our people are cursed! Come out in judgment, oh God, and hide their sins, wickedness and abominations from before Thy face!'

"Also, my son, the Nephite army of Zenephi has taken what little food the Lamanites left. Because of this, many widows and their daughters in Sherrizah now wander about looking for food, and many of our old women faint by the road and die. My army is weak, and the Lamanite armies are between us and Sherrizah. All who have run to Aaron's army have fallen victim to the awful brutality of the Lamanites.

"Oh, the depravity of my people. They are without order and without mercy. I have only the strength of a man, and I can no longer enforce my commands. They have become strong in their perversion, and they are all brutal, sparing no one, old or young. They delight in everything evil. The suffering of our women and children in this land is worse than anything. It cannot be spoken, neither can it be written.

"And now, my son, I will write no more about this horrible scene. You know the wickedness of this people—that they have no principles and are past feeling. They are more wicked than the Lamanites. If I recommended them to God, He would smite me. But my son, I recommend you to God, and I trust in Christ that you will be saved. I pray to God that He will spare your life to witness the return of His people to Him, or to witness their utter destruction. I know they will perish unless they repent and return to Him. And if they perish, their destruction will be like that of the Jaredites because of the strong desires of their hearts for blood and revenge. Even if our people are destroyed, we know that many of our brethren have deserted over to the Lamanites, and that many more will. I am writing these few things in case I do not see you again. But I trust that I may see you soon, for I have sacred records to give you.

"My son, be faithful in Christ, and do not let the things I have written cause you to sorrow or weigh you down to death, but rather, may Christ lift you up. May His suffering and death, the showing of His body to our fathers, His mercy, long-suffering and the hope of His glory and of eternal life rest in your mind forever. And may the grace of God the Father, whose throne is high in the heavens, and our Lord Jesus Christ, who sits on the right hand of His power, until all things become subject to Him, be and abide with you forever. Amen."

10 - Moroni writes to people in the latter-days...

Now I, Moroni, will engrave some things that I feel will benefit my brethren, the Lamanites. I want them to know that more than four hundred and twenty years have passed since the sign was given of Christ's coming.

I will hide these records after I write a few very direct words to you, my brethren and sisters (the latter-day Lamanites). When you read these records, if in God's wisdom you should read them, I invite you to remember how merciful the Lord has been to His children, from the creation of Adam and Eve down until the time when you will read these records. I also invite you to think carefully about these words, and to trust the feelings of your heart.

After you do this, I urge you to ask God, the Eternal Father, in the name of Christ, if these records are true. If you ask with a sincere heart, having faith in Christ, then He will show you that they are true, by the power of the Holy Ghost. For by the power of the Holy Ghost you may know the truth of all things.

Whatever is good is also just and true, and nothing that is good denies Christ, but acknowledges that He lives! You may know that He lives, by the power of the Holy Ghost. I urge you not to deny God's power, for He works by power according to the faith of His children, just as He always will.

Again, I urge you, my brothers and sisters (the latter-day Lamanites), not to deny God's gifts, for they are many. They all come from the same God, who gives them to His children through His Spirit to profit them.

One person may be given wisdom by God's Spirit so that he may teach wisdom. Another may be given knowledge by the same Spirit so that he may teach knowledge. By God's Spirit, some are given very great faith. To others, gifts of healing are given. Another may be given the gift to work mighty miracles. To yet another, God's Spirit gives the gift to prophesy of all things. Others are given the gift of seeing angels and spirits who are sent to teach them. Some are given the gift of speaking all types of languages, while others are given the gift of interpreting languages.

All these gifts come by Christ's Spirit to different people according to His will. Remember, every good gift comes from Christ, and He is the same yesterday, today and forever. Remember, that all these spiritual gifts will never be taken away as long as the world exists, unless the people stop believing.

There must be faith, hope and charity, for unless you have these three things, you cannot be saved in God's kingdom. If you have no hope, you are in despair, and despair is the result of sin. And Christ truly said to our fathers, "If you have faith, you can do anything necessary to further my work."

Now I speak to all people from the ends of the earth: If the day comes that God's power and gifts are not among you, it will be because of unbelief. If this is your condition, then you are cursed, for in such a condition, there will be no one that does good among you—not even one. And if there is even one among you who does good, he will do it by God's power and gifts. Whoever does away with the gifts of God and then dies is cursed, for he dies in his sins and cannot be saved in God's kingdom. I write according to Christ's words, and I do not lie.

Remember these things, for the time will soon come when you will know that I have not lied. You will see me at the bar of God, and the Lord will say to you, "Did I not declare my words to you, written by this man, as one crying from the dead, even as one speaking out of the dust?" I write these things so that the prophecies will be fulfilled, for this book will go forth from the mouth of the everlasting God, and His word will call to all people from generation to generation. God will show you that what I have written is true. Again, I urge you to come to Christ and to hold on to every good gift. Do not touch the evil gift nor the unclean thing.

Awake, and arise from the dust, oh Jerusalem. Put on your beautiful robes, oh daughter of Zion. Strengthen yourselves and increase your influence forever, that you may no longer be confused—that the covenants of the Eternal Father, which He made to you, oh house of Israel, may be fulfilled. Come to Christ and be perfected in Him. Deny yourselves all ungodliness. If you deny yourselves all ungodliness and love God with all your might, mind and strength, then His grace is enough to make you perfect in Christ, after which you cannot deny God's power.

And if you are made perfect in Christ, and do not deny His power, then you are sanctified in Christ by God's grace. This is done because of the Father's covenant—the shedding of Christ's blood, which takes away your sins and makes you holy and spotless.

Now I bid farewell to all. Soon I will rest in God's paradise, awaiting the resurrection, when my spirit and body will be reunited, and I will be brought triumphantly through the air to meet you before the pleasing bar of the Great Jehovah, the Eternal Judge of both the living and the dead. Amen.

- THE END -